Zimbabwe Emergency

Journal of the Zimbabwe Vigil in London

by
Dennis and Rose Benton

Copyright © 2017 Dennis and Rose Benton
ISBN 978-1-9998156-2-2

Published in the UK by
The Zimbabwe Vigil
www.zimvigil.co.uk
co-ordinator@zimvigil.co.uk

Cover photo by Guy Benton captures an ambulance outside the disheveled Embassy on 1st October 2016.

All proceeds from the sale of this book will go to the Zimbabwe Vigil.

Group photo June 2017

Vigil Co-ordinators June 2017

Group Photo June 2017

Preview

Chasing Mugabe through Paris . . .
Exposing Mugabe's hired prostitutes in Lisbon . . .
Getting Mandela to condemn Mugabe . . .
Forcing King Mswati to flee his London hotel . . .
Sweeping Zambia's president out of London . . .
Pouring South African wine down the drain . . .
Betrayed by Tsvangirai . . .
Harassed by the CIO . . .
Joined by Archbishop Pius Ncube . . .
Attacked by naive Caribbeans . . .
Blocking Chinamasa's fundraising in London . . .
Despair as MDC walks into rigged 2013 elections . . .

About the authors

Dennis was a reporter on the Herald but spent most of his working life with the BBC World Service. He is Vigil press officer. Rose was born in Zimbabwe and was appointed Co-ordinator at the start of the Vigil. They met at the University of Cape Town.

Dedication

'Joyce got up at 5 am to get to the Vigil. She expected to be back in Manchester at 11.45 pm to catch a connection home' (28th August 2004). This journal is dedicated to all those like Joyce who have made sacrifices to campaign with us for free and fair elections in Zimbabwe.

Index

Introduction	1
Chronology	4
Beginnings	9
2016	22
2017	73
2004	93
2005	100
2006	116
2007	137
2008	165
2009	189
2010	201
2011	217
2012	235
2013	251
2014	279
2015	305
Glossary	325

Introduction

In the fifteenth year of the weekly Vigil under the windows of Zimbabwe House in London, we produce this journal in the hope that real change is in sight and the country can embrace a future free of the malignant Mugabe influence.

Diaries are windows into the past. Unlike an historical account, they speak of what is happening in the context of what is known at the time: jewels reflecting all manner of things.

The Vigil's weekly diaries that we have selected and summarised here will show how events have unfolded as seen by the diaspora in the UK. They cover a time of economic disintegration, periodic political violence, growing oppression and political polarisation. We hope they will remind people of the dangers of further co-operating with Zanu PF's divisive legacy.

As we edited the diaries, it became clear that readers might miss important developments because we had not explicitly mentioned them at the time, or we had treated them elliptically. This was because it was not the purpose of the diaries to tell people what they already knew, but to comment on things that were happening – drawing attention to those things we thought were escaping sufficient scrutiny. We have tried to overcome these deficiencies with background information where we thought it would be useful.

We are proud to have kept going a decade after being told we were the longest-running regular protest in London. So what? Well, we believe in the true liberation of Africa, in real freedom, where people can express themselves without fear. There are good signs that this is coming, even though these are still faint in Zimbabwe.

In brief, the diaries show how the opposition Movement for Democratic Change let down its supporters by joining the so-called Government of National Unity imposed by South Africa after the stolen 2008 presidential elections. How within days Mugabe showed his contempt for the Global Political Agreement and arrested Roy Bennett, the nominated deputy agriculture minister, on spurious charges.

Introduction

The Vigil believed that the MDC should immediately have walked away from the agreement. Indeed, our view was that the MDC should not have accepted what we regarded as an unworkable arrangement in the first place and that Tsvangirai should have taken the open door to Botswana and formed a government in exile after being forced by Zanu PF violence to withdraw from the second round of the presidential election.

For the duration of the unity government the Vigil provided a critical, and often lonely voice as Tsvangirai and his ministers trotted around the world claiming that all was well in Zimbabwe. While they were enjoying the hollow trappings of office – Tsvangirai chasing from skirt to skirt, continually demanding more luxurious homes and holidays – the MDC wasted its energies on the four year long constitution-making process foisted on them by blinkered donors.

Readers of the diaries will see how the Vigil constantly warned the MDC that the 2013 elections would be rigged, urging them not to take part in the sham. Before the election day we wrote this diary: 'With only four days to go before the elections, the Vigil 'commends' President Mugabe on his 'credible' re-election for another 5 year term as he approaches his 90th birthday. Despite overwhelming evidence that the elections on 31st July are being rigged, the SADC Summit on 20th July had four 'commendations' and a 'credible' in its brief four-point communique released after meeting to consider complaints by the MDC about the election arrangements.'

They say the leopard never changes its spots. Our fear is that, with the departure of Mugabe, the people of Zimbabwe may again have the Zanu PF leopard foisted on them in some form or other. For the likely results be warned by these pages.

As this journal goes to press, after 37 years of Zanu PF rule, Zimbabwe is one of the poorest and most corrupt countries in the world with astronomic unemployment, mass starvation and failing public health and education services. The jewel has become a stone around the neck of Africa.

The journal takes us up to mid-2017. Diary entries since then can be seen on our website. The entry on 29th April 2017 includes this point:

Introduction

Zimbabweans are among the poorest people in the world according to a report this week by AfrAsia Bank. It puts Zimbabwean wealth per person last year at US$200. By comparison, wealth per capita in South Africa was US$11,300, Namibia US$10,800, Botswana US$6,700, Angola US$3,600, Zambia and Tanzania US$1,200, Mozambique US$800 and the DRC US$400. (The index didn't include Malawi, Lesotho and Swaziland.) The report said: 'Notably, back in 2000, Zimbabwe was one of the wealthiest countries in Sub Saharan Africa on a wealth per capita basis, ranked ahead of the likes of Nigeria, Kenya, Angola, Zambia and Ghana. However, now it is ranked well behind these countries.' The report continued that contributing factors to Zimbabwe's poor performance included the erosion of ownership rights which, it said, were key to facilitating wealth creation. 'Business owners are unsure as to whether their businesses or property will still belong to them a year down the line, which creates a situation where no one will take the chance of investing in the country.' The report went on to speak of political intimidation, election fixing and the banning of independent media which made it impossible for investors to tell what was happening, and pointed to a brain drain caused by 20% of the population fleeing the country (see: http://www.afrasiabank.com/en/afrasia-bank-africa-wealth-report).

The Vigil diaries have attracted a wide readership. When the Zimbabwean newspaper was launched the diary became a regular feature. It was soon picked up by other publications and websites. The exiled Short Wave Radio Africa carried regular interviews with the Vigil, as did the BBC, Voice of America, Vatican Radio and other broadcasters. The Vigil became a voice of the diaspora, wrestling with all the problems facing Zimbabwe.

The full diaries are availabe on our website: www.zimvigil.co.uk. Photos from 2007 are available on our flickr page: https://www.flickr.com/photos/zimbabwevigil/.

Chronology

1964 – Ian Smith of the Rhodesian Front (RF) becomes prime minister. Tries to persuade UK to grant independence.

11th November 1965 – Smith unilaterally declares independence (UDI) under white minority rule. International economic sanctions imposed.

1972 – Guerrilla war against white rule intensifies, with rivals Zanu (predominantly Shona) and Zapu (predominantly Ndebele) operating independently.

1978 – Smith yields to pressure for negotiated settlement. Elections for transitional legislature boycotted by Patriotic Front made up of Zanu and Zapu. New government of Zimbabwe Rhodesia, led by Bishop Abel Muzorewa, fails to gain international recognition and liberation struggle continues.

1979 – All-party talks at Lancaster House in London lead to a peace agreement and new constitution, which guarantees white minority rights.

1980 – Robert Mugabe and his Zanu party win British-supervised independence elections. Mugabe is named prime minister and includes Zapu leader Joshua Nkomo in his cabinet. Independence Day 18th April.

1982 – Mugabe sacks Nkomo, accusing him of preparing to overthrow the government. North Korean-trained Fifth Brigade deployed to crush what Mugabe said was a rebellion by pro-Nkomo ex-guerrillas in Midlands and Matabeleland provinces. Many thousands of civilians are brutally killed over next few years.

1987 – Mugabe, Nkomo merge their parties to form Zanu PF, ending the violence in southern areas.

1987 – Mugabe changes constitution, becomes executive president.

1998 – Economic crisis accompanied by riots and strikes.

1999 – Economic crisis persists, Zimbabwe's military involvement in DR Congo's civil war becomes increasingly unpopular.

February 2000 – President Mugabe suffers defeat in referendum on draft constitution. Squatters seize hundreds of white-owned farms in a violent campaign to reclaim what they say was stolen by settlers.

June 2000 – Parliamentary elections: Zanu PF narrowly fights off a challenge from the opposition MDC led by Morgan Tsvangirai, but loses its power to change the constitution.

July 2001 – Finance Minister Simba Makoni publicly acknowledges economic crisis, saying foreign reserves have run out and warning of serious food shortages. Most western donors, including the World Bank

and the IMF, have cut aid because of President Mugabe's land seizure programme.
February 2002 – Parliament passes a law limiting media freedom. The European Union imposes sanctions on Zimbabwe and pulls out its election observers after the EU team leader is expelled.
March 2002 – Mugabe re-elected in presidential election condemned as seriously flawed by the opposition and foreign observers. Commonwealth suspends Zimbabwe from its councils for a year after concluding that elections were marred by high levels of violence.
April 2002 – State of disaster declared as worsening food shortages threaten famine.
June 2002 – 45-day countdown for some 2,900 white farmers to leave their land begins under terms of a land-acquisition law passed in May.
12th October 2002 – Zimbabwe Vigil starts
March 2003 – Widely-observed general strike is followed by arrests and beatings.
June 2003 – Morgan Tsvangirai is arrested twice during a week of opposition protests. He is charged with treason, adding to an existing treason charge from 2002 over an alleged plot to kill Mugabe.
December 2003 – Zimbabwe pulls out of Commonwealth after the organisation decides to extend suspension of country indefinitely.
October 2004 – Tsvangirai is acquitted of treason charges relating to an alleged plot to kill Mugabe. Still faces a separate treason charge.
January 2005 – US labels Zimbabwe as one of the world's six "outposts of tyranny".
March 2005 – Zanu PF party wins two-thirds of the votes in parliamentary polls. MDC says election was rigged against it.
May-July 2005 – Tens of thousands of shanty dwellings and street stalls are destroyed as part of Murambatsvina 'clean-up the chaff' programme. The UN estimates that about 700,000 people left homeless.
August 2005 – Prosecutors drop remaining treason charge against Tsvangirai.
November 2005 – Zanu PF party wins an overwhelming majority of seats in a newly-created upper house of parliament, the Senate. The opposition MDC splits over its leader's decision to boycott the Senate poll.
December 2005 – UN humanitarian chief Jan Egeland says Zimbabwe is in "meltdown".

Chronology

September 2006 – Amid galloping inflation, riot police disrupt a planned demonstration against the government's handling of the economic crisis. Union leaders are taken into custody and later hospitalised, allegedly after being tortured.

December 2006 – ZANU PF approves a plan to move presidential polls from 2008 to 2010, effectively extending Mugabe's rule by two years.

February 2007 – Rallies, demonstrations banned for three months. Ban extended in May.

March 2007 – Tsvangirai is hospitalised after his arrest at a rally. One man is shot dead as riot police disperse the gathering.

May 2007 – Warnings of power cuts for up to 20 hours a day while electricity is diverted towards agriculture.

June 2007 – Zanu PF and MDC hold preliminary talks in South Africa.

March 2008 – Presidential and parliamentary elections. MDC claims victory.

May 2008 – Electoral body says Tsvangirai won most votes in presidential poll, but not enough to avoid a run-off against Mugabe.

June 2008 – Run-off goes ahead. Mugabe declared winner because Tsvangirai pulled out days before poll, complaining of intimidation. Russia, China veto a Western-backed UN Security Council resolution to impose sanctions.

July 2008 – EU, US widen their sanctions against Zimbabwe's leaders.

September 2008 – Mugabe, Tsvangirai sign power-sharing agreement. Implementation stalls over who gets top ministerial jobs.

December 2008 – Zimbabwe declares national emergency over a cholera epidemic and the collapse of its health care system.

January 2009 – Government allows use of foreign currencies to try stem hyperinflation.

February 2009 – Tsvangirai is sworn in as prime minister, after protracted talks over formation of government.

March 2009 – Tsvangirai's wife is killed in a suspicious car crash. He is injured. Retail prices fall for the first time after years of hyperinflation.

June 2009 – Constitutional review begins. Tsvangirai tours Europe and US to drum up donor support.

September 2009 – One year after power-sharing deal, MDC remains frustrated and alleges persecution and violence against members. Arrival of EU and US delegations seen as sign of thaw in foreign relations. Both maintain stance on targeted sanctions. IMF provides $400 million support.

Chronology

October 2009 – Mugabe calls for new start to relations with West.
January 2010 –Tsvangirai calls for easing of targeted sanctions, saying the unity government's progress should be rewarded. Zimbabwe's High Court rejects a SADC Tribunal ruling against Mugabe's farm seizures.
March 2010 – New "indigenisation" law forces foreign-owned businesses to sell majority stake to locals.
August 2010 – Zimbabwe resumes official diamond sales amid controversy over rights abuses at the Marange diamond fields.
September 2010 – Tsvangirai accuses Zanu PF of instigating violence at public consultations on new constitution.
December 2010 – Zanu PF party nominates Mugabe as candidate for next presidential election.
February 2011 – EU eases sanctions on Zimbabwe by removing the names of 35 of Mugabe's supporters from a list of people whose assets had been frozen.
March 2011 – Tsvangirai says unity government rendered impotent by Zanu PF violence and disregard of power-sharing deal.
August 2011 – General Solomon Mujuru, one of the country's most senior politicians, dies in a suspicious house fire.
November 2011 – The Kimberley Process, which regulates the global diamond industry, lifts a ban on the export of diamonds from two of Zimbabwe's Marange fields.
December 2011 – Mugabe says he will run in the next elections. He condemns the current power-sharing government as a monster.
February 2012 – EU lifts sanctions on some prominent Zimbabweans, while retaining the travel restrictions and the freeze on the assets of Mugabe. Constitutional Select Committee completes draft of new constitution, but Zanu PF and MDC continue to quarrel about the details.
April 2012 – Political violence on the rise, with MDC complaining that its rallies have repeatedly been shut down.
October 2012 – Rights activists say repressive structures instrumental in 2008 electoral violence are being reactivated. Tsvangirai threatens to pull out of unity government, citing violence against his party's members.
January 2013 – Talks involving Mugabe and Tsvangirai reach a deal over a new draft constitution.
March 2013 – New constitution approved by an overwhelming majority in a referendum. Future presidents will be limited to two five-year terms.

July 2013 – Presidential and parliamentary elections. Mugabe gains a seventh term in office and his Zanu PF party three-quarters of the seats in parliament. MDC dismisses the polls as a fraud.

August 2013 – The US responds to calls from southern African leaders for the West to lift all sanctions on Zimbabwe by saying that it will not do this unless there are further political reforms in the country.

September 2013 – The MDC boycotts the opening of parliament presided over by Mugabe in protest at what it says was a rigged election.

August 2014 – Grace Mugabe, the president's wife and a political novice, is nominated as the next leader of Zanu PF's Women's League, fuelling speculation that she may succeed her husband.

December 2014 – Mugabe sacks Vice-President Joyce Mujuru and seven other ministers after accusing them of plotting to kill him. Mujuru denies the allegation, but is later expelled from Zanu PF.

January 2015 – Mugabe is chosen as chairman of the African Union.

9th March 2015 – Human rights activist Itai Dzamara abducted by security agents.

March 2016 – Mugabe says $15 billion looted from Marange diamond mines.

13th / 14th July 2016 – Two day protest in Harare by ThisFlag movement.

August 2016 – Chaos in Harare as police attack demonstrators near parliament demanding that Mugabe must go. Days earlier the war veterans' association withdrew support for Mugabe.

28th November 2016 – Bond notes issued.

July 2017 – Mugabe amends constitution to gain power over judiciary.

Beginnings

The Vigil started in 2002 to draw attention to human rights abuses in Zimbabwe. From the beginning it saw itself as a coalition of groups, not owned by any one party, and has always welcomed people from other organisations who agree with its mission statement:

'The Vigil, outside the Zimbabwe Embassy, 429 Strand, London, takes place every Saturday from 12.00 to 18.00 to protest against gross violations of human rights in Zimbabwe. The Vigil which started in October 2002 will continue until internationally-monitored, free and fair elections are held in Zimbabwe.'

As the Vigil found its feet and the magnitude of the task it had set itself became clear it was agreed to amend the time on the street to 14.00 – 18.00 to allow for post-Vigil meetings which had become an important feature.

The Vigil was described by the Observer newspaper after a few years as the largest regular demonstration in London. By this time it had became a well-known feature on the busy Strand near Trafalgar Square and Charing Cross station. Tour guides started to point it out. But the singing and dancing, colourful banners and posters make it difficult to miss.

Attendances varied from week to week. On some occasions it attracted hundreds of supporters and sometimes it was down to a handful. This has usually been because of transport problems caused by bad weather because many people travel some distance to take part, setting out in the early hours by coach, facing as much as 24 hours away from home.

But the only Saturdays when there has been no gathering have been those which coincided with Christmas Day as public transport is limited and anyway few passers-by are around. On these rare occasions we hold a 'virtual Vigil' meaning we remember it in our prayers and leave appropriate notices on the four maple trees from which we string our banners: 'No to Mugabe, no to starvation' and 'End murder, rape and torture in Zimbabwe'.

Beginnings

The early years of the Vigil, looked at in retrospect, show a blythe assumption that Mugabe and Zanu PF were so obviously wrong that they could not survive for long. Not alone, the Vigil has been proved wrong by underestimating Mugabe, who has been adroit dealing the cards in Zimbabwe.

The decision to start the Vigil was made by the Central London branch of the recently formed Movement for Democratic Change which used to hold regular forums on Mondays at the George pub down the Strand. One forum was addressed by Tony Reeler, the Zimbabwean human rights activist, and another by Roy Bennett the MDC MP. They urged us to draw public attention to the rapidly developing Zimbabwean crisis. Zimbabwe was then in the throes of violent farm seizures and brutal suppression of the emerging opposition. The two speakers reminded us of the anti-apartheid protests which had been held outside South Africa House in London. There was strong support at the forum for the idea of starting a Vigil outside Zimbabwe House and the first one was held on Saturday 12th October 2002.

In those days there was a big input from white Zimbabwean exiles but the balance gradually changed as more and more black Zimbabweans joined the diaspora. Now the weekly protest is 95% black Zimbabweans, perhaps because white Zimbabweans have been more quickly absorbed into the mainstream in the UK and have found it easier to make new lives outside Zimbabwe. Or they simply despaired of the situation and moved on.

Here is the first report on the Vigil, which appeared in the newsletter of the UK arm of the Movement for Democratic Change of 8th November 2002, a few weeks after the first Vigil:

SINGING IN THE RAIN
We thought it would be tough as winter draws on. Six hours outside the Zimbabwe High Commission in London every Saturday is some commitment. After a buoyant launch on 12th October, the next two Vigils drew a good attendance – but the weather was fair (for the time of year in England!). The 2nd November was a different matter: steady rain. Would anyone get out of bed for this? But that Vigil was the best ever. If it rains, you have to sing and dance to keep your spirits up. And much to

the surprise of passers-by, a party was going on in the rain outside the High Commission.

The Vigil has come of age. Make the most of it – it's only going on for a limited period: until there's agreement on free and fair elections in Zimbabwe. And that can't be far off. All signs are that Mugabe is finished, despite his pay rise! In one week the Zimbabwe dollar plunged from 950 to the US dollar to 1800. Oil supplies are again precarious as bills go unpaid. Let's hope the death rattle is short.

In the meantime we will party every Saturday from 12.00 to 18.00, singing and sharing food and getting the latest news from home from the unending stream of refugees – some of the estimated two-and-half million people who have fled Zimbabwe. Zim House is once again the place to go – not just for the joy of meeting friends but also because we are making an impact. Thousands of passers-by have signed our petition asking the UN Security Council to send a team to investigate human rights abuses in Zimbabwe:

*'**A petition to the UN High Commissioner for Human Rights and the UN Special Rapporteur for Torture about human rights abuses in Zimbabwe:** We are deeply disturbed at growing human rights abuses in Zimbabwe. There are daily reports of torture by the authorities in Zimbabwe, involving the Central Intelligence Organisation (CIO) and Zanu PF militia. Now the police themselves are increasingly involved, reflecting a growing breakdown of law and order. Independent observers in Zimbabwe (the Amani Trust) have recorded thousands of cases of political abuse, including beatings on the soles of the feet and suspected dissidents being burnt or given electric shocks by electrodes attached to genitalia and inserted in the ear. Many cases of ruptured eardrums have been seen as well as evidence of sexual torture, including the rape of young children. Please will you draw this to the attention of the UN Security Council and urge it to send a team to Zimbabwe to investigate these gross violations of human rights.'*

We all know the situation in Zimbabwe is catastrophic. It is up to us to raise awareness in Britain so that the government here and the European Union in general will be forced to make it a priority. Why should they lag behind the United States?

Beginnings

Initially, our campaign against Mugabe was hampered by his propaganda over the land issue: that the opposition was working for white farmers and that Britain was responsible for all Zimbabwe's troubles. The famine changed the perspective a bit. Surely it was obscene to destroy commercial farming when people were starving? No, came the answer from Zanu PF, this was just Blairite propaganda . . . but the murders, the torture, the rapes, the brutal suppression of any dissent? Despite Mugabe's desperate attempt to muzzle the press, the truth still gets out. Let's make sure everyone knows of the horrors being perpetrated in Zimbabwe. And that the MDC is about having a government that respects the constitution and human rights.

The newsletter went on to publicise an extra demonstration.

ZIMBABWE HUMAN RIGHTS DEMONSTRATION
Hundreds of human rights campaigners and Zimbabwean exiles are supplementing the Vigil and staging a demonstration outside the Zimbabwe High Commission from 12.00 – 14.00 on Saturday 9th November 2002. Buses will bring supporters from as far afield as Manchester.

The demonstration is in support of MDC leaders who are to begin appearing in court on 11th November to answer allegations of treason against the illegitimate Mugabe regime – allegations which they strongly reject. (The party leader, Morgan Tsvangirai, is himself not expected to face trial until February.)

The MDC sees the trials as a further attempt to stifle dissent in Zimbabwe amid growing opposition to the brutal and corrupt regime. The threat of starvation in Zimbabwe has now become a reality – especially for opposition supporters and their families, who have been denied international food aid by Mugabe. People are dying of malnutrition and others are being killed, tortured and raped by thugs of the ruling Zanu PF.

One of the latest victims was Learnmore Jongwe, former MDC Secretary for Information and Publicity, who was murdered by the authorities last month while being held in custody. Demonstrators will pay tribute to his memory.

Beginnings

The next issue of the MDC newsletter on 8th January 2003 reported on the Vigil's progress after three months:

A THORN IN MUGABE'S FLESH
The country's starving. People are grubbing in the wild for anything to eat. The only plentiful thing in Zimbabwe is state terror. Keep quiet or you'll be beaten to the point of death – or beyond. Oh, there's one more thing that's plentiful – new 4-wheel drives for the Mugabe cronies.

The Zimbabwe representative may have been greeted as a hero at the ANC conference in Stellenbosch, but things are changing, as the Kenyans have shown. Mr Mugabe may still open the batting for Zimbabwe, but he still has a few other niggles. One of them, we hear, is SW Radio Africa based in London, which broadcasts an alternative view to those back home bombarded by Zanu PF lunacy.

The other niggle, so we are told, is the Vigil mounted outside the Zimbabwe High Commission in London every Saturday from 12.00 – 18.00. Why is Mugabe bothered? Is it because we gave our leaflets to the children arriving for a party there? The kids certainly thought our Vigil – with the drumming, singing and dancing – was more interesting than the "party" games inside. And some of the parents seemed to agree. Several signed our petition calling on the UN to send an inspection team to Zimbabwe to investigate human rights abuses.

That Saturday we collected 1,500 signatures. Of course we can't expect much from the UN – after all they elected Zimbabwe to a human rights committee . . . But it's a petition everyone can sign, even the (white) fellow who came and argued that, of course, land must be handed over to the people . . . But for each of these simple-minded souls there are a hundred others, from all over the world, who show surprising concern for a country many of them have never visited – including the Boston University student studying African Affairs who had never heard of Zimbabwe! Americans, Australians, Danes, Estonians . . . you name it . . . we even had a former Zimbabwean judge signing.

We have going on for 9,000 signatures since the Vigil started in mid-October – just people passing through the busy Trafalgar Square / Charing Cross area. The whole world goes down the Strand! First they hear us: our amplifier can reach above the Saturday bustle. You may hear a Zimbabwean protest song or a refugee talking about how she/he was tortured. And we have had a number of them there – with the scars and neck braces to prove it.

Or their attention may be drawn by the visuals: the dancing – you must keep warm in the English winter! Or it may be the posters, some listing the dead victims of the Mugabe regime. Or the main attraction may be our rain shelter – the green tarpaulin like a Bedouin tent billowing between 4 trees which seem to have been specially planted for us outside the High Commission, itself so symbolic with its castrated Epstein sculptures. Or it may be the colourful mix of people, black and white, young and old. As you would expect in London, there are a good few passionate whites – Zimbabweans and others who have adopted the cause in horror at the atrocities Mugabe is inflicting on his own people. But the demonstrators who attract the most attention are the new refugees, who have helped to nose Zimbabwe towards poll position in the crush of asylum seekers. With them it is like being back in Africa. In the brief time they have in London before being dispersed to different parts of the country they come and join us. The numbers vary but passers-by seem to know instinctively that something is deeply troubling them to force them to leave the sunshine.

Anyway the Vigil is going better than we had hoped with winter here. Six hours outside in the cold is a bit sapping. Mind you, they are busy hours – handing out leaflets, passing over petition forms, explaining and sometimes comforting people anxious for news of relatives. We offer a contact point for Zimbabweans in London, somewhere they can find friends and get help (it might just be a warm coat).

We were inspired by the anti-apartheid vigil outside nearby South Africa House which helped to focus attention on South Africa. It is ironic that we are being driven now to stage demonstrations there as well in protest at South Africa's support for Mugabe. The anti-apartheid protest went on for years. We are certain we will not have to wait so long for a return to the rule of law in Zimbabwe with internationally-monitored, free and fair elections.

Here is another extract from the MDC newsletter of 8th January 2003:

Beginnings

WORLD CUP CRICKET
From a publicity point of view the proposed match between England and Zimbabwe in Harare on 13th February has been a godsend. It has given the media something they can get their teeth into – even the tabloid press, which seldom pays much attention to Zimbabwe. World Cup cricket has stepped into a minefield – but the explosions won't do Mugabe any good. Popular outrage in London was reflected by the hundreds of people who signed a petition against the matches at the Saturday Vigil outside the Zimbabwe High Commission.

Among those who helped form the Vigil was Ephraim Tapa, a former leader of the Zimbabwean civil service trade union and one of the founders of the MDC. He had to flee in early 2002 after being tortured by the regime and joined the Central London branch of the MDC. He was soon elected branch chairman going on later to be elected chair of the MDC UK and Ireland before being deposed by MDC President Morgan Tsvangirai in October 2007 – a move apparently timed to coincide with the Vigil's 5th anniversary. In brief, Tsvangirai wanted money sent direct to him rather than through the party structures.

The Vigil has always seen its purpose as drawing attention to the situation in Zimbabwe and has run many petitions – notably the one to the UN calling for an investigation of human rights violations in Zimbabwe signed eventually by some 100,000 passers-by. One purpose of the petitions is that they draw in passers-by to engage with us.

The Vigil has also lobbied Parliament and staged numerous demonstrations, including at the Africa / Europe summit in Lisbon in December 2007 and the AU / EU summit in Brussels in April 2014.

One of the earliest demonstrations was against Mugabe's visit to Paris in February 2003. Here is a report:

A day in Paris - Friday, 21st February 2003
Sitting in a police holding cell in Paris, I write. 11 of us detained. For peacefully protesting, for calling for the arrest of Mugabe for torture, for trying to make the world aware of our anger at Chirac allowing this banned dictator into France, flouting the EU's travel ban.

Beginnings

With only a few hours sleep behind us, we had arrived early in Paris and headed to the Ministry of Justice where we joined forces with members of Act Up and the Pink Panthers, gay activists who share our anger at Mugabe's presence in France. Our protest was broken up by the police who arrived quickly and outnumbered us completely. But not before our chants and shouts had been caught on camera by the international press.

From there, we had walked through Paris to the Magistrate's Court, the French among us warning us not to wave banners while walking for fear of arrest. We were there to serve papers prepared by Peter Tatchell giving grounds for the arrest of Mugabe. Our attempts to protest were foiled by armed police, who, repressively circling, told us to disband. We couldn't protest, no chanting of slogans, no waving of banners. Peter and Tom Spicer, an 18 year old victim of torture at the hands of the Mugabe regime, served the papers, as no more than two were allowed inside . .

We caught the metro to the Champs-Elysees, a swift walk up towards the Arc de Triomphe, and right to the Zimbabwe Embassy, to spend the intervening hours supporting Act Up in their protest. They threw condoms filled with dramatic red liquid at the walls and then themselves down onto the road to stop the police who were were gathering in force from dragging them away. 'Mugabe, arrete,' their angry defiant cries reached us as we approached. Joining their protest on the periphery, aware that if we were arrested now we would not make our four o'clock rendezvous outside the (Mugabe's) hotel. We fell back as they were dragged away, the press filming their distress and rough handling at the hands of the police.

From there back down the Champs-Elysees, and into the road on which Mugabe's chosen hotel stood. A road lined with shops, filled with designer goods – Gucci, Prada – the price of which the average Zimbabwean could hardly dream of, but its first lady routinely wears. Outside the hotel the press had gathered at the ready. We waited there for Peter. But our arranged time passed, and we could see the press getting restless, nothing happening, nothing to report. So we made our move. Rushed forwards, shouting and waving our banners. Yelled until we were hoarse. 'Arrest Mugabe, arrest Mugabe for torture.' 'Arrest

Beginnings

Mugabe, arrest Mugabe for torture.' 'Chinja, Maitiro.' 'Murderer, Murderer'. 'Mugabe must go.' 'Arrest Mugabe, Save Zimbabwe.'
The media's cameras trained on us. The police circling, jostling us, ripping the flags and banners from our hands. Slowly we were pushed further and further from the hotel entrance. Again more police than protesters, not asked to disband but slyly rounded up behind barriers, enclosed in a makeshift cage. Still we shouted, arousing the curiosity of passers by. And then a police bus arrived and one by one we were escorted onto it. To be taken where, we did not know. None of the police would tell us: 'just to take your identity'. We pushed our faces against the clear sections of the window, past the press and Peter Tatchell who must have arrived as we were being rounded up.

And then, a winding sirened journey (reminiscent of Mugabe's passing through the streets of Harare – a high speed motorcade) past the Eiffel Tower, up the Champs-Elysees and by the Arc de Triomphe, and into a suburb none of us knew. A tour of Paris unexpected. We were surprisingly jubilant. Messages came through on our phones from London, from South Africa, from Ghana and from Harare. We were on Sky, the BBC; the news had gone around the world. We had been seen.

Herded then out of the bus and into a holding cell where first our cameras were taken, then our mobile phones, and then our bags. Telling us nothing of how long we would be held, what would happen . . .

We were finally released after 8 o'clock, the policewoman on duty taking all our details and a group statement. She seemed embarrassed by our being detained. Our possessions were returned but not our flags and banners. 'Must be destroyed' we were told, much to our disbelief. And then it was a mad rush to get to the airport, a combination of metro and taxi getting us there just in time. On board we had champagne and each of us gave a toast 'To the next time' 'To change at home' 'To the end of a brutal regime'.
Sarah Davies

This Paris excursion was closely followed by one of the Vigil's most successful demonstrations when we hired a double decker bus to visit various places in London including Parliament to deliver a petition.

Beginnings

Freedom Bus – Wednesday 26th February 2003
A sunny early Spring day and an open-top red London bus, festooned with Zimbabwean flags, banners and posters denouncing murder, torture and rape under the Mugabe regime; it was a heady combination and with the top deck crowded with singers and drummers, it certainly turned many heads as it drove around central London for five hours on Wednesday 26th February. The occasion was the delivery of a petition calling on the UN Security Council to send a team to investigate human rights abuses in Zimbabwe. The petition was signed by close on 16,000 passers-by who stopped to support the protest Vigil outside the Zimbabwe High Commission, held every Saturday from 12.00 to 18.00 since last October. 16,000 signatures may not sound a lot compared to some widely-distributed petitions – but it meant a person signing every twenty seconds or so during the vigils.

About 60 of us – including supporters from Scotland, Bedfordshire, Coventry, Hertfordshire and Southend – set off raucously from the High Commission on our bus tour with much blowing of whistles and banging of drums. First stop was the House of Commons to present a copy of the petition to Clare Short, Secretary of State for International Development,

who – together with a number of other MPs from both the main parties – had agreed to receive us in the historic lobby of the House, despite an important debate that day on Iraq.

Ms Short paid rapt attention to Ephraim Tapa, chairman of MDC UK's Central London Branch, who handed over the petition on behalf of a group of six torture survivors. Mr Tapa told her, "There is no argument, no history, no post-colonial baggage, no politics or rhetoric that can explain or justify what has happened to myself and my compatriots here today. There are countless more in Zimbabwe who have not had the good fortune to escape from Mugabe's reach, who live and die in fear and humiliation every day." Mr Tapa pointed out that more than 3 million Zimbabweans have been forced into exile by deliberate starvation, state-sanctioned violence, murder, torture and rape – all to maintain Mugabe's political power. He added that support for the Zanu PF regime by some members of the non-aligned movement and the Commonwealth was utterly disgusting and misguided.

In her reply, Ms Short promised to do all in her power to work for change in Zimbabwe and said she was confident that this would come soon. But, beyond these words, it was the interest and concern that she showed that impressed the 40 or so Zimbabweans who had left the bus to deliver the petition. She spoke privately to the torture survivors, putting her arm around one young woman who recounted her story, and the meeting went on for much longer than scheduled.

After this it was light relief to rejoin the bus for a riotous journey through central London and down Oxford Street, packed as usual with shoppers from all over the world. By now our bus driver was no longer the anxious man he had been at the start: he had come to realise that all the hooting behind him was because of a poster on the back of the bus "Toot to stop Mugabe". As the bus made its slow way down Oxford Street surprised drivers and even cyclists had flyers thrust at them. Pedestrians smiled and waved – some of them risking life and limb to grab a flyer. One fellow looking very disapproving demanded who was in charge – only to hand over a £20 note. Down Park Lane we got a friendly wave from the world champion boxer Chris Eubank as he left an hotel.

Beginnings

On to the UN office at Millbank Tower, where people crowded to the windows to see the singing, dancing and drumming as we waited to present the petition. A UN representative, George Armstrong, told us the UN was aware of the urgency of the situation and promised the petition would be given high priority. Back to the bus and on to the Commonwealth Secretariat and then the South African High Commission, where demonstrators sang a rousing song demanding that President Mbeki do something about Zimbabwe. The High Commission staff seemed nonplussed – but visitors in Trafalgar Square were fascinated by the singing and dancing. Copies of the petition were also delivered to the Nigerian High Commission, to the office of the European Parliament and to the French Embassy. But, predictably, we were stonewalled at Zimbabwe House. Put it in the letterbox said the security man. A quick check established there was no letterbox. Well, the message had already been delivered!

A strong element in the early days of the Vigil was a young (mainly white) group aligned to the far left Socialist Workers. They wanted the Vigil to be part of the broad left agenda, embracing international Marxists, the Palestinian cause and particularly the anti (Iraq) war coalition.

A majority at our Monday gatherings of the Central London branch of the MDC felt that, while we may be sympathetic to these causes, our focus must be Zimbabwe and we should not dissipate our energies on other struggles. We questioned: if material from one other group was to be displayed at the Vigil, why material from any other group should not be allowed?

The Monday MDC meetings became fractious. One of the Socialist Workers, chosen as acting chairman, remarked after a vote against him: 'It doesn't matter. I'll just call another meeting.' The situation became so bitter that the police were called to investigate an anonymous threatening telephone message. The police reported that the call had come from a public call box near the home of one of the radical leftists.

Members of the far left had been given responsibility for the Vigil's website and refused for a long time to relinquish control even though

Beginnings

they were producing no material. This is why the weekly diaries did not start until June 2004 when control of the website was regained.

The journal takes us until mid-2017 when we faced renewed efforts to undermine the Vigil. We begin with the diaries of 2016 / 2017 because they are likely to be of most immediate interest. Afterwards we follow a chronological pattern from the earliest diaries in 2004 onwards, with each year prefaced by highlights. A glossary can be found at the back.

2016

Highlights

23rd January: former Botswana president criticises Mugabe.
30th January: NHS doctor evicts white farmer.
February: state of emergency declared over food shortages.
February: Mugabe splashes out on 92nd birthday party.
March: Mugabe says $15 billion looted from diamond mines.
March: clashes between war veterans and police.
7th May: announcement that Zimbabwe to print money again.
June: activists in Harare stage round-the-clock protest against worsening situation.
13th June: Zimbabwean doctor's UK medical centre closed.
18th June: Vigil appeals to Botswana for help.
5th July: Vigil besieges Finance Minister Chinamasa on money-raising trip to London.
9th July: fears grow that West to bail out Mugabe.
13th / 14th July: Two day protest in Harare by #ThisFlag movement.
23rd July: war veterans denounce Mugabe.
6th August: Vigil launches petition to UN for transitional authority.
26th August: chaos in Harare as police attack demonstrators.
17th September: MDC MP Eddie Cross tells Vigil of international plan to replace Mugabe with reformists.
October: dismissed Vice-President Mujuru talks in London of her new party's plans for reform.
October: Zim activists denied visas to speak in UK.
28th November: bond notes issued.
December: Zanu PF Conference nominates Mugabe to stand in 2018 elections.
December: Grace Mugabe in dispute over $1.3 million diamond ring.
December: Mugabe family fly to Singapore on $6 million holiday.

Vigil Diary Excerpts

Thirst for human rights – Saturday 2nd January: A representative of the Vigil and our sister organisation the Restoration of Human Rights has been on an undercover visit to Zimbabwe during which he travelled extensively. He reported finding a thirst for human rights. He said he had spoken at many meetings, including in the Zanu PF heartland of Mashonaland West. Among those attending were university lecturers as well as pastors who said they were prepared to speak from the pulpit about human rights. Our envoy said that while he was in Harare he tried to renew his expired passport under a provision in the new constitution providing for dual citizenship. But when his name was entered into the computer a message flashed up 'Threat to national security' originating from the CIO Directorate. The lady processing his claim asked anxiously 'What have you done?' When he said he was a human rights campaigner she said: 'No it's political. Just go now or it has to be referred to security.'

Indigenous hot air – Saturday 9th January: As far as producing hot air is concerned the Vigil is confident that Zimbabwe is a world beater. With swarms of political parties quacking away like ducks on steroids, it is one industry in which we can more than compete. So it comes as a surprise that in the 'clarified' indigenisation guidelines (ensuring black control of companies) the government has seen it necessary to include air among the affected categories. The guidelines were the product of Indigenisation Minister Zhuwao, nephew of Mugabe. But even Zhuwao is outdone for hot air by Zanu PF spokesman Simon Kaya Moyo who says his party has done 'extremely well' over the past two years with 'the generality of the population feeling the effects of ZimAsset'. We suppose the hot air has at least kept them warm in winter . . . As the Vigil marked the passing of ten months since the abduction of Itai Dzamara on 9th March, we were encouraged to hear the message of Pastor Patrick Mugadza who has called on Mugabe to step aside and hand power to an interim authority. He said 'Fear has gotten us to where we are. Dzamara was a seed and many Dzamaras will come up if I disappear.'

Appeal for UN aid – Saturday 16th January: The United Nations is understood to be considering a Zimbabwean request to provide emergency aid for Mugabe's 92nd birthday celebrations in Masvingo next month. UN East and Southern Africa spokesman, Idi Ott, said UNFED had been expecting a request for help because of the severe drought affecting Sub-Saharan Africa. He said there had been surprise at UN headquarters at the lateness of the request because it normally takes some months to mount an international appeal of this magnitude. A Zanu PF spokesman was reassuring: 'People need have no fear for Comrade Gushungo. He is well-fed and there will also be enough food for the whole Politburo as well'.

Time to intervene? – Saturday 23rd January: With the Mugabe regime seemingly determined to use any means to cling to power despite the deepening crisis in Zimbabwe, the outside world must be prepared to think the unthinkable. Former Botswana President Festus Mogae was clear in an interview that sovereignty has limits. He made no direct reference to Zimbabwe but his message was unmistakeable. Here is part of what he had to say: 'Sovereignty has limits like any other right. A leader cannot kill and harass his people and hide behind sovereignty. A true leader does not kill, but protects his people. We still have leaders in Africa who think they are indispensable, larger than life and more important than their countries. That must stop. If a leader loses control, the world will and should intervene to save the people'.

No African country has the will or capacity to intervene to avert disaster in Zimbabwe and Mugabe's all-weather friends China and Russia will prevent any action by the UN. So it's up to Zimbabwe's real friends – the countries that keep on putting their hands in their pockets – to help in spite of Zanu PF's bile. Only this week Rural Development Minister Abednego Ncube told traditional leaders that they had not received their November and December allowances because of (long gone) Western sanctions. This is the cloud cuckoo land that Zanu PF is living in, supported by back-slapping Western diplomats having the holiday of their lives. The Vigil thinks the West must stop propping up this evil regime and instead prepare plans to avert the slide into violence born of poverty and desperation.

British doctor seizes farm – Saturday 30th January: After months besieged on their farm at Centenary, 20 police armed with AK 47s on Friday forcibly evicted Phillip Rankin and his wife. The farm has long been coveted by British medical practitioner Dr Sylvester Nyatsuro and his wife Veronica, who are reported to be connected to Grace Mugabe. Mrs Nyatsuro is alleged to have planted invaders on the farm when she was over last year on a visit from the UK. The police refused access to lawyers acting for Mr Rankin, loaded his furniture onto lorries along with Mr Rankin and drove off before he could harvest his crops.

The behaviour of the Nyatsuros has disgusted Zimbabwean exiles in the UK and the Vigil is to stage another protest outside their Nottingham clinic and will also be running the following petition to Prime Minister David Cameron: *Zimbabwean exiles in the United Kingdom and sympathisers are appalled by the behaviour of Dr Sylvester Nyatsuro and his wife Veronica who run the Willows Medical Centre in Nottingham. Dr Nyatsuro is a British citizen, long resident in this country, yet he has illegally seized a farm in Zimbabwe owned by a white Zimbabwean farmer, Mr Phillip Rankin, who bought it with the approval of the Mugabe government. Dr Nyatsuro and his wife are reported to be connected to Grace Mugabe. We are puzzled why a British doctor should want a farm in Zimbabwe since he and his wife are apparently in full-time employment here and have no known farming expertise in a country facing starvation. We ask your government to consider revoking Dr Nyatsuro's citizenship on the grounds that 'it was obtained by means of fraud, false representation or concealment of any material fact'. We also question his suitability to run an NHS clinic in Nottingham while farming in Zimbabwe.*

Pressure mounts on farm looter – Saturday 6th February: More than 60 exiled Zimbabweans and supporters yesterday took part in a protest outside the clinic in Nottingham run by a Zimbabwean immigrant doctor who has seized a farm in Zimbabwe. Demonstrators were not surprised to see a notice on the front door saying the clinic was closed because of 'unforeseen circumstances'. But people were in the building because someone from the clinic called the police and complained we were taking pictures of them through the window. We replied that pictures were being taken of us from the clinic. A Vigil supporter posted this letter to Dr Nyatsuro through the clinic's letter box: *'As fellow Zimbabweans we wish to express our disgust at your abuse of British hospitality. You work as a doctor for the NHS but feel free to steal a white-owned farm in Zimbabwe in your spare time. We have tried to meet you to discuss this matter but all we got were lies, evasion and legal threats. So we return to your clinic to draw the attention of your patients and the wider community to your greed and hypocrisy. If you wanted to have a farm in Zimbabwe why are you here? Get out of the UK and don't* *come back.'* Many motorists hooted in support of the demonstration when they drove past and the Vigil engaged many local people about the issue. We have already written to the local NHS Commissioning Group drawing attention to the matter with copies to the General Medical Council and the Department of Health. Ironically another white farmer has also been driven off the land. But we have no sympathy for this farmer, Yvonne Goddard. She had been funding Zanu PF until the party bigwigs simply decided to take everything – a fate we fully expect to be visited on themselves in due course.

A no-brainer – Saturday 13th February: Having waited until Mugabe returned from his sacred month-long Christmas holiday abroad, the government finally got around to admitting what it had persistently denied and declared a state of emergency because of food shortages. The Vigil's sister organisation ROHR expressed the desperation in Zimbabwe by taking part in a Valentine's march in Harare. We received this message from a ROHR member: 'The march started at the corner of Inez Terrace and Speke Avenue. We marched into Julius Nyerere then into Nelson Mandela singing the national anthem. As we approached Second

Street towards Parliament, where we intended to place a bouquet, we encountered the full force of the vicious riot police. They beat up people badly with baton sticks. Three people are hospitalized at Westend Hospital. One ROHR member is in a bad state.'

Earlier in the week, speaking at the official launch of the aid appeal, Vice-President Mnangagwa spoke of a food disaster as if it had suddenly arisen although experts had been warning of it for at least the last six months. Perhaps he made the mistake of believing the lies of Agriculture Minister Mad Made who said only recently that Zimbabwe had plenty of food in stock. Mnangagwa will also no doubt back Mad Made's insistence that any aid should not include GM food. So donors beware: you could be wasting your money sending us poisonous food when people can starve in a non-GM way. Mnangagwa was precise about Zimbabwe's requirements, which he said amounted to $1,572,009,953. This billion plus included money to repair irrigation equipment and livestock support and restocking, as well as soap, pharmaceuticals and three dollars for sanitaryware. In short, Zimbabwe needs everything except GM food. Mugabe may not acknowledge it, but people are already starving. Perhaps Mugabe will call off his $800,000 92nd birthday bash next week to devote the food to the suffering masses. It's what they call a no-brainer . . . obviously the right thing. But the Vigil fears that in Zanu PF's case no-brainer must be taken literally.

Internal contradictions – Saturday 20th February: With Dr Grace now openly described as a witchdoctor, it came as no surprise that Mugabe was magically transported to the Vigil to try to raise some of the $800,000 apparently wanted for his 92nd birthday party with its 92 kg cake. That the party is being held at the Zimbabwe Ruins is entirely appropriate. What may seem less appropriate to donors is spending so much feeding Mugabe at a time when Zimbabwe is appealing for $1.5 billion to help the starving. The birthday boy – played by Fungayi Mabhunu in our Mugabe mask – turned up sleepily at the Vigil holding upside down one of our posters 'Where is Itai Dzamara?' He was presented with several cakes and a colourful birthday painting showing Mugabe drowning in a tide of blood. Pinned to the painting were Zimbabwean hundred trillion dollar notes worth two quadrillion, five hundred trillion Zimbabwe dollars. Surely enough for anyone's party. Mugabe was surrounded by Vigil supporters carrying posters such as:

'Pay Mugabe in his own currency', 'Let Mugabe eat cake', and 'Emergency appeal for Mugabe's birthday party'.

Mugabe was fresh from making a televised address in Harare to appeal for an end to factionalism in Zanu PF following clashes in Harare between war veterans and riot police. Perhaps with Grace in mind, he spoke of the need 'for a whip of discipline'. The clashes prompted war vet leader Mutsvangwa to make an extraordinary attack on Grace who he suggested was under the influence of occult powers. Perhaps this was one of the things Mugabe had in mind when he spoke of 'contradictions' in Zanu PF. A more obvious contradiction came in an answer given by Agriculture Ministry Secretary Ringson Chitsiko when he was questioned about the food situation by the parliamentary committee on agriculture, which asked why Zambia had surplus maize when it was also affected by El Nino weather conditions. The difference, Chitsiko said, was due to 'serious farming in Zambia at commercial level'.

The contradictions between the public and private faces of the ruling party have been shown in a new light by ousted Vice President Joice Mujuru in a lengthy interview with the UK Sunday Times. 'I think this is pointing to the end', said Mujuru. 'He no longer has the energy to tell them to stop, and no one listens to him. He has no respect now – from anybody. It's painful.' According to Mujuru, Mugabe often falls asleep in cabinet meetings. 'He would speak for 15 minutes then nod off and I would then chair the meeting, with everyone ignoring the fact he was asleep.' Asked about Mugabe's accusations that she had consulted witchdoctors about his death, she said: 'I have never used magic. A head of state using his platform to lie and believing stories about frogs being kept in a calabash, and if one dies then he will die? I said to myself, "What a backward man."'

Kick out Zanu PF – Saturday 27th February: Some of the UK's main newspapers published lengthy articles today on the Nottingham doctor, Sylvester Nyatsuro, who has seized a farm in Zimbabwe. The articles coincided with the presentation of the Vigil's petition to 10 Downing Street calling on the UK to revoke Dr Nyatsuro's British citizenship. What prompted the two papers to revisit the story was the emergence of photographs which showed Dr Nyatsuro and his wife Veronica socialising with Grace Mugabe. As the Daily Mail put it 'Grinning with

Mrs Mugabe, GP who was handed white couple's farm'. The photograph was seen as disproving the Nyatsuros' denial that nepotism had played a part in the allocation of the farm to someone who has become a British citizen and lived in the UK for the past 15 years. The mass circulation Daily Mail has been assiduously digging away at the scandal. That it has now been joined so enthusiastically by the upmarket Daily Telegraph perhaps reflects the Telegraph's irritation at the Nyatsuros' earlier blustering legal threats against the paper which prompted it to drop a previous story from its website. The same Zanu PF bullying tactics were made against the Vigil but we have not been deterred from demonstrating outside their Nottingham clinic to show their patients what hypocrites the Nyatsuros are. Our latest protest yesterday was attended by 50 from as far afield as Edinburgh and Portsmouth. A Daily Mail journalist interviewed us. She then tried to ask Veronica Nyatsuro some questions, only to be pushed angrily away.

Many of the Nottingham demonstrators turned up to support the presentation of the Vigil petition addressed to Prime Minister Cameron. It was accompanied by this letter: *Dear Prime Minister: Zimbabwean exiles in the United Kingdom and supporters ask your government to look at the case of Dr Sylvester Nyatsuro, a GP running a clinic in Nottingham with his wife Veronica. Dr Nyatsuro is from Zimbabwe but has lived in the UK for the past 15 years and is now a British citizen. The Sunday Times says he came here as an asylum seeker but this has not stopped him from violently seizing a farm in Zimbabwe owned by a Zimbabwean citizen, Phillip Rankin and his family. We are not aware that Dr Nyatsuro has any farming knowledge or whether he intends to relinquish his Nottingham practice so we wonder what justification he has to take over one of the last remaining white-owned farms in Zimbabwe, beyond being given the go ahead by the Mugabes with whom he and his wife are reported to have connections. The Zimbabwe Vigil draws your attention to the starvation threatening millions of Zimbabweans and the urgent need to resuscitate agriculture and asks you whether 'slimming expert' Dr Nyatsuro is a person likely to further this goal. We believe that he and his wife are Mugabe predators and Dr Nyatsuro's citizenship should be revoked because we believe it must have been obtained under false pretences.*

Interesting times – Saturday 5th March: There is apparently an old Chinese warning against living in 'interesting times' . . . interesting meaning dangerous, troubled, violent, precarious, unstable etc: in brief, all the 'interesting' conditions that now prevail in Zimbabwe. So hard luck to us after a week which saw the unveiling of Joice Mujuru's People First Party and the suspension from Zanu PF of War Veterans' Minister Mutsvangwa. Both events were overshadowed by Mugabe's announcement that $15 billion had been looted from the Marange diamond fields and by the government's chaotic seizure of the Chiadzwa diamond mines owned by Mugabe's pals. 'We wuz robbed,' claimed Mugabe. 'Where has all the money gone?' feigning not to have noticed the diamonds on the soles of the feet of his well-shod wife and well-heeled cronies and all-weather friends. Chief friend Comrade China says it is offended and hopes it's all been a mistake. 'We hope that the Zimbabwean side would earnestly safeguard the legitimate rights of the Chinese companies and employees, according to the local laws and the 'Agreement on the encouragement and reciprocal protection of investments between China and Zimbabwe,' Chinese ambassador Huang Ping said. Laws? Agreement? It appears the Chinese were born yesterday. But anyway it must mean farewell to the long-promised 'mega deals' with China which we were told would usher in the promised land. Zimbabwe is floundering with little sign of meaningful reform and sustainable, broad-based recovery says the International Crisis Group. 'Upbeat economic projections by international institutions are predicated on government rhetoric about new policy commitments and belief in the country's potential, but there are growing doubts that ZANU PF can "walk the talk" of reform. Conditions are likely to deteriorate further due to insolvency, drought and growing food insecurity,' it says.

On a cold rainy day, the Vigil welcomed human rights activist Ben Freeth on a brief visit to the UK. He went on to speak at the Zimbabwe Action Forum held after the Vigil and was encouraging about our work. He said the situation at home was dreadful and remarked that he recently went back to see his stolen farm and found there were no crops, the irrigation system had been destroyed and his former workers were unemployed and impoverished. He warned that Zanu PF would be looking to control people by exploiting British and American food aid for party-political purposes. 'The British tax payer will be paying to keep Mugabe in power'. Ben said he was sceptical about the sudden conversion to enlightened democrat of die-hard Zanu PF thieving functionary Joice Mujuru. He recalled how she and her murdered husband General Solomon Mujuru had deceived and stolen their farm from its previous owner who had been forced to flee the country with only one suitcase. He was critical of the European diplomats living in what he called the 'Harare bubble' and said how difficult it was to get any of them to go out and see things for themselves.

Culture of denial – Saturday 12th March: Where is Mugabe? The government's mouthpiece the Herald says he has gone to a cultural festival in India (accompanied by the Foreign Affairs Minister and a planeload of overpaid lackeys). The fact that the obscure festival was not even attended by the Indian President didn't matter. The Vigil knows that this is probably all a cover for another trip to his doctors in Singapore. The International Monetary Fund has concluded its latest consultations in Harare leaving the door ajar to new loans to help bankrupt Zanu PF. The IMF seems to think that promises of reform by the regime are bankable. Zimbabwean ministers like Chinamasa can promise the moon but no one can deliver except Mugabe. And, as he has shown over civil servants bonuses, he will not make any decision which will imperil his hold on power.

The culture of denial in Mugabe's Zanu PF is shown by the party's brazen hypocrisy over the abduction of human rights activist Itai Dzamara. We welcome the statement by the US Embassy in Harare on the anniversary of this outrage demanding justice. We urge the United States to take the advice of Bob Corker, Chairman of the Senate Foreign Relations Committee, who called on President Obama to prevent new lending to Zimbabwe unless there is meaningful progress to restore the rule of law and improve human rights. The Vigil believes that any financial help to prop up Mugabe's odious regime will simply prolong the suffering of the people of Zimbabwe. It was good to see old friends from the MDC UK who joined us today to mark one year since the abduction of Itai Dzamara. For Vigil supporters it was the second Dzamara demonstration in a week following a protest outside the Embassy on 9th March, which was the actual day he was seized.

Mugabe's 'hit and run' – Saturday 19th March: President Mugabe, stung by the growing opposition of war veterans, complained at a rally in

Bindura 'some of you are going as far as China telling them that we need a new leader'. The comment is ironic given reports that the nonagenarian is soon to go on yet another jaunt to the Far East – this time to Tokyo – which some might think shows an absence of leadership. The Herald will no doubt tell us that the trip is as important as the Indian cultural festival that Mugabe used as a pretext last week to go to Singapore to see his doctors. But what credulity has the Herald? This week it splashed a story that a majority of Zimbabweans approve of Mugabe's leadership – only for it to emerge a day later that the paper was repeating a dodgy two-year-old report. Contrary to the Herald's delayed 'scoop', it is clear that even the war veterans have fallen out of love with Mugabe even though he assures us all is under control. No one will starve he told supporters at the rally. 'The food is there and what is slowing distribution is the challenge we are facing in transportation', he said. To alleviate the transport problem, the district development fund had adopted a 'hit and run' concept and has ten trucks going around the country moving food from the grain marketing board depots to the public. Ten trucks? All solved then!

The great demise – Saturday 2nd April: There is growing concern in the diaspora about the wellbeing of Zimbabweans when Mugabe goes. The people the Vigil worry most about are those who have been led to believe that Mugabe is semi-divine. For them the loss will be cataclysmic. Mugabe has gone to see his doctors in Singapore twice in the last few weeks. We must be brave. Others have gone through similar trauma. We remember the mass hysteria in North Korea at the departure of the Great Leader Kim Jong Il, whose people had been led to believe that he could never get ill. Scenes of public grief were broadcast around the world. Zimbabweans must show we are made of sterner stuff. We expect Harare to come to even more of a halt when the great transition occurs. So outside help will be urgently required to minimise grief-related suicides and post-traumatic stress disorders. To do our bit, we in the diaspora are appealing to the United Nations to prepare to send teams of bereavement counsellors who could fan out across the country. Para-psychotherapists could even be air-dropped in remote areas.

The Vigil's approach is two-pronged. We have also written to the American Ambassador in London urging the US to oppose any IMF / World Bank loans to Zimbabwe until the situation is clarified. Surely no-one wants the money to end up in the wrong hands? Here is our letter: *Dear Ambassador Barzun, With the Mugabe regime nearing its end, Zimbabwean exiles in the UK wish to convey our reservations about the apparent readiness of the International Monetary Fund to advance new loans to Zimbabwe. We ask what purpose this financial injection will serve when there is no clear idea of who will receive the money? We draw your attention to the latest index of economic freedom which concludes that Zimbabwe remains one of the most repressed economies in the world due to rampant corruption and government mismanagement* . . .

Can of maggots – Saturday 9th April: Zimbabweans in exile join in demanding a commission of inquiry into the involvement of Zimbabweans in offshore tax havens and believe it will open a can of maggots that have been sucking dry the carcase of our economy. The leaking of millions of documents from the dodgy Panamanian law firm Mossack Fonseca has exposed the involvement of Zanu PF financiers Billy Rautenbach and Nicholas van Hoogstraten. This was predictable but it is also alleged that Mugabe himself has used the firm to hide his vast wealth in havens around the world. The MDC MP Eddie Cross says Mugabe's personal wealth is estimated at over $3 billion gained from all sorts of activities in Zimbabwe and the region. He adds: 'The disclosure by Mr. Mugabe that some $15 billion in revenues had somehow vanished from the Marange diamond fields between 2008 and 2015 reveals the extent of these activities. He is known to own, directly or indirectly, luxury homes in South Africa (Sandton and Durban North), Hong Kong, Singapore and Dubai as well as in Harare.'

The Japanese commentator Ken Yamamoto, who closely follows Zimbabwean affairs, describes Mugabe's disclosure as: 'the mother of all scandals'. He says: 'With the stolen $15 billion, Zimbabwe could have provided its economy a huge bailout, funding refurbishment of railways infrastructure, construction of power plants, construction and expansion of national highways, a bailout to the sinking industrial sector, provided clean water in cities, funded alternative agriculture and processing industries and invested in clean energy.' Yamamoto goes on: 'For a 92-year old man whose leadership has wasted an entire generation to laugh and crack jokes while talking about such grand theft under his watch is a vulgar insult to millions of jobless Zimbabweans and millions more who are presently being fed by donors.' He concludes: 'This kind of plunder must immediately make Zimbabwe pass a vote of no confidence in Mugabe and his government. If this theft does not cause Zimbabweans to demand that he resign, then nothing else will. In that case, going forward, Zimbabweans must just be left to their own devices and the donors currently feeding the population must just take their efforts to other countries. The country cannot be helped. And no more of this nonsense that Zimbabweans are the most literate people in Africa.'

War veteran and former Zanu PF insider Margaret Dongo also has no illusions about the greed and corruption in Zanu PF. In a recent interview with the Daily News she said: 'I left Zanu PF in 1995, and watching from the terraces I am seeing people fighting for a dwindling gravy puddle. The party is a sinking ship and it's all about who has power now to access more of the little loot left before the inevitable big bang.' She went on to say: 'The 90 per cent unemployment obtaining in the country, the starving masses that the government is unable to feed, the dilapidated infrastructure all around, the serious shortage of drugs, deteriorating education standards, poor sanitary facilities are all a result of Zanu PF's misrule.'

36 years of destruction – Saturday 16th April: As we marked Zimbabwe's 36th independence anniversary, exiles in the UK were joined by Mugabe himself outside the London Embassy. His Excellency, in the form of Fungayi Mabhunu in our Mugabe mask and carrying a poster reading '36 years of me. What else can I destroy?' answered some of our questions. The first was how he justified spending $20 million on foreign trips so far this year at a time when the economy is alleged not to be booming. 'Well, this trip to London is costing nothing', he said. 'As you may know I have recently had to make one or three essential visits to the Far East so I have collected lots of air miles'. Our second question to his well-travelled Excellency was about the 300 cattle that he announced he had donated to the African Union last year to reduce the AU's dependence on Western aid. 'It just struck me that no one had ever thought of a gift by way of cattle to the AU', he said, brushing aside reports that none of the beasts had been sent . . . Mugabe was then asked about Zanu PF's rejection of genetically modified food – a move condemned by Zimbabwean farmer Nyasha Mudukuti in an article in the Wall Street Journal: 'So my country – a country that can't feed itself –

will refuse what millions around the world eat safely every day . . . we're apparently better dead than fed'. The nonagenarian went on: 'What some people don't realise is the effect of illegal sanctions. As well as inflicting aids on Africa and causing our drought, the West is now determined to exterminate us with genetically modified organisms (GMOs) so that they can control us like they do the troublemakers who caused chaos in Harare on Thursday in an attempt at regime change'. The Vigil is pleased to see that our sister organisation ROHR was prominent among those which took part in the MDC demonstration on Thursday.

Emperor with no clothes – Saturday 23rd April: The newish American Ambassador to Harare, Peter Harry Thomas Jnr, has quickly got the hang of Mugabe, speaking this week of his 'wicked sense of humour'. Commenting on Mugabe's sanctions mantra, Mr Thomas showed he had come to realise that the President is a joke. Hans Christian Anderson's 'The Emperor's New Clothes' is a story about a vain emperor who is tricked into wearing what he is told are clothes that are invisible to those who are stupid. Everyone raves about his clothes until a child cries out 'he isn't wearing anything at all'. It often takes an outsider to say that the emperor has no clothes. People were merely puzzled as Mugabe bowed to a picture of himself at his Independence Day address. They pretended not to see he was exposing himself. Zanu PF supporters didn't dare see the humour when Mugabe told them that the economy was on a rebound, with firms reopening for business and creating jobs. They didn't even laugh when he said: 'My government is determined to translate political independence into meaningfulness by attending to the socio-economic needs of our people'. Even claims that bankrupt parastatals such as Air Zimbabwe and National Railways of Zimbabwe had come out of the woods, failed to draw a smile, let alone his comment that 'progress has been made in the development of social infrastructure in health, education and housing'. Nobody laughed when he promised to improve the wellbeing of government workers so that they can earn salaries above the poverty datum line. Perhaps they did not get the 'wicked' joke that he has promised the International Monetary Fund to halve the government wage bill this year. There was not even a giggle when he concluded 'one of the greatest tributes we can pay to Zimbabwe is to shun corruption, regionalism and nepotism'. Mind you many people also didn't get the joke when he promptly flew off to the United States for the ceremonial signing of the UN climate change agreement and droned on as usual about invisible sanctions against Zimbabwe when signatories – mainly lower-ranking officials – were supposed to keep their remarks to 40 seconds. But those at the UN meeting realized that Mugabe had not travelled all the way to New York for a mere 40 seconds . . . he and his cronies no doubt had serious shopping to do for some more new clothes.

Déjà vu again – Saturday 30th April: May Day is celebrated around the world to honour workers. Indeed, Zimbabwe calls it Workers' Day. But the MDC says it should now be rebranded Vendors' Day instead. MDC spokesman Obert Gutu says there is nothing to celebrate given the depressing state of the economy. Zanu PF, he pointed out, had failed to create the 2.2 million jobs it promised at the 2013 elections. Instead it had created 2 million 'vendors and loafers'. An equally gloomy view came from People's Democratic Party spokesman Jacob Mafume: 'The nation is facing insurmountable challenges underlined by a decaying economy, high unemployment and total collapse of service delivery, a ravaging drought and general hopelessness among the generality of the people,' he said. 'About 98% of youths are in the informal sector, 60% of the industries which we had operating in 2010 have shut down, 83% of our people live on less than $1 a day and our women still die while giving birth because our hospitals lack basic facilities and medicines.'

Even people in work are suffering from the economic meltdown as banks struggle to find cash. As Radio Voice of the People puts it 'it's déjà vu again' with many workers reliving the nightmare of 2008 when banks imposed daily cash withdrawal limits. Back then the financial collapse led of course to the South African-brokered coalition government which pulled the country back from the abyss but saved Mugabe. The Vigil fears that this time Britain and the international community will come to the rescue of Mugabe with mad new lending to a totally corrupt and self-serving regime. The announcement this week of a conference to be held in London in July to discuss a proposed deal between Mugabe and the International Monetary Fund and the World Bank confirms the Vigil's suspicions that once again the UK has misread the situation in Zimbabwe. You could say it is déjà vu yet again. Former finance minister Tendai Biti's People's Democratic Party has accused the British Ambassador in Harare, Catriona Laing, of lobbying the US State Department to support Mugabe's bid for renewed IMF funding, warning her that appeasing Zanu PF is 'tantamount to riding a leopard'. What does Ms Laing think that Mugabe's gang will do with the money apart from paying the Israeli Nikuv company to rig the next elections as usual? Wouldn't it be better to wait until Zanu PF actually implements the new constitution and better still after free and fair elections before they give Zimbabwe more money. As it looks at the moment there are strong indications that Zanu PF will again resort to violence in the run up to the elections in 2018.

The megabus arrives? – Saturday 7th May: There is a saying in the UK that you can wait ages for a bus and then several will come along together. It seems the same thing happens with news about Zimbabwe reported in the foreign press. There was a drought in stories about Zimbabwe for years but now the buses are coming regularly. Not long ago we had Cecil the lion capturing world attention. Then everyone was fascinated by the extravagant parties given for nonagenarian Mugabe as if he were Louis XVI, with Grace his Marie-Antoinette advising the hungry to eat cake (shortly before the royal couple were downsized by a head). The buses have continued coming, with widespread interest in Zimbabwe selling off wild life. As Fox News headlined: 'Zimbabwe's drought cash crunch forcing the nation to sell its animals'. (Thinking of Zimbabwe selling off its wild life, its nurses, its graduates, its women to Kuwait, suggests there may be room for a sell off of politicians from among its dozens of parties.)

Among journalists there is a saying 'a nose for news'. You would think that Zimbabwe is now positively stinking because they have jumped in force on the latest bus with the announcement that Zimbabwe is to print money again. BBC: 'Zimbabwe to print its own version of US dollar', Bloomberg: 'Zimbabwe introduces new currency angering everyone', International Business Times: 'Zimbabwe to print its own US dollars amidst severe cash shortage and deepening economic woes'. The world thinks that this smells – its the megabus – and it expects to see, as the Vigil diary put it last week, déjà vu again, with the Zimbabwe Reserve Bank sending out runners onto the streets to buy up US dollars with worthless bits of paper as inflation rises again into the billions. And perhaps King Mugabe and co being downsized . . .

Facing reality – Saturday 14th May: Exiled Zimbabweans in the UK welcomed remarks this week by US Ambassador to Zimbabwe, Peter

Harry Thomas Jr, who called for full implementation of the constitution, an up-to-date voters' roll, the elimination of corruption and a 'reliable' court system. Speaking to journalists in Harare, Mr Thomas said this was critical if Zimbabwe is to have free and fair elections in 2018. He added: 'We don't want to see violence; we don't want to see intimidation. We want to see people who are given the opportunity to campaign without fear of harassment and the start is full implementation of the 2013 constitution'. So far so good. But the Vigil would like clarification of Mr Thomas's assertion that the US is 'in support of Zimbabwe's re-engagement with the international financial institutions'. What exactly does this mean? Zimbabwe desperately needs money, sure. The reason is clear: Mugabe and his cronies have stolen everything. There is pervasive corruption at all levels as well as institutionalised incompetence. An example: Health Minister Dr David Parirenyatwa says his ministry needs $65 million urgently to buy drugs. He said the Treasury approved a budget of $450,000 for Midlands province but it was given only $3,000 – and that was also to cover patients' food and utility bills . . . Vice-President Mphoko of course blamed Western sanctions.

The Vigil's fear is that 're-engagement' with the International Monetary Fund and World Bank means approval of some creative bookkeeping to deal with Zimbabwe's debt to these institutions allowing the imploding regime to access more loans to enable it to steal yet another election. Having been turned down by his 'all-weather friends' Mugabe has been left with no option but to try to con money from the enemy and has come up with a plethora of promises from dealing with corruption to a land audit and compensation for white farmers, from halving the state wage bill to reforming bankrupt parastatals. All this is fantasy as there is no real will or capacity to achieve these goals. The IMF has recently toughened its hitherto craven language about the regime. We want it to get even tougher and tell Mugabe that new money will only come if the West is at long last allowed in to observe the elections and judge whether they have been free and fair. As we have pointed out before, the stakes are high. Zanu PF has long been a malignant influence in the region as is shown clearly by recent developments in South Africa. Witness the paranoia of ANC Secretary-General Gwede Mantashe, facing growing opposition to his party, parroting the line that the West is pushing for 'regime change' in South Africa. Where did we hear that before?

Waving the flag – Saturday 21st May: The suggestion that the Zimbabwean government is looking at ways of 'taxing' the diaspora may be fanciful but it is clear that both Zanu PF and the opposition are looking hungrily at the money earned by the millions of Zimbabweans who have fled Mugabe's economic Armageddon. The government, we were told this week, has drafted a Diaspora Policy which seeks to tap into exiles' remittances estimated at $1.8 billion a year – way more than the country is attracting in foreign direct investment. It is typical of the Zanu PF mentality that the government should think it has a claim to any of this money. It's bad enough that hundreds of thousands of family members in Zimbabwe have become so dependent on remittances – indeed appealing for ever more help. We now learn from a prominent opposition member that their own attempt to raise money from the diaspora for an election war fund has met with little response. Can they be surprised given their dismissive attitude to the diaspora down the years? To them the diaspora has only ever been a cash cow. If the government does try to 'tax' the diaspora we must consider how we can pay in 'bond' notes.

Wednesday 25th May: Africa Day – a large group from the Vigil went to a performance of a play about Zimbabwe 'After Independence' at the Arcola Theatre in London. The play examined the land question in Zimbabwe and the theatre was packed. Our group danced, sang and drummed afterwards to an appreciative audience in the theatre bar including members of the cast. The producer Chris Foxon sent us this email afterwards: *'Just a quick note to express an enormous thanks for joining us last night. It was a fabulous event and I hope it helped raise awareness of your work. Certainly the audience loved it, and our cast were blown away.'*

The big stink – Saturday 28th May: Fresh from his 'million man' charade in Harare, Mugabe flew off on Air Mugabe to enjoy being the only President from the 79 members of the Organisation of African, Caribbean and Pacific States to attend a meeting in Papua New Guinea. Apparently not even the Papua New Guinea President was attending. Papua New Guinea? If you consult the atlas you will find it is part of an island east of Indonesia and north of Australia. A spokesman for PNG (as it is known to those who have consulted the atlas) said his country was keen to raise its international profile because not many people knew where it was. 'They think it is part of Africa' he said. Well, Air Mugabe knows where PNG is: conveniently close to Mugabe's doctors in Singapore. It's been more than a week since he last saw them so surely more injections are due – apart from changing the nappy of his grandson. Mugabe was accompanied by the usual large delegation which included Grace of course, Industry and Commerce Minister Mike Bimha and Foreign Affairs Minister Simbarashe Mumbengegwi. Permanent secretaries Ambassador Joey (yet another) Bimha and George Charamba, among the usual flunkies, helped fill the Air Mugabe plane. The PNG is popular for its diving and other leisure facilities. But the Vigil is worried that Mugabe's insatiable trips abroad are believed to have cost the country $80 million this year. How come he is squandering this money when thousands of hungry, deluded Zanu PF youth were left to make their own way home from the 'million man' march?

Jacob Mafume, spokesman for Tendai Biti's People's Democratic Party, said: 'Mugabe suffers from an excessive attention seeking sickness. He is like a man who messes up his own house with his waste and keeps leaving the house because the house smells'. This struck a chord with us because an article has appeared in the London Times on this theme, even mentioning Mugabe. The article about dictators talked of the overpowering stench at the French King Louis XIV's palace at Versailles. The palace had 700 rooms but no functioning lavatories for nearly 200 years. Even then the soon to be executed Queen Marie Antoinette was said to have been drenched by the contents of a chamber pot emptied from an upper window. The place apparently stank more than Chitingwiza. The writer of the article noted 'eventually people cease to be awed by dictator display and start to laugh at it . . . beneath every showy dictatorship lies a secret cesspool. When the smell becomes overpowering the revolution starts'. Mugabe must be aware of the big stink at home.

Protest 'against black oppression' – Saturday 4th June: The Vigil salutes the activists who are staging a sixteen-day round-the-clock protest in Harare's Africa Unity Square against Zimbabwe's worsening economic and political situation. The protest was launched on Wednesday when eleven people from the Zimbabwe Activist Alliance and other civil society organisations bedded down in the square. They included Patson Dzamara, brother of missing activist Itai. Lynette

Mudehwe, coordinator of the Activist Alliance, called for the rejection of bond notes. Linda Masarira, of our sister organisation ROHR and leader of Zimbabwe Women in Politics Alliance, said the government had shown it did not care for the needs of the people especially women. She complained of 'black oppression'. The Secretary-General of the National Students' Union, Makomborero Haruzivishe, also joined the protest, saying they were tired of watching while the fruits of Zimbabwe were being squandered by just a few individuals. The Occupy Africa Unity Square facebook page today said they had come under attack early this morning by fourteen men. It said Lynette was grabbed and her ID taken out of her wallet. After inspecting it, they wiped their fingerprints off and returned it, clearly indicating that they were trained. One disabled woman, Naspar Manyau, was indecently assaulted and tipped from her wheelchair towards the stove at which she had been warming her feet. The men grabbed blankets and other possessions and several activists were attacked and injured.

Patson Dzamara on Monday released a photograph of what looked like his brother with his hands tied behind his back and a bandage around his head. He told a news conference: 'Some individuals from within the evil establishment volunteered information regarding who abducted Itai Dzamara, why and where he was kept. The heinous act was executed by state security agents, in particular the military intelligence.' The revived Occupy Africa Unity Square protest, together with Pastor Evan Mawawire's #ThisFlag campaign with its 'hatichada, hadichatya' slogan, reflects widening unrest at the government's failure to turn around the economy. Some fifty civic organisations under the banner of the Zimbabwe National Agreement Platform have also urged the public to reject bond notes. Spokesman Bishop Ancelimo Magaya said that following the illegitimate 2013 elections Zanu PF wanted to reintroduce the Zimbabwe dollar to fund their 2018 election campaign. 'The decision to print bond notes will not help anyone but the political leaders. We are certain they are making massive withdrawals to relocate their wealth outside the country.'

Mugabe strikes at activists – Saturday 11th June: As activists at the Vigil commemorated the fifteenth month since the abduction in Harare of Itai Dzamara, we displayed a new poster – this one condemning the arrest on Wednesday of his brother Patson. He was arrested along with four other activists while taking part in a revived protest in Africa Unity Square originally started by Itai. More were detained later in a clear move to close down the protest, which has been gathering increased support as the economy slips towards the cliff edge. The Facebook page of Occupy Africa Unity Square was defiant, saying the protest would continue: 'We have been attacked, robbed, beaten, detained without charges, arrested on trumped-up charges, denied bail by charging outrageous amounts, smeared in the Herald. All of this for 10 days of activism, for demanding the freedom hard-earned at independence, and subsequently sold down the river'.

Our friends at the Swaziland Vigil confronted the Swaziland High Commissioner, Mrs Dumsile T Sukata, when she was driven away to attend the ceremony of Trooping the Colour. They pushed a poster against a rear window of her car showing a picture of King Mswati III with the wording 'Wanted for Human Rights Abuses'. She desperately tried to close the window blinds.

On Friday we were alarmed to hear that Vigil supporter Emmaculate Tshuma was to be deported that day. She was in a Home Office van outside Heathrow airport. Kenya Airways' telephone lines were overloaded with calls telling them not to take Emmaculate back to Zimbabwe. In the end she was not sent home.

PRESS RELEASE: British medical centre run by Zimbabwean doctor closed – Monday 13th June: A medical centre in Nottingham run by a black Zimbabwean doctor has been closed. Zimbabwean exiles have staged repeated demonstrations outside the clinic in protest at the doctor's violent seizure of a white-owned farm in Zimbabwe. In February the Zimbabwe Vigil protest group presented a petition to 10 Downing Street calling on the government to consider revoking the British citizenship of Dr Sylvester Nyatsuro, who runs the Willows Medical Centre with his wife Veronica. Dr Nyatsuro has lived in the UK for 15 years and lives with his family in a large and luxurious house nearby valued at around £750,000. They say that they were simply allocated the farm by the Zimbabwe government and denied any nepotism was involved. But photographs emerged showing the couple socializing with Grace Mugabe. The Vigil also drew the matter to the attention of the National Health Service which has responsibility for the clinic. Last week inspectors from the Care Quality Commission visited the centre and took immediate action to close it until further notice. Patients are being directed to other practices. The UK government says the question of Dr Nyatsuro's citizenship is being looked at by the Home Office. The Vigil argues that they are clearly Mugabe supporters and citizenship could have been obtained by means of fraud or false representation. The Nyatsuros have no known farming experience.

SADC save Zimbabwe – Saturday 18th June: With Zimbabwe's army going unpaid while the government tries to find the money, the Vigil delivered a petition to the Botswana High Commission in London on Tuesday calling for the help of the Southern African Development Community to avert disaster in Zimbabwe. A Vigil delegation was given a courteous reception at the High Commission which accepted a letter to pass on to President Ian Khama as Chair of SADC.

Our letter said: *'In the last 15 years or so Zimbabweans have increasingly looked to Botswana as a model of good governance. We have been comforted that Botswana could always be relied on to speak the truth to President Mugabe – even if it was a lone voice. We are grateful for your patience in the face of the influx of Zimbabwean refugees and other problems we have caused you as our country's economy collapsed. You have been a true friend and we will not forget your solidarity with our suffering people. Your predecessor, former President Festus Mogae, was quoted by the UN recently as saying: 'Sovereignty has limits like any other right. A leader cannot kill and harass his people and hide behind sovereignty. A true leader does not kill but protects his people. We still have leaders in Africa who think they are indispensable, larger than life and more important than their countries. That must stop. If a leader loses control, the world will and should intervene to save the people.' We of the Zimbabwe Vigil have been protesting outside the Zimbabwe Embassy in London for the past 14 years demanding an end to human rights violations and calling for free and fair elections. We fear that our country could be torn apart as President Mugabe clings to office into his nineties with no designated successor. In your closing months as Chair of the Southern African Development Community we submit to you the following petition calling for SADC intercession to avert disaster. The petition has been signed by thousands of people from all over the world who have passed by our Vigil outside the Embassy.*

'To the Chair of the Southern African Development Community (SADC), President Ian Khama of Botswana *We wish to alert you to alarming threats by the military in Zimbabwe to employ violence against people opposed to the Zanu PF regime. The threats come amid worsening splits in the party and rising popular outrage at the demolition of the homes of the poor and the imposition of pre-paid water meters for an unreliable supply. The Commander of the Presidential Guard Brigadier-General Anselem Sanyatwe has threatened force to stop ousted Vice-President Joice Mujuru from opposing Mugabe. He told his troops 'Professionalism is over . . . Zanu PF should rule forever'. The national army commander Lieutenant-General Phillip Sibanda later warned that 'the Zanu PF axe' could be wielded again. You will be aware that Zimbabwe has recently been judged the worst governed country in SADC. Bad governance has destroyed the economy, reducing people to desperation while the ruling elite drive past in their luxury cars from their mansions to the expensive restaurants. There is growing resentment. Provocative moves by the military could cause an explosion of anger. We call on SADC to prepare to intervene to stop a meltdown.'*

We remember how SADC facilitated the government of national unity after the violent 2008 elections, arresting catastrophe. It is not for Zimbabweans in the diaspora to prescribe what any solution should be but we want a government that observes the rule of law and will conduct free and fair elections. We believe this is the key to the restoration of Zimbabwe.

Zanu PF's London sales pitch – Saturday 25th June: Exiled Zimbabweans are to picket a conference in London on 5th July at which Zanu PF will try to persuade the world that it is reforming and should be bailed out with Western loans. The meeting comes as the bankrupt regime hopes to convince the International Monetary Fund that it is serious about implementing the constitution adopted in 2013. The Vigil will be outside the meeting to tell any prospective investors the real reasons why Zimbabwe has run out of money and why the world should be sceptical about any assurances given by the likes of Finance Minister Chinamasa, Minister of Macro Economic Planning and Investment

Promotion Obert Mpofu (unaccountably one of the richest men in Zimbabwe) and Mike Bimha, Minister of Industry and Commerce. They are listed to speak at the conference along with Reserve Bank governor John Mangudya. The meeting has been organised by Africa Confidential, a fortnightly newsletter covering politics and economics in Africa. Explaining the conference, Africa Confidential says Zimbabwe 'is on the brink of finalising an historic deal which will end a decade and half of sanctions and unlock substantial new funds for economic growth and development'. This comment indicates from which perspective the organisers are coming.

Contrary to Africa Confidential's assumption, the MDC T MP Eddie Cross says the sudden announcement that Zimbabwe is introducing a new local currency (bond notes) has exposed the real state of affairs and the IMF realises it has been deceived and the regime's liabilities are much greater than previously revealed. As an indication of Zanu PF's intentions, Mr Cross cites a new bill tabled in Parliament this week to reinstate the powers that the new constitution had stripped from the Minister of Local Government to suspend and dismiss the elected leadership of local authorities. He says 'In preparation for the next election – expected in 2018 – the minister (who is also the Political Commissar of Zanu PF) has been instructed to cripple and even remove as many MDC T controlled Councils as he can'. Mr Cross continues: 'It clearly demonstrates that Zanu PF has no intention at all of implementing the new constitution. Secondly, it shows that they know that they cannot win a free and fair election and are therefore strengthening their defences against the MDC. The voters roll is still under military control and is managed, not by the Electoral Commission as provided in the constitution, but by a secretive company called Nikuv from Israel. The Minister of Local Government has announced his intention of settling up to 250 000 members of the "youth" wing of his party in urban areas using urban and state land and allocating these people small plots at virtually no cost to themselves. 'You do not need an imagination to understand that the programme of fear and coercion, and the control given by the fear of being removed from your allocated stands, is now being extended to all urban centres and the newly settled people will be used for political purposes and controlled violence against all opponents.'

Mr Cross concludes: 'What does this all indicate? Very clearly it says that the leopard that has been courting the IMF and the international community in the past three years, has not changed its spots in any way. The consequences for the country are disastrous. They are again taking money out of our accounts and replacing it with a worthless form of virtual money. Their economic policies are destroying what little is left of a once diversified and sophisticated economy. They are clearly not going to allow a democratic election any time soon and the wholesale theft of resources by a tiny, military and civilian clique is continuing. I am afraid that the days of trying to whitewash this leopard and to persuade it to change its ways are over. We have no choice but to take matters into our own hands and effect real change in our country. The best solution would be an internationally supervised election without a voters roll as soon as possible. If this is not facilitated by the region, then the streets will have to make the required decisions. We the citizens of this country, really have no choice.'

Mugabe's vultures descend on London – Saturday 2nd July: Mugabe's Finance Minister Patrick Chinamasa has admitted that Zimbabwe is broke. 'Right now we have nothing', he said in France on his way to London. The Vigil has called on supporters to demonstrate outside the Royal Institute of International Affairs on Monday at which Chinamasa is to speak and at a conference in the City of London on Tuesday to be addressed by Chinamasa and other representatives of the regime including Mangudya governor of the Reserve Bank of Zimbabwe.

We will hand out the following leaflet at Chatham House: **No to Mugabe's lies:** Exiled Zimbabweans are picketing this meeting at which Mugabe's Finance Minister Patrick Chinamasa will try to persuade you that the ruling Zanu PF party is reforming and should be bailed out with Western loans and investment. He is part of a larger Zanu PF delegation touring Europe in a desperate attempt to raise money. The meeting comes as the bankrupt regime hopes to convince the International Monetary Fund that it is serious about implementing the constitution adopted in 2013.

The Zimbabwe Vigil is here to explain the real reasons why Zimbabwe has run out of money and why the world should be sceptical about any assurances given by the likes of Chinamasa. We draw your attention to this recent article by the Times correspondent in Harare.

'*Shopkeepers struggle with 'multicurrency' Mugabenomics – Jan Raath, Harare: 27/06/2016.*'
Having had triple heart bypass surgery two years ago, Stelio Haralambos, who runs a little store, ought to avoid stress. He came to what was Rhodesia in 1966 as a barber from Lesbos but switched to running a shop.
Mr Haralambos has endured a series of economic crises since independence in 1980 but nothing quite like the one now. After Zimbabwe's currency vanished in hyperinflation in 2009, the US dollar became the official money. But seven years later, and with the country importing twice as much as it exports since President Mugabe destroyed agriculture and industry, there is a shortage of greenbacks, so the central bank has introduced a "multicurrency" system.
Customers entering Mr Haralambos's store for a morning scud, Zimbabwe's soupy traditional beer, can offer payment in up to seven currencies — US dollars, sterling, Chinese yuan, Japanese yen, Australian dollars, South African rand, Indian rupees and the Botswanan pula. In the store the day's exchange rates will not have arrived so Mr Haralambos has to do the calculations. You can just about pick up the fibrillation of his heart from the other side of the scratched old glass-topped counter.
The banks have tried to ration cash at ATMs but the daily withdrawal limit dwindles steadily. Slow, winding queues are the order of the day. It is the latest absurdity created by Mugabenomics. Other countries borrow but Zimbabwe cannot. Mr Mugabe once borrowed unsustainably and, worse, he doesn't pay back.
Country people, who long for the days of the Zimdollar, have to deal with notes carrying Chinese or Japanese characters. And the township con-artists revel in the opportunity to profit from the confusion. It gets worse. The central bank governor has announced that he will introduce a "bond note", equal to the US dollar, in October. Economists are trying to find out if it will be currency, money, legal tender, negotiable instrument, treasury bill or promissory note — but the governor is not saying. The only conclusion economists can reach is that it is a piece of paper.
The reaction has been a collective nationwide, "No." The bond note is seen as a government attempt to solve the cash crisis by issuing another

form of the Zimdollar, whose value will plunge instantly on appearance. No one has forgotten the instant impoverishment caused by hyperinflation as the value of hard-earned wages, income and investments shrank. Police do their best to boost national outrage. They have become a force of uniformed highwaymen. Anywhere you go, you risk being stopped at a roadblock. On the 275-mile stretch between Bulawayo and Victoria Falls last week, there were 16. At each one police search for faults to fine you — for not having the latest stamp on your fire extinguisher indicating its last service, for example. Zimbabwe must be the only country where you can be fined $20 for a dirty car. I hide my cash so I can say that I can't pay.

Government coffers are nearly empty. Civil servants' pay days have been repeatedly postponed since late last year and the 40,000-strong army, as well as the police and prison service, were told last week that paydays had been pushed back by two weeks.

This week the government was due to present its plan to repay $1.8 billion to the International Monetary Fund, the World Bank and the African Development Bank, which would, theoretically, have allowed Zimbabwe to start borrowing again. However, Algeria, which was to have lent $1 billion, has backed off. Not that Mr Mugabe seems to care. He said last week that the cash crisis, "is a temporary problem which should be behind us soon". Mr Haralambos would best be advised to retire to Lesbos.'

PRESS RELEASE: Chinamasa besieged in London – Monday 4th July: Zimbabwean Finance Minister Patrick Chinamasa was besieged in London by angry Zimbabwean exiles and had to be rescued by a vanload of police. Chinamasa was speaking at the Royal Institute of International Affairs at Chatham House on a desperate visit to Europe to try to raise money for the bankrupt Zanu PF regime. Protestors from the Zimbabwe Vigil and its sister organisation Restoration of Human Rights in Zimbabwe picketed Chatham House with posters reading: 'No to Mugabe's lies', 'Don't prop up the Mugabe regime', 'Don't lend money to thieves' and 'Zimbabweans reject odious debt'. It became apparent that Chinamasa and his companions were afraid to come out and face the music. The demonstrators deterred an attempt to exit from a side door of Chatham House and eventually the police arrived and provided a safe corridor for Chinamasa and his friends to access the Zimbabwean Ambassador's car amid jeers from protestors, fired up by messages from home of mounting unrest in all urban areas. We were not impressed by the Chatham House official who refused to allow our supporter David Wilkins to sit on the steps. David is blind and has hearing difficulties. Part of his condition is that he has weak ankles. They said he should sit in the park across the road but he wanted to stay with us.

PRESS RELEASE 1: Chinamasa confronted again – Tuesday 5th July: Zimbabwean demonstrators confronted Chinamasa for the second time in two days when he arrived for a money-raising conference in London on Tuesday. Chinamasa was driven up at about 8 am to a side door of the conference venue in the financial district. If he thought he would evade Vigil protesters he was mistaken. Vigil co-ordinator Fungayi Mabhunu spotted ZIM 1, the Ambassador's car, and when Chinamasa got out Fungayi demanded to know what he had done with the $15 billion Mugabe says has disappeared from diamond revenues. 'He was really shaken', said Fungayi. The Vigil was congratulated on its work by the former coalition's finance minister Tendai Biti. 'Well done guys you are doing a good job', he said when he arrived for the conference. He was happy to be photographed with us and took a bundle of our leaflets to hand out at the meeting. Congratulations also came from Zimbabwean journalist Peta Thorneycroft who was covering the conference which Zanu PF hopes will help get loans and investment to make up for the $15 billion it has looted.

PRESS RELEASE 2: Chinamasa trapped in London – Tuesday 5th July: Zimbabwean demonstrators lay down in the road outside the conference in London addressed by Chinamasa preventing him from leaving for more than an hour. The minister had hoped to escape in an ordinary taxi after his arrival in the ambassador's car ZIM 1 was ambushed by Zimbabwean exiles. The minister's taxi was backed up by other cars so was unable to escape the one way road and he had to wait until the demonstrators were lifted bodily by the police to clear the way. The demonstration at the conference began before 8 am and ended at about 7 pm. Chinamasa was expected back for the last session but did not reappear. Sources at the conference told the Vigil that Chinamasa had been challenged by Professor Stephen Chan of the School of Oriental and African Studies: 'Why are you begging money from the British government?' Tendai Biti, the former coalition's finance minister, is said to have told Chinamasa bluntly that he was lying. Vigil supporters and others from ZAPU and MDC agreed to hold another demonstration outside the Embassy on Wednesday in response to the #ThisFlag call 'Shut Down Zimbabwe'. #ThisFlag is calling for everyone to stay at home but in our case we won't stay at home but will be outside the Embassy in solidarity with our families at home.

West to rescue Mugabe? – Saturday 9th July: The West seems hell-bent on saving the beleaguered Zanu PF regime – in spite of a Zanu PF minister accusing Western embassies of fomenting the mounting unrest. The West apparently believes that there will be regional chaos if the regime collapses. Behind the re-engagement process between the West and Zimbabwe is the International Monetary Fund which has been persuaded by Zimbabwe's promises of economic reforms and says the country is capable of quick growth if it can only get some cash. The word is that new loans will only come after reforms have been made but the Vigil can't see how Zanu PF can undertake reforms. For instance, would this involve a 50% cut in the government wage bill as recommended? We do not believe this can be delivered as it would undermine Zanu PF's support base. Many others are equally sceptical. The Zimbabwean economist Tony Hawkins says 'the IMF is being taken for a ride'. An article in the latest edition of the UK's Economist headlined 'Bailing out bandits' makes clear its view that a lifeline for

Mugabe is 'a bad idea'. It says 'The West is pinning its hopes on those they see as 'reformist' elements in Zanu PF. Vice President Mnangagwa, despite his genocidal history, is seen as one of them, along with Finance Minister Chinamasa, who made a poor impression at a money-raising conference in London's financial district on Tuesday.'

The Zimbabwean academic Alex Magaisa was at the conference and says Mugabe and Zanu PF can't believe their luck at the prospect of new loans. He says Western countries must not delude themselves into thinking that they are dealing with a different creature or that it is in the interests of ordinary Zimbabweans. Dr Magaisa said that as the conference was taking place the songs and chants by Vigil protestors outside could be heard, prompting laughter when Chinamasa claimed 'political stability'. Former Finance Minister Tendai Biti said Zimbabwe needed a national transitional authority to stabilise the situation and arrange new elections. The MDC T has called on the Southern African Development Community to intervene as it did after the violent 2008 elections. This echoes the call by the Vigil, which last month delivered a petition to Botswana, the current Chair of SADC.

The Vigil received several messages of congratulations including one from Eddie Cross MP: *'Thank you Team Zimbabwe once again for doing your country proud – I think we sunk this ship well and truly'*.

PRESS RELEASE: Enough is enough – Wednesday 13th July: Zimbabwean exiles demonstrated outside the Embassy today in support of a two-day #ShutdownZimbabwe called by Pastor Evan Mawarire of the #ThisFlag protest movement. Demonstrators – some draped in the Zimbabwe flag – demanded that charges be dropped against Pastor Mawarire, who was arrested in Harare on Tuesday accused of inciting violence. One poster read: '36 years of freedom: no free speech, no freedom. Free Evan Mawarire'. About 150 people were there to hear a demand that there should be no western aid to prop up the Mugabe regime. The demand was made by Ephraim Tapa who said: 'We want Mugabe to go and a transitional authority to organise free and fair elections monitored by the international community'.

PRESS RELEASE: Standing still is suicide – Thursday 14th July: The second day of solidarity demonstrations outside the Embassy was one of the biggest gatherings held by the Vigil in 14 years of campaigning for an end to human rights abuses and free and fair elections. We were joined by gay rights campaigner Peter Tatchell famous for his attempt to make a citizen's arrest of Mugabe on visits to London in 1999 and Brussels in 2001 when he was savagely beaten by Mugabe's bodyguards. We were also joined by a white Zimbabwean family who brought a striking poster reading 'Moving forward is perilous, moving backwards is cowardice, staying still is suicide'.

Parallel Universe – Saturday 16th July: The Zimbabwean diaspora was interested to hear from Home Affairs Minister Ignatius Chombo that we are being used by Western countries to promote alarm, despondency and unrest in the motherland where all is 'calm and peaceful'. Chombo is cushioned by his vast wealth. He seems to be living in a parallel universe inhabited only by the Mugabe mafia. They appear to be too far gone to see that it is the state that they have created that promotes 'alarm, despondency and unrest' – a state that can charge a pastor with treason for wearing the Zimbabwe flag and working for nation building without hate. Whatever the delusions of the dying regime, the bottom line is that it has run out of money. Once again the army has been told that they cannot be paid on time. Eddie Cross, the MDC T MP, says the crunch appears to be imminent. 'The regime has its back to the wall in Harare and I see no way out . . . The regime has falsified the financial position of the state and the IMF talks have collapsed leaving the regime in Harare totally reliant on the international community for emergency support.'

Veneer peels – Saturday 23rd July: As the Zanu PF regime crumbles its veneer of constitutionalism is rapidly peeling off. Any opposition to Mugabe is now seen as treason. Even the regime's storm troops – the war veterans – have now been accused of being traitors for questioning Mugabe. The accusation came from the top civil servant in the veterans' ministry, retired Brigadier-General Asher Tapfunaneyi. He was responding to a statement by the War Veterans' Association after a 7-hour leadership meeting. The statement accused Mugabe of entrenching dictatorial tendencies, egocentrism and misrule and said it would not support his re-election campaign. The war veterans criticised the oppressive attitude shown towards peaceful protesters. This highhanded unconstitutional behaviour is shown by its treatment of Linda Masarira of the Vigil's sister organisation the Restoration of Human Rights in Zimbabwe who was arrested on 6th July during the peaceful shutdown protest and has since been detained in Chikurubi prison. Linda came to public attention as a member of the Occupy Africa Unity Square protest when she memorably said 'We are sick and tired of being sick and tired'. She appeared in Mbare Magistrate's Court on Friday and was remanded in custody until Tuesday 26th July although her lawyer pointed out that her constitutional rights had already been violated by the prosecution's delay in bringing her to court.

Demonstration in support of Linda Masarira – Tuesday 26th July: ROHR and Vigil protesters demonstrated outside the Embassy today in support of Linda Masarira who was appearing in court in Mbare on trumped up charges. She was further remanded in custody until 11th August. The demonstrators rang the bell and slipped in posters to the surprised doorman. The Ambassador's car ZIM 1 was parked outside with a window slightly open. The protesters pushed the remaining posters into the car before they left.

'Charming' psychopath – Saturday 30th July: The 'charming' side of Mugabe was not in evidence when he addressed a splinter group of 'war veterans', padded out with bussed-in youths, at a hurriedly-arranged rally to denounce war veteran leaders who last week issued a statement condemning his regime. 'Charming' was the word used by a former British ambassador, Deborah Bronnert, some years back, after presenting her credentials to Mugabe. She is not alone in being taken in by the psychopathic megalomaniac. The Vigil tired of hearing MDC ministers in the bogus coalition spouting the same deluded line. 'Charming' Mugabe certainly was not when he outlined the punishment he had in mind for the 'treasonous' war veteran leaders being rounded up by security agents.

'We will punish them in a very big way', he said, going on to recall how holes had been dug for enemies during the liberation struggle. 'We kept them underground like rats . . . it is the same thing we are going to do here in Independent Zimbabwe'. Mugabe added that the police belonged to Zanu PF and would be used to crush any protests by his enemies, especially church leaders dabbling in politics. 'The police are ours and they shall see to it that these small party protesters are thrown in jail so they can taste the food there . . .'

It appears that many police share this view. A contingent of police recruits said Mugabe was 'the real angel Gabriel sent by God to deliver Zimbabwe and Africa'. They pledged their support for Mugabe at a passing out parade after a year of indoctrination at Morris Depot in Harare. 'Like Jesus Christ, who was crucified by a people whom He saved, you have innocently grappled with all forms of persecution', they declared. 'Because of you, Zimbabwe is a land of peace and tranquillity, equity, equality, freedom, fairness, honesty and the dignity of hard work. You have been attacked for championing the cause of the people, justice and equality, for denouncing racial segregation, immorality, corruption, human rights abuse and violence'

As war veteran leaders joined protesters in jail and #ThisFlag pastor Evan Mawarire fled into exile, the Vigil believes Mugabe now has little chance of securing British support in his desperate attempt to persuade the International Monetary Fund to bail out his regime. The Vigil believes the 'charm' of the psychopathic megalomaniac has now faded like the allure of his idols Kim Jong-Il, Chairman Mao, Stalin and Hitler.

Vigil petitions UN for transitional authority – Saturday 6th August: Exiled Zimbabweans are to appeal to the United Nations to prepare to intervene in Zimbabwe as the bankrupt regime teeters on the verge of violent unrest. The Vigil today launched the following petition to the UN Secretary-General: *With mounting unrest in Zimbabwe, we urge you to appoint a Special Representative to prepare the ground for a UN Transitional Authority to take over from the failed Mugabe regime. We look to the Special Representative to initiate comprehensive negotiations so that the UN Transitional Authority can assume control of Zimbabwe's administrative structures – foreign affairs, defence, security, finance and communications – to ensure a level playing field conducive for credible national elections.*

The petition is the fruit of the late Vigil supporter Clifford Mashiri, an academic and former diplomat whose funeral took place in London on Tuesday. Clifford said 'Arguably, governance would change in Zimbabwe by virtue of a UN Security Council resolution giving mandate to the UN Transitional Authority in Zimbabwe (UNTAZ) which will only withdraw after free and fair elections have been conducted.' In recent months there have been proposals from various quarters in Zimbabwe for some kind of transitional authority and – in the absence of any initiative by the Southern African Development Community – the Vigil believes Clifford's ideas offer a way forward.

Supporters might have seen an article on the dodgy Zimeye website in which the Vigil was criticised for not allowing Stendrick Zvorwadza to address us last week. Our refusal to give a hearing to this charlatan was because he still pretends to be the leader of ROHR and has yet to account for £2,000 we entrusted to him in 2008 to hand over to an orphanage we were supporting in Zimbabwe, as well as computers, phones and cameras for the ROHR office in Harare.

Another demonstration for Linda – Thursday 11th August: About 20 people gathered singing and drumming outside the Embassy today to demonstrate in support of ROHR member Linda Masarira, who is facing trumped up charges in Harare. During the demonstration the protesters were angered to hear that Linda had been further remanded in custody until 25th August, unable to get home to her children. It is reported that 'Lynda looked visibly sick when she appeared in court today because she is allegedly being denied access to medication.

End of road for Mugabe – Saturday 13th August: President Mugabe was symbolically put on trial at the Vigil and ordered to leave office for crimes against the people and economy of Zimbabwe. He had earlier been 'arrested' by human rights activist Peter Tatchell, who had unsuccessfully tried to make a citizen's arrest of Mugabe in London in 1999 and Brussels in 2001. Mugabe was brought to the Vigil along with first lady Grace and the governor of the Reserve Bank John Mangudya from the south coast resort of Brighton, where the three had gone incognito to get treatment under the National Health Service and apply for state benefits.

Peter Tatchell successfully arrests Mugabe

A group of Vigil / ROHR supporters and other exiled Zimbabweans left Brighton for London with the prisoners on Friday and walked 30 miles before camping overnight on a farm. On Saturday they continued for a further ten miles, singing Zimbabwean songs as they passed the Houses of Parliament and 10 Downing Street before joining the Vigil, where Mugabe was handed over to a judge outside the Embassy. He was found guilty of treason and offered a pistol so he could make an honourable exit. But, cunning as always, he collapsed against the Embassy door to claim diplomatic immunity. The Vigil has alerted the British authorities to examine all Zimbabwean diplomatic baggage very carefully, looking particularly for a 92 year old with corns and blisters from a long walk.

The judge released Grace and Mangudya to the local social services. It is understood that both have applied for asylum on the grounds of diminished responsibility caused by stupidity. Latest word is that Grace has asked the UK immigration authorities for training as a typist and Mangudya has asked for a UK government loan to study arithmetic and economics at O level.

Final looting spree? – Saturday 20th August: It looks like the Mugabe regime is preparing for a final looting spree to mop up the dollars remaining in the economy. Despite earlier denials, Reserve Bank Governor Mangudya, has now admitted that the bond notes piling up at the bank will be used to pay wages. It will be a windfall for the Mugabe cronies.

Whether Mugabe himself really knows what is happening is doubtful. His physical condition is now so poor he has had to pull out of a trip to Ghana where he was to receive a Lifetime Africa Achievement Award – testament only to the ignorance of those who awarded it. Probably Mugabe still believes in the fantasy world of the Herald, which said this week Zimbabwe is poised for an economic take-off – reminiscent of the Zambian space ship of a few years ago which ended up in the branches of the nearest tree.

The regime faces its biggest challenge so far if a massive protest in Harare planned by the combined opposition parties goes ahead on Friday. The riot police showed on Wednesday that they mean business when a demonstration in Harare against the introduction of bond notes ended with blood on the streets. Pastor Evan Mawarire of #ThisFlag movement saw the brutal face of the regime himself and fled the country. He said he had been warned to leave or be killed. His wife had been threatened with rape and its clear his children were also in danger.

We at the Vigil have some information of our own about the police reign of terror. Here's a message from a member of our sister organisation ROHR: *'Hi guys. Thanx so much for the caring messages I got during my dice with state security over a nothing. They tried to frame me on very silly allegations that I was inciting violence and causing public disorder. They authored very derogatory papers with my name, phone number and address at the bottom and threw them around at night. They were shockingly pasted on walls at Zanu PF offices and buildings around the offices. Was called to a CID office where there were CIOs as well. Was heavily abused verbally and threatened when they were profiling me. No charges were laid against me but was warned that they will come back for me when they are finalising their paperwork. Though a bit disturbed psychologically, that's what they wanted, I am fine physically and unsafely at home and unmoved. The guys are cunning and very good at intimidating and threatening. Your messages and calls really raised my spirits and got me to realise that there is a bigger family out there.'*

Demonstration for Linda – Thursday 25th August: Vigil supporters demonstrated outside the Embassy again when Linda Masarira of ROHR appeared in court in connection with political activism. Linda has been in jail for the past two months and was again remanded in custody until Wednesday 31st August. Linda is in poor health and has been denied bail despite having young children.

Topsy-turvy land – Saturday 27th August 2016: The Mugabe 'official' view of the chaos in Harare on Friday is that it was the work of paid demonstrators for the imperialist West aiming at regime change. And, as everyone has learnt from the Herald, regime change is un-African. This is not just a Zanu-PF attitude. Zuma, mired in corruption, spouts the same mantra. In fact there are all too many African leaders who view political opposition and any threat to their position as treasonous, justifying a change in the constitution to make this impossible. In the topsy-turvy land of Zimbabwe, it was as if the demonstrators were the ones wielding the batons, indiscriminately spraying teargas around and blasting people with water cannons or worse. One would have thought it was the police who had been ordered by the High Court to stop a peaceful demonstration instead of being specifically told 'not to interfere'. If nothing else, Friday's events show graphically how law and the constitution count for nothing in Mugabeland.

In a vivid account, the opposition MP Eddie Cross describes how he was on his way to take part in the protest when he was warned that it was dangerous to go any further. 'I proceeded to the collection point through rock strewn roads, burning tyres and saw running battles between young people and the police. I saw water cannons in action with blue dye in the water and one machine putting out a fire . . . I left the area and drove to Parliament to wash my face and get the tear gas out of my eyes. Then I tried to go back but was completely blocked by cars fleeing the battles in the central business district. Subsequently the street battles raged over much of the city, business closed down and the streets deserted. The army was deployed and helicopters were put up to monitor the people. Was there any need for this? Absolutely not! I had participated in four previous marches and had not felt for one instance any threat or danger. Just cheerful thousands celebrating their right to protest at the state of crisis through which we are all living. The violence was instigated by the police who were totally responsible for what followed'.

The Care Quality Commission has condemned a medical centre in Nottingham which was closed in June after the Vigil staged a series of protests outside. The clinic was run by Zimbabwean doctor Sylvester Nyatsuro and his wife Veronica, who earlier this year violently seized a farm in Zimbabwe owned by a white couple. The Commission described the clinic as chaotic and noted that there was a culture of fear with staff being reprimanded and shouted at by management. It said an unregistered health care assistant had been passed off as a doctor at the clinic and allowed to carry out examinations. Dr Nyatsuro has lost his job for which he was paid more than £100,000 a year. It is not known how much his wife earned as the practice manager.

Unlamented dictator – Saturday 3rd September: The news leaked out quickly despite the security clampdown. It always does. After all, it was not unexpected. The old tyrant had been felled by a stroke: probably dead, but anyway finished. It had been a long time coming. No one was sure what would happen next. Who would take over? There were several obvious candidates but which one would move first? Fresh in the memory was the sudden death of Malawi's President Mutharika in 2012. As the Vigil recorded at the time, his corpse was flown to South Africa, ostensibly for medical treatment but really just to buy time for his inner circle to work out what to do. This tyrant left a difficult legacy. Long decades of brutal oppression to elevate him to the status of a near deity. There was talk of opponents being boiled. The country was ruined. Well at last he is gone. The official announcement when it came was brief. President Karimov is dead, the only President Uzbekistan has had since independence. The Uzbek government described him as a great statesman who had brought 'peace, stability, prosperity and progress'. Will we soon be hearing similar nonsense about Mugabe?

After a week of frenzied police violence against demonstrators and passers-by in Harare, the Zimbabwe Action Forum met after the Vigil to discuss the worsening situation. Ephraim Tapa, who has just returned from a clandestine visit, spoke of the worsening corruption he found. He said he had been told that euthanasia was being practiced in hospitals on those too poor to pay for life-saving treatment.

Deluded Mugabe – Saturday 10th September: A thousand years ago the Danish ruler Cnut became King of England. He is remembered today for sitting on a throne on the seashore, surrounded by courtiers, and ordering the tide to retreat. King Canute, as he is better known, was not mad. He was making the point that – however powerful he was – some things were beyond him. Mugabe's rebuke to the judiciary for allowing demonstrations against his misrule illustrated his belief that the constitution is his to interpret. He is the law. He is the state. His powers are unlimited. The Vigil waits with interest to see how he reacts when he wakes up and hears about Chinamasa's sacking of 25,000 state workers, cuts in pay and allowances – and even scrapping the sacred bonuses. Last year Mugabe ordered the tide to retreat – and Chinamasa duly complied and restored bonuses. This year there simply isn't the money to do this again

Thanks to Fungayi Mabhunu who appeared at the Vigil in Mugabe mask and judge's wig to demonstrate with the help of a 'button stick' the reality of power in Zimbabwe. He was surrounded by Vigil supporters carrying posters saying: 'Chief Injustice Mugabe', 'Mugabe says protest is treason' and 'Mugabe: I am the law'.

Protest outside Embassy - Friday 16th September: over 40 exiled Zimbabweans gathered at the Embassy to demand 'Mugabe must go' in support of protests back home. Flowers were laid at the door of the Embassy for Itai Dzamara who was abducted and disappeared 18 months ago.

Mugabe a 'walking corpse' – Saturday 17th September: The Zimbabwean opposition MP Eddie Cross says the international community is backing Vice-President Mnangagwa to take over from 'walking corpse' Mugabe in the next few months. Mr Cross was speaking at the UK Parliament on Thursday during a trip to Europe. He said South Africa was backing a road map for change in Zimbabwe – a road map which had also been embraced by the US, the UK and European Union and even China. The plan envisaged the immediate retirement of Mugabe to be replaced by Mnangagwa who would be tasked with managing comprehensive reforms to ensure a level playing field allowing free and fair elections in 2018. Mr Cross said Mnangagwa had the support of the military and the principal power brokers in Zimbabwe. He said financial support for Zimbabwe would be dependent on reforms being implemented and the diaspora of 4.7 million being allowed to vote. All voting would be on the simple basis of an identification document. He added that he was confident MDC T would get 70% of the vote.

Eddie Cross at the Zimbabwe Vigil with Ephraim Tapa

In Parliament with Eddie Cross

Ten Vigil supporters were at the meeting in a parliamentary committee room overlooking the Thames. They were pleased when Mr Cross mentioned the Vigil at the meeting, saying 'we are really proud of you guys – how you have struggled all these years'. Mr Cross was invited to attend the Vigil, where he was presented with a Vigil cap in appreciation of his long and courageous service to Zimbabwe. But Vigil supporters expressed their reservations about trusting Mnangagwa, who was implicated in the Gukurahundi genocide of the 1980s. Mr Cross was told the Vigil's view is that the United Nations should be asked to help set up a transitional authority, as outlined in our current petition. The Vigil produced its own version of the new Mugabe statue displayed in Zimbabwe with Fungayi Mabhunu in our Mugabe mask demonstrating how the 'walking corpse' was still exercising his malignant influence – off on another tour leaving the country in flames after scrapping Chinamasa's latest attempt to satisfy the international financial world by reigning in government spending.

Pinocchio paper – Saturday 24th September: Botswana's President Ian Khama deserves the Nobel prize for doing the unthinkable: telling an African leader to step down because he has passed his sell-by date. The Herald's reaction is that it is un-African for a fellow African president to criticise Mugabe. So it responds by calling President Khama 'queer'. That really is 'un-African' . . . The Vigil, on behalf of Zimbabweans, apologises to President Khama, who has helped to make his country an island of good governance and prosperity in an ocean of corruption and inefficiency. President Khama will no doubt already know that Mugabe's mouthpiece the Herald is like Pinocchio, the puppet in the children's story whose nose grows longer every time he tells a lie. So he will not be surprised if the Herald's nose is now so long as to stretch all the way to Botswana.

We believe the Herald would be a worthy winner of the Ig Nobel Prize awarded every year at Harvard University as an alternative to the Nobel Prize. After all, this year an award went to a team for their psychology paper 'From Junior to Senior Pinocchio; a Cross-Sectional Life Span Investigation of Deception'. They were chosen for 'asking a thousand liars how often they lie and for deciding whether to believe those answers'. In fact, the Herald would qualify for two Ig Nobel awards. A second one went to Japanese researchers 'for investigating whether things looked different when you bend over and view them between your legs'. The Ig awards for the Herald would be suitable (and timely) – they carry a cash prize of a Zimbabwean ten trillion dollar note.

Who's the tortoise now? – Saturday 1st October: On Friday Botswana celebrated 50 years of independence. There has been a transformation. In 1966 it was the poor relation in the region. Some of us at the Vigil recall travelling through Botswana by train about this time, making lengthy unexplained stops in the middle of nowhere, only for someone to suddenly emerge from the semi-desert with a tortoise for sale.

Today the tables have been turned. It's poor Zimbabweans who emerge everywhere to sell handicrafts, wild fruit and vegetables, simcards, second hand clothes . . . soon to be joined by US dollars when the threatened bond notes appear. Far from being the backward relatives the Batswana now have a much higher standard of living than Zimbabweans though their country has far fewer resources. The Gross Domestic Product per head of population – a standard measure of wealth – was $953 for Zimbabweans in 2013. The figure for Botswana was $7,315.

Why has this happened? Mugabe blames it on sanctions but the Vigil believes the simple answer is Mugabe and his rapacious elite. Robert Guest of *The Economist* wrote in his 2004 book, *The Shackled Continent*, 'In the last 35 years, Botswana's economy has grown faster than any other in the world. Yet cabinet ministers have not awarded themselves mansions and helicopters — and even the president has been seen doing his own shopping.' Botswana was described today as 'an island of peace, tranquillity and wisdom' by the writer Alexander McCall Smith in a BBC radio interview. McCall Smith has made Botswana famous abroad with wry tales of Precious Ramotswe and her No. 1 Ladies' Detective Agency. If only he would turn his attention to Zimbabwe, where he was born. How about this plot for a farce: a High Court judge who overturns an illegal police ban on demonstrations is accused by the Chief Justice of having taken a bribe, police hover in the background as Zanu PF youth provoke violence in Harare to be blamed on demonstrators, a student leader is arrested for holding a poster asking for jobs at a graduation ceremony, people are threatened with jail for displaying the Zimbabwean flag, people abducted, tortured . . .

Too far-fetched? Not in Zimbabwe. The Mugabe regime is what the Japanese observer Ken Yamamoto would describe as a fence post tortoise: 'When you're driving down a country road and you come across a fence post with a tortoise balanced on top, that's a fence post tortoise. You know he didn't get up there by himself, he doesn't belong up there, he doesn't know what to do while he's up there, he's elevated beyond his ability to function, and you just wonder what kind of dumb arse put him up there to begin with.'

We were glad that ROHR activist Linda Masarira has been released at last after being incarcerated for nearly three months on trumped up charges.

Unrepentant Mujuru – Saturday 8th October: There was no breast-beating or wringing of hands when Zimbabwe People First leader Joice Mujuru made a wooden pitch for respectability at the Royal Institute of International Affairs at Chatham House in London on Thursday. Of the abuses committed during her 34 years in the Mugabe inner circle she confessed to nothing, admitting only 'guilt by association'. Certainly no repentance. She had been kicked out as Vice President, she said, because she was a 'moderate' who favoured restoring relations with the West. (Not, as Mugabe alleged, being a 'witch'.)

But it was nevertheless a bit magical that Mrs Mujuru arrived at Chatham House in what we were told was the Ambassador's car – an unheard of courtesy to an 'opposition' figure (let alone a 'witch' of the West). What was equally surprising was the small group of prosperous-looking Mujuru supporters with sparkling new banners gathered outside the front door. Surprising because Vigil supporters – perhaps less well-dressed and suspected of being less welcoming – were herded behind a metal barricade on the far side of the road, watched over by two police officers.

On this occasion a few Vigil supporters were allowed into Chatham House to hear what was going on. They say Mujuru made all the right noises (reading from a prepared script): 'We want a government responsive to the needs of the citizens . . . there is a generational disconnect . . . country ruined by mismanagement of old guard . . . we will respect the constitution , , , repeal repressive legislation , , , observe property rights . . . restore collateral value of land . . . pay compensation, repeal indigenisation . . . reduce corruption . . . depoliticise, privatise parastatals . . . allow dual citizenship . . . diaspora vote . . . '

It could have been a party political broadcast for the Vigil. But we wouldn't choose anyone with her history in Zanu PF to deliver it. Our supporters at the Chatham House meeting didn't get a chance to ask her the question: 'What do you know about the election rigging?' At the very least the Vigil wants the full details from the Zanu PF defectors so that the world knows that all elections in the last two decades have been cooked. The Vigil certainly welcomes Mujuru to the ranks of the struggle for democracy. But we remain deeply distrustful of those who have been for so long close to the heart of Zanu PF evil. 'Peace and reconciliation?' The question remained unaddressed at the Chatham House meeting.

Nothing allowed – Saturday 15th October: On the eve of a visit to London, the human rights activist Patson Dzamara was arrested for – as he put it – 'sitting in a public park'. Patson – brother of abducted Itai Dzamara – was chatting in Harare Gardens with a few others. One of the others was Linda Masarira, mother of five, only recently released from jail for taking part in protests. They were all bundled into a truck by police officers. When they demanded to know the charge, the police were apparently clueless saying only that it was an 'instruction from above'. The group of six were released on bail on Saturday to stand trial on Monday. Prosecutors accused them of abusing and insulting some law enforcement agents by likening them to dogs and puppets.

Vigil supporters in the UK who have received invitations to attend a meeting in the UK Parliament on Wednesday to be addressed by Patson wonder whether this is a clumsy effort to stop him travelling to London. Or is it just routine intimidation? The Mugabe regime is now so paranoid that it has given up any pretence of observing the constitution. Waving the flag or even wearing clothes in the national colours is an offence. But when it comes to brazen corruption by the elite the police are suddenly powerless. An attempt to arrest higher education minister Jonathan Moyo for stealing public funds was halted by Mugabe himself. So much for the fight against corruption . . .

Everything must fall? – Saturday 22nd October: To paraphrase the famous observation by the German pastor Martin Niemöller: 'First they came for Rhodes, then they came for Isaac Newton, next they'll come for the constitution itself'. The Rhodesmustfall campaign which started at Cape Town University calling for the removal of a statue of the nineteenth century imperialist was seen by many to be rather silly but nevertheless understandable. Then students took their reforming mission further, seeking to scrap what they see as a 'Eurocentric' science curriculum in favour of traditional African theories. In particular, they dismissed Newton's work as colonial. The students have stopped short of calling it a 'Newtonmustfall' campaign perhaps realising this might validate Newton's law of gravity. Zimbabwean students have rather more pressing problems to face than removing Rhodes from his grave in the Matopos. And as far as decolonising science is concerned, they learnt to be sceptical of assertions that diesel comes from rocks in Chinhoyi.

But that doesn't seem to apply to Mugabe's nephew Patrick Zhuwao who seems ready to reject not only Rhodes and Newton but the constitution itself, asserting that Zanu PF is the state and it can use state resources to fund party projects. Zhuwao is not alone among Zanu PF leaders with this mindset. Vice President Mnangagwa, addressing a Zanu PF rally ahead of the Norton by-election, said the electorate should not waste their votes on an opposition candidate as that person would not access state resources to develop the constituency. He added that, after doling out agricultural land, Zanu PF was now providing residential stands to its supporters. More ominously, Social Welfare minister Prisca Mupfumira told starving Norton residents that they risked losing out on food aid if they were not Zanu PF members. So much for the constitution . . .

Zim activists denied UK visas – Saturday 29th October: A leading British parliamentarian has said it is disgraceful that prominent Zimbabwean civil rights campaigners are being refused visas to visit the UK to talk about the struggle against Mugabe and his Zanu PF regime. Kate Hoey, Chair of the All Party Parliamentary Group on Zimbabwe, was speaking at the Royal Geographical Society in London on Wednesday at a meeting of the Mike Campbell Foundation which was set up to address injustices involved in Mugabe's land seizures. She said a visa had been denied to one of the speakers invited to the gathering, Gift Konjana, who had been detained more than thirty times and his home petrol-bombed for helping destitute farm workers. Other activists refused visas include Pastor Evan Mawarire, leader of the #ThisFlag protest, now exiled in the United States, who had been invited to address the parliamentary group as well as to speak at the Royal Institute of International Affairs. Another excluded activist was Patson Dzamara, brother of the abducted Itai, who was also due to speak to the parliamentary group.

Ms Hoey said the British government was letting in representatives of the Mugabe regime, including people who had been involved in killings, as well as other tainted people such as Joice Mujuru, but was more and more turning away seasoned campaigners for change. Kate said the British Ambassador to Harare Catriona Laing was angry at the refusal of visas and had taken the matter up with the relevant government department. The problem appeared to involve financial guarantees regarding their stay in the UK.

A speaker from Zimbabwe who was able to get a visa was Bishop Ancelimo Magaya, founder of Grace Ablaze Ministries International, making his first visit to the UK. The Bishop, who is blind, received a standing ovation for his speech in which he said the people of Zimbabwe were 'wounded and despondent'. He spoke of abductions and a tired dictatorial leadership holding on to power by brutality. Mugabe had mastered the art of giving the impression that he allowed democratic elections but they were all rigged and people intimidated. 'Diplomats don't see this', he added. In answer to a question from one of the 28 Vigil supporters at the meeting, the Bishop said people in the diaspora were automatically regarded by the regime as sell-outs and were liable to be treated as such when they returned home. Anyway, there was nothing for them if they did go back.

Another speaker at the gathering was Professor Craig J Richardson, an American economist and author of a book 'The Collapse of Zimbabwe in the Wake of the 2000 – 2003 land reforms'. Asked by a Vigil supporter to comment on studies by British academics Ian Scoones and Joseph Hanlon painting land reform in a positive light, Professor Richardson said 'The studies I have seen were carried out in a specific area and were unrepresentative. The growth they showed was because they were starting from zero, giving a misleading impression'.

Belshazzar's feast – Saturday 5th November: The meeting between Mugabe and Zuma in Harare on Thursday was a surreal encounter between the doomed and the damned. 'His Excellency President Zuma brings with him a cloud of hope and integrity' gushed Zanu PF, adding that Zuma was walking in Mugabe's footsteps. They ignored the dark cloud of hopelessness in South Africa over the rampant corruption which has damned his presidency. And as far as 'integrity' goes, the Vigil supposes that Zanu PF must have its own definition of this word. Just ask Jonathan Moyo, who didn't even bother to go to court on Friday to answer for his defrauding of state funds – even though he had given an undertaking to be there. As for the doomed Mugabe, he is already booked in next month for more monkey gland injections in Singapore. In the meantime, state television was banned from showing him tottering to the lectern at the Zuma meeting. The Daily News quotes Zanu PF insiders as saying it could be 'mene, mene, tekel and parsim' time for Mugabe (the words appearing on the wall during Belshazzar's feast). They were interpreted by the Prophet Daniel to mean 'God has numbered the days of your kingdom and brought it to an end . . .' Angry South Africans must hope that Zanu PF is right that Zuma really is 'walking in Mugabe's footsteps' and that his banquet too is about to end.

Campaign against visa refusal – Saturday 12th November: The Vigil has launched a petition to the British Prime Minister, Theresa May, following the refusal of visas to Zimbabwean human rights activists invited to address audiences in London. The petition reads: *'Exiled Zimbabweans and supporters appeal to the UK government to allow Zimbabwean civil rights campaigners to take up invitations to visit the UK so that they can tell the world about the worsening situation in Zimbabwe. A number of prominent activists have been denied entry* *although members of the Mugabe regime have been given visas despite having a history of human rights abuses.'*

A new onslaught – Saturday 19th November: The ruthless crushing of the latest anti-government demonstration in Harare, combined with news that the army is recruiting thousands more soldiers, suggest that Zanu PF's strategy for stealing elections has not changed. The scenario is confirmed by the announcement that the diaspora will only be allowed to vote in 2018 if they return home to register and stay on or return again for the ballot – despite the lauded 2013 constitution giving every Zimbabwean the right to vote. The Zimbabwean diaspora is believed to number some 4 million – the overwhelmingly majority of voting age. The registered electorate at home is put at around 6.6 million, so the diaspora would have a decisive say. Rita Makarau, chair of the Zimbabwe Electoral Commission, said that the electoral laws had not yet been aligned with the new constitution introduced three years ago. The Vigil thinks that this is a step that Zanu PF is never likely to take, making our constitution a hollow mockery.

The Vigil is not surprised that six activists were shot at and beaten up ahead of Friday's planned demonstration against the introduction of 'bond notes'. Ishmail Kauzani, who was driving one of the two cars containing the activists when they were blocked by unmarked pick-up trucks, said he managed to escape into the night under a hail of gunfire. 'They were firing on us when we were still driving - many, many shots. It was like a war zone, a barrage of bullets', he said. Although the Vigil was not surprised by the regime's ambush we were surprised at the lack of wider support for the demonstration given the opposition's promises to confront Mugabe on the streets.

The final nail – Saturday 26th November: Despite the government's last minute hesitation, the Reserve Bank has announced that it is to release its monopoly money on Monday – widely seen as the final nail in the coffin of the Zimbabwean economy. Human rights lawyer Irene Petras said that the authorities have 'illegally, immorally and inhumanely set about destroying Zimbabwean lives for a second time' – a reference to the hyperinflation era which ended with the abandonment of the Zimbabwean currency in 2009. The Reserve Bank says $10 million of bond notes in denominations of $2 and $5 are to be issued, along with $2

million worth of $1 dollar bond coins. But few believe it will stop there. Because Zimbabweans have lived through this asset stripping before, they know exactly what to expect. Savings will be wiped out by rapidly depreciating
Mickey Mouse money for the benefit of the elite which will externalise all remaining US dollars in the country. The move is likely to be badly received by the army. Reuters news agency says it has seen a report by the Central Intelligence Organisation warning Mugabe that introduction of bond notes would cause his downfall.

There has been widespread unrest at the move although the promised 'mother of all demonstrations' against bond notes last week failed to gain support amid allegations that money collected for the Harare protest was misappropriated. It is reported that this prompted Tajamuka to pull out of the demonstration at the last moment. Zimbabwe People First spokesman Jealousy Mawarire said as much as $100,000 may have been involved. He said: 'As long as the struggle is commercialised we will always have these solo sporadic selfie moments disguised as demos'. Others talk of activists 'milking donor funds' and 'living large'. The accusations come as no surprise to us. We ourselves refuse to have anything to do with one of the protest leaders because of our own experience working with him. This person certainly fits the bill of being a 'selfie activist': always in the photograph, in the news, known to all the journalists, ready with a quote. We at the Vigil marvel at how he seems to have a 'get out of jail free' card. With no visible means of support, he nevertheless pops up regularly in the UK, always impeccably dressed, hustling for money. The social media protest movements need to beware the bad apple effect.

A dead parrot – Saturday 3rd December: The dead parrot sketch from Monty Python's Flying Circus says everything we need to know about the new bond notes. For those who are not familiar with this old BBC television comedy, the sketch is about a customer who goes into a pet shop complaining that he had been sold a dead parrot. The shopkeeper says the parrot is not dead, just resting after a long squawk. The Zimbabwean economy seems to the Vigil to be a dead parrot. With police rushing to crush any sign of dissent over the introduction of bond notes, it was left to the diaspora in London to show the contempt with which Zimbabweans regard the latest Zanu PF rip-off. The Vigil was particularly angered by the abduction and torture of Ishmael Kauzani after the abortive bond note protest in Harare on Wednesday. He is a member of our sister organisation Restoration of Human Rights in Zimbabwe and is in hospital in a critical condition. 'Mugabe uses bond notes to buy wheelchair' read one of the posters in our demonstration outside the Embassy today during which Fungayi Mabhunu in our Mugabe mask was pushed around the Vigil in a wheelchair. A central message was a display of Zimbabwean $100 trillion notes. Bond notes were shown as the successor to the dead, deceased, defunct Zimbabwean currency in the form of Mickey Mouse monopoly money.

'We are Zimbabwe' – Saturday 10th December: 'L'etat c'est moi' (I am the state) was a remark by King Louis XIV that reflected the despotic regime before the French Revolution, when the people lived in poverty, lorded over by a rich aristocracy. Now we hear the same thing from the Zanu PF elite. 'We are Zimbabwe' was the response of Grace Mugabe's son and son-in-law to protests when they illegally seized three properties in Harare. In effect: 'you can do nothing about it. We can do whatever we want.' Court documents about Grace's purchase of a $1.3 million diamond ring last year – said to be a present from Mugabe – showed the complete contempt with which the Mugabe mafia regard the rule of law. The properties belonging to a Lebanese diamond dealer were seized in a dispute after Grace decided she didn't want the ring after all. Perhaps the diamond was too small. Among the questions we want an answer to are: how was Grace able to send the $1.3 million to Dubai from her Harare bank despite exchange controls? When she decided she didn't want the ring, how could she so confidently order the repayment to be deposited in a Dubai bank account rather than returned to Harare – when this amounted to illegal externalisation of money?

Disgraceful Zimbabwe – Saturday 17th December: After his tireless work this year, travelling long distances to promote Brand Zimbabwe around the world, President Mugabe could not hide his disappointment at Zanu PF's Conference in Masvingo. All too little had been achieved at home while he had been away, he noted sadly. There had been too many juvenile squabbles in Zanu PF and silly protests from dissidents despite the hundreds of top of the range cars provided. And more cars were still to come. Of course, he said, he would like to retire and milk his cows. But the sad truth was that everyone else in Zimbabwe was either deluded or naughty. 'So we just have to soldier on to ensure continued prosperity and economic growth in line with ZimAsset.' Zanu PF agreed with the President and confirmed support for his sacrificial offer to stand for re-election in 2018. The party is fortunate because he will still be just under 100 when that presidential term ends so he will be able to stand again.

Expensive holiday season – Saturday 24th December: As Zimbabweans tighten their belts at another bleak Christmas, President Mugabe is taking a month-long rest in Singapore. He left Harare by chartered plane on 20th December accompanied by his family, aides, security people and $6 million from the Reserve Bank which will have to last them until the end of January. The holiday may cheer up Grace Mugabe who must have been annoyed to have been ordered by the High Court to return Harare properties she seized from a Dubai diamond dealer in a dispute over a $1.3 million gem she thought was not good enough. Zimbabweans can relax for a while because the government has closed down for seasonal celebrations and will do nothing for five weeks or so. Then it will spring into life to prepare for the President's 93rd birthday party in February.

Stony road ahead – Zimbabwe Vigil Diary: 31st December: As we begin a new year it is difficult to imagine that it will be a happy one in Zimbabwe. Even optimists will find it hard to see anything but a stony road ahead. We at the Vigil in the depths of a British winter are further chilled by the bleak analysis of Prince Mashele, executive director of the Centre for Politics and Research in South Africa. He argues that 'Western' values of accountability, political morality, reason and so on are not African and that it is idle to hope that Africans will have democracies of the type existing in Europe. He says: 'People must not entertain the illusion that a day is coming when SA will look like the US. Our future is more on the side of Zimbabwe, where one ruler is more powerful than the rest of the population.' He goes on: 'How else are we to explain the thousands of people who flock to stadiums to clap hands for a president who has violated their country's constitution? . . . In a typical African country people have no illusion about the unity of morality and governance. People know that those who have power have it for themselves and their friends and families.' As we embark on 2017, we at the Vigil cling to the hope that Mashele is too pessimistic and that, having gone through so much suffering, Zimbabweans, given the chance, will find the road to freedom.

2017

Highlights

January – Protesting pastor Mawarire arrested.
February – 93 kg cake for Mugabe's birthday feast.
March – French Ambassador defends Mugabe government.
July – Mugabe amends constitution to gain power over judiciary.
August – Former South African president in secret talks in Harare. Mugabe takes a billion dollars to build own university. Grace attacks woman in Johannesburg.

Zimbabwe Vigil Excerpts

Mugabe's contempt for Zimbabwe – Saturday 7th January: Happy and content must be the land whose president is secure enough to fly off on holiday with bucket and spade and doesn't even leave a forwarding address. Zimbabwe is obviously one such haven of peace and stability. Vice-President Mnangagwa, 'acting Boss', indicated as much when he disclosed that he was unable to ask Mugabe whether the late provincial governor Peter Chanetsa qualified as a Hero because he couldn't get hold of the Hero-in-Chief for his ruling. So poor old Pete will have to wait in the fridge until the Boss gets home and decides whether Pete can have a plot in Heroes' Acre. By then he will deserve hero status anyway because the Boss apparently has plans to flit all over the place before he drops by in Harare again to replenish his funds.

Give Grace a million dollars – Saturday 14th January: Zanu PF has defied the old saying that you can't have your cake and eat it. The party has been chomping away for 37 years and believes there is an inexhaustible supply of cake. But now comes the sad case of Grace Mugabe's million dollar diamond. The poor woman was conned. She says she paid up but the Lebanese businessman didn't deliver the right gem. Zimbabweans en masse have been conned for 37 years so we must sympathise with her predicament. Especially as it was such a romantic idea of the President to give her a ring to mark 20 years of wedded bliss. And as Grace noted: 'This was hard-earned money saved over the years .

. . It's a lot of sacrifice that my husband did from our farming and dairy business.' It certainly must have been some sacrifice: getting up before dawn every day to milk the cows. And then there's the ploughing to do . . . No wonder the old man falls asleep when he gets to the office. The Vigil has a brilliant suggestion: why doesn't the 21st February Movement use the million dollars it is raising for Mugabe's 93rd birthday bash to buy a ring from a non-Lebanese businessman? That way Grace could lose her ring and still have it!

Grace the Trump of Zimbabwe – Saturday 21st January: The $1.35 million diamond recently bought by Grace Mugabe was only the sparkler on top of a $7.5 million spending spree. Grace is known to have also recently paid $4.5 million for a large property in Borrowdale close to the mansion where the Mugabes live, in preference to State House. A local resident said: 'We understand Grace wants to develop many upmarket homes in a security estate.' Property magnate Grace is also spending money on a private school complex near Mazowe village on land seized from an old white couple fifteen years ago. A teacher there said pupils, mostly boarders, were charged $3,700 a term. The complex is below a huge luxury home Grace finished building last year. Dr Grace is reported to have taken about a dozen other properties, mostly white-owned farms, since 2001. Robert has lagged behind, seizing only about six farms for himself. But then he is getting on a bit. Revelations of Grace's spending spree came as it emerged that the Mugabes are paying up to half a million dollars a year on renting a ten bedroom house in Dubai.

Mugabe's mega delusions – 28th January: Zimbabwe's Christmas holidays drew to a close on Friday with the fleeting return to Harare of President Mugabe after six weeks gallivanting around the world. The government can now turn its attention to the main business facing the country: preparations for the President's 93rd birthday party next month. The two Vice-Presidents, accompanied by a variety of cabinet ministers and senior officials, were at the airport to brief the presidential couple on preparations for the celebrations. They obviously had good news as Mugabe was said to have been in high spirits. He assured them that his holiday had not been all frolics. He had, for one thing, interrupted it to see China's President Xi, who had assured him he would help as much as possible with the mega deals agreed some years ago. Unfortunately, Mugabe had no news of a mega financial bailout to pay its mega workers and enable the country to pay for its mega imports. The Vigil believes this is a mega problem and all the government's mega promises are mega delusions. As if to prove it, the mega welcoming delegation returned to the airport today to say a mega farewell to the President who, having refilled his mega wallet, flew off to Addis Ababa for a mega African Union meeting on 'Harnessing the Demographic Dividend for Investment in the Youth'. The youth of Zimbabwe await the outcome with bated breath.

BIZARRE: Pastor arrested – Saturday 4th February: 'Jailed for protesting' read one of the posters at the Vigil as we gathered in outrage at the arrest of Pastor Evan Mawarire, leader of #ThisFlag movement, on his arrival home from sanctuary in the United States. BIZARRE seems to be the headline of choice for some websites to grab your attention. The scoop may be 'goblins having sex with teachers in school' or 'woman gives birth to frog baby'. Well here's the Vigil's 'scoop': human rights activist faces 20 years in jail for saying he doesn't like the government. His lawyer Fadzayi Mahere posted: *'Pastor Evan Mawarire has been classified as a "D" Class remand prisoner and is being detained at Chikurubi Prison where convicted murderers are held, instead of the normal remand holding centre. This is not about Pastor E as an individual but it's a battle for the soul of Zimbabwe. Are we a constitutional democracy – where free speech, free assembly, free conscience and political rights are respected – or not?'*

Protest in support of Evan Mawarire – Friday 17th February: More than 40 demonstrators from the Vigil, ROHR and the MDC gathered outside the Embassy when the trial of Pastor Evan Mawarire was scheduled to start. The protest was in support of all human rights activists in Zimbabwe being harassed by the authorities in defiance of their constitutional rights.

End Mugabe's parties – Saturday 18th February: Zimbabwean exiles marked Mugabe's 93rd birthday by launching a new petition to the Southern African Development Community appealing to them to ensure free and fair elections next year. The petition reads: *The countdown to next year's elections in Zimbabwe has begun but no electoral reforms have been made and we fear the elections will once again be rigged. The increasingly incapacitated nonagenarian Robert Mugabe has already* *been nominated to stand for another five year term as Zimbabwe President while the country faces mass starvation and a collapsed economy with astronomic unemployment. We appeal to the Southern African Development Community to insist that SADC election principles are observed to ensure a level playing field for all political parties. Furthermore, we call on SADC election observers to be free from political pressure to rubberstamp a rigged poll.* Mugabe himself, in the form of Fungayi Mabhunu in our mask, was at the Vigil in his wheelchair. Wearing a superman bib, he sank a Beelzebub of birthday wine and tucked into his birthday cake, scornful about our petition, saying he believed his disciples in SADC would support Grace's proposal that, even if he died before the election, his name should still be on the ballot form because he was so popular that people would feel cheated if they could not re-elect him.

Grotesque birthday feast – Saturday 25th February: The Mugabe family and their cronies feasted on a 93 kg cake at a requisitioned school in Matobo where local people live in desperate poverty, their children starving. The grotesque party for Mugabe's 93rd birthday was particularly insulting to the local people because the venue is so close to the graves of victims of Mugabe's Gukurahundi genocide of the 1980s. Mugabe at 93 is fast failing. But he is the only thing Zanu PF can rally around. When Grace recently said he could stand for re-election next year even if he is dead, people laughed. Then it dawned on everyone that the Mugabes were deadly serious. After all, whole cemeteries of skeletons over 100 years old were on the voters' roll for the 2013 elections. They all voted for Mugabe then and will no doubt be even keener now that he himself is approaching 100. It wouldn't be surprising if he was already gearing them up to go canvassing for him in the dead of night. No use locking your doors, they will simply walk through them. It is well know that Mugabe is keen on the occult. He said it was because Mai Mujuru was trying to put spells on him that he had to get rid of her. For her part, Grace Mugabe, as befits someone with a doctorate, takes a more scientific view. She wisely warns girls that they are more likely to get pregnant than boys and cites her evidence: 'If you look at the statistics, girls have nearly 100% chance of getting pregnant, while boys have nearly zero chances of falling pregnant. This means girls have to be extra vigilant'.

2017

Xenophobia Protest – Wednesday 1st March: Vigil supporters staged a demonstration outside South Africa House against the renewed xenophobia in South Africa. They handed a petition to the Deputy High Commissioner Golden Neswiswi.

Fears of election rigging – Saturday 4th March: There are growing fears that Zanu PF is already busy preparing to steal next year's elections. Suspicions have been heightened by the government's move to seize control of the new biometric voter registration process. It had been agreed that the process would be handled by the United Nations Development Programme but the bankrupt Zanu PF government suddenly announced it would itself pay for it, taken as a clear sign that it intends to nobble the whole process. The move comes amid complaints that traditional leaders are again being coerced to support Zanu PF and that voters are being warned that the biometric system will enable Zanu PF to see how they vote.

The Vigil has now submitted its petition to the UN calling for intervention to ensure a level playing field in the Zimbabwe elections. Here is our letter to the UN Secretary General, António Guterres: 'We respectfully submit a petition calling on the United Nations to intervene in Zimbabwe. The petition reads: *With mounting unrest in Zimbabwe, we urge you to appoint a Special Representative to prepare the ground for a UN Transitional Authority to take over from the failed Mugabe regime. We look to the Special Representative to initiate comprehensive negotiations so that the UN Transitional Authority can assume control of Zimbabwe's administrative structures – foreign affairs, defence, security, finance and communications – to ensure a level playing field conducive for credible national elections.* The petition has been signed by thousands of people who have passed by the Zimbabwe Vigil which has been held outside the Zimbabwe Embassy in London since 2002 in support of free and fair elections. In addition, many more have endorsed it online. Mugabe's Zanu PF party has been in power since independence 37 years ago and has reduced Zimbabweans to poverty and starvation. Polls have been blatantly rigged and, with no electoral reforms in sight, it is certain that the 2018 elections will again be stolen by a combination of rigging, bribery, intimidation and violence. In the past the bogus polls have been routinely endorsed by the Southern African Development Community and the African Union despite all the evidence of malpractice. We fear that if it happens again there will be an explosion of anger by people driven to desperation and this will have serious consequences for the region as a whole.'

What should the West do? – Saturday 11th March: With scarcely 15 months to go before Zimbabwe's next elections, it seems that the Western world has no strategy to avert continued Zanu PF misrule. What's new, you may ask, and why are we singling out the Western world? Well, it's because the other power blocks do have a strategy: it is to support Zanu PF. Our 'all-weather' friends China, Russia, the Middle East etc have no interest in promoting democracy in Zimbabwe. Neither does the South African government or Africa in general. Witness Mugabe's zombie trip to Ghana for their 60th independence anniversary celebrations. Zimbabwe had no working planes so Mugabe hired one in Bahrain to take his usual '$5 million a time' retinue on a trip through which he slept most of the time. So those hoping for change are looking to the West. But the outlook here is poor as well. Western countries must know that the next elections are going to be rigged. After all, most of them have embassies in Harare and their envoys can't spend all their time attending each other's national day festivities. The opposition, civil society – and even expelled former Zanu PF leaders – have all explained how the elections will be stolen. The way it always has been. Well, says the West, we will be stern and tell Mugabe to change his ways . . . And if Zanu PF steals the elections we will bleat loudly. But we won't break off diplomatic relations, stop aid money which props up the regime or even impose any more of those problematic sanctions. So it will be business as usual, probably with Tsvangirai roped in again to do what the MDC have already shown they can do: revive the rapidly collapsing economy so that Zanu PF can get rid of them again.

Fake news – Saturday 18th March: Donald Trump won the US presidency partly because he persuaded ordinary Americans that there was an alternative truth to that being presented to them by the mainstream media. Anything he didn't like he dismissed as 'fake news'. This is not a new phenomenon, as Zimbabweans must know well. The government controlled press is adept at fake news. Take Friday's report in the Herald about the UN Human Rights Council's meeting in Geneva. It begins: 'Zimbabwe scored big here when the United Nations adopted its November 2016 Universal Periodic Report highlighting the human rights situation in the country, as member-states applauded Government efforts and commitment at ensuring enjoyment of various rights by citizens.' Talk about alternative reality! If you look into the composition of the Council you will find that it is packed with serial human rights abusers such as North Korea, China, Iran, Belarus, Turkey, Venezuela and Cuba. There are many African member countries as well but they vote in shameless solidarity with brother Africans. These countries predictably ignored a submission by human rights organisations expressing concern that human rights defenders in Zimbabwe 'continue to face harassment, arbitrary arrests and torture for exercising their freedoms to assemble and of expression'.

Also dwelling in an alternative world is former Vice President 'Dr' Joice Mujuru whose failings were forensically examined by Stephen Sackur of the BBC Hardtalk programme. 'What a plump chicken I see before me', he might well have thought as he plucked another feather from Mugabe's long-time bag carrier. What emerged from the interview was a woman whose husband had been murdered by her boss but who nevertheless chose to hang onto her job. The ancient Greeks would have seen this as a subject for a tragedy. For Zimbabweans it is just life. Joice showed herself to be lying and self-serving. She bleated: 'I could do nothing. I was not guilty. I was only Vice President. I knew nothing. I spent my 30+ years in government only doing good for people etc.' By the end of the interview the chicken feathers were knee deep in the BBC studio.

Neither up nor down – Saturday 25th March: Like the Grand Old Duke of York, Morgan Tsvangirai marched his men up to the top of the hill on Wednesday. And, as goes the English nursery rhyme, he promptly marched them down again. 'Circumstances dictate the situation and today is not the day to stage street protests', he told supporters in Harare campaigning for electoral reforms. But, the Vigil asks, if not now, when? Yes, the police had predictably placed last minute obstacles in the way of the protest. Can anyone see the day coming when they won't? Seen from afar, it looks like the protestors simply bottled out. But what right do those of us safely in the diaspora have to criticise activists at home? After all, according to the French Ambassador in Harare, we are just helping to spread a negative portrayal of Zimbabwe. Ambassador Richard Boidin has been in Zimbabwe for a couple of months so he thinks he knows what's what. He reportedly told the Herald 'the reality of Zimbabwe is very different from what you have when you are outside'. The Ambassador was speaking after paying a courtesy call on Senate President Comrade Edna Madzongwe with members of a French parliamentary Zimbabwe friendship association. Boidin continued: 'For example, the two members of the association have been here since yesterday and what they have seen here they have not seen in the media outside'. Pretty smart, the French. Barely a day in Harare and the delegation has concluded that the Zimbabwean independent media and the international press are producing 'fake news' about the situation. Envoys like Boidin call into question why about a dozen European Union countries have embassies in Zimbabwe and another half dozen are represented by consulates. To crown it all there is even an embassy of the European Union itself. What can they possibly be doing, apart from enjoying the sunshine? It's not the media that's fake, Mr Boidin. It's self-satisfied, time-serving, patronising functionaries who are 'neither up nor down'.

Rule by Grace – Saturday 1st April: People who settled on Arnold farm in Mazowe back in 2000 thought they were protected by the rule of law when Grace Mugabe started sniffing around. When armed police arrived with officials from the Land Ministry and started demolishing their homes they took recourse to the High Court, where a judge granted an application to prevent their eviction. Vindicated, they went back to the farm with the court order – only for the police to brush it aside, saying they took their orders only from their superiors. In other words, the court order counted for nothing. Residents were forced onto trucks and dumped some 40 kilometres away, without food or water and far from their children's schools. The dispossessed residents went on to appeal for intervention by the Southern African Development Community, meeting in Swaziland under the chairmanship of King Mswati, asking it compel the Zimbabwean government to respect the rule of law. The Vigil is sorry for these poor people. Sorry because they have been badly treated. Sorry because there is no rule of law in Zimbabwe when it comes to the interests of the elite. Sorry because Mswati is an acolyte of Mugabe. And even sorrier because SADC is an irredeemable joke. A joke at which no one laughs.

Dokora's Muslim syllabus – Saturday 8th April: The diaspora was surprised to learn from Education Minister Lazarus Dokora that Islam was Zimbabwe's biggest religion in 1980 and was the country's 'designated' indigenous faith. According to Dokora, Christianity was only the fourth religion when Mugabe took over, behind not only Islam but Judaism and Hinduism as well. We in the diaspora don't remember many Muslims around when we lived there. Precious few Jews either, for that matter, though there were certainly Indians. It was Christianity that was the prevailing faith – and that was even before the spectacular rise of the Profit Ministries. It's the time of year when Christians start thinking of 30 pieces of silver. The Vigil suspects Lazarus Dokora wouldn't even rise from the dead for that. But he's getting millions for selling out the country. The learned minister said he has managed to get a 'loan' of $20 million from the Organisation of Petroleum Exporting Countries (OPEC) to build the first 17 of 2,000 Muslim schools planned for Zimbabwe. Money was being raised from other 'international partners' for 66 other Muslim schools, the sites for which had already been chosen. OPEC's dominant member is Saudi Arabia which finances Muslim schools in the West and is known for promoting Islamic fundamentalism of the type adopted by the bloody Boko Haram in Nigeria and Al Shabaab in Somalia. Is this what we need in Zimbabwe?

London protest at Zanu PF misrule – Saturday 15th April: The Vigil is to mark Zimbabwe's Independence Day by a demonstration outside the Embassy in London next Saturday in protest at Zanu PF's misrule. At the same time, Zanu PF in the UK has invited people to join anniversary celebrations they are holding in the small town of Aylesbury some 50 miles from London. They seem to have plenty of money as they are offering 'free entry, free food, free parking, free entertainment'. Noticeably, they describe themselves as 'UK based Zimbabweans'; it is only hidden away in small print that the hosts are Zanu PF UK.

ROHR in Zimbabwe is taking a leading role in a new initiative, a 'peace bandwagon', to prevent violence and make space for democracy – the Zimbabwe Peace Actors' Platform (ZimPAP). The initiative has moved on considerably since it was started in December last year. ZimPAP will be launched in Mashonaland East province on 17th April with a peace soccer tournament and registration of volunteer civilian friends for peace. Here in the UK, ROHR has been actively fundraising for ZimPAP.

Bitter fruits – Saturday 22nd April: '37 years of Zimbabwe Independence' read one poster. '37 years of Mugabe slavery' read another. Exiles in the UK marked Zimbabwe's national day with a mixture of anticipation and fear – the bitter fruits of 'liberation'. The fear was that – despite news of reconciliation between Tsvangirai and Welshman Ncube – the opposition was facing an insurmountable obstacle posed by Zanu PF's control of the election process. 'The 2018 election results are already declared', said former Finance Minister Tendai Biti at a meeting in Parliament in London. He said he could not support Tsvangirai and was in favour of a transitional authority to rescue the wreckage of Zimbabwe and prepare for real elections. He insisted that Mnangagwa – the favourite of the West – could play no prominent role in Zimbabwe's future because of his bloodstained record.

Saturday 29th April: Zimbabweans are among the poorest people in the world according to a report by Afrasia Bank. It puts Zimbabwean wealth per person last year at US$200. By comparison, wealth per capita in South Africa was US$11,300, Namibia US$10,800, Botswana US$6,700, Angola US$3,600, Zambia US$1,200, Mozambique US$800 and the DRC US$400. (The index didn't include Malawi, Lesotho and Swaziland.) The report said: 'Notably, back in 2000, Zimbabwe was one of the wealthiest countries in Sub Saharan Africa on a wealth per capita basis, ranked ahead of the likes of Nigeria, Kenya, Angola, Zambia and Ghana. However, now it is ranked well behind these countries.' The report continued that contributing factors to Zimbabwe's poor performance included the erosion of ownership rights which, it said, were key to facilitating wealth creation. 'Business owners are unsure as to whether their businesses or property will still belong to them a year down the line, which creates a situation where no one will take the chance of investing in the country.' The report went on to speak of political intimidation, election fixing and the banning of independent media which made it impossible for investors to tell what was happening, and pointed to a brain drain caused by 20% of the population fleeing the country.

Saturday 6th May: President Mugabe laughed at the suggestion that Zimbabwe is a fragile state. The question was put to him on Thursday at the World Economic Forum on Africa held in Durban. 'That isn't true', he snorted. 'Zimbabwe is the most developed country on the continent after South Africa. We have a bumper harvest, not only of maize but also of tobacco and many other crops. We are not a poor country.'Mugabe's head then slumped on his chest as he returned to dreamland – before he could be told of the violent clashes on the tobacco sales floors in Harare, where riot police fired teargas at desperate farmers demanding payment for their crops. They complained 'hurumende yedu haichadi vanhu yakutirwisa Smith aiva nani' (The government is now fighting us; the Smith regime was better.)

Overcoming fear – Saturday 13th May:

Supporters of Restoration of Human Rights gathered at the Vigil to give a send-off to ROHR activist Sipho Ndlovu who will be cycling through England for seven days to raise funds for the Zimbabwe Peace Actors' Platform (ZimPAP). Sipho will cover 324 miles from Nottingham to London, calling at Leicester, Birmingham, Oxford, Southampton, Reading and Slough. ZimPAP was formed by ROHR International together with 18 other Zimbabwean civil society organisations, including Heal Zimbabwe, the Catholic Commission for Justice and Peace and Amnesty International. Its aim is peace-building and the prevention of violence around next year's elections.ROHR President Ephraim Tapa was enthusiastic about the initiative, which he said would curb voter manipulation by encouraging co-operation across the political divide to overcome fear. During the week Ephraim and others from the Vigil and ROHR had a meeting in London with visiting Senator Michael Carter of MDC T, which discussed ways of reassuring rural voters that they could safely support the party of their choice. Senator Carter, his wife Judy, as well as two sons and a grandson, joined us at the Vigil, taking part in the singing and dancing.

Former Finance Minister and presidential candidate Simba Makoni dismissed Mugabe's recent denial that Zimbabwe is a fragile state. Makoni said the economy was collapsing: 'Government can't pay its workers. Hospitals and schools are sustained by donors. We have the highest ratio of graduate informal traders in the world,' Makoni tweeted. 'Up to one third of the population are economic refugees. It is estimated that approximately three million Zimbabweans are living in South Africa, many of them illegally. Public infrastructure is decrepit and dysfunctional. National roads are pot-holed. For nearly 20 years, people who fed themselves before have survived on food aid. The economy shrank to 40 percent of its size in 10 years,' he said.

The wet road to freedom – Saturday 20th May:
The Zimbabwean diaspora gave ROHR activist Sipho Ndlovu a hero's welcome when he arrived at the Vigil after a marathon bike ride through to raise money to stop political violence in Zimbabwe and teach people in the rural areas what their voting rights are. Sipho braved roads flooded by heavy rain on his 324 mile ride from Nottingham to London, which took in six other towns. He said some of the roads were like rivers. The weather took a toll on his bike and also his phone, which he was relying on for navigation. Fortunately members of Restoration of Human Rights in Zimbabwe were waiting to meet him at the end of each day and they arranged to have the bike fixed and lent him a phone, as well as organising food, dry clothes, a hot bath and a place to sleep.

Rotten to the core – Saturday 27th May: Figures are important, particularly for Zimbabwe where they simply don't add up. Let's start with Mugabe's trip to the Mexican resort of Cancun less than a week after he returned from seeing his doctors in Singapore. Mugabe travelled by chartered airliner with an entourage of three dozen people. All of them received a daily allowance of at least $1,000. Some would have got considerably more, among them three cabinet ministers who would be obliged by the dignity of their office to stay in the best suites in the most expensive hotels. That will prove to Mugabe's opponents that Zimbabwe is doing alright, won't it? Why were they in Mexico? One wonders if it was just for the expenses. The routine UN meeting on 'disaster risk reduction' was attended by only the odd head of state like Mugabe who, this time, was apparently denied his usual grand-standing opportunity. Mugabe is said to have left Mexico 'not too pleased' before the conference ended. His entourage was presumably 'not too pleased' at losing some per diems out of the millions of dollars in cash that Mugabe takes with him every time he moves (or is this cache only for his own expenses?). Some more figures: last year Mugabe made more than 20 trips abroad, spending $36 million in ten months according to the finance ministry. This year has seen no slowdown.

MDC T legislator Eddie Cross, in an article on corruption in Zimbabwe, says 'I can think of four ministers in Government whom I am prepared to say are honest and not involved in any material corruption – but the rest, 30 of them, are rotten to the core and do not miss an opportunity to make a margin on anything over which they have control.' He continues: 'The evidence of corruption on a massive and pervasive scale is everywhere – estates of homes that would look good on a Hollywood Boulevard. Ministers, earning a few thousand dollars a month, accumulating tens of millions of dollars of property, luxury cars with wives and girl friends swimming in luxuries of every kind. Even Mr Mugabe, who earns a very modest salary, has luxury homes in Harare, Zvimba, South Africa, Dubai, Singapore, Hong Kong and Malaysia. The Head of a Medical Aid Society that provides medical cover to the Civil Service; steals US$35 million in three years, is fired and no further action is taken.' Perhaps it's time Mr Mugabe gave up his travels and paid some attention to what is going on at home.

Best educated idiots? – Saturday 3rd June: Zimbabweans love myths. One of the proofs is the popularity of the suave, sharply-dressed salesmen promising them everything they pray for. Like Mugabe. Here we bump into one of the great myths of our age: 'Zimbabweans are the best-educated people in Africa'. If this was ever true it is surely impossible to claim this today with our run-down schools and malnourished pupils and our premier university's two-month doctorate for Grace Mugabe. This is not to say our people are stupid. Far from it. Zanu PF is proof of this. Their well-oiled 2018 election strategy is already underway. It is felt everywhere. Mbare for instance is out of bounds to the MDC. Not that there is anything new in the strategy, but they have the intelligence to just go on repeating what works. This is shown in the experience of our sister organisation Restoration of Human Rights in Zimbabwe which was given the old run-around when they applied to the police for clearance for their constitutional right to stage a peaceful demonstration in Harare at the end of May. For weeks they were made to report to Harare Central to receive clearance only to be turned down at the last minute and threatened with arrest.

Who needs wheels? – Saturday 17th June: When it comes to straight talking, Zimbabweans don't have to look much further than the Manicaland Provincial Affairs Minister Mandi Chimene, who welcomed Mugabe to Mutare for a Zanu PF Youth Rally. 'Some of you think I have taken weed', she said. 'Do I look like someone who took weed today?' Mugabe said nothing. You could say he sat stoned-faced. Vice President Mnangagwa however, who was sitting next to him, must have had difficulty suppressing a smile. Chimene, speaking as it were from on high, urged Mugabe to end the divisions in the party over the presidential succession. 'We end up seeing crocodile smiles because of the divisions,' she snorted. Chimene proceeded to demonstrate that she was in full possession of her senses by accusing ministers in the province of looting. She went on: 'If it means going down with you, we fall together Comrade President.' Mugabe, who is quite capable of falling down by himself, made no response to this offer. But he would hardly have been reassured by Chimene's undertaking the previous week to youth leaders preparing for the rally. She promised them they would have no trouble with police road blocks. 'You said some vehicles do not have wheels, but I will make sure you will not be harassed.' Who needs wheels when you have mbanje power?

Victims of 'sovereignty' – Saturday 24th June: As Zimbabwe embarks on the final lap before the next elections, all indications are that it will be a repetition of the stolen 2013 polls, nodded through by an acquiescent outside world. Vice President Mnangagwa, speaking on a money-raising trip to South Africa, insisted that the elections would be free and fair, saying electoral reforms had been made to level the playing field, such as the introduction of biometric voter registration. But this is belied by a report that the Zimbabwe Electoral Commission will still use the database set up by the notorious Israeli company Nikuv International, which was accused by the opposition of helping Zanu PF rig the voters' roll in the last elections. Renewed support for the Zimbabwe status quo came from former South African president Thabo Mbeki, who said political leaders who had 'outstayed their welcome' must be shown the door – but only by their own people, adding that he would fight any South African who stood up to say Mugabe must go. 'It's none of your business' he insisted. This is the spurious 'independence solidarity' rhetoric which he and other antediluvian leaders have used to legitimise brutal undemocratic regimes – ignoring all evidence of oppression and happily sacrificing the welfare of the people on the altar of sovereignty.

Walk for peace – Saturday 1st July: Thirty people joined the Vigil at the Embassy after a 15-mile walk to raise funds for the Zimbabwe Peace Actors' Platform (ZimPAP) which seeks to train civilian peacekeepers for next year's elections. Waving posters, they were singing as they came to join us down the Strand, conveniently closed to traffic by demonstrators complaining about financial 'austerity' in the UK.

A graphic insight into Zimbabwean-style 'austerity' in the rural areas comes from a pastor in the Bulawayo area who is supported by members of the Vigil. Asked in an interview about the mood of the people, he said: *'They are sad, very depressed. The only time they are happy is when they receive food from us.'* The pastor went on: *'There is a lot of witchcraft going on around Zim as well as in the church. The reason is because of suffering due to the economy collapsing. Most businesses have closed down and people can't get jobs so can't get money to pay their bills or buy food or school fees or get treated for their illnesses. There is a high level of corruption and as a result people seek the services of false prophets and nyangas.'* The pastor added: *'Jealousy is widespread among families because they cannot meet their basic needs, especially if one part of the family has children supporting them from outside the country. Because the needs are so great people are just looking out for themselves and neglecting other relatives. Married couples are breaking up bitterly and often the children are deserted. I have many times tried to bring some new street kids back to the family but often the parents don't even want them. The children say they are happier to be away from the relatives. Very old people are also deserted by the family members who leave and never send anything for them. I have many grandparents now. Another thing that is difficult for me is children dying from malnutrition. At the cemetery in Luveve the ground is spreading with children's graves. According to traditional beliefs if a child is less than three months the women are expected to bury the child, especially very elderly women. This is very difficult to watch. These things keep us on our knees.'*

Reality and delusion – Saturday 8th July: Manicaland Provincial Affairs minister Mandi Chimene appears to have been smoking weed again. Only a few weeks after raving about mbanje to Mugabe at his Mutare rally, she has come up with a proposal to lie to attract tourists. Chimene urged those involved in tourism in Manicaland to claim that an Indian tourist who mysteriously disappeared three years ago while climbing the sacred Inyangani mountain would return one day. 'Some of them will wait for him to meet them' she said, adding: 'We need strategies if we are going to survive in this industry'. Mandi's attitude is in keeping with Zanu PF's deceitful short-termism: reality is an illusion. One minute Vice President Mnangagwa assures prospective South African investors that land invasions are over than, incited by Mugabe, the remnants of a farm developed by a white family over the last 80 years are seized – and by none other than the presiding bishop of the Pentecostal Assemblies of Zimbabwe. As the Vigil has long pointed out, the delusional world of Zanu PF – with their alternative reality – has gained a foothold in the UK where a professor at London University's School of Oriental and African Studies Stephen Chan has published a book claiming that, despite opposition complaints of election rigging, Mugabe would have won the 2013 elections anyway – and furthermore the elections had taken place under relatively 'credible' conditions. Asked by the Vigil to justify this conclusion, Chan said he had 'crunched the numbers'. The Vigil questions how you can 'crunch' the voters intimidated into voting for Mugabe or the opposition voters moved off the voters' roll by the rigging company employed by the Mugabe regime when even the Zimbabwe Electoral Commission says it doesn't have a copy of the 2013 voters' roll?

Campaign of fear – Saturday 15th July: Fears of violence are growing as the 2018 elections approach. The fears are especially acute in rural areas such as Gutu West constituency, where a local NGO reports that Zanu PF intimidation has triggered panic in the entire community. Villagers says a former chief, George Chivhande Serima, now a Zanu PF ward chairman, has warned them of severe punishment if they support opposition parties. People are being ordered to submit their names and national registration details to village heads. MDC MP Eddie Cross says: 'the entire rural population is living under a regime of terror built up over many years by Zanu PF. The level of intimidation and control is extraordinary and includes beatings, targeted abductions, rape, threats, the use of traditional leaders and threats of expulsion from their homes. It includes close supervision of voting and collective punishment for communities or villages who are known to support, in any way, the opposition.' The MDC said teams had been deployed from the Registrar General's office to conduct voter registration ahead of the legal voter registration process by the Zimbabwe Electoral Commission. The Zimbabwe Human Rights Association expressed grave concern over the rise in political conflict in the country and said 'political developments should be taken seriously by the international community to avert a slide into more violence'.

Mugabe's non-stop party – Saturday 22nd July: You must hand it to the Mugabes – they know how to party. No expense spared. No distance too far to travel. No diamond ring too big. No guilt. No conscience. In fact, no hypocrisy because they don't understand the word. To them it's entitlement. It was the sense of entitlement that reeked more than the smell of mbanje from the luxury apartment in the affluent Sandton area of Johannesburg from which Mugabe's party-loving sons Robert Jnr and Chatunga Bellamine were evicted after a late night brawl over women which left one of their guards with a broken leg and shattered arm and the apartment trashed with cigarette burns, whisky, champagne and red wine-soiled carpets. One source quoted by the Zimbabwe Independent said the boys lived 'a carefree life of luxury, partying and over-indulgence. Money never seems to be a problem with the lucky Mugabe family. Zimbabwe may be rated poor by some people but for the Mugabes it has always been a land of milk and honey. The President himself, continuing his neurotic attempts to escape the country, spent $4,588,990 on travel in January, $ 4,250,630 in February and $4,119,638 in March – $13 million in the last 3 months for which data is available. Not bad for a 93 year-old who can hardly walk.

Lunatics in charge – Saturday 29th July: Four years after the vaunted new constitution was approved in a national referendum, Zanu PF has forced through an amendment restoring the President's power over the choice of the Chief Justice and other top judges. Considering that much of the 2013 constitution has still to be implemented, including the right of a vote for the diaspora and the right to demonstrate – it is ominous that the first amendment further undermines the rule of law. The amendment was moved in the House of Assembly by Vice President Mnangagwa, who is favoured by the West (and China) to take over from Mugabe as the 'sane' element in Zanu PF. The MDC in Parliament found Mnangagwa anything but reasonable. It pointed out that the parliamentary move was clearly violating the express views of the nation, the independence of the judiciary and the principle of separation of powers.

Crunch point in Zimbabwe? – Saturday 5th August: The mysterious visit to Zimbabwe this week by former South African president Thabo Mbeki, a long-time Zanu PF supporter, is a clear sign that things have reached crisis point in Zimbabwe. An unprecedented feature of the lightning visit was a meeting between Mbeki and Zimbabwe's security chiefs at a time of growing differences between them and Mugabe over the succession issue. Service chiefs are believed to be pressing him to name Vice-President Mnangagwa as his successor and they were reported to have had a meeting with Mugabe on Monday urging him to settle the issue to end the increasingly bitter conflict in Zanu PF. Last week, Mugabe publicly berated the generals for interfering in the political process. 'There are secret manoeuvres going on', he said. At the same party meeting Grace Mugabe called on him to name his successor, saying the party would rally behind his anointed 'horse' – clearly a reference to herself! The Vigil welcomed the agreement to reunite the MDC in an alliance with other parties to confront Zanu PF in next year's elections.

Mugabe's University – Saturday 12th August: The Mugabe family have dramatically expanded their property empire in the Mazowe area by giving themselves a billion dollars of government money to build a new university there to be called the Robert Gabriel Mugabe University with themselves as the trustees. It will be convenient for their two sons, Robert Jnr and Chatunga Bellarmine, who were recently thrown out of their luxury flat in Johannesburg after a drunken and drug-fuelled party. The pair seem to have continued their profligate ways on a visit to Harare. The Zimbabwe Independent says they left patrons at Club 1+1 stunned by their extravagance, keeping tables in the VIP section overflowing with champagne and whiskey. One patron said he counted 51 bottles, costing an average of $190 each. Robert's studies at the University of Johannesburg seem to have been a bit of a fantasy, with lectures hardly ever attended – certainly not in the morning when his chauffeur was rarely required. So a local uni run by mum and dad far away from the fleshpots of Joburg and 40 kilometres from Harare would seem to be suitable. And since Grace got her doctorate from the University of Zimbabwe after a few weeks' work, it shouldn't be too difficult for the boys to match this at their own place, so to speak. 'The influence of champagne and whiskey on cognitive function' might make a PhD thesis. Or perhaps closer to Grace's interest, 'The effect of privilege on child development'.

Disgraced First 'Lady' – 19th August: The undignified flight from South Africa of the disgraced Zimbabwean First 'Lady' after viciously attacking a young woman in Johannesburg has made her an object of derision throughout the world. Grace's crazed attack tells a lot about her sense of being above the law – fostered by the impunity with which the Zanu PF elite plunder and abuse Zimbabwe and her people. Grace lost her cool when she went to see her two dissolute sons at a Johannesburg hotel and apparently found yet another party going on. She lashed out with an electrical extension cord leaving a 20 year old model Gabriella Engels bleeding from head wounds. When police began criminal investigations, President Mugabe appealed to his friend Zuma to grant retroactive diplomatic immunity. But Grace may not be off the hook. A group supporting Ms Engels say that if the South African authorities do not hold Grace to account they will help a private prosecution. This would cause serious embarrassment if Grace was to visit her new acquisition – a luxury house in Johannesburg costing about $3.5 million.

Zanu PF's contempt for justice was illustrated this week when President Mugabe said people implicated in the murder of white farmers during the land seizures would never be prosecuted.

For subsequent diaries see www.zimvigil.co.uk. Now we go back to pick up the story from our earliest diaries.

2004

Highlights

5th June: first Vigil diary.
24th July: Roman Catholic Archbishop of Bulawayo attends Vigil. 'Keep up the pressure', he says.
15th October: MDC leader Morgan Tsvangirai acquitted of plotting to kill Mugabe, although he still faces another treason charge.
30th October: MDC MP Roy Bennett imprisoned for eight months after altercation with a Zanu PF minister in Parliament.
21st November: Morgan Tsvangirai speaks to the diaspora in London at meeting organised by the Vigil.

Vigil Diary Excerpts

Saturday 5th June: Welcome to the first Vigil Diary. We were joined from Zimbabwe by the MDC National Chairman, Isaac Matongo, visiting the Vigil after addressing the MDC UK District assembly held at the Springbok Bar near the Vigil. Exuberant MDC members from all over the country joined the Vigil after the assembly and kept it going well beyond its closing time because we stayed to catcall Zimbabwe Embassy officials when they emerged at what they thought was the end of the Vigil. They looked very crestfallen.

Saturday 12th June: The Vigil was dominated by the visit to the UK by the Governor of the Reserve Bank of Zimbabwe, Gideon Gono. He is here to raise funds for the Mugabe regime through his Homelink initiative. Zimbabweans in the UK are furious that the British Government has allowed him in and not expanded targeted sanctions to include him. The Vigil was extended well into the evening so we could protest while a reception took place at Zimbabwe House hosted by Gono. Catcalls, whistles, singing, dancing and drumming increased in volume as Zimbabwean officials arrived. The message of our protest was that, however tempting the exchange rate offered by the Homelink roadshow, Zimbabweans in the diaspora should not succumb as they will be propping up the regime and perpetuating human rights abuse in

Zimbabwe. Some of our supporters managed to sneak in to the reception. They reported that Gono's presentation was very short and he did not take any questions.

Saturday 19th June: Today the Vigil expressed solidarity with the WOZA protests in Zimbabwe – Women of Zimbabwe Arise – to mark world refugee day. The protest was made more poignant when we received texts from Zimbabwe to say a number of protesters there had been arrested. It was good to be joined by Geoff Hill, author of 'The Battle for Zimbabwe', who has a new book on Zimbabwe coming out shortly. After our protest last week we were cheered to receive text messages from Johannesburg that Zimbabwe Reserve Bank Governor Gono had been routed by Zimbabwean protesters there.

Saturday 26th June: The UN day drawing attention to torture was marked at the Vigil today. More than a hundred people joined an informal procession from St Martin-in-the-Fields church in Trafalgar Square to lay flowers at the Vigil in solidarity with Zimbabwean torture survivors. Zimbabwe was named by the Law Society in London as the worst country in the world for torture two years ago – and things certainly haven't got better since then. The church service was addressed by Beatrice Mtetwa, a human rights lawyer, and Evelyn Masaiti, an MDC MP, among others. Among the visitors during the day was Andrew Meldrum, whose new book on Zimbabwe, "Where We Have Hope", was launched in London yesterday. The Vigil was the third in as many days. On Thursday and Friday Zimbabweans gathered outside Zimbabwe House to mark the anniversary of the stolen Parliamentary elections of 2000.

Saturday 24th July: One of the most memorable Vigils in the 21 months we have been gathering on Saturdays outside Zimbabwe House. Placards we had made said it all: "Welcome Pius Ncube – voice of the oppressed". The Roman Catholic Archbishop of Bulawayo, outspoken critic of the Mugabe regime, spent one and a half hours with us, comforting those on bended knees who sought his help. The Archbishop signed our petitions and spoke of his pain at seeing so many Zimbabweans driven from their homes. 'Don't be discouraged. Keep up the pressure,' he exhorted us. The crowd of exuberant Zimbabweans was joined by a number of pastors, Including two Methodist ministers. One of them, 85-year-old Merfyn Temple, jailed last year in Zimbabwe, carried a placard around his neck: 'Ashamed to be a Methodist'.

Saturday 31st July: Racist abuse. Most of our regular supporters had gone off to the wedding of the MDC's UK representative, Dr Brighton Chireka, in Surrey. So it was three murungus (whites) who had to confront a succession of 'Africa for the Africans' British Caribbeans. 'You white people leave black people alone'. Human rights abuses? 'It's all white propaganda'. Normally we have black faces in the early part of the Vigil who disarm this sort of abuse. Fortunately our faithful local (black) dustman intervened and signed our petitions (as he does every week). A nun carrying a 3 foot high Madonna and child on her way to gospel singing in the open air (it touched 30 degrees today) dropped by – some continuity with Archbishop Pius Ncube's visit last week. Some of us attended the service at Westminster Cathedral last Sunday at which he preached. The congregation broke into spontaneous applause. Several of those who attended spoke to him after the service and It was clear that he felt the Vigil was enormously important.

Saturday 21st August: As we write this, a sadza party is going on in Bermondsey to mark the departure from London of some of the Vigil's most faithful supporters. They include our inspirational singer and drummer, Patson Muzuwa. With the high cost of everything in London, It's tough here for Zimbabweans and we hope they will find it easier in Leicester. Patson spent an hour today explaining the situation in Zimbabwe to an ill-informed Rasta.

Saturday 28th August: A passing tribe of Italian boy scouts was fascinated by the singing and dancing. They probably got some badge for joining in. Talking about joining in: Joyce from Manchester got up at 5 am to be with us at the start of the Vigil. She expected to be back in Manchester at a quarter to midnight to catch a connection home. And Joyce wasn't alone: we had another from Manchester and also supporters from Leeds, Derby, Hastings and Luton. People make great sacrifices to be at the Vigil. Two white Zimbabweans dropped by. It was sad to see how they had given up and felt there was no future for them in Zimbabwe.

Saturday 4th September: Our 100th Vigil and we were favoured by the gods – 28C with a brilliant cloudless sky. But it was discouraging to have yet another Zimbabwean couple passing by who asked us why we were bothering when there was no hope of change. Our view is we must try and keep Zimbabwe in the public eye at a time when it is fading out of the news.

Saturday 11th September: Big competition today: (mainly white) Zimfest with beer, braai, sport and talk. The Vigil sent two representatives to Zimfest to put forward our message. They reported back that many there had not heard of the Vigil.

Saturday 18th September: Farewell to the Springbok (formerly the aptly named Bad Bob's) the pub/club just up the road from the Vigil. They have been sympathetic supporters, allowing us to store our gear there and providing a friendly place for donations to be counted in a transparent manner – and for our occasional celebrations in the louche lounge, Lillie's Bordello! We arrived to collect our things for the Vigil only to find the Springbok had been closed without notice. Bad Bob's revenge? Fortunately someone let us in. We were heartened by messages from the US of vigils being opened there based on our model.

Saturday 25th September: Geoff Hill, author of 'Battle for Zimbabwe', was with us from the start and helped to set up the Vigil. He was very bullish about the situation back home, having just been in South Africa where he says hundred of thousands of Zimbabweans have emerged into the open and expressed their opposition to the Mugabe regime. His assessment was that there had been a sea-change in the SADC attitude to Zimbabwe. He donated some T-shirts from Zimbabweans in South Africa.

Saturday 2nd October: After a fellow from the Congo had swaggered past repeating Mugabe's mad message to the UN: 'Bush is God and Blair is his prophet', and a regular passing delivery driver shouted yet again: 'God bless Mugabe', it was encouraging having two Zimbabweans from Switzerland under our leaky tarpaulin asking advice on how to get active there. We were pleased to welcome a sympathiser from Togo, all too familiar with ranting megalomaniacs like Mugabe. But we were most touched by the man in the wheelchair, who persevered for five minutes to sign our petitions. (On last reckoning our petitions are signed every 30 seconds or so, so he is the equivalent of ten . . .)

Tuesday 12th October: Today is the second anniversary of the Vigil. So we arranged to have our petition to President Mbeki calling on him to take a tougher line on Mugabe delivered on this day. Our delegation was met courteously by South African diplomats. The petition had been signed by more than 22,000 people. Our delegation was also well received by the Nigerian High Commission. We also delivered copies of the petition to Mozambique and to Mauritius, which hosted the recent summit of the Southern African Development Community, which adopted recently a protocol on good governance which has been ignored by Zimbabwe even though they signed up to it.

Saturday 16th October: The highlight of our week was a special Vigil in support of Morgan Tsvangirai on Friday – the day of the verdict in his treason trial. We had loads of news coverage. The Vigil was mounted with the active support of the MDC UK District and they managed to get through to Morgan by phone to tell him about it. He was very touched that a special Vigil was being held for him. It was opportune to be there also because the infamous Zimbabwe Homelink programme seemed to be having a reception in the Embassy. Before coming to the Vigil, other supporters attended a meeting in Kensington Town Hall 'Rebuilding Africa'. The meeting was told by a Mugabe man that Zimbabwe was now free and people in the diaspora should send money home through this wonderful scheme Homelink. An enraged Vigil supporter stormed up to the speakers and declared 'You chase us from Zimbabwe and now you follow us here for our money'. She went on to say 'You can't rebuild Africa until the dictators have gone'.

Saturday 30th October: Vigil supporters were upset by the jailing of our friend, Roy Bennett, the MDC MP.

Saturday 21st November: Morgan Tsvangirai received a tumultuous reception when he addressed a gathering of the diaspora and MDC supporters in London. The eager crowd filled the main hall of Friends' House (Quakers). Morgan made it clear that the party's decision on whether to take part in the March parliamentary elections was still on hold. He said no opposition party in the region would accept the electoral arrangements in place in Zimbabwe. Nevertheless, the way ahead remained through the ballot not the bullet. Outlining the situation at home, he said the Zanu PF regime had destroyed jobs and food production, turning the country from a breadbasket to a basket case and producing the fastest shrinking economy in the world. Tsvangirai was introduced by Ephraim Tapa, Chair of MDC Central London Branch, which hosted the event. Mr Tapa said the Branch's weekly forum was the first point of call for many in the diaspora who were later relocated from London. It was also showing the way with the Vigil which has been taking place outside the Zimbabwe Embassy every Saturday for more than two years.

(Background information on the Tsvangirai meeting: in organising this meeting, the Vigil, through the Central London MDC branch, faced resistance from elements close to Tsvangirai. We filled the large venue with supporters only to be told at the last minute, when people had already arrived, that leading figures were being swept off to a secret preliminary meeting on the other side of London. We were left waiting for hours for them to return without a word. We believe the problem lay with Welshman Ncube, who was then the Party's Secretary-General. We also had repeated requests for an interview on the prime television Frost Show but kept on being told that Tsvangirai would not do it. We believe Welshman was sabotaging our efforts.)

Saturday 27th November: The arrogant posturing of the England cricket authorities was displayed for all to see at the Vigil today. They argue that the England team was obliged to tour Zimbabwe for contractual reasons following Zimbabwe's tour here last year. Well, we dug up some of our banners from nearly two years ago and put them up again today: "Murder, rape and torture: it's not cricket" said one. We vividly recall how we tried to stop the last England tour to Zimbabwe: our petition to the English cricketing authorities, our invasion of Lords . . . They said then they could do nothing . . . and yet still entered into a further deal involving Zimbabwe.

But it certainly wasn't all cricket at the Vigil today. The UK government has acted quickly following its announcement that it was ending the suspension of expulsions of failed Zimbabwean asylum seekers after a two-year moratorium. We are, of course, aware that Zanu PF have been coming here because they can no longer survive in Zimbabwe but we are doing all we can to ensure that Mugabe opponents are protected and have launched the following petition to the Home Office. *'Please make sure that you are not sending home Zimbabweans whose lives are at risk because of their support for the Zimbabwean opposition party, the Movement for Democratic Change, or because they are perceived to be opponents of Zanu PF. the ruling regime.'* Vigil supporters rushed to Gatwick Airport to help Crispin Kulinji, an MDC activist in Zimbabwe, who was an early victim of the asylum decision. Crispin was not put on the plane.

Saturday 11th December: Well, nobody could describe the Vigil as being a money-spinner today – a thief ran off with our takings just as we were packing up! But the Vigil has never been about collecting money: it is about raising awareness and today we introduced an extra petition calling for the release of Roy Bennett. Highlight of the day was a parade of 200 Father Christmases. Just as well they didn't bring us a present – it would probably have been stolen as well!

2005

Highlights

January: The US labels Zimbabwe as one of the world's six 'outposts of tyranny'.
31st March: Zanu PF claims two-thirds of the votes in parliamentary elections. Opposition says they were rigged.
9th April: Prince Charles shakes hands with Mugabe in Rome.
28th May: Operation Murambatsvina ('clean out the trash'). Tens of thousands of shanty dwellings and street stalls are destroyed. UN estimates it left about 700,000 people homeless. (The Guardian newspaper in the UK described it as sensible town planning.) The MDC says it was aimed at destroying its base in the urban areas.
4th July: Vigil launches boycott of South African produce at London meeting of NEPAD (New Economic Partnership for Africa's Development). Pours South African wine into the gutter and tramples South African fruit outside Guildhall.
2nd August: Prosecutors drop remaining treason charge against Tsvangirai.
6th August: Freed from jail, Roy Bennett visits Vigil – which he describes as 'a fire in Mugabe's bum'.
25th / 26th November: Zanu PF wins overwhelminging majority in newly-created upper house of parliament, the Senate. MDC splits over Tsvangirai's decision to boycott the poll. British government spells out its Zimbabwe policy in letter to Vigil.
10th December: UN humanitarian chief says Zimbabwe 'in meltdown'.

Vigil Diary Excerpts

Saturday 22nd January: The British Government's decision to resume the deportation of failed Zimbabwean asylum seekers overshadowed the Vigil. As we were gathering we heard that Dumi Tutani, a member of the Vigil co-ordinating team, had been taken into custody. Dumi has been an active supporter of the Vigil since its start and is also a member of the MDC's Central London Branch Committee.

Saturday 29th January: A big demonstration outside the Home Office against the deportation of failed Zimbabwean asylum seekers was attended by many of our regular supporters. The deportations have galvanised Zimbabweans here. The latest news we have was from a contact who was on a BA flight back to Harare on Thursday. The contact said that a large number of the passengers were deportees, some of them in handcuffs.

Monday 14th February: A Valentine's Day protest in sympathy with WOZA (Women of Zimbabwe Arise) was held outside the Embassy. Latest reports say that some 40 women have been arrested in Bulawayo for demonstrating they favoured love rather than violence.

Saturday 19th February: Cold – perhaps the coldest it's been this winter. The tone was set by a supporter from Sheffield, William, who took a four hour coach journey to help start up the Vigil. The new newspaper The Zimbabwean has reported an initiative from the Vigil urging Zimbabweans in the United Kingdom to register to vote in the UK elections expected in May to express their dismay at the lack of action by the UK government over Zimbabwe's deepening crisis. (Zimbabweans are allowed to vote in UK elections as Commonwealth citizens even though Zimbabwe has left the Commonwealth because the British government has not got around to changing the legislation.) Business at the Zimbabwe Embassy was brought to a halt the other day when a group of Zimbabwean citizens including representatives of the Vigil asked to see the voters' roll ahead of the Zimbabwe general elections called for March. Embassy staff refused access and proceeded to close the doors for the day, turning away all callers including workmen and couriers.

Saturday 26th February: We had with us Remus Makuwaza, MDC Director of Elections. Remus is here to discuss arrangements with the MDC in the UK before the Zimbabwe elections – twinning with Zimbabwean branches and financial support. He was an inspiring presence at the Vigil. We, in the United Kingdom, must always remember the bravery and self-sacrifice which is involved in opposition politics in Zimbabwe.

Saturday 5th March: Remus Makuwaza was with us again on his last day before leaving the cold of the UK for the heat of the Zimbabwe elections, in which he is contesting Makoni West. Andi Osho, from Full Frontal Theatre, also spent the afternoon with us. Her group is mounting a production in London about Zimbabwe. She interviewed some of the people at the Vigil about their experiences at the hands of the Mugabe regime.

Saturday 12th March: The Vigil was busy this week handing over a petition we have been running for the past several months urging international action to try to ensure that the elections in Zimbabwe are free and fair. The petition signed by more than 10,000 people passing by the Vigil was handed over yesterday at the London High Commission of Mauritius, the current chair of the Southern African Development Community. A Vigil delegation had a meeting with the High Commissioner and his Deputy and we expressed our fears that the SADC election protocol was being flouted in Zimbabwe. They promised to pass our views on. On Wednesday, the House of Lords had a debate on Zimbabwe, which was described as a 'failed state'. The debate was led by Baroness Park, who has taken a close interest in Zimbabwe, and who was given a copy of our petition, to which she referred in her speech. Copies of the petition have been sent to all the other SADC countries and international organisations.

Saturday 19th March: A gloomy winter suddenly gave way to brilliant sunshine. But the Vigil was overshadowed by a big demo in Trafalgar Square against Western intervention in Iraq. We were disappointed that so few of the partying demonstrators paid much attention to the Vigil despite a recent statement by Unicef that Zimbabwe has the highest child death rate in the world. The situation in Zimbabwe is getting lots of coverage in the media but there is a complete absence of any ideas on how the world should react. As the Vigil ended, the Zimbabwean Ambassador, Simbarashe S Mumbengegwi, was speaking at a public meeting nearby organised by the Communist Party of Great Britain. One of the Trafalgar Square people dropped off leaflets with us on his way to that meeting. It read 'With the Zimbabwean elections just around the corner, imperialism is once against stepping up its propaganda efforts against the Zimbabwean State . . . Their dearest wish is to oust Zanu PF and replace it with an administration that will willingly submit to the unlimited plunder of Zimbabwe's resources by the multi-nationals'. No doubt imperialism is to blame for the child death rate in Zimbabwe!

Saturday 26th March: The start of a momentous week for Zimbabwe and a busy one for the Vigil. Today we hosted an MDC rally organised by the UK District Chair, Washington Ali. It was addressed by the Liberal Democrat spokesman for International Development, Tom Brake – so we have now been supported by senior MPs from all three main political parties in the UK. The Vigil's next project is an all-night Vigil on Wednesday, 30th March, from 8 pm until polling opens in Zimbabwe – 6 am, British Summer Time. This is to express our support for South Africa's trade union federation, COSATU, which is staging protests on the eve of the Zimbabwe elections. On election day, Thursday, 31st March, we will be set up as a mock polling station during voting hours, 6 am to 6 pm BST to mirror the voting hours in Zimbabwe. We will have transparent ballot boxes with mock ballot papers. But ours will not be filled in, in advance, by the army. The Vigil wants to draw attention to the failure of the Mugabe regime to allow free and fair elections and the disenfranchisement of millions who have fled the country. The votes will be handed in to the Embassy on Friday, 1st April – appropriately April Fools' Day.

Thursday 31st March: Overwhelming support for the MDC. That was the result of the parliamentary elections – at least at the one polling station where a free and fair internationally-monitored ballot took place, namely the mock election outside the Zimbabwe Embassy in London. Scores of exiled Zimbabweans cast their symbolic vote in London and 94.2% of them backed the MDC. The mock polling station drew hundreds of passers-by to sign the Vigil's petition calling for genuine elections in Zimbabwe, including votes for half the electorate now in exile. Among people dropping by – he spent quite some time with us – was Professor Terence Ranger, the distinguished historian, who has taught at the University of Zimbabwe.

Saturday 9th April: A picture of Prince Charles shaking hands with Mugabe at the Pope's funeral took pride of place on the Vigil table. Poor fellow (Prince Charles, that is) obviously couldn't tell one black man from another ... Our caption read 'They all look the same to me'. Well, we are not the same and that is what the Vigil is about: trying to educate the British government that they can't continue their own insipid version of South Africa's "quiet diplomacy". Mugabe making a mockery of EU sanctions by being allowed to go to Rome can only underline the point.

Saturday 16th April: Today we marked the 25th anniversary of Zimbabwean Independence with our four maple trees draped with black cloth to symbolise the death of democracy in Zimbabwe. We introduced a new petition today asking the British government under no circumstances to legitimise the new regime in Zimbabwe: 'NO SHAKING HANDS WITH MUGABE – The latest elections in Zimbabwe were once again stolen by the Mugabe regime with the connivance of its neighbours. Retaliation is now being meted out to people who supported the opposition. We urge the British government to end Mugabe's reign of terror and halt his drive for legitimacy: 1) bring the matter to the UN Security Council, 2) make it a priority during Britain's term as President of the EU and G8 (group of leading industrial nations), 3) put pressure on South Africa to allow democracy in Zimbabwe, 4) extend targeted sanctions against Mugabe's cronies.'

Saturday 23rd April: The Vigil was cheered by the last-minute rescue of one of our supporters, Tafara, who escaped being deported on Tuesday. A group of us – galvanised by a good friend of Zimbabwe, the Rev Dr Martine Stemerick – persuaded a Kenyan Airways flight attendant to refuse to co-operate with sending him back to Zimbabwe. One of our supporters today reported how he had been threatened by the CIO at our pre-election overnight Vigil. He also said that sons of the Zanu-PF bigwig Patrick Chinamasa, along with other thugs, had visited someone at his home and warned him against supporting the Vigil. We are collecting evidence to present to the police to support a complaint made by us to the government some time ago about the activities of the CIO in the UK and the presence in this country of so many Zanu PF people, including close family members of the Zimbabwe regime.

Saturday 30th April: The Vigil joined forces with other groups to express determination to step up the struggle – despite the stolen elections. The UK Chair of the MDC, Washington Ali, appealed to all to join what he called the new liberation struggle. Speaking at the Vigil, he said the battle would have to be waged from abroad. "We are fighting a dictator and you have never seen a dictator lose an election." Among other speakers was Julius Mutyambizi of the Zimbabwe Human Rights NGO Forum, who urged the diaspora to think of themselves as exiles rather than refugees. We will return, he said, but freedom in Africa has always been brought by blood.

Saturday 14th May: Morris dancers, a mad Caribbean boxer and a white conspiracy theorist – we had it all today. We were subjected to an anti-western rant from a one-eyed Rastafarian with the word 'fear' shaved into his scalp. It was the usual "leave Africa alone" business. As always, the overwhelming majority of the people at the Vigil were black – but they were dismissed as "house boys" not able to appreciate the inspired leadership of Comrade Mugabe. A broadly similar view was taken by a politics student from Bristol University who said: everything written on Zimbabwe in the West was propaganda funded by M16. Then we encountered three well-rounded Zambians who – asked to sign the petitions – said 'It's all lies'. Oh well: at least we had the support of the Morris men with their colourful costumes and traditional folk dancing.

Saturday 21st May: There was jubilation when Dumi Tutani arrived at the Vigil. He was held high while everyone danced, sang and cheered. Dumi was released on bail earlier in the week from Dover Removal Centre. Our petitions in support of Dumi went far afield – some were filled in and posted from Zimbabwe and Germany. The joyous end to the Vigil followed a tempestuous start. Almost before we had put up our first banner, we were under attack from more Mugabe supporters – didn't we realise we were puppets of the West?

Wednesday 25th May: Zimbabwean exiles demonstrated outside the Embassy to mark Africa Day. They heard the Chair of the UK arm of the MDC and other speakers call for intervention by the UN to save Zimbabwe from becoming a 'failed state'. MDC supporters from as far away as Wales, Birmingham, Leicester, Hastings and Reading joined the protest, organised by MDC UK and supported by the Vigil.

Saturday 28th May: Abuzz with street gossip from Zimbabwe, the word is that the regime is now eating itself, destroying the informal economy and tearing down the homes of the people. Cathy Buckle from Zimbabwe informs us 'Opposite the hospital eight or ten women, many with children at their feet or babies on their backs, (used to stand) selling fruits and vegetables to nursing staff, patients and visitors. Their stalls were substantial and made of treated gum poles with thick plastic sheeting overhead to protect them and their produce from the weather. Here you could buy bananas and apples, avocado pears, cucumbers, cabbages, tomatoes and almost any fruit or vegetable in season. They have gone, chased away by police.' The feeling at the Vigil was one of deep foreboding. While we were safe, those at home were being deprived of the very basics of life: their homes and livelihood.

Friday 10th June: A group responded to a last-minute appeal to gather outside the Embassy to express solidarity with the call for a protest in Zimbabwe. We distributed the following flyer: 'OPERATION MURAMBATSVINA (DRIVE OUT TRASH). The Zimbabwe Vigil is outside the Embassy today in support of their brothers and sisters protesting at home against a new onslaught from the Mugabe regime. In retaliation for their support of the opposition MDC in the recent rigged elections, Mugabe is destroying the homes and livelihoods of poor people in cities and towns throughout the country in an attempt to drive them back to the rural areas where they can starve out of the public eye.' With our makeshift posters we must have looked the sort of street scene Mugabe calls trash. A threatening CIO agent, the size of a bulldozer, spent the whole day glowering at us from the Embassy doorway as if he wanted to demolish us.

Saturday 11th June: The heavy media coverage given to Mugabe's scorched earth policy ensured that the Vigil was besieged by people eager to sign our petition demanding that South Africa stops supporting the Mugabe regime. The Vigil committee met earlier on Saturday to approve our new project – a call to boycott South Africa because of Mbeki's support for Mugabe. This is the advance notice we will be sending to the media. 'ZIMBABWEAN EXILES CALL FOR BOYCOTT OF SOUTH AFRICA: Zimbabweans in the United Kingdom are to stage a protest on 4th July 2005 to call for a boycott of South African products in protest at the South African Government's support of the Mugabe regime. The Zimbabwe Vigil is to pour South African wine into the gutter and trample South African fruit into the pavement outside the Guildhall in London, where African and Western leaders are meeting to discuss help for Africa. The demonstration aims to draw on the resonance of the anti-apartheid protest against South Africa when many people refused to buy South African products. The Guildhall meeting has been organised by NEPAD (New Economic Partnership for African Development) and is to report by video link to the African Union Summit in Tripoli being held on 4th and 5th July. The objectives of NEPAD – mainly involving Western investment in Africa – have been promoted by President Mbeki of South Africa, who has promised that NEPAD will, in return, deliver good governance. Zimbabweans are dismayed that South Africa has accepted the rigged Zimbabwean parliamentary elections of 31st March, are appalled by the treatment of Zimbabwean exiles fleeing to South Africa and alarmed that South Africa is even now providing military equipment to the Mugabe regime. The NEPAD meeting is to be followed by the summit in Scotland of G8, the group of leading industrial countries. The Zimbabwe Vigil is to present the Chairman of the meeting, Tony Blair, with a petition demanding action to ensure that South Africa: 1) allows democracy in Zimbabwe, and 2) honours its UN commitment to humane treatment of refugees.'

Saturday 18th June: The Vigil was augmented by members of Women of Zimbabwe Arise who had been asked by the leadership back home to join others in the diaspora to mark World Refugee Day by protesting outside their embassies. During the Vigil, we were disturbed to hear that 30 WOZA women had been arrested for demanding a halt to Operation Murambatsvina during a street protest in Bulawayo. A highlight of our day was an inspirational talk by Lucia Mativenga, first Vice-President of the Zimbabwe Congress of Trade Unions and Secretary for the MDC Women's wing.

Saturday 25th June: We should have expected it but were surprised by the media coverage: BBC TV, Channel 4 News, Sky TV, Press Association and SW Radio Africa. The camera people were there before we had properly set up. Of course Zimbabwe has been given saturation coverage in the UK recently – not only as a result of Comrade Mugabe's Murambatsvina but also because of the campaign to save Vigil supporter Crispen Kulinji from deportation. Happily Crispen's expulsion has been suspended and it looks as if the UK may be forced to rethink its policy of sending failed asylum seekers back. We had with us Lovemore Madhuku, Chair of the National Constitutional Assembly and Co-ordinator of the Broad Alliance. He was interviewed at the Vigil by the BBC and others.

Sunday 26th June: A ceremony was held to mark the UN day in support of torture victims. Zimbabweans carrying flowers walked in procession from a special church service at St Paul's, Covent Garden to Zimbabwe

House, where the flowers were laid on the doorstep. A sombre Vigil was then held in the bright sunshine and interested passers-by were given details of the savage treatment meted out by the Mugabe regime to anyone standing in its way. Many expressed outrage at the readiness of the UK government to deport Zimbabweans in the worsening situation. Hundreds of people signed the Vigil's petition warning Mr Blair not to give in to President Mbeki and legitimise the Zanu PF tyranny. Earlier, the congregation at St Paul's was addressed by Dr Lovemore Madhuku who gave an update on the violence in Zimbabwe.

Saturday 2nd July: We were pleased to learn during the week that Roy Bennett is out of prison. We got a message of support from his wife for our planned anti-Mbeki demonstration on Monday: 'Wonderful, well done. Regards Heather'. This endorsement is particularly important as the Vigil was started partly at the request of Roy Bennett when he addressed the MDC Central London Forum three years ago. After last week's media blitz it was a comparatively quiet Vigil – if you can count a Gay Pride March and a Liberal invasion as quiet. We were pleased that the National Executive of the Liberal Party took time to join us.

Monday 4th July: Delegates attending the NEPAD meeting at the Guildhall were confronted by a noisy group of about 40 Zimbabweans calling for a boycott of South Africa. Trevor Manuel, South African Finance Minister, must have been discomfitted at such banners as: Mbeki supports a tyrant, NEPAD supports tyranny in Zimbabwe, Quiet diplomacy condones genocide.' We were armed with new stickers 'Don't buy South African, Save Zimbabwe'. We are going to plaster thousands of these all over the country until Mbeki disowns Mugabe. We were particularly pleased to have the SABC filming the entire demonstration and took pains to explain that we are not anti-South African but determined to make our point that President Mbeki can make all the difference if he recognises publicly what is going on next door. The BBC was there to see us pouring South African wine onto the ground and trashing South African fruit. Afterwards our petition was sent to Prime Minister Tony Blair with the following letter: *'We respectfully submit a petition signed by several thousand people urging the UK government to take stronger action against the Mugabe regime. Among our suggestions is that pressure be put on President Mbeki to condemn what is going on in Zimbabwe as a clear violation of the Southern*

African Development Community's obligations under the New Partnership for Africa's Development. For our part, the Zimbabwe Vigil is launching today a call for a boycott of South African products in an attempt to persuade the South African government to end its policy of denial.'

Saturday 9th July: It was great to have Crispen Kulinji back at the Vigil after his release on bail from detention. His hunger strike made him the most famous Zimbabwean in the UK – an opposition supporter who had suffered under the Mugabe regime and was at real risk if returned to Zimbabwe: the complete challenge to the Home Office. Everyone had a story of the London (terrorist) bombings and we were inspired by the London spirit: we will not be moved.

Saturday 23rd July: Reports that Mugabe is going to China this weekend to raise money prompted us to launch a new petition: ***'CHINA – DO NOT PROP UP MUGABE:** We understand that the aim of President Mugabe's visit to China is to seek an emergency loan to prop up the collapsing Zimbabwe economy. We advise the government of China that we will support any decision by a new democratic government in Zimbabwe to disown such debts to China incurred by the Mugabe regime, including payment for armaments recently supplied.'* Zimbabwe is reported to owe so much money to Dutch banks that the banks are considering trying to take possession of a number of Zimbabwean assets around the world – including the London Embassy.

Friday 29th July: We've had all sorts of demos with drumming, dancing and singing. But we have never had a demo with meditation. Well, we put this right today with a demo outside the Chinese Embassy in London in protest at Beijing's handout to prop up Mugabe. We joined members of the Falun Gong, a Chinese spiritual movement which has been protesting silently around the clock for the past two years. They were an inspiration and made us feel so welcome. The Falun Gong can speak at first hand of the Chinese Communists' contempt for human rights. Already advertised on the BBC Newsnight programme, we had a variety of media (including New Tang Dynasty TV, a global TV station run by overseas Chinese – banned in China) to record our protest at Zimbabwe being sold off to the thugs of Beijing. Among material which found its way to our table was a China Daily News comment: 'The Zimbabwe economy is described as collapsing despite the UK economy being far worse'. So now you Zimbabweans know what the future holds – certainly don't come to the UK! And we wouldn't bet on China either. We tried unsuccessfully to present our petition. We'd already been advised that the Chinese government does not want any encounter with democracy but we will stick the petition in the post nevertheless.

Saturday 30th July: In line with Mugabe, the Vigil has also adopted a 'Look East' policy. As a consequence of our demo outside the Chinese Embassy on Friday, we had the same Chinese TV team filming the Vigil: the dancing and singing and banners and posters – particularly those warning the Chinese government against bailing out Zanu PF. Quite independently, a Chinese passer-by spent some time studying our banners. He went off with one of our flyers and returned some minutes later to say, "'I agree with everything but you shouldn't say 'the Chinese' it should be 'the Chinese government'". A good point!

Saturday 6th August: 'A fire in Mugabe's bum' was how Roy Bennett described the Vigil. The former MDC MP is visiting the UK after being freed from jail in Zimbabwe. He spent the day at the Vigil, which he partly instigated at a meeting in London three years ago. Roy expressed disappointment that more Zimbabweans were not attending the Vigil. After his gruelling eight months in prison, he said he was disgusted that Zimbabweans abroad were not taking the opportunity to draw attention to the situation. "It is your country. We are in meltdown and you must fight for your rights. We need to be at one to rebuild Zimbabwe." Wearing the Vigil t-shirts which we presented to them, Roy and his wife, Heather, took part in a symbolic 'queue for freedom' of Vigil supporters stretched out along the pavement from the door of the Embassy.

Saturday 13th August: Zimbabwean journalist and writer Geoff Hill was with us. His new book 'What happens after Mugabe' is selling well. We were pleased to have Francesca Toft with us on her 15th birthday. She is not Zimbabwean but has relatives in Zimbabwe and asked her parents to bring her to the Vigil for her birthday treat. On her wrist was a homemade wristband saying 'Make Mugabe History' – this is an idea we hope to carry forward.

Saturday 27th August: A pretty average Vigil. What's an average Vigil? Well, for a start, some fantastic dancing – this time by a recent supporter, Mqhubele. His dancing, often balletic on his toes, seemed to express the anguish of the people in Zimbabwe. He ended up lying on his back playing a drum. The weather was pretty average too: no rain and no sun, not too warm and not too cold. As usual, we drew supporters from far and wide – a family from Bedford, an MDC official from Leicester, a sympathiser from Birmingham. Also, as usual, we had some Zanu / CIO people. A typical Vigil also has the following – a sympathetic African from another country (in this case an Eritrean who said 'We are suffering from the same problems'); an enthusiastic "do-gooder" (in the best sense of someone who is genuinely trying to help). In this case a very sympathetic chap from East London, Mark, who takes a close interest in Africa and has kindly offered his support; and a core group of supporters, many of them just out of detention. These are people who have suffered because of their opposition to Mugabe and inspire us to continue our weekly Vigil.

Saturday 3rd September: People came from all over Britain to pay tribute to Remus Makuwaza who died in hospital in London after a long illness. Remus was an important figure in the MDC (Director of Elections) and the party's leadership in Harare has paid heartfelt tribute to his work. For us at the Vigil he was an inspirational person. Those who were there will never forget how he spent a cold day with us at a Vigil sparsely attended but fired by his passion. He was already so fragile we kept piling coats on him until we thought he would suffocate. His determination gave us all the message: we must never give up the struggle. The Vigil contributed money to send the body of our friend back to Zimbabwe.

Saturday 24th September: Many supporters had difficulty getting to the Vigil today because of the latest anti-Iraq war demo. Roads were closed, helicopters hovered overhead. But it turned out to be a subdued event. As Vigil people arrived they remarked that our drumming and singing could be heard way above the musicians from Trafalgar Square. Among the loudest singers was Ben Evans whose theatrical production "Qabuka" is being staged at the Soho Theatre in London in October. It is based on the experiences of Zimbabweans in exile described as 'a postcard from the edge which tells their stories with song, dance, humour and mischief'. Among those taking part in the play is our supporter Patson Muzuwa from Leicester. We were pleased this week to receive a letter from the Human Rights Office of the United Nations in response to our petition about human rights abuse in Zimbabwe. It appears that the petition has been discussed on several occasions and we have now been invited to present detailed evidence.

Saturday 1st October: An urgent call to the British Government to get Zimbabwe discussed at the United Nations came from the British MP Kate Hoey at the Vigil today. Kate is Chair of the All-Party Parliamentary Group on Zimbabwe and recently made a clandestine visit to see at first hand the devastation caused by Mugabe's "Operation Murambatsvina". She said she couldn't believe how much the situation had deteriorated in the two years since her previous visit and pressure should be kept up on South Africa to use its influence over Zimbabwe. She said the Vigil had succeeded in keeping Zimbabwe in the spotlight.

Saturday 8th October: Members of WOZA Jenni Williams, Magodonga Mahlangu and Siphewe Maseko arrived with their bags direct from the airport on a visit sponsored by Amnesty International. They have been an inspiration for us. We gave them each a Vigil t-shirt and they put them on immediately despite being knocked out by their flight. They led us in some WOZA songs and then joined in our regular singing and dancing. Unhappily, we were disrupted by the CIO at the end. They are doing all they can to disrupt our activities. We had half a dozen police at the end after one of the disrupters tried to throw a punch at one of our supporters. As the situation in Zimbabwe worsens, we expect increasingly hysterical responses from the dying regime.

Thursday 13th October: It was supposed to be a symbolic 'walk' from the Zimbabwe Embassy to Downing Street in solidarity with those back home, including Morgan Tsvangirai, who had been walking to work in brotherhood with people suffering from the collapsing economy. But it was toyi-toying all the way. Immediately we left the Embassy we seemed to form a phalanx and the appearance of 40 or so Zimbabwean exiles high stepping and singing past the Grenadier Guardsmen on their horses in Whitehall surprised passers-by. We gathered across the road from Downing Street still singing and dancing until Kate Hoey MP arrived to lead our delegation into No 10 to hand over our petition 'No

Shaking Hands with Mugabe' calling on Mr Blair to bring Zimbabwe to the attention of the UN Security Council.

Saturday 29th October: A very lively Vigil this week right from the start, with a sizeable crowd from Leicester swelling our ranks. For the last few weeks the Vigil seems to have been getting bigger and bigger. We experienced a rare piece of London tradition as a Pearly King and Queen walked past, stepping in time to the drums of Africa. The Pearly King and Queen are an old working class tradition. They wear suits covered in mother-of-pearl buttons. The Vigil's influence is expanding to China. Since our demonstration outside the Chinese Embassy against Mugabe's begging visit to Beijing, we have had a warm relationship with the Falun Gong spiritual movement who maintain a daily protest outside the Chinese Embassy against human rights abuses in China. They have now expanded their activities near the Vigil.

Saturday 19th November: The Vigil has made a contribution towards sending home the body of one of the Zimbabwean asylum-seeking hunger strikers protesting against being sent home Lizwane Ndlovu, who died last week. She has left behind two young children in Zimbabwe.

Friday / Saturday 25th / 26th November: We had a taste of what so many back in Zimbabwe are experiencing: homelessness. For us it was voluntary and temporary – but nevertheless it wasn't easy spending the whole night outside the Embassy in freezing weather. Our protest was at the waste of our nation's resources on the puppet Senate. We were joined by Washington Ali, Chair of the MDC-UK District, who said the Senate elections should not be contested because of the unlevel electoral playing field. Those who arrived for the normal Vigil were inspired by the determination and spirit of those who had seen through the night and yet were still singing and dancing. We were cheered by news that the US has greatly extended its targeted sanctions against Mugabe's cronies and are confident the EU will follow suit.

Lord Triesman, Minister for Africa, told the Vigil that the Zimbabwe situation must be addressed by concerted international action. He said: 'Thank you for your letter of 13 October to the Prime Minister about Zimbabwe enclosing a petition. I am replying as the Minister responsible for Africa. We are fully aware of the appalling situation in Zimbabwe and share your concerns. The Foreign Secretary, the Prime Minister and I have all made statements, repeatedly, condemning the latest outrages and detailing the actions we have taken in response. The Prime Minister discussed Zimbabwe with G8 leaders at Gleneagles. They issued a statement underlining the strength of international concern. It called for an end to the (Murambatsvina) campaign, an assessment of the damage, and respect for human rights and the rule of law. We will continue to speak out, and raise international concern, until the Government of Zimbabwe ends the bad policies and bad governance it currently pursues.

Zimbabwe remains a high priority for this government and we continue to believe that external pressure, particularly from within Africa, coupled with support for organisations working for the restoration of democracy within Zimbabwe, offers the best hope for encouraging reform. We have therefore taken every opportunity to raise Zimbabwe with African leaders, encouraging them to recognise and respond to the full horror of what is happening in Zimbabwe. We welcome efforts by the African Union to engage President Mugabe through first a Special Envoy and then the nomination of former President Chissano to facilitate talks of national unity. We regret Mugabe's rejection of both efforts but will continue to work with our African and UN partners and together consider what further steps must now be taken to press for the return of democratic governance in Zimbabwe.

We and our EU partners have also expanded the scope of the targeted measures first adopted in 2002. These measures include a travel ban and assets freeze on Zimbabweans close to Mugabe's regime, as well as an arms embargo. There are now 126 names on the targeted measures list. Regarding the increasing of sanctions, we will consider other measures as and when appropriate. Concerted international action is the only effective option. We are also working directly with the UN Secretary General. Kofi Annan has said he is increasingly concerned by the human rights and humanitarian impact of the recent demolitions of what the Government of Zimbabwe has called illegal settlements. His Special Envoy, Anna Tibaijuka, issued a hard hitting report on 22 July, emphasising the scale of the humanitarian crisis and the direct role the Government of Zimbabwe has played in creating it. Supported by a number of partners, we ensured that the report was discussed at the UN Security Council on 27 July and again on 4 October.

We will continue to work with our African and UN partners and together consider what further steps now must be taken to press for the return of democratic governance in Zimbabwe. We are also concerned about the humanitarian impact on innocent Zimbabweans. DFID (Department for International Development) has responded to the latest evictions by committing £1 million to a co-ordinated international response mainly through the International Organisation for Migration and UNICEF. This has so far reached over 23,000 beneficiaries, and includes food, blankets, soap and other essential items. Emergency water and sanitation facilities are being provided where appropriate and child protection activities are being put in place. In total, DFID spent some £25 million in Zimbabwe in 2004 / 05. DFID will contribute £30 million in 2005 / 06, through multilateral agencies and Non Governmental Organisations (NGOs), making the UK one of the three largest donors in Zimbabwe. We expect to increase the UK spend on HIV prevention, care and mitigation to around £1.5 million over the next year. I hope this is helpful.'

Tuesday 6th December: The recent murder of Zimbabwe farmer Don Stewart was brought very close when we realised he was the father of Vigil supporter Cathy Stewart. Cathy sent us the following statement: 'Early on Sunday morning, my wonderful father Don Stewart was murdered by intruders at his farm just outside Harare. My dad died as he had lived, on the land that he loved with a passion. He was a true African, unhappy anywhere other than Africa.'

Saturday 10th December: A good crowd to mark UN International Human Rights Day. Graphic pictures of Mugabe victims underlined our message that the UN must do more than feed the starving. It must take action to bring Mugabe to justice. Posters reminded passers-by that the crisis is worsening: 'Evicted and Forsaken', 'Rights under Siege', 'Desperate Plight of Homeless'. To mark the occasion we unveiled our new updated banner 'Mugabe wanted for Murder' listing the victims of state-sponsored violence. Many people out shopping for the festive season expressed deep concern about the deteriorating situation. They were shocked by comments made by the UN Emergency Relief Co-ordinator, Jan Egeland, after his visit to Zimbabwe. He said: 'The situation is very serious in Zimbabwe when life expectancy goes from more than 60 years to just over 30 years in a 15-year span - it's a meltdown, it's not just a crisis, it's a meltdown'.

2006

Highlights

25th February: Vigil submits evidence of torture to the UN Human Rights Office.
May: Year-on-year inflation exceeds 1,000%.
9th May: Welshman Ncube's front man Arthur Mutambara speaks in London.
28th May: Tsvangirai addresses London meeting organized by Vigil.
9th September: Ephraim Tapa of the Vigil elected MDC UK Chair.
13th September: Riot police disrupt Harare demonstration against the economic crisis. Union leaders taken into custody and tortured.
12th October: Vigil presents petition at Parliament calling for UN intervention in Zimbabwe.
28th October: Vigil supporters confront South African Foreign Minister in London.
9th December: Letter to President Chirac of France asking him not to invite Mugabe to the French / Africa summit in Cannes.

Vigil Diary Excerpts

Saturday 14th January: The Vigil has been the recipient of some interesting gifts. Today a supporter from South Africa brought some lavatory paper featuring Mugabe and his lolling tongue. Our donor says loads of it is being taken back to Zimbabwe from South Africa. Perhaps it will end up at State House given the shortages. Another gift came in the post today - packs of playing cards which have been created by a coalition of civic groups concerned about freedom in Zimbabwe. The five of spades, for example, shows rural chiefs on their knees with their mouths in the Zanu PF trough, the ace of diamonds has 'Robber Mugabe' on his throne surrounded by bags of gold and jewels. The joker is Jonathan Moyo depicted as a snake with two heads.

Saturday 21st January: No sooner had we set up shop with our banners and flags and 'Mugabe wanted for murder' poster than we were overwhelmed by supporters. Soon we had helicopters overhead. We drummed and sang even louder. It turned out that the helicopters were tracking a whale which had swum up the Thames in a desperate attempt to join us. A supporter from Leicester, Richard, came to the Vigil with his tag – an electronic monitoring system offered to asylum seekers in place of detention.

Saturday 28th January: The depths of winter, with an icy wind from Siberia. Today we had two asylum seekers wearing tags. In addition to Richard who came last week, we also had Tsitsi. She gave us her weekly schedule of times she has to be at home: Monday, 9 – 11 am and 9 – 10 pm; Tuesday, 1 – 2 am; Wednesday, 10 – 11 am and 3 – 4 pm; Thursday, 12 – 1 pm (report to police at 2 pm); Friday, 10 – 11 am and 9 – 10 pm; Saturday, 12 – 1 pm and 9 – 10 pm; Sunday, 5 – 6 am. The Vigil received a reply this week to a letter to the Foreign and Commonwealth Office asking for a meeting to discuss the Zimbabwean situation, They have given a positive response. Their letter said, 'We share your views about Zimbabwe. The situation is appalling, as Mugabe continues with his disastrous policies. We will keep international pressure on the Government of Zimbabwe until reform takes place.'

Saturday 11th February: The space between the four maple trees outside Zimbabwe House has become too small. We are now regularly spilling outside our bannered enclosure into the rest of the small piazza in front of the Embassy. We were glad to welcome Patricia, the daughter of Jairos Jiri, who did so much for the disabled in Zimbabwe.

Sunday 12th February: Julius Mutyambezi-Dewa of the Vigil took the opportunity to expose the renegade Bishop of Harare Nolbert Kunonga when he addressed a special service for Zimbabwe at an Anglican church in Kent today. He was pleased to meet a Zimbabwean choir at the Church. The congregation raised over £700 for Zimbabwean causes.

Saturday 18th February: One of our supporters, Tsungi, has just lost her mother and this news rather overshadowed our day. She was the seventh of her family to die in the present crisis.

Saturday 25th February: Supporters came from all over the country to join the Vigil on a bright but icy day with a piercing Arctic wind which twice overturned our table, sending copies of our petition flying down the Strand. The 70 or so people who braved the elements were pleased to hear that the Vigil has now submitted its evidence on torture to the Human Rights Office of the UN in Geneva. We were invited to contribute following a petition we submitted to the UN about abuses in Zimbabwe. The bulky dossier we have sent them includes personal testimonies from a number of our supporters detailing their torture. As it considers this matter, we are stepping up the pressure with a new petition demanding UN intervention as the situation spirals out of control. We had with us Kudaushe Matimba, a former member of the Bhundu Boys, who gave a star performance on the drums.

Saturday 11th March: A late winter snowfall covered much of Britain. The Vigil escaped but naturally, with our supporters so widely dispersed, it affected our numbers. Everyone was abuzz with reports of the so-called arms find in Zimbabwe: there was a general feeling that it was another desperate attempt by the Zanu PF regime to divert attention from the MDC's Congress in Harare next week.

Saturday 18th March: The MDC in the UK joined the Vigil to protest at the arrest of a number of senior MDC members ahead of the MDC Congress. The gathering was angry at the threat to the last vestiges of democratic space, with the wave of violence unleashed against MDC supporters. There were new reports of police torture.

Saturday 25th March: Two of our stalwarts, Ephraim Tapa and Julius Mutyambezi-Dewa, went to support our sister vigil in Bristol on their launch day. Ephraim welcomed them to the 'Vigil family' and spoke of the need to see ourselves as Zimbabweans rather than cling to a tribal identity. The Bristol Vigil attracted some Zimbabwean passers-by, once again showing how Zimbabweans are dispersed all over the place.

Saturday 1st April: We had with us Adella Chiminya, whose husband, Tichaona, was one of the first MDC victims of the Zanu PF regime. He was Morgan Tsvangirai's campaign manager and was burnt to death by Mugabe's people six years ago while police stood by. His name features on the roll of honour displayed at the front of the Vigil under the headline 'Mugabe wanted for murder'. The recent shortage of stories about Zimbabwe in the British press has been broken with a vengeance with a two- page spread in the Sunday Times: 'Desperate mothers throw away 20 babies a week as Zimbabwe starves'. We doubt whether it will make much impact on the pointy-shoed Zimbabwean ladies seen going in and out of the Embassy today with their expensive shopping bags.

Saturday 15th April: Mugabe Must Go Now was the Independence Day message from the UK. The Vigil hosted a highly-charged demonstration by the MDC-UK. The demonstrators' demands were summed up by Crispen Kulinji, whose torture by the Mugabe regime was part of our recent submission to the United Nations Human Rights Commission in Geneva. Crispen received a letter from Geneva this week acknowledging the evidence we had sent in support of our petition about torture in Zimbabwe. The UN tells us that our evidence has been sent to the authorities in Zimbabwe for their response. We await it with bated breath! As well as marking Independence Day, the demonstration was in solidarity with other MDC demonstrations around the world, particularly Canada, and with the MDC mass rallies in Zimbabwe. During the week Vigil delegates had a useful meeting with Foreign and Commonwealth Office officials.

Saturday 22nd April: Bathed in gentle, warm sunshine, we were joined again by the Rev Dr Martine Stemerick whose filmed reports about what is happening in Zimbabwe provide such powerful ammunition for our cause. Also with us was Wiz Bishop just returned after a trip to Zimbabwe with a thick wad of Zimbabwean bank notes which we displayed as only buying half a loaf of bread in Zimbabwe.

Saturday 29th April: Lots of past supporters returned to the Vigil. They were senior members of the MDC in the UK who had broken away from the party in support of the pro-Senate faction in Zimbabwe. This faction led by Welshman Ncube opposed the decision by Party President Morgan Tsvangirai against taking part in the elections for the Senate. Whatever the differences, they expressed full support for the Vigil's mission to campaign for free and fair elections. We are now sure that winter is over: we saw our first bagpiper of the year. His playing prompted Vigil dancers to do a Zimbabwean version of the Scottish reel. The bagpiper was so enthusiastic that he took a kilt out of his bag and put it on. Our ladies were surprised to find that what men are reported to wear under their kilts is true.

Saturday 6th May: Passers-by were fascinated by a new feature of the Vigil – a board with Zim $42,000 fanned out showing how much half a loaf of bread cost.

Tuesday 9th May: Mutambara feeds us alphabetti spaghetti – The Vigil was asked to report for the Zimbabwean on a London meeting addressed by Professor Arthur Mutambara who had been plucked from academic obscurity in the United States to front the breakaway MDC faction led by Welshman Ncube. Here is what we wrote:

While Morgan Tsvangirai has been braving the heat of the kitchen in Zimbabwe his rival Arthur Mutambara has been dining in the US on Malcolm X, accompanied by a vintage Che Guevara. These were the fashionable (well, 30 years ago) names he offered at his London meeting when asked who had inspired his new political career. Some of us expected heroes closer to home. Mandela for instance. But it tells us quite a lot about Mutambara and his political philosophy: from the head and not the heart, opportunist and morally vacant.

A forceful speaker and commanding presence, Mutambara looks the part but his strategy sounded like the Alphabetti Spaghetti we used to feed our children: pasta shaped into letters and drowned in tomato sauce. Straight from the tin. The easy option. Not very healthy - full of e-numbers. And the letter E was as far as he got in articulating the way forward for Zimbabwe. (Even our children got to Z.)

Mutambara's big idea was as soggy as spaghetti. We will contest the elections in 2010, he said, but we will identify the methods Zanu PF has used to rig the elections of 2000, 2002 and 2005 and work to counter them. Where has he been? Downing too many Che Guevaras? He seemed not to know that the MDC has identified exactly how the voting has been rigged and has been challenging this in the Courts since the year dot.

Should this strategy fail, the Mutambara Party will have not only a Plan B, but a Plan C, D and E ready to put into effect. Of course he couldn't divulge them to the 250 or so people present. They would have to take their Alphabetti Spaghetti on trust. But some people were hungry now. They complained they couldn't wait until 2010. Would Zimbabwe still exist then or would everyone be in Jozi or Unit K? Mass action, jambanja, the audience demanded. He insisted it must be constitutional and democratic. Not much sign here of Malcolm X and Che Guevara.

And even Plan A began to look like Alphabetti Spaghetti in the sky when he let slip: "South Africa will turn a blind eye to vote rigging if they think we are not ready for government, or even help the rigging." Mutambara seems to have been told by Mbeki how to behave in grown-up African politics: Tell the West they are strategic partners (ie give us money) but remember we are a sovereign state and can do what we like (ie ignore neo-colonialist human rights). And remember stick together at all costs. Mutambara seems to have taken this to extremes already ("Mugabe has put in many years of work. He will be judged very favourably by history.")

Every bit as economically illiterate as Mugabe, Mutambara came up with the inspired idea of asking our friends in China to invest in Zimbabwean factories so we can export Japanese technology to the world (putting Chinese workers out of jobs). "We want to be equal to the EU and America in 20 years," he declared. His Pan-Africanist rhetoric may endear him to the political dinosaurs of Africa but will they attract Western investors? "No puppetry," thundered the robotics professor. Talking of puppets ...

Saturday 13th May: The Vigil dancers were interested to see the Morris Men – English traditional dancers who gather in Trafalgar Square on the second Saturday of May. A London group, the Westminster Morris Men, wearing their distinctive costume, performed several intricate dances in the space next to the Vigil. We are always humbled by the trouble people take to come and join us. Nomuhle with her toddler came all the way from Liverpool and Tafara from Manchester. Hats off to Dumi who still pitched up despite a train delay which meant it took him four and a half hours to come to London from Southampton.

Saturday 27th May: We sent a representative to a news conference at Parliament addressed by the MDC leader, Morgan Tsvangirai. It was hosted by the Parliamentary Group on Zimbabwe, chaired by Kate Hoey, MP, who spoke highly of the Vigil as representing the Zimbabwean diaspora. Mr Tsvangirai warned that if the democratic route failed the forces of violence, civil war and anarchy would take over. The Vigil also sent representatives to the Dignity Period Fund Raiser organised by Action for Southern Africa on Friday night. It was addressed by Thabitha Khumalo, women's secretary of the ZCTU (Zimbabwe Congress of Trade Unions), who spoke movingly about her own abuse at the hands of the Mugabe regime.

Sunday 28th May: Scores of Vigil supporters from all over the UK turned out for the MDC UK's London meeting for Morgan Tsvangirai. It made Vigil Co-ordinator Dumi's day when he was greeted by the MDC Secretary-General Tendai Biti with 'You must be Dumi of the Vigil'. No doubt he had seen pictures in the Zimbabwean of Dumi's exuberant dancing. Another Vigil Co-ordinator Rose was glad to be remembered by Mr Tsvangirai from the last meeting she helped arrange for him at the Friends' Meeting Housing in London in November 2004. Mr Tsvangirai spoke about the MDC's recently unveiled Road Map aimed at resolving the Zimbabwe crisis. The message was that Mugabe must be forced to the negotiating table for talks about a transitional authority, a new constitution and free and fair elections. The MDC leader urged an intensified isolation of the Mugabe regime and said South Africa must do more to resolve the Zimbabwe crisis. Mr Tsvangirai indicated that he was disappointed at the failure of Zimbabweans in the diaspora to rally more strongly behind demonstrations such as those organised by the Vigil. "You must contribute," he urged, "after all you are part of the struggle".

Saturday 3rd June: We were joined by a lady who was tempted to buy one of our 'Make Mugabe History' wristbands but said her family wouldn't approve. They are Mugabe supporters even though they are claiming political asylum here – unfortunately you can't lose your family, she said.

Saturday 24th June: The deposed mayor of Harare, Engineer Elias Mudzuri, was at the Vigil. Mr Mudzuri, the General Organising Secretary of the MDC, is in the UK to help sort out the MDC UK structure. He was very supportive of the Vigil and urged everyone to attend. He signed our petition which he said was in line with the MDC agenda. **'A petition to UN Secretary-General Kofi Annan about human rights abuses in Zimbabwe**: We are deeply disturbed at the deteriorating situation in Zimbabwe. It seems as if the international community does not care that a rogue government can hold its people hostage. In the past six years up to a quarter of the population have fled the country. Half of those remaining face starvation. Any dissent is stamped on. The UN's special envoys have seen this for themselves and condemned the regime. We urge the UN Security Council to take measures to help free the suffering people of Zimbabwe.'

Monday 26th June: The Vigil was well represented at a service at St Martin-in-the-Fields in Trafalgar Square, to mark the UN International Day in Support of Victims of Torture. Arnold Tsungu, Director of the Zimbabwe Lawyers for Human Rights, outlined the worsening situation. Three Zimbabwean torture survivors brought home to everyone the horror of what is happening in Zimbabwe. After the service we processed, bearing flowers and singing hymns, to the Zimbabwe Embassy where the flowers were laid on the steps of the Embassy. Earlier in the day, Vigil supporters attended a meeting at the House of Lords commemorating the victims of organised violence and torture in Zimbabwe. The meeting was to launch two reports relating to torture, one by the Centre for the Study of Violence and Reconciliation on Zimbabwean asylum seekers in South Africa, and one by the Zimbabwe Human Rights NGO Forum on the outcomes of torture cases brought to the courts.

Saturday 1st July: We had the Reverend Dr Martine Stemerick, who has done so much to promote the Zimbabwean cause, with us to help start up the Vigil on a boiling hot day. She went on to see the Zimbabwean theatrical production "Qabuka" and one of the stars of the show, Patson Muzuwa, was at the Vigil to tell her about it. It opened this week to an enthusiastic reception: many people at the preview on Wednesday were deeply moved by its sensitive depiction of the trials of Zimbabweans in exile.

Sunday / Monday: 2nd / 3rd July

The Vigil and other Zimbabwean organisations, in conjunction with the Refugee Council, took part in a 24 hour demonstration outside the Asylum and Immigration Tribunal in London at a hearing to consider Home Office evidence that it is now safe to send home Zimbabwean refugees.

Saturday 8th July: Sadly we have two deaths to report of relatives of supporters – an indication of the collapse of Zimbabwe's health service. The Vigil is increasingly in touch with activists around the world. Givemore Chari, the Bindura students' leader, has been corresponding with us. He reports that he is now safely in South Africa after crossing the Limpopo in fear of his life. He wrote 'What the Vigil is doing is greatly appreciated by all students and Zimbabweans'.

Saturday 15th July: An extra vibrancy was added by Patson who sang non-stop for two hours. And this was before going on stage for the last night of a successful run of the Zimbabwean theatrical production, 'Qabuka' in which he stars.

Saturday 22nd July: The Vigil was attended by women chairs of MDC UK branches. They were introduced by Suzeet Kwenda-Ruwona, Women's Chair of the MDC UK Executive. She said how sad it was that so many Zimbabweans in the UK were in denial: they would try and pass themselves off as South Africans or even West Indians. Another speaker was Adella Chiminya whose husband was burned to death in 2000 by Zanu PF. She said women must take a leading role to change Zimbabwe and urged more people to come to the Vigil, which she said was making an impact back home. The speakers were introduced by Ephraim Tapa, Chair of MDC Central London Branch. This week he learned that his younger brother had died in Harare – a victim of the failing Zimbabwean health service. His funeral was today. Ephraim's brother collapsed while doing the family shopping and for three hours there was no help. The police were called but said they had no petrol. An ambulance passed by but wouldn't take him because he had no money. When he got to hospital the doctors were on strike. Ephraim managed to contact a family friend, a doctor, who rushed to the hospital to help but it was all too late. This man could have lived if treated in time. He had five children and was also looking after three children of a deceased sister. Ephraim, himself a torture victim, is the sole surviving sibling of four.

Saturday 29th July: The Vigil has received this email from Zimbabwe. *'I want to tell you of the most terrible incident I witnessed yesterday and this is truly indicitive of the hatred, savagery and total disregard for all human rights and the law, perpetrated by Police. I had to take a witness to Mabelreign Police station at 3pm - there was one car in the car park,* *an accused on the ground near the car and four plain clothes (one with an FN over his shoulder), one Cst. and one militia in police uniform. The accused, a small man of about 40, had already been bashed, the left side of his face was like a football. So the Cst. starts shouting at him and punching the swollen side of his face. Then the militia starts his ranting, pulls the accused onto his side on the tar mac and leaning over him starts punching him in the face and ribs and then kicking him . . . I was physically ill afterwards and said many prayers for that accused last night. BUT he is one of thousands that experiences the absolute savagery, torture and barbarity of the so called Police/cio/cid on a daily basis. There is absolutely NO RECOURSE – now . . . Only two months ago, our daughter had to get a form signed at Mabelreign police. She was in the charge office and an accused, screaming in agony, was being beaten on the feet by a militia cop in full view of Lindsay. She asked the cop why they were doing this "he stole a tube of toothpaste from the supermarket".'*

Saturday 5th August: Much anxious discussion at the Vigil following the court ruling overturning the ban on sending home Zimbabwean failed asylum seekers. A senior member of the Vigil, Ephraim Tapa, cautioned people to be careful to whom they turned for help. 'There are wolves in sheep's clothing,' he warned, 'they will take your money and give you bad advice'. Asylum seekers who could not show that they were genuinely politically involved would have difficulty getting asylum in Britain.

Saturday 26th August: There was such a crush we had to make room by taking down two of the banners penning us between the four maple trees. "Wake up World! Zimbabwe is Dying!" and "No to Mugabe and No to Starvation" gave way before the bursting dancers. A bus brought down a large contingent from Leicester. Separate groups came from Manchester, Newcastle and Leeds. The Vigil was further augmented by WOZA supporters whose graphic photos of recent "sheroic" demonstrations drew lots of attention from passers-by.

Saturday 9th September: One of the Vigil founders, Ephraim Tapa, has been elected Chair of MDC-UK at a meeting in Oxford overseen by members of the leadership in Harare. Ephraim, who for the past four years has been Chair of MDC Central London Branch, aims to unite all

Zimbabweans in the diaspora. The Vigil thinks that he certainly has the credentials: a founding member of the MDC and head of the Zimbabwean civil service trade union, he was spirited out of Zimbabwe after being abducted, tortured for 21 days and almost killed in Mutoko while on MDC duty during the 2002 Presidential elections.

Monday 11th September: Isaac Matongo, MDC National Chairman, spoke at the Zimbabwe Central London Forum about the decision by Mr Tsvangirai to march on Parliament and how they were met by a sea of people on the route. 'Mugabe was shocked, the police were shocked. The police ran away when we arrived at Parliament. Where were they when we wanted to be arrested?' He praised the Vigil and said 'The diaspora must work and be active.' He encouraged everyone to support a solidarity demonstration in support of mass action in Zimbabwe which was to take place on Wednesday outside Zimbabwe House. The MDC National Chairman was accompanied by Grace Kwinje, Deputy Secretary for International Affairs. She said those back home needed to know that the women in the diaspora were watching their efforts and reporting to the international community.

Wednesday 13th September: A telephone conversation with Grace Kwinje in Harare galvanised people during the special Vigil in solidarity with today's Zimbabwean anti-Mugabe protest. She said she had been seized and beaten by the police along with many others. We had seen her only the other day in London. Our demonstration in support of the call by the Zimbabwe Congress of Trade Unions was well-attended. One Embassy employee spent a long time photographing the protest on his mobile phone. The Ambassador phoned the police to complain and was told that we had every right to protest and had permission to be there. There was a general demand to protest outside the South African High Commission and we toyi-toyied to Trafalgar Square carrying posters 'Mbeki – Zimbabwean Blood on Your Hands', 'Mugabe wanted for Murder'. We arrived singing and dancing to be met by an aggressive security guard. Somebody at the High Commission must have called the police because several police bikes suddenly appeared – they were advised by the protestors that we had obtained permission from Charing Cross Police for a 30 minute protest outside the South African High Commission to inform them of the violent arrests of our leaders in

Zimbabwe and ask for their intervention. The police were happy to leave us there.

Saturday 16th September: We had with us Vigil founder member Addley, whose sister Grace Kwinje was arrested during the Harare demonstration on Wednesday. Grace had a phone conversation with Addley today and told her that she was covered in cuts and bruises from her violent treatment while under arrest. Addley was not the only one of us affected by this latest trauma. We were relieved to hear that Lovemore Matombo, ZCTU President, along with the others had been released. On Wednesday, we had his niece Mercy with us in tears when she heard he'd been arrested and beaten. As we hear from SW Radio Africa: 'The victims, including ZCTU President Lovemore Matombo and Secretary General Wellington Chibhebhe told the medical team that when they were arrested on Wednesday, "they were taken two at a time into a cell and beaten by five policemen in uniform, who beat them for at least an hour if not more." The arrests happened in Harare as people gathered for a mass demonstration against low salaries, high taxes and workers' lack of access to anti-retroviral HIV/AIDS drugs. Describing the injuries Dr Matchaba Hove said; "Chibhebhe himself had obvious lacerations on the top of his head and his shirt was full of blood. His hands were obviously swollen and the left hand – it was very clear that he had an obvious fracture. They all had severe bruises to the limbs, backs, buttocks and they said to us they had been thoroughly beaten the very day they had been picked." He said Lovemore Matombo's hands and his back are swollen. Lucia Matibenga, the ZCTU First Vice President, was bleeding from the ears. Matchaba Hove named some of the others injured; Moses Ngondo and Rwopedza Chigwagwa had fractures of the forearm, Tererai Todini a broken finger and Nqobizita Khumalo a fractured leg.' These torturers must not think they can get away with it forever. The people know who they are and they will be brought to justice.

Friday 22nd September: Leaders of British trade unions turned out in pouring rain today to protest outside the Zimbabwe Embassy against the ill-treatment of trade unionists. The demonstration was part of a worldwide protest by labour movements in response to the brutal suppression of peaceful protests organised by the trades union movement in Zimbabwe. The President of the Trades Union Congress (TUC),

Alison Shepherd, said they wanted to demonstrate the depth of their support for fellow workers in Zimbabwe. She said there had been a long and close relationship with the Zimbabwe Congress of Trade Unions and they were watching the situation in Zimbabwe with great anxiety. Leaders from a number of unions took part in the protest, joined by members of the Vigil.

Saturday 23rd September: Two nieces of Lovemore Matombo, the ZCTU President, were with us and said they had spoken to their uncle, who was in a lot of pain. We were encouraged by the Reverend Nicholas Mkaronda, who is co-ordinator of the Crisis Coalition of Zimbabwe based in South Africa. He addressed the Zimbabwe forum on Monday and said how much the Vigil is appreciated by people back home. Nicholas gave graphic details of the brutality inflicted on the activists on Wednesday. One of our Vigil supporters attended a service at Rochester Cathedral where there was a Zimbabwean choir. She reported that the Cathedral has frozen its relationship with the Anglican diocese of Harare because of the lunacy of the Bishop of Harare, Norbert Kunonga, who recently cancelled all church services so that everyone could pray to him. It was also heartening that when one of our supporters managed to phone an ill lady in the rural areas in Zimbabwe to whom she had sent money for medical treatment, the lady was overwhelmed to hear the sound of the Vigil going on. One of our strongest Vigil supporters, Siphewe Masora, organised a vigil in Middlesbrough last Saturday. She reports that about 30 people attended from Middlesbrough, Newcastle and Stockton in the north of England. We are sending two representatives to Germany, where Zimbabweans there have asked for our help in setting up a vigil.

Saturday 30th September: Waving a flag at the end of the Vigil was 2 year old Tatenda Tsikire. His mother, Caroline, has been in jail for the past 4 months for working with bogus papers. Hopefully they will be reunited before Christmas when Caroline will have served half her sentence. We are puzzled why someone like Caroline is parted from her young child and jailed when the UK government is desperate to make room for new criminals in prisons . . . and when two asylum judges have been accused in a case involving hiring an illegal worker. We are appealing to the British government to allow Zimbabwean refugees here to be allowed to work to support themselves until such time as they can return home. The Vigil was also glad to be invited to help brief Gabriel Jugnet, the new French Ambassador to Zimbabwe, who takes up the post on 11th October. We were impressed that he is taking trouble to gather information from Zimbabweans in the diaspora.

Saturday 7th October: Passers-by were all very supportive. Many of them were aware of the clandestine visit to Zimbabwe recently by Kate Hoey, the Chair of the All-Party Parliamentary Group on Zimbabwe. It was given wide publicity on television and in the newspapers, and people were shocked at the brutal treatment of peaceful trade union demonstrators.

Vigil presents petition demanding UN action – Thursday 12th October: Time is fast running out for Mugabe said Kate Hoey, Labour MP, Chair of the UK All-Party Parliamentary Group on Zimbabwe. She said she had seen on her recent clandestine trip to Zimbabwe a swelling tide of people who were saying Mugabe must go. "It's the beginning of the end" she told the Vigil. Kate Hoey was speaking at a demonstration outside Parliament during which she was entrusted with a petition signed by many thousands of people from all over the world who had passed by the Zimbabwe Vigil held outside the Zimbabwe Embassy every Saturday afternoon. The petition calls on the UN Security Council to intervene in Zimbabwe. It was handed over by Vigil Co-ordinator, Dumi Tutani, and Kate is to deliver it to a UN representative in London. Kate was serenaded with Zimbabwean protest songs by some 40 Vigil supporters, who had sung and danced their way in brilliant sunshine from the Zimbabwe Embassy ending up in the shadow of Westminster Abbey. Supporters carried posters "Vigil 4 Freedom" reflecting the fact that the demonstration marked the 4th anniversary of the Vigil.

Saturday 14th October: Today's anniversary Vigil was the biggest gathering we have ever had – and probably the biggest Zimbabwean protest ever held in the UK. We had to take down one of our banners to accommodate the pulsating crowd – many of them wearing black armbands to mourn the death of freedom back home. A heaving mass of Zimbabweans sang and danced to 3 drummers. We had supporters from all over the UK: Ernest caught the overnight train from Glasgow, Kuchi was there from South Wales, a bus load of supporters came from Leicester and there were large groups from Liverpool (including Dorcas who made the journey twice this week), Manchester, Wolverhampton, Oxford and Milton Keynes. Ephraim Tapa, Chair of the MDC UK, drew loud applause when he criticised the South African government's policy towards Zimbabwe. He accused them of double standards: they were besieged by Zimbabweans seeking refuge and yet were denying that there was a crisis in Zimbabwe. 'Quiet diplomacy', he said, 'is a sham and the campaign to change South Africa's attitude must be our priority'.

Saturday 28th October: Vigil supporters sent out a clear message to the South African government this week: we will harass you until you stop supporting Mugabe. Alois and Wellington from Brighton and Ethel from Liverpool, among others, were waiting for the Vigil to start. Both Alois and Wellington were booted out for interrupting a lecture in London on Wednesday given by the South African Foreign Minister, Dr Nkosazana Dlamini Zuma. Alois said 'We were sickened to hear Dr Zuma talk about international solidarity when her government is refusing to show solidarity with the persecuted people of Zimbabwe'. After stewards removed Alois from the auditorium, the veteran human rights campaigner Peter Tatchell, another Vigil supporter, unfurled a placard behind Dr Zuma reading 'Mbeki's shame. ANC betrays black Zimbabwe'. As Peter was conducted out, Wellington cried from the balcony, 'Why do you (Dr Zuma) and your government persist with quiet diplomacy when it has failed to deliver?' The South African Foreign Minister sat silent even when other Vigil supporters appealed to her for support for the terrible plight of Zimbabwean women, saying, for instance, that they had no sanitary towels. They were also evicted. Dr Zuma's refusal to comment on the Zimbabwean situation in spite of taunts 'Tell us what you think of Zimbabwe?' undermined the credibility of South Africa's new membership of the UN Security Council. She went so far as to say that Zimbabweans in Britain had no right to speak about the situation in Zimbabwe – apparently forgetting that she herself had spent part of the apartheid era in exile here. Her hypocrisy did not pass unnoticed by the audience at the London School of Economics. While she scuttled away through the back door, many who'd come to hear what South Africa had to say stayed behind at the protest outside to see what Zimbabwean exiles had to say.

Saturday 4th November: Once again the Vigil had to divide its resources to encompass the protest at what is happening in Zimbabwe.

Some of us engaged the public passing by the Vigil to and from a big rally in Trafalgar Square demanding action on global warming. We found many sympathisers among the climate change people – they seemed to know that what was needed in Zimbabwe was Mugabe change. Other Vigil supporters went to hear speakers at a meeting organised by Action for Southern Africa in support of the ZCTU (Zimbabwe Congress of Trade Unions). At the ACTSA meeting, Lord Triesman, Minister for Africa, was emphatic: the British government could not stand aside while Zimbabweans starve. It had contributed £38 million to feed the starving in the last financial year and was doing everything it could to help the people of Zimbabwe. It was urging the UN and EU to continue engagement on the issue. He said President Chirac of France was keen to host a conference for the African Union and wanted to invite all African leaders including Mugabe to attend. The British government's attitude is that EU sanctions against Mugabe and his cronies should be maintained. The main speaker at the meeting was Lovemore Matombo, one of the ZCTU leaders who was beaten up with his colleagues by Zanu PF thugs after their recent attempt at a democratic protest.

Saturday 18th November: 'Dead by 34.' This was the front page splash in the Independent yesterday. It went on: "This is the fate of women in Zimbabwe where they now have the world's lowest life expectancy after 26 years of Mugabe". At the same time British television showed a harrowing account of life under Mugabe with prostrate people being beaten by the thugs of the ruling regime. In addition we had Al-Jezeera, the new international television channel, in their inaugural broadcast showing the desperate plight of Zimbabweans. Vigil supporters were surprised at a new poster in the Embassy window 'Go to Victoria Falls, Zimbabwe's true wonder is back'. We all wondered where the Victoria Falls had been – perhaps flooding into South Africa. We adorned the window with a copy of the Independent front page "Dead by 34" and a picture of Mugabe with Dracula teeth saying "Who said the devil has no son, well now he has." Many Vigil supporters signed letters to the President of the ANC Youth League condemning his recent pro-Mugabe comments. Some statistics from the Independent article:
- 4 million the amount the population is thought to have fallen since the last population census in 2002. Current estimates put it at 8 million.

- 50% the amount Zimbabwe's economy has shrunk since 1999.
- 73 million, the size of Zimbabwe's tobacco output in millions of tons. In 2000 it was 734 million.
- Infant mortality has doubled since the 1990s.
- An estimated 3,500 people are dying every week – the figure is more than those dying in Iraq, Darfur or Lebanon.
- Life expectancy for women is 34. It was 65 just over a decade ago. It is much lower than in neighbouring countries: in Zambia, life expectancy for women is 40; in Mozambique, 46; in Botswana, 40; in South Africa, 49. Even in Afghanistan women can expect to live until 40.

Saturday 25th November: The Vigil ended with a bang tonight. At 6 pm (8 pm Zim) we banged a pot as loudly as we could for two minutes in solidarity with similar protest actions back home. "Our pot is empty. Food, food. We are hungry. Come and feed from empty plates," was the message. Passers-by were confronted by our new poster:

ZIMBABWE LEADS THE WORLD
- Highest inflation at around 2000%. The IMF predicts 4000% inflation in 2007.
- Fastest shrinking economy
- Lowest life expectancy – 34 for women, 37 for men (source UN)
- Highest number of orphans per capita (source UNICEF)
- Death rate 3,500 per week – exceeds: Darfur, Iraq, Afghanistan
- 80% unemployment
- 80% below poverty line
- Half the population starving
- 24%+ HIV Positive – 90% HIV infection rates in the army

WELL DONE MR MUGABE

This litany of distress was underlined by the Archbishop of Bulawayo, Pius Ncube, who visited the UK this week and seemed despondent at the lack of international will to deal with Zimbabwe. The Vigil's mission is to alert the world to the crisis in Zimbabwe. Our supporter Sue Toft from Tunbridge Wells, with the support of her MP, Sir John Stanley, is the latest to challenge the British government to do more to resolve the situation. She was told by the government, 'At this stage we judge that insufficient members of the United Nations Security Council would be prepared to support such a referral.' This was in response to a request that Mugabe should be arraigned before the International Criminal Court. South Africa is one of the African non-permanent members of the Security Council, along with Ghana and Congo-Brazzaville, and our efforts will be focused on reminding them of their obligations. This week the Vigil and the Zimbabwe Central London Forum sent letters to African members of the UN Human Rights Council asking them to raise a motion against human rights abuse in Zimbabwe at the 3rd session of the Council at the end of November.

Saturday 2nd December: Only the second week into our cooking pot protest and we are already running into trouble. Two of our wooden cooking sticks have been beaten to death. The pot beating, along with the drumming and singing, made a potent backdrop for interviews for a radio which is doing a programme about the Vigil. Vigil supporters also made their views known at a meeting in London this week addressed by the Deputy Foreign Editor of the Independent newspaper, Daniel Howden, who gave a damning report of his recent visit to Zimbabwe. Daniel told us that the "country is emptying out". He had noticed that there was a whole missing generation of people between about 25 and late middle-age who had left the country, been jailed or died. He explained that the reason that Zimbabwe did not get more international press attention was because it was a country slowly dying and there was no immediate news peg. Our young English supporter Francesca Toft, continuing her patient lobbying, reported that she had received a reply this week from Hilary Benn, the Secretary of State for International Development, in response to her latest approach to the government about the Zimbabwe situation. Mr Benn said "I applaud your participation in the Zimbabwe Vigil". He said the British government continued to provide humanitarian assistance to Zimbabwe and had give £120 million since the present crisis emerged in 2001 / 2002. Initiatives currently being scaled up included programmes to assist orphans and vulnerable children and improving access to anti-retroviral drug treatment for people with HIV Aids.

Saturday 9th December: Even more cooking pots today. Everyone seems to be bringing them to beat the needs of Zimbabwe. People who passed the Vigil took the opportunity to bang a pot hanging from one of our four maple trees. Children found this great fun – but many of the parents had heard of the brutal treatment meted out to WOZA supporters. We showed a graphic photo of the injuries inflicted on one of the WOZA ladies in Bulawayo. The awful situation in Zimbabwe was underlined this week by the Zimbabwe Human Rights NGO Forum report that more than 15,000 cases of organized torture and violence have been documented in Zimbabwe since 2001. A notice about this was stuck on the Embassy window on their new poster 'Go to Victoria Falls, Zimbabwe's true wonder is back'. (Perhaps the Falls had fled to Zambia because of torture.)

The Vigil's deputation (Ephraim Tapa and Wiz Bishop) to our friends in Germany was given an open-hearted welcome. They were guests of the Harare-Munich Municipal Partnership, which has in effect frozen dealings with the authorities in Zimbabwe but are very supportive of Zimbabweans. Ephraim expressed outrage at the activities of the Zimbabwean Ambassador in Berlin who has targeted all Zimbabwean asylum seekers in Germany telling them that they are not allowed to take part in political activities. Our delegation reported that ordinary German people are appalled by what is happening in Zimbabwe. Videos taken in Zimbabwe left them in tears. Unfortunately we have to report that the CIO is very active in Germany as elsewhere.

The Vigil has been advised by sources in the British and French governments that the French government may invite Mugabe to a France / Africa summit in Cannes in February. We have written a letter to the French Embassy to pass on to the new French Ambassador to Zimbabwe pressing him to do all he can to prevent this. We are also asking supporters to send a letter to President Chirac along these lines: *The excesses of the Mugabe regime are getting worse: I need only mention the brutal treatment of trade union leaders when they tried to hold a peaceful protest on 13th September (this was applauded by Mr Mugabe), the re-launch of Operation Murambatsvina which destroyed the homes and livelihoods of the urban poor and more recently the vicious suppression of a peaceful march by women on 29th November. At a time when the country is spiralling into deeper chaos as a result of Mugabe's inhumane policies, we find it extraordinary that France can consider entertaining this cruel man. A French government invitation to Mugabe (in contravention of EU targeted sanctions) will dismay Zimbabweans worldwide. At a time when we are told that people are dying in their* *thousands not just from AIDS, lack of medication and lack of food, but from despair and hopelessness, this sends a message that the French government is prepared to overlook gross human rights abuses in Zimbabwe. If Mugabe's visit goes ahead it will lend him legitimacy and send the wrong signals to would-be dictators in Africa and elsewhere. The visit will also present Mugabe with an opportunity to once more claim on a world stage that he is not to blame for what is happening in Zimbabwe – France will be complicit in this deception. We understand there is considerable pressure on you from leaders of the Southern African region to invite Mugabe. We beg the French government not to give in to unprincipled pressure. Call their bluff – most of them will find it very hard to resist an all-expenses paid trip to the Riviera!*

Supporters are also sending the following letter to MPs: *I am writing to ask for your support in ensuring that the European Union holds its Common Position against the regime of Robert Mugabe and his cronies in Zimbabwe. The EU adopted the position in 2002 and it has been renewed year after year as Mugabe's oppression has increased. The reasons for holding the sanctions on Mugabe have never been stronger – yet some members of the European Union seem to be willing to let the sanctions, and their morals, drop. The sanctions do not affect the freedom or economic well-being of the people of Zimbabwe, they only affect individuals closely associated with the Mugabe regime. If we let these sanctions drop then we will be condoning the torture of the trade unionists in September and the wanton economic destruction of Zimbabwe that has led to an average life expectancy for women of only 34 years, the lowest in the world. The EU cannot been seen to condone these actions and I ask you to stand in solidarity with the Zimbabwean people to ensure that we do not allow Mugabe to travel to the EU; that his European assets are kept frozen and that we do not deal arms with a regime that is causing so much suffering.*

Saturday 16th December: It's that time again and this year we had even more Father Christmases visiting the Vigil. Well over a hundred of them came past in their regimental uniform – though this time some of the girls were wearing a new Mother Christmas outfit. They probably found the false beards too scratchy. They were again very supportive, signing our petition and our letter to President Chirac and joining in the singing and drumming. A new poster greeted passers-by: "President of Death now President for Life". The Mugabe regime's desperate attempts to cling to power by postponing the 2008 presidential election brought much derision at the Vigil.

Saturday 23rd December: The Vigil marked the end of a busy week. Vigil supporters participated in carol singing on Tuesday evening in Trafalgar Square in aid of a Zimbabwean orphanage. Others turned up on Wednesday evening to sing carols outside Zimbabwe House. Both nights were bitterly cold, with fog blanketing London. Friday saw the beginning of the "Long March" by our supporters, Free-Zim Youth. Banging one of our drums, they marched to half of the High Commissions in London of the Southern African Development Community to demand action on Zimbabwe. Small coffins symbolising the death of democracy were delivered to the buildings. They were pleased to be joined by supporters from other African countries as well as passers-by. Free-Zim Youth plan to visit the other High Commissions in the New Year.

Saturday 30th December: We were debating whether to put up our tarpaulin in view of threatening weather when it suddenly bucketed down. We had to frequently prod the tarpaulin with an umbrella to release the trapped water – sometimes onto some innocent passer-by. The last Vigil of 2006 was certainly the wettest for some time and the erratic blasts of wind tested our knot-tying abilities on our banners and tarpaulin but passers-by stopped to sign our petition and give us encouragement. One man called by and said "I've seen you here for 5 years". We have become a fixture. We hear the tour guides on the open deck buses passing along the Strand saying "and this is the Zimbabwe Vigil". At times the weather made it impossible for us to drum and sing, but Ephraim, MDC UK Chair, spoke of how people in Zimbabwe looked at the Vigil diary every week to see what was happening in London.

2007

Highlights

2nd February: Demonstration outside French Embassy against inviting Mugabe to Franco-African summit in Cannes.

3rd March: 350 people protest at Vigil at Mugabe's plan to postpone presidential election.

14th March: Protest at Embassy over the brutal treatment of opposition demonstrators, including Tsvangirai.

March: Vigil agrees to set up a separate organisation the Restoration of Human Rights in Zimbabwe (ROHR).

18th April: Petition to South Africa House calling for action against human rights abuses in Zimbabwe.

June: Zanu PF and MDC hold preliminary talks in South Africa.

23rd June: Tsvangirai visits UK: tells people to come to the Vigil.

August: ROHR sets up provincial structures in Zimbabwe.

September: British Prime Minister Brown says he will not attend AU / EU Summit in Portugal if Mugabe is there.

13th October: Vigil breaks with MDC.

7th – 9th December: Vigil demonstrates in Lisbon against attendance of Mugabe at AU / EU Summit.

Vigil Diary Excerpts

Saturday 13th January: We interfaced with thousands of people coming past the Embassy who had attended a 'Russian Winter Festival"' which took over Trafalgar Square. Many stopped to look at our laminated full page article "Zimbabwe, the land of the dying children." from last week's UK Sunday Times. They were shocked to learn that Zimbabwe has been reduced to such an abysmal state. Other recent stories tell of women dying in childbirth because of hospital staff strikes and three illegal miners dying of exhaustion and starvation after being forced by police to work filling up trenches for six days without food.

Saturday 20th January: Welcome back to Caroline who was freed last month after spending six months in prison for working with bogus papers. She brought her small son Tenda, who had looked so subdued when his father brought him to the Vigil while she was locked up.

Saturday 27th January: 'UN Holocaust Memorial Day'. Mugabe is not, as far as we know, putting people in gas ovens but what is happening in Zimbabwe is a holocaust nevertheless. Zanu PF's Didymus Mutasa made it known some 3 or 4 years ago that they wanted a population of only 6 million 'of our people'. They have been busy working for this ever since. A Chinese UN official who had just been to Zimbabwe stopped to talk to us. He said they are doing everything in their power to ensure that emergency humanitarian aid is not being abused.

Friday 2nd February: Vigil supporters took part in a demonstration outside the French Embassy in London demanding that France stop sitting on the fence about Zimbabwe. The demonstration was organised by ACTSA to put pressure on the French government following suggestions that it might invite President Mugabe to the Franco-African Summit in Cannes. The demonstration was attended by Kate Hoey MP who said it was important that sanctions were renewed when the matter came up again in Brussels later this month. The bulk of the demonstrators were trade unionists, including some prominent union leaders who expressed outrage at the brutal treatment of trade unionists in Zimbabwe.

Saturday 3rd February: Welcome back to Jeff Sango. He was released only yesterday after serving half of a nine month sentence for having a bogus passport. He looked better than ever and blamed this on the good food he'd had in Canterbury Jail. Jeff said the Archbishop came to visit the prisoners on Christmas Day. A brilliantly sunny day brought a good crowd of supporters including people from Wolverhampton, Bradford, Leeds, Blackburn, Manchester, Birmingham, Sussex, Luton and Bristol. Everyone was kept busy either with the singing and dancing and drumming or with sending our 'Make Mugabe History – Free Zimbabwe' postcards to Mugabe for his birthday. They were given to us recently by the Bristol Vigil. We posted a batch to Mugabe last week and we have even more to send him this week. One of the messages: 'Happy birthday, you are way past retirement age – go with grace!'

Saturday 10th February: First at the Vigil was Juliet from Manchester. She left home at 7 am for her long journey. She told us her asylum claim had been turned down. We are supporting an appeal. It was disturbing to hear from Juliet that her 73 year old sister in Matabeleland is eating only once in two days. Her sister told her 'If I get food today I won't eat tomorrow, I will save it for the day after'. Francesca, our English schoolgirl supporter, was also in touch with Zimbabwe this week. She was surprised when a friend in Zimbabwe mentioned the Vigil and asked him how he knew about it. His reply was 'everyone knows about the Vigil'.

Saturday 17th February: The Vigil was happy to host WOZA in launching its people's charter in the UK. We were pleased that the French government has announced it will not invite President Mugabe to the French / African summit in Cannes. We can now reveal that the French Embassy in London gave us assurances of this after our lobbying. We are already involved in engaging Portugal about their apparent intention to invite Mugabe to the AU / EU summit which we understand will be held in Lisbon later this year.

Saturday 24th February: The Vigil marked Mugabe's birthday celebrations with a performance by Zimbabwean protest singer Viomak, who sang several songs from her new album. It came as no surprise that the Zimbabwean Embassy did not accept her invitation to attend the launch of the new album. Viomak bought pizzas and soft drinks for our supporters – in contrast to the Mugabe's obscene birthday feast in Gweru where there was food for the bigwigs while the ordinary people went away hungry.

Saturday 3rd March: A wave of MDC supporters swept down from Trafalgar Square to join the Vigil. MDC UK had called on supporters all over the country to converge here to express disgust at Mugabe's attempt to postpone the presidential election till 2010 and in solidarity with MDC activists back home who are being treated with psychopathic brutally for peaceful protest. It turned out to be probably the biggest Zimbabwean gathering ever held in the UK. We reckon more than 350 people came from all over the UK. We were happy to have with us Sally Keeble, the MP for Northampton North, who has visited Zimbabwe and knows of the suffering of our people. We are pleased to hear that another Zimbabwe Vigil is starting in the UK. The new Vigil will be in Belfast.

Saturday 10th March: For the second week in a row hundreds of Zimbabweans gathered at the Vigil to protest at the rapidly deteriorating situation back home. The immediate draw was a rally in Trafalgar Square organised by ACTSA to mark the role of women in the struggle for freedom and justice. The rally was supported by British trade unions and the main speaker was Lovemore Matombo, President of the ZCTU. He said the worsening poverty in Zimbabwe was hurting women most of all and protecting women was protecting the nation. At the close of the rally there was a mass toyi-toyi to the Vigil accompanied by the Vigil drums. The Vice-President of the ZCTU, Lucia Matibenga, told the Vigil that, despite talk of divisions, various groups in Zimbabwe were working together under the Christian Alliance to campaign for change.

Wednesday 14th March: The Zimbabwe Embassy in London was closed today. What a surprise. About 200 Zimbabweans distraught at the brutal treatment of opposition activists in Zimbabwe found no one to answer their questions. All we saw was an anxious face behind a twitching curtain. We wanted to know why the regime in Zimbabwe had meted out the vicious treatment which had left so many MDC and other activists severely injured. Pictures of their injuries have horrified the world and we were swamped by the media. The demonstration called by the MDC UK was easily the biggest ever held on a weekday by Zimbabweans in London. Big enough to alarm the Embassy people. They had asked the police to ban the protest because they said 2,000 people were coming to attack the Embassy. The police had to explain once again that Britain is a democracy and that people are allowed to gather and express their views. For the first time in five years of Vigil protest there were barriers round the Embassy rather than containing demonstrators.

Saturday 17th March: With hot news coming in from Zimbabwe while the Vigil was underway we felt a bit like a news service, relaying information to the BBC and others. It is no secret that one of our supporters is Grace Kwinjeh's sister so we knew immediately when the police stopped Grace and Sekai Holland from flying to South Africa for treatment of the injuries they received in custody. Other informed sources phoned to tell us about the CIO hijacking of the body of Gift Tandare, the MDC activist shot dead last Sunday by the police. We regard it as part of our job to keep the media informed about what is going on in Zimbabwe. Coverage of Zimbabwe in the British media has been enormous and most outlets also reported Wednesday's demonstration outside the Embassy. Being St Patrick's Day, as well as the final day of the Six Nations rugby tournament, there was a high-spirited feeling in London, but the Vigil sobered up people passing along the Strand with our graphic pictures of a beaten-up Morgan Tsvangirai, Sekai and Grace. Many people who stopped to sign our petition expressed disgust at the failure of African countries to condemn Mugabe's criminality.

Friday 23rd March: The Vigil was asked by the Sunday Herald, a Scottish newspaper, for an article on 'What the West should do about Zimbabwe'. Founding Vigil member Dennis Benton submitted the following:

WHAT THE WEST SHOULD DO ABOUT ZIMBABWE
The sudden explosion of the Zimbabwean crisis into popular demands for action has thrown the British government onto the back foot. It would be unfair to say that the government has not been engaged on the issue but it has been on a hiding to nothing. What can it do? It could send a planeload of troops and solve the problem overnight. But there are various obstacles to this, chiefly that it would be regarded in Africa and in the third world generally as neo-colonialism. Mugabe and much of Africa have found it convenient to blame colonialism for the desperate straits to which corrupt and inept leadership has driven their countries over the past half century. Secondly, most of the world does not give a damn about Africa so any attempt in the United Nations and other bodies to do anything about Zimbabwe will be vetoed by the self-serving interests of the second world. After all, they will say, Mugabe is not the world's worst leader: look, for instance, at North Korea or Burma. The reason why we must do something about Zimbabwe is that, unlike North Korea and Burma, it was a success and can be so again. As President Nyerere of Tanzania told Mugabe at independence: 'you are inheriting a jewel'. The people are intelligent and hard-working, educated and cultivated. The land is beautiful and full of possibilities. When its people began to turn against Mugabe some ten years ago he began to act like a

cornered rat and jettisoned all respect for the law. Despite this, there was little the West could do to rein him in. Targeted sanctions were imposed, preventing him and his cronies travelling to Western Europe, the United States and some members of the Commonwealth, and support from the World Bank was suspended. Since then Western governments have been scratching their heads how to make Mugabe's life more difficult. Here are some suggestions which have been floating around and are now being considered as the situation worsens:

- *Extend the targeted sanctions to include, for instance, the children of Mugabe and his cronies. They have destroyed Zimbabwe's education system and should not escape the consequences.*
- *Secure the appointment of a special rapporteur on Zimbabwe through the UN or some other agency to compile a dossier on those perpetrating the violence to drive home to them that they cannot act with impunity and that punishment will come.*
- *Generally increase pressure on African countries to honour their commitment to observe and protect human rights. There have been some welcome signs in the last week or so from the Zambian President and others that Africa's defensive solidarity on this issue is crumbling.*
- *In particular, suspend aid to countries such as Malawi and Namibia which are supporting Mugabe. It was not too long ago that Mugabe was invited to Malawi to open a highway named after him. The West should make it clear that they are not going to pay people to kick us and their own people in the teeth.*
- *Impose a sports boycott. It's an affront that Zimbabwe should be taking part in the Cricket World Cup when the Zimbabwean cricket authorities are controlled by Mugabe.*

Saturday 24th March: It was a relief to find Zimbabwe House still intact when we arrived at the Vigil. On Wednesday a dozen or so Zimbabweans staged a sit-in: staff fled in panic though the demonstrators only wanted to present a petition to the Ambassador. When they refused to leave they were arrested but were released at the end of the day without charge. At the same time a demonstration was held by our supporters Free-Zim Youth outside the nearby South African High Commission demanding an end to Mbeki's support of Mugabe. We have not been impressed by the comments this week of the South African

High Commissioner, Lindiwe Mabuza, that South Africa is not guilty of inaction. No doubt a noisy supporter of the Anti-Apartheid Movement herself, she said 'Noisy posturing has not and will not work'. We will make it work.

Saturday 31st March: Disappointed is too mild a description of the feeling at the Vigil following the SADC meeting on Zimbabwe. Supporters were outraged at what was seen as cowardly betrayal by our neighbours. It was agreed we would immediately run a new petition: 'We record our dismay at the failure of the Southern African Development Community to help the desperate people of Zimbabwe at their time of trial. We urge the UK government, and the European Union in general, to suspend government to government aid to all 14 SADC countries until they abide by their joint commitment to uphold human rights in the region.' We do all we can to encourage humanitarian aid but it is difficult to explain to the British taxpayer why they pay Malawi to employ guards to stop people defacing signs on the new highway Malawi has named after Robert Mugabe. Our supporters in Free-Zim Youth claimed another scalp this week when they confronted Angola's Ambassador to the UK in his own Embassy. They wanted to establish the truth of reports that Angola has agreed to send 3,000 of its para-military forces to Zimbabwe to shore up Mugabe's tottering regime. The good news is that the Ambassador denied this. The bad news is that the Vigil is getting reports from Zimbabwe that some of the perpetrators of violence do not appear to be Zimbabweans as they can't speak either Shona or Ndebele. We had an interesting visitor today, Brian Haw, who has been staging a non-stop demonstration for six years in Parliament Square over Iraq. He briefly left his patch to visit a fellow activist being held in our local police station. He joined in the singing and dancing and expressed sympathy for our cause.

During March the Vigil agreed to a proposal by Ephraim Tapa to set up a separate organisation, the Restoration of Human Rights in Zimbabwe (ROHR), to be the Vigil's face on the ground in Zimbabwe. Ephraim was subsequently appointed to lead the organisation, which would be supported by its own membership in the UK.

Wednesday 4th April: 32 Vigil supporters joined Action for Southern Africa and the Trades Union Congress outside the Zimbabwe Embassy in support of a general strike by the Zimbabwe Congress of Trade Unions.

A senior Labour MP, Michael Meacher, was with us together with the human rights campaigner Peter Tatchell.

Wednesday 18th April: Some 200 or so exiled Zimbabweans staged a running demonstration in London to mark the 27th anniversary of Zimbabwean independence. The demonstraters, organised by MDC UK, gathered at the Zimbabwe Embassy behind the Zimbabwe Vigil banner "End Murder, Rape and Torture in Zimbabwe". They then moved on to the nearby South African High Commission, where a petition was handed in calling on South Africa to recognise the reality of human rights abuses in Zimbabwe. The Chair of MDC UK, Ephraim Tapa, said President Mbeki's quiet diplomacy seemed to be quiet protection of Mugabe. Traffic was stopped to allow the demonstrators to their next rallying point opposite the Prime Minister's residence in Downing Street where another petition was handed in. This asked the British Government to put pressure on South Africa to do what Mr Tapa called 'the right thing'. The climax of the demonstration was outside Parliament, where the final petition was handed to Kate Hoey, the Chair of the Parliamentary Group on Zimbabwe. She recalled that the last petition she had received from Zimbabweans had been handed over by the Vigil. It called for UN involvement in Zimbabwe and she read from a reply she had received from Britain's Permanent Representative at the UN, Sir Emyr Jones Parry, in which he said he would strive to maintain focus at the United Nations on Zimbabwe. Demonstrators returned to the Zimbabwe Embassy where they were addressed by Lucia Matibenga, Women's Chair of the MDC in Zimbabwe and Vice-President of the Zimbabwe Congress of Trade Unions, who said SADC must be questioned why there was no democracy and human rights in Zimbabwe.

Saturday 21st April: 'Each time a man or a woman stands up for justice, the heavens sing and the world rejoices.' This was the theme of our special Prayer Vigil for Zimbabwe. We were addressed by two pastors from Zimbabwe, Useni Sibanda and Promise Manceda, of the Zimbabwean Christian Alliance (ZCA). The ZCA spearheads the Save Zimbabwe Campaign, the umbrella organisation from which the MDC and civic bodies in Zimbabwe are working for change. Useni Sibanda, who is co-ordinator of the ZCA, praised the Vigil for its consistency and said it was a time for unity. Among other speakers were pastors from Nigeria and Ghana.

Saturday 12th May: We had with us Hilary FitzPatrick: 'On 8th May my 70 year old husband was beaten by riot police in Harare. My husband together with many other lawyers had responded to Mrs Beatrice Mtetwa's (President of the Law Society) appeal to the legal community to congregate at the High Court of Harare with the intention of a peaceful march to Parliament to protest at the earlier arrest of two human rights lawyers, namely Mr Muchhadeha and Mr Makoni. My husband together with many other lawyers responded to Mrs Mtetwa's call. Zimbabwe's riot police also responded and descended on the High Court. Mrs Mtetwa, Mr Micah, another law councillor whose name is not known to me and my husband were assaulted at the High Court, thrown into a pick-up and dragged to a vlei area near the Harare prison. Dragged out of the pick-up and ordered to lie down, my husband refused to do so. Accordingly he was beaten to the ground. During the commotion, Mr Micah made a run for it and leaped onto the bonnet of a passing vehicle. The result was that a growing number of vehicles stopped and observed the activities of the riot police with horror. Ultimately the riot police made off, leaving their victims behind. I salute the courage of my husband and all those showing the courage to resist the human rights abuses of the Mugabe regime.'

Saturday 19th May: We gathered to commemorate the second anniversary of Operation Murambatsvina, the brutal campaign in which Mugabe's troops and police bulldozed people's houses indiscriminately throughout urban areas, displacing 700,000 people to an uncertain future and disrupting the livelihoods of around 2.7 million people. Two years on, most of those affected remain unaccounted for. We used rubble in a physical display of the effects of Murambatsvina, along with some very graphic photographs of the devastation.

Saturday 26th May: The Vigil marked Africa Day with a sad sense of betrayal. The latest kick in the teeth for Zimbabweans has been the election of Zimbabwe as Vice-Chair of the Common Market for East and Southern Africa, Africa's largest trading bloc. We always get South African visitors passing by because of our close proximity to the South African High Commission. It was interesting to note the different attitudes of two of our South African visitors today. One young man who had arrived in London only a few hours beforehand saw our "ANC loves Mugabe" poster and asked if we hated the ANC. Our response was that we were unhappy about their support for Mugabe: in five years of protest we had not once heard a member of the South African government condemn him for the human rights abuses in Zimbabwe. Our South African friend was very sympathetic. The second South African visitor was a bad-tempered woman who was irritated by the number of Zimbabwean refugees in South Africa.

Saturday 2nd June: A British Caribbean passer-by was spitting with impotent rage at our protest. 'You are licking the arses of the whites', he said. While African governments continue to pay lip service to solidarity with Mugabe it is clear they are embarrassed and the black press around the world is beginning to be critical of his brutality and hypocrisy – including some newspapers in the West Indies. It has driven the head-in-the-sand diehards hysterical. They are so wedded to the image of Mugabe as the great liberator that they are in a state of denial and continue to swallow Zanu PF propaganda however absurd. Mugabe is reported to have paid over US$1.6 million to the London-based magazine "New African" to counter bad publicity emanating from the 11th March beatings. Our Caribbean critic was faced by Vigil supporters who have themselves been tortured and have had relatives killed by the regime. But he would not be shaken from his prejudice and neither will the man who drives the van for Global Foods who always hurls insults at us as he drives past. It is partly to stand against brain-washed people like these that we hold our demonstration every Saturday outside the Embassy.

Saturday 9th June: The Vigil celebrated the news that two supporters have been given their papers this week to stay in the UK. They are Co-ordinator Dumi Tutani and Fungayi Mabhunu. Dumi has been at the forefront of the Vigil's activities since it started five years ago.

Saturday 23rd June: An hour into the Vigil there were only three people there, including Vigil co-ordinators Dumi and Rose. It was testimony to Morgan Tsvangirai's pulling power. The MDC leader (together with Lovemore Madhuku of the National Constitutional Assembly) was addressing a meeting in Luton some 35 miles north of London and Vigil supporters were keen to hear what he had to say about this crucial time in Zimbabwe, with the economy in freefall and talks underway aimed at breaking the political impasse. With less than half an hour of the Vigil to go we were joined by two carloads of supporters from the Luton meeting. Among them was Patson from Leicester who said that Mr Tsvangirai had told the Luton gathering that people must come to the Vigil if they want to help liberate Zimbabwe. Patson said the venue was too small and many couldn't get in.

(The Vigil was asked to arrange a location in central London for this meeting as had become customary but elements in the MDC seemed to have other objectives.)

Tuesday 26th June: 'Mugabe must pay for his sins' said the Zimbabwean academic and human rights campaigner John Makumbe at a church service in solidarity with torture victims in Zimbabwe. Mr Makumbe told the gathering in the historic St Paul's Church in Covent Garden that the Zimbabwean regime had invented new forms of torture. He went on: 'There is a price to pay for freedom and Zimbabweans are paying the price'. Mr Makumbe said that one day there would be a Truth and Reconciliation Commission under which those who had committed atrocities would be called to account. The service, marked the United Nations International Day in Support of Victims of Torture. It was conducted by the Rev Graham Shaw, a Methodist Minister formerly from Bulawayo, who said torture is now considered routine in Zimbabwe. Brita Sydhoff, the Secretary General of the International Rehabiliation Council for Victims of Torture, said that in the past six years 25,000 human rights violations in Zimbabwe have been documented and the situation is worsening. The Zimbabwean poet and writer, Chenjerai Hove, said he had cried when he had seen pictures of the brutality meted out to opposition activists. After the service, the congregation sang their way in procession to the Zimbabwe Embassy to lay flowers on the doorstep in tribute to the bravery of Zimbabwean torture victims.

Saturday 30th June: Two old Mugabe themes at the Vigil – gays and cricket. Despite the attempted mass murders in London on Friday, life went on more or less as normal today. Some roads were closed in the search for more bombs, but the annual Gay Pride march went ahead as planned. We are always pleased that so many of the people on the march sign our petitions and express such concern for Zimbabwe. Vigil supporters were also pleased at the outcome of the cricket meeting in

London. The International Cricket Council has launched an investigation into the finances of cricket in Zimbabwe because of the looting by the current bosses. We were going to hold a protest at the meeting at the request of FreeZim Youth, but FreeZim suddenly made an about-turn and called for everyone to accept the Zanu PF case. We are puzzled as to why FreeZim Youth feel that giving the Zimbabwean cricket authorities more money will help cricket on the ground in Zimbabwe. Surely they know it will just go into the pockets of Zanu PF cronies? It seems, from an article in Zimdaily, now that FreeZim Youth are safely in the UK they have identified 'the real enemy' as the UK. FreeZim Youth are quoted incoherently as saying 'We have a crisis here of Zimbabweans in diaspora who have to face hard life with no legal status, no accommodation, no access to health, young Zimbabweans subjected to all forms of abuse and cannot (return for?) obvious reasons yet we have a host nation that says its so much concerned about the humanitarian crisis in Zimbabwe, well charity begins at home'.

Monday 2nd July: The Israeli Intelligence Agency Mossad has been accused of rigging elections for Mugabe. The University of Zimbabwe political scientist John Makumbe told a meeting in London that if the MDC is to win the next election it will be necessary to get Mossad out of the country; they were operating a computer company in Harare as a front and would rig any election for money. Dr Makumbe added that he didn't know if the Israeli government was involved but observers say it is known that Israel has supplied Mugabe with military equipment and a man with Mossad connections was involved in the attempted treason frame-up of the MDC leader Morgan Tsvangirai. Dr Makumbe is a member of the Save Zimbabwe Campaign, the umbrella organisation from which the political opposition, the church and civic bodies in Zimbabwe are working for change. He was asked to address the Central London Zimbabwe Forum about the split in the MDC (over the creation of a Senate). He said that with the help of Zanu PF the two factions were going in different directions. Dr Makumbe added that, in his view, the MDC faction led by Morgan Tsvangirai was the strongest political party in Ziimbabwe. As for the current discussions through South Africa's President Mbeki, Dr Makumbe said that Mugabe was going through the motions. He said he believed Mr Mbeki was serious about getting rid of Mugabe but didn't want to see the ousting of Zanu PF.

Saturday 14th July: The mother of one of our supporters, just over from Bulawayo, broke down when she described how things were there. There has been a lot of coverage in the media here of the deteriorating situation but it was good to briefed by a former reporter from the banned Daily News. When not singing and dancing, people at the Vigil were busy signing a letter to the Portuguese Ambassador in London over the possibility that Mugabe might be invited to an EU/AU summit in Lisbon in December: *'We, the Zimbabwe Forum and the Zimbabwe Vigil, wish to express our concern at the possibility that your government may invite Mugabe to Portugal for the sake of appeasing African governments. While we agree that the EU should not in principle be seen to determine the composition of the African delegation, we find it imperative that you continue to voice your disapproval of electoral fraud and disrespect of human rights which prompted the targeted sanctions against Mugabe – Decision 2002/148/EC. Any failure to apply the targeted sanctions will legitimise Mugabe's government, betray the suffering masses of Zimbabwe and make you accomplices to the human rights abuses In Zimbabwe. We therefore call upon the EU to beg South Africa and the SADC region to take concrete steps to ensure that Zimbabwe reforms itself and adheres to internationally acceptable standards as a condition for its inclusion at the EU / AU Summit.'*

Thursday 19th July: Vigil supporters attended a House of Commons debate on Zimbabwe. One question addressed by several speakers was the possibility of Mugabe attending the EU / AU Summit. The former Conservative Foreign Secretary, Sir Malcolm Rifkind, said the UK should not attend the Summit if Mugabe took part. President Mbeki came in for strong criticism for what was seen as his years of inaction over Zimbabwe. The Chair of the All-Party Parliamentary Group on Zimbabwe, Kate Hoey, said Zimbabwe's neighbours were turning a blind eye to the humanitarian disaster if they were not actually cheerleaders. She and several other MPs were in favour of the possible suspension of government to government aid to Southern African countries supporting Mugabe.

Saturday 28th July: Among visitors was Kate Hoey MP. She arrived wearing her Vigil t-shirt so she fitted in well when she took a turn on the drums . . . not to mention joining in with the singing and dancing. She was happy to stand on the pavement handing out our flyers. A German supporter, Jenny Kuhlmann, said how impressed she was that such a senior politician had shown such solidarity with us and taken part in all our activities. Ms Kuhlmann is doing a PhD in African Studies in Leipzig and came over to join us after following our activities on the internet. Supporters were angry at the latest outrageous behaviour by the Zimbabwe police. The attack on activists was widely reported here. What appalled everyone was that mothers were separated from their babies to make it easier for the police to beat the women.

Saturday 4th August: Part of what we try to do, with pictures and laminated newspaper reports, is show how serious the situation is in Zimbabwe. One of our supporters, Edwin Dube, testified at first hand to the decline of the Zimbabwean health service. He said his mother had died on Tuesday after being admitted to Harare Hospital last month when a cough developed into pneumonia. He said the hospital had been unable to offer her any real help beyond putting her on a drip and giving her mild painkillers. The family even had to organize a private ambulance to take her elsewhere for X-rays.

Tuesday 7th August: A Zimbabwean journalist, Ottis Mubaiwa (formerly Herald, Daily News) attended the Vigil last Saturday and was invited to write his own diary. Here it is: *'Date: 04/08/2007. Venue: outside Zimbabwe Embassy in London UK. Attendance approximately 100. Brave drum beating, dancing, ululating and singing activists denouncing the oppressive and brutal rule of tyrant Robert Mugabe. This section of the road stood to a standstill as Vigil activists went through their paces. Our songs centred on the need for a new independence in Zimbabwe. Leaflets were handed out to willing passers-by; some signed a petition to be forwarded to the South African leader Thabo Mbeki who holds a key to Mugabe's reforming. Our songs also touched on the human rights abuses by Mugabe – the self-styled believer in violence boasting of degrees in the trade. This has been the norm every Saturday for the past 5years. I salute the co-ordinators of the Vigil for bringing this idea of Saturday demos to enlighten/remind the international community of the deteriorating economic and political situation in Zimbabwe.'*

Saturday 11th August: Well over one hundred people came to the Vigil – despite being blacklisted by the Zimbabwean government! We were

surprised to be thought of as sufficiently important to figure on their radar taking in some 40 or so websites perceived as unfriendly by Zanu PF. It's sad evidence of their paranoia. Supporters were kept busy signing the following letter to President Thabo Mbeki of South Africa ahead of the SADC Summit in Lusaka to report on his mediations in Zimbabwe: *'Dear President Mbeki. We are encouraged by your stated desire to promote free and fair elections in Zimbabwe next March. However we fear that the reality on the ground is not conducive to these aims for the following reasons:*
1. *The Registrar-General's Office is conducting voter registration in a way widely perceived as partisan.*
2. *The registration excludes Zimbabweans who have fled the country – a large proportion of the electorate.*
3. *We are disturbed by the declaration by the armed forces that they will ensure Robert Mugabe is re-elected.*

We doubt whether there can be free and fair elections unless these matters can be addressed and call on you and other SADC leaders to take steps to ensure democratic space in Zimbabwe and that Zimbabweans in the diaspora are allowed to vote. We are disturbed at numerous reports of ill-treatment of Zimbabwean asylum seekers in South Africa, most recently by vigilante action by white farmers. We urge you to afford protection to our people in their time of trial. We fear that the situation in the region may not be conducive to the holding of the World Cup in 2010 if Zimbabwe is allowed to descend even deeper into crisis.'

Saturday 18th August: Everyone was disgusted by the television pictures from Lusaka showing the ignorant support for Mugabe at the opening of the SADC meeting. We are bewildered that our African brothers and sisters cannot see what is really happening in Zimbabwe, forcing so many people into exile. We had with us at the Vigil today a young man who told us of the horrific situation of Zimbabweans in South Africa -- of Zimbabweans there being driven to crime, including soldiers who had deserted with their weapons. He spoke of the exploitation of Zimbabweans fleeing across the border and said they were referred to as ATMs (bank cash machines) because they are always having to fork out bribes. Several supporters noted that the Portuguese deputy foreign minister indicated at the Lusaka meeting that Mugabe would be invited to the AU / EU Summit in Lisbon in December. It was agreed that the

Vigil would write to the British Prime Minister, Gordon Brown, asking him to stay away from this summit if Mugabe attends.

Friday 24th August: The Zimbabwean journalist Ottis Mubaiwa, who is now based in Birmingham, spoke of his dismay at the behaviour of SADC leaders. He wrote 'Outlined below are some of SADC's standards breached by Mugabe: 2.1.1: Full participation of the citizens in the political process, 2.1.2: Freedom of association, 2.1.3: Political tolerance, 2.1.4: Regular intervals for elections, 2.1.6: Equal opportunity to exercise the right to vote, 2.1.7: Inepedence of the judiciary and impartiality of the electoral institutions, 2.1.8: Voter education, 4.1.1: Constitutional and legal guarantees of the freedom and rights of citizens, 4.1.2: Conducive environment for free, fair and peaceful elections, 4.1.3: Non-discrimination in voters' registration, 6.1.3: Unhindered access to and communicate freely with the media, 7.1: [The member state holding the elections shall] take the necessary measures to ensure the scrupulous implementation of the principles, 7.3: [The member state holding the elections shall] establish impartial, all-inclusive, competent and accountable national electoral bodies staffed by qualified personnel, 7.4: [The member state holding elections shall] safeguard the human and civil liberties of all citizens, 7.5: [The member state holding elections shall] take all the necessary measures and precautions to prevent the perpetration of fraud, rigging . . . 7.6: [The member state holding the elections shall] ensure the availability of adequate logistics and resources for carrying out democratic elections 7.7: [The member state holding elections shall] ensure that adequate security is provided to all parties participating in elections, 7.8: [The member state holding elections shall] ensure the transparency and integrity of the entire electoral process. I wonder how on earth the SADC leaders can applaud Mugabe in the light of his abuse of power?

Saturday 25th August: A post-Vigil planning meeting was held at our local pub to organise our parallel Vigil next Saturday when Vigil supporters will be demonstrating at Zimfest. This is a largely white event held in London every year and we want to encourage people there to give more support to the struggle. We are having a stand there with banners, petitions and leaflets.

During August ROHR set up provincial structures in Harare, Masvingo, Midlands, Bulawayo, Mashonaland Central, Manicaland and Mashonaland East. They also held a mass rally in Hatcliffe.

Saturday 1ˢᵗ September: Two London Vigils today. A detachment was sent down to Zimfest on the southern outskirts of London to try to galvanise people attending this annual day out for Zimbabweans. They took with them some of our banners along with one of our drums, and set up a stall. Up to 50 Vigil supporters attended Zimfest during the day. They reported some difficulty in getting the hundreds of people there to think about the situation in Zimbabwe rather than beers and braais, sadza and games. Unfortunately our supporters at Zimfest were not able to properly duplicate the Embassy Vigil as they were given no space / opportunity for the usual rousing singing and dancing. But supporters were glad to meet Jenni Williams of WOZA. Back at the Embassy we were happy to keep the flag flying. Among those who stopped for a chat was a Zimbabawean whose cell phone ringtone was a recording of Mugabe's speech to the Johannesburg Earth Summit in 2002 at which he said: "So Blair, keep your England and let me keep my Zimbabwe". What has he done with it? Well, according to Equatorial Guinea President Teodoro Obiang Nguema Mbasogo on a visit to Harare his fellow dictator Mugabe has produced 'an agriculture sector which is one of Africa's most developed . . .'

Tuesday 4ᵗʰ September: The Zimbabwe Vigil sent the following letter to the Zimbabwean in response to their editorial in the last edition. *'EDITOR – You rightly observe in your leading article last week that there are no economic sanctions against Zimbabwe and that trade continues with the vilified UK and US. You could have added that these countries are also the biggest aid donors to Zimbabwe. All SADC leaders must realize this. No, there is a different dialectic in play. What they mean by sanctions is the refusal of the IMF/World Bank to give Mugabe any more money unless he changes his Gaderene economic policies. Mugabe and his colleagues in SADC do not accept that these bodies – funded largely by the West – have the same obligation as ordinary bank managers to see that their investments are not wasted. SADC (also funded largely by the West!) is to launch an "it's not fair "campaign although it has itself indicated it will place conditions on any financial help it may give Zimbabwe. The African Development Bank has gone* *further, refusing Mugabe more money until he pays off his arrears. Even best friend Angola is not prepared to send any more oil until its bill is paid. SADC says "sanctions harm the image of Zimbabwe" and Mugabe and his cronies are being denied their "right" to travel to Europe and the US to demand more money with no strings attached so that they can maintain themselves in the style to which they have become accustomed. Theirs is the rhetoric of entitlement: "We are sovereign countries and you are acting illegally if you do not give us money to do with as we like". President Mbeki adds ominously: "It is clear that some are treating human rights as a tool for regime change." Quite so. The Zimbabwe Vigil is to mark its 5th anniversary in October by submitting a petition calling on the UK and other European nations to suspend government-to-government aid to all SADC members until they abide by their joint commitment to uphold human rights. We want this money diverted to help the suffering people of Zimbabwe.'*

Saturday 8th September: The Vigil participated in a worldwide protest to raise awareness of the plight of Zimbabweans struggling for freedom and democracy. The protest was organised by the International Literature Festival of Berlin which selected poems and prose written by Zimbabweans to be read in public in more than 40 countries. The readings were also to be broadcast around the world. Some of our event was recorded by Tererai Karimakwenda of SW Radio Africa. The first reading was Elinor Sisulu's introduction to a new edition of 'Gukurahundi in Zimbabwe: A Report on the Disturbances in Matabeleland and the Midlands 1980–1988'. Elinor Sisulu said 'Speaking about Rwanda, South African President Thabo Mbeki said: "A time such as this demands that the truth, the whole truth and nothing but the truth should be told. It should be told because not to tell it is to create the conditions for the crime to recur."' It was followed by a poem by Chenjerai Hove – 'Nights with Ghosts - A Child's Letter from the Rubble' (written after Operation Murambatsvina. 'dear samueri, my friend, i will never see you again; maybe i will. but i shall not know until father finds us a new address. addresses! we have none anymore. we are of no address. now that i have written this letter, where do i post it to? shall i say, samueri, care of the next rubble harare?'

Friday 14th September: ROHR demonstration dispersed by police and thirteen people arrested, spending four days in custody during which time they were tortured.

Saturday 15th September: Everyone seemed to have seen the television report filmed secretly in Zimbabwe which was shown on the BBC on Thursday, including many passers-by who expressed great anxiety about the situation. The Ugandan-born Archbishop of York, Dr John Sentamu, also saw the report and has called for tough sanctions to bring down what he called the racist Mugabe regime. The Vigil contacted Dr Sentamu recently and we are glad he has taken up the question of Zimbabwe so boldly. Representatives of the Vigil had been invited to watch the programme with the reporter responsible, Sue Lloyd Roberts. She was anxious to get our feedback. Sue said she was horrified to see how the situation had deteriorated. One image from her report that struck everyone's heart was the picture of a starving child whose skin was coming off and whose hair was falling out.

Thursday 20th September: Vigil supporters joined a trade union demonstration outside the Embassy in support of a two-day stayaway called by the Zimbabwe Congress of Trade Unions. The demonstration was attended by about 70 people, including many leading trade unionists. The General Secretary of the Trades Union Congress, Brendan Barber, was there and said 'Zimbabwe's people are suffering from Mugabe's appalling economic mismanagement, corruption and brutal repression. They are standing up for their rights, and we must stand with them.'

Saturday 22nd September: Another big crowd with many new faces – not surprising given the British media's saturation coverage of the Zimbabwe meltdown. Every day there have been detailed reports in the papers and on television and radio. There was unqualified support for Gordon Brown's announcement that he would not attend the AU / EU summit in Portugal if Mugabe attends. The Vigil notes that Mr Brown is to approach the UN Security Council and the UN Human Rights Council to send representatives to Zimbabwe to see the situation for themselves. Both bodies have been sitting on Vigil petitions calling for this signed by many thousands of people. A supporter, Sue Shaw, wrote to the Archbishop of York thanking him for speaking out about Zimbabwe. She received the following reply from his office 'The Archbishop has seen your e-mail and, like you, believes that the time for African solutions has now passed and we should be working towards imposing sanctions that are targeted against those purveyors of misery whose luxury is bought at the cost of unbearable poverty.'

Saturday 29th September: The day started early for Vigil Co-ordinator Rose, who was invited to speak at a Quaker meeting at the local Friends House. They were discussing Africa and were anxious to have someone from the Vigil to speak about our activities and what's happening in Zimbabwe. She was asked her personal opinion on what should be done and said 'Support the Vigil petition for suspension of government to government aid to SADC countries until they honour their human rights obligations and instead use the money to support the suffering in Zimbabwe. They could also follow the Archbishop of York's suggestions and toughen up sanctions that hit the Zimbabwean kleptocracy'. The Vigil diary thinks it's about time we had a gossip column and we have two items. We learnt today from an insider that staff at the Embassy have not been paid for eight months. Our source said people were making do by doing odd jobs. We suspect they are doing more than this. There are plenty of ways that diplomats, being able to pass freely through border controls, can make a good living and we are told by another source that there is certainly no shortage of mbanje in Luton, where there are many Zimbabweans. As one of our supporters said "it is not so much an axis of evil as an axis of petty crime". He was referring to the story told to us by a man who passed by the Vigil today. He said he had just been released from prison in Latvia where he had met a Cameroonian who was serving 20 years for dealing in counterfeit US dollars emanating from North Korea. The Cameroonian said the money had been given to him by Zimbabwean diplomats in Abu Dhabi and Canada.

Saturday 6th October: The situation in Zimbabwe was brought home to us by Agnes Zengeya who reported that her brother, a 35 year old school sportsmaster, had just died for the lack of a hospital drip. Another of our supporters, Fungayi, reported that his elderly, frail mother in Mubare had been forcibly conscripted to walk to the airport to greet Mugabe.

Saturday 13th October: Our fifth anniversary! It was good to have recognition for our long commitment – shortly after we arrived the place was swarming with media: BBC, Channel 4, Sky News, the Press Association and others. There was even a report in Kenya.

The main event of the afternoon was the presentation of our petition to Kate Hoey MP calling on the European Union to suspend aid to SADC. Kate criticized SADC countries for keeping quiet about Zimbabwe and congratulated the Vigil on its years of dedication.

She later went on BBC radio to defend the petition, pointing out that our target was not humanitarian aid but government-to-government aid. We received an encouraging letter from Morgan Tsvangirai: 'As you meet to mark five years of a continuous presence and unity of purpose, demonstrating your revulsion with the situation at home, may I take this opportunity to record my deepest appreciation over the work you have done so far. Your vigils have kept a flicker of our struggle burning. Your vigils have highlighted the plight of desperate Zimbabweans to the world. Through your vigils you have shown a deep sense of patriotism and solidarity with us at home. Together you fought hard with us in our struggle. We are now on the home stretch, nothing has no end. Get ready for a New Zimbabwe. Prepare yourselves for a new society as we take on the Mugabe regime in this final and decisive phase of the struggle'"

Given Mr Tsvangirai's strong endorsement of the Vigil it is doubly puzzling that elements within the MDC UK (who paid for Lovemore Moyo, the MDC Chairman, to come over) chose the day of our anniversary for an MDC UK meeting for Mr Moyo to discuss dissent within the party in the UK. This meeting could have easily been called for another day and we know that many MDC members who felt compelled to attend this last minute meeting had been planning to come to the Vigil and the social event afterwards. Since Mr Moyo was in the UK on the day of the anniversary, why did he not join us as his predecessor, Isaac Matongo, used to? We can't believe he didn't know.

Well, the Vigil knows who the true activists are in the UK and who are the self-servers who bicker and jockey for position in countless meetings.

(While the Vigil was marking its anniversary a cabal in the MDC UK leadership voted Ephraim Tapa out as Chair. He believes they were acting for senior party leaders in Harare who objected to his insistence on financial accountability. Many at the Vigil ended their membership of the MDC in response and since then the Vigil has kept its distance from the party although we co-operate when asked.)

Saturday 20th October: We were encouraged at the worldwide publicity given to our fifth anniversary and there has been no let up in media interest. We were amused to be described in the Herald as being led by Kate Hoey to whom we presented our petition, and as an arm of the Gordon Brown government. The Herald seems to be particularly upset that we support Mr Brown's decision not to attend the AU / EU summit in Portugal in December if Mugabe goes. Well here's a scoop for them – the Vigil's letter to the Portuguese Presidency of the EU calling on the organization to suspend aid to SADC countries. The letter goes on to say: *'We must explain that the aid we are discussing is not humanitarian or food aid but balance of payments support, which is all to often misappropriated. We would like all the money saved to go to help the starving people of Zimbabwe. We regret to note that Portugal – Africa's oldest colonial partner – is still to meet its promised aid commitments and seems intent on inviting Mr Mugabe to attend the EU / AU summit in Lisbon in December. We believe there is no justification in lifting the EU travel ban on Mr Mugabe and cannot see how either Europe or Africa would benefit from the embarrassing spectacle of this old fool strutting on the world stage and blaming everyone else for the catastrophic situation in his country. We ask Portugal to stand shoulder-to-shoulder with the people of Africa and not with leaders who abuse human rights. Tell Mugabe to stay at home and mend his ways. If other African leaders choose to rally behind this tyrant they will further expose themselves to shame. Earlier this year the Vigil interceded with the French government which proposed to invite Mugabe to a Franco-African summit in Cannes. We are glad to say that President Chirac decided in the end not to invite Mr Mugabe and African leaders did not go ahead with their threat to boycott the meeting. We do not expect them to pass up on a free trip to your lovely capital on this occasion.'*

Saturday 27th October: A grey day – brightened by the unexpected appearance of Judith Todd, straight from an overnight flight from Cape Town. She is here to promote her book "Through the Darkness". "I'm so grateful for the work of the Vigil", she said. Judith has been an inspiration to generations of Zimbabweans, consistently fighting for freedom and democracy against successive oppressive regimes. Judith said she'd taken the title of her book from a poem by Eddison Zvobgo written in prison. *'A **Time to rise:** It's six, my son, and time to rise; The sun has shot through the darkness . . . Should you fall, rise with grace, and without Turning to see who sees, continue on your road Precisely as if nothing had ever happened; For those who did not, the ditches became graves . . . The end of the road is what we have our sight on.'* We have now sent letters to all 27 EU members about our petition and are writing to SADC members. We were pleased to have with us Patson Muzuwa who has been working hard in support of Zimbabweans on hunger strike in Yarlswood Detention Centre. They are threatened with deportation to Malawi because they arrived in Britain on bogus papers bought from the Malawi Embassy in Harare.

Saturday 3rd November: We were glad Judith Todd took the time to be with us again despite her busy schedule. She is to give the Cambridge Commonwealth Lecture "Zimbabwe – a troubled past and present: a challenge for the Commonwealth'.

Saturday 10th November: It was the Lord Mayor's Show today – the 800-year-old procession by the new Lord Mayor of the City of London, the financial heart of the capital. We were thrilled to see the Household Cavalry ride past. They were followed by a jeep with 4 soldiers including a black soldier who surprised us by saluting the Vigil! Judith Todd visited us again and brought with her a petition launched by the Royal Commonwealth Society asking that the Commonwealth Heads of Government Meeting in Uganda later this month should discuss Zimbabwe. This ties in very well with our own initiative, a letter to the Commonwealth Secretary-General: *'Dear Mr McKinnon, We write to express our hope that the plight of Zimbabweans will be discussed at the Commonwealth Heads of Government Meeting in Kampala on 23 – 25 November. We are grateful for your efforts on behalf of Zimbabwe in the past. The insults directed at you by the Mugabe regime should be seen as* *compliments. We are sure the Commonwealth understands that it was not the people of Zimbabwe who walked out of the Commonwealth in 2003 but only Mugabe. We look to our brothers and sisters in the Commonwealth to help us because we have been failed by the United Nations. Over the years we have sent it petitions signed by scores of thousands of people asking for help to stop human rights abuses in Zimbabwe but the UN seems to have done nothing. Now the European Union has decided to ignore its travel ban on Mugabe and instead invited him to the EU / AU summit in Lisbon in December. They seem to have been blackmailed by an African threat to boycott the meeting if Mugabe is not allowed to attend. We know that the EU is worried about the tidal wave of immigrants coming from Africa. But we believe that the solution does not lie in accommodating dictators like Mugabe but by dealing with the problems of corruption and human rights abuses to improve living conditions at home. It is no coincidence that the International Monetary Fund this week announced that economic growth in Sub-Saharan Africa is expected to increase this year by about 6% – except for Zimbabwe which is expected to fall by about 6% – clear evidence of bad governance.'*

Saturday 1st December: Once again we had an enormous attendance – more than 200 Zimbabweans from all over the UK. The main subject of discussion was the EU / AU Summit in Lisbon. The Vigil has booked for 29 of our supporters to go. Many of our most committed supporters wanted to come but lacked the right travel papers. They will be at our usual London Vigil to support us from a distance. We have heard from informed sources that we should try and track members of the Zimbabwean delegation to try and establish in which banks they deposit their stolen money and to whom they sell their Marange diamonds. We were pleased that Judith Todd found time for a farewell visit. She is to speak about the Zimbabwe situation in the United States, where her new book is being launched.

Friday - Sunday 7-9 December: Zimbabwe Vigil Diary in Lisbon and London: A Vigil team of about 30 grabbed the attention of the media during the EU / AU summit in Lisbon. Our demonstrations were shown on television all over the world. In Britain we were on BBC, ITV, Channel 4, Sky News . . . We gave interviews to broadcasters and other journalists from all over the place: Finland, the Czech Republic, Voice of

America . . . In addition we were tracked for a TV documentary to be shown later. In Lisbon itself we became minor celebrities because we were on television every day. People greeted us when they saw our Vigil t-shirts (it was lovely weather). They agreed with our stand: 'Super Bastardo' was how Mugabe was described by one of our taxi drivers who had seen us on TV. We staged demonstrations near the Summit meeting on all 3 days we were in Lisbon and, in between, plastered the city with our posters contrasting the living conditions of the poor in Zimbabwe to Mugabe's new mansion.

On our first morning, on Friday, Fungayi Mabhunu and Farayi Madzamba were roped in by the group Crisis Coalition to play the roles of Mugabe and Sudan's President Bashir for a stunt in which they were shown in bed with President Sarkozy of France and Chancellor Merkel of Germany – the suggestion being that these two leaders were being soft in dealing with tyranny. The four playing the roles wore very realistic masks: no doubt many of you will have seen pictures in the papers showing them surrounded by Vigil supporters. (The stunt seems to have worked because both Sarkozy and Merkel were later reported to have been pretty tough with Mugabe!).

On Saturday, the opening of the Summit, we staged a seven hour protest while our supporters in London held the normal Vigil outside Zimbabwe House. We wondered whether we would get any publicity at all given the saturation coverage our anti-Mugabe campaign had already received but the CIO came to our rescue. They arranged a pro-Mugabe demonstration with the notorious George Shire ('Widening Participation Officer' of St Martin's College of Art in London). Among his supporters were several young women from Guinea-Bissau who had obviously been paid to take part. We tried to talk to them but they knew no Zimbabwean languages. Someone who could at least speak English was a Jamaican woman from Brixton in London who shouted racist abuse at her own MP, Kate Hoey, who joined us for the day. The Jamaican asked us 'Are you African? Why are you being used by whites?' The only person who managed to shut the Shire group up was Adella, wife of Tichaona Chiminya who was burnt to death by Mugabe agents in 2002. She said "You have left my children fatherless"—referring to the murder of her husband . . . The pro-Mugabe demonstration guaranteed we would achieve our aim and keep Zimbabwe on top of the Summit agenda. Armed police separated us from the Mugabe group, who were penned in on one side of the square, together with Gadaffi supporters flown in for the Summit. We were kept on the other side, together with anti-Gadaffi demonstrators and a group demanding freedom for Cabinda in Angola. By the end of the day we were firm friends with the other antis: the Libyans gave us their loudspeaker when they left and the Angolans gave us their t-shirts. This was after both groups joined us in singing 'Nkosi Sikilele'. Media interest was further heightened when police wrestled to the ground and arrested two pro-Mugabe people when they tried to cause problems. We ended Saturday by displaying a huge banner saying 'Mugabe you would be more welcome in the Hague – a reference to the International Criminal Court. We invited everyone to sign it. The banner had earlier been flown over the beach area; unfortunately, permission was refused to fly it over the Summit itself.

On the final day of the Summit, we staged another demonstration in case the Mugabe hirelings were there. But Mugabe had obviously decided that enough had been spent on a losing cause and the money could be better spent stocking up on electricity, water, bread and other essentials from the local boutiques. Only the Gadaffi supporters were on the other side of the square – but they have oil money! As everyone says, if only Zimbabwe had oil (rather than diesel coming from the rocks).

Saturday 15th December: We have received a reply from the British government in response to the petition we sent the Prime Minister on our 5th Anniversary calling on the EU to suspend government to government aid to SADC countries until they carry out their obligation to protect Zimbabwean human rights. The reply goes: *'Thank you for your letter of 30 October to the Prime Minister on behalf of the Zimbabwe Vigil Coalition and for forwarding their petition. I am replying as Minister for Africa. Let me pass on our admiration for the Zimbabwe Vigil Coalition for reaching their fifth anniversary. The fact that over 5,000 people have signed the petition you have forwarded confirms the public's strength of opinion regarding the situation in Zimbabwe. Recent media reports have graphically shown what a desperate and tragic position Zimbabwe is now in. This is due entirely to President Mugabe's policies which continue to punish ordinary Zimbabweans already suffering from unemployment, food shortages and hyperinflation. Thank you for your words of support regarding the Prime Minister's decisions that neither he not any senior government member will attend the EU/Africa Summit in December if President Mugabe attends. We want the EU/Africa Summit to go ahead and to be successful. The Summit can and should deliver progress on peace and security, growth, development, governance and climate change. President Mugabe's attendance at the EU/Africa Summit will undermine the substantive business and dominate the media profile of the event overshadowing the important discussions taking place. We will continue to make this point in our contact with EU and AU states. The UK government sees a resolution to the crisis in Zimbabwe as a top priority. We are committed to doing everything we can to ensure a better future for Zimbabweans: a democratic and accountable government, respect for human rights and the rule of law, and policies that ensure economic stability and development, not humanitarian misery. We believe President Mugabe must change his policies, which are hurting rather than helping ordinary Zimbabweans already struggling from hyperinflation, mass unemployment and food shortages. Political change must come from within Zimbabwe. Yours The Rt Hon Lord Malloch Brown, Minister of State.'*

Saturday 22ⁿᵈ December: Famous faces at the Vigil today. We reckon we could field a reasonable Zimbabwe soccer team. With us were: Memory 'Gwenzi' Mucherahowa (former Dynamos FC captain and manager), Joe 'Kode' Mugabe (former CAPS United captain and former Sporting Lions coach), Blessing Nkatia (Dynamos), Panganayi Kuzanga (Black Aces and Grain Tigers) and our regular supporter Moses Kandiyawo (Acadia United, Air Zim, Sporting Lions). While constructing our football team we could also plan a new band with the brilliant talent Zimbabwe is exporting. Willard Karanga (trombonist for Thomas Mapfumo) said how dreadful it was that everyone was being forced into exile. He said several members of the band that toured the US with him were now seeking asylum in the UK. 'Our music is not allowed in Zimbabwe', he said. Also with us was Fungai B Gahadzikwa (mbira player with the band Ambuyo Biula Dyoko). On the last Vigil before our 6ᵗʰ Christmas loads of people took enormous trouble to be with us. We took the banners down before the end because we could not fit everyone in between the four maple trees outside the Embassy. When we gathered to sing the national anthem at the end we filled the whole piazza again.

Saturday 29ᵗʰ December: Our last Vigil of 2007. It's now our sixth New Year. People ask what drives us to continue. Here's one reason: with us today we had Guguzinhle Khumalo. We asked her to write her story for us. "I live in Romford, came to the UK in December 2004. I was abducted and taken to the Gwanda Green Bombers' Camp in 2002 and trained in combat. I was raped multiple times and had a child (girl) who is still in Zim with my mother. I had to flee because they threatened and beat me up so much. I left for South Africa and came here. I have never seen my daughter since I left her when she was 1 year, 7 months. I am now joining the Zimbabwe Vigil cause. Hopefully we will bring Mugabe and his evil associates down. People are suffering and we are suffering – enough is enough. I am 23 years old with no life at all. I don't think this is right. I want to go to school and be someone. For now I can't do that. What about the future of my daughter?" Guguzinhle also said that when she tries to talk to people here about what happened they can't believe it. What future is there for our land unless we all stand up and protest as the Vigil does week after week. We have gone through our register and we find that our average attendance per Vigil this year has been 107.

2008

Highlights

29th March: Vigil stages mock poll as Zimbabwe holds presidential and parliamentary elections.
April: Violence intensifies and inflation rate passes 100,000%.
May: After long delay, Electoral Commission says Tsvangirai won most votes in presidential poll but not enough to avoid a run-off against Mugabe.
9th June: Archbishop Tutu accepts Vigil petition on visit to London.
22nd June: Tsvangirai pulls out of presidential run-off complaining of violence and intimidation.
25th – 26th June: Vigil gets Mandela, on a visit to London, to speak out on Zimbabwe. He talks of 'failure of leadership'.
27th June: Election run-off day. Mugabe declared winner.
July: EU / US widen sanctions against Zanu PF leaders.
20th September: Power-sharing agreement but implementation stalls over who gets top jobs. Resignation of Mbeki.
26th November: Vigil condemns dishonesty and hypocrisy of South Africa and the 'elders'.
December: Zimbabwe declares national emergency over a cholera epidemic and the collapse of health care system.

Vigil Diary Excerpts

Saturday 5th January: Over 200 people attended our first Vigil of 2008. Our young English supporter Francesca Toft, who is tireless in campaigning for Zimbabwe, received a letter this week from the Archbishop of York, John Sentamu, in which he says 'Please be assured of my continuing prayers for the people of Zimbabwe and for all those who pray, march and protest to help resolve this desperate situation.' Dr Sentamu, from Kampala, recently cut up his dog collar in protest at Mugabe's human rights abuses. We are planning to ask the Archbishop to accept our petition to pass on to the UN Secretary-General. The petition reads 'We are deeply disturbed at the deteriorating situation in

Zimbabwe. It seems as if the international community does not care that a rogue government can hold its people hostage. In the past six years up to a quarter of the population have fled the country. Half of those remaining face starvation. Any dissent is stamped on. The UN's special envoys have seen this for themselves and condemned the regime. We urge the UN Security Council to take measures to help free the suffering people of Zimbabwe.'

Vigil faces bully-boy tactics – Thursday 17th January: The Vigil has contacted Charing Cross Police about threats to disrupt the Vigil on Saturday. The following is our confirmatory email to them. 'To confirm our conversation today about the demonstrations on Saturday: We suspect the group behind the rival demonstration is responsible for a campaign to misinform our supporters that the Vigil has been cancelled and as you know the Vigil is going ahead as usual this Saturday. This group has refused to co-operate with the Vigil and has drawn up a programme which they seek to impose on us. It is like allowing the Socialist Workers' Party to stage a demonstration at a Labour Party gathering. We will do our best to ensure that the day passes peacefully but fear that they are trying to disrupt us. They talk of bringing a thousand people but we suspect that – like the supposed presence of the Archbishop of York – this is just fantasy (we have it on good authority that the Archbishop will not be in London this Saturday). Anyway, we will be grateful for a police presence. As you know we have asked for this very seldom in going on six years. Thank you for your help and support during this long campaign.'

Saturday 19th January: A massive and very busy Vigil. We estimate that at least 500 were there, filling the entire piazza outside Zimbabwe House. Among them were MDC members who had marched from Trafalgar Square behind a huge banner 'Zimbabweans want free and fair elections 2008'. The banner was donated to us and it will be a centrepiece of our Vigils in the weeks leading up to the elections. It was by far the biggest demonstration that we know of held outside the Zimbabwe Embassy and made an important statement at this crucial time in Zimbabwe. The London Observer newspaper, in a review of protests in London, described us as the largest regular demonstration.

(We arrived at the Embassy for the Vigil full of foreboding. It turned out that the problem was Hebson Makuvise, Tsvangirai's uncle, who had been appointed his representative in the UK (later to be ambassador to Germany). He arrived with MDC members from a rally in Trafalgar Square and marched up to Vigil co-ordinator Rose Benton waving his fist in her face shouting 'How dare you call me a bully boy'. We refused to be bullied and in the end we worked together. Our report at the time did not mention this altercation to avoid embarrassing the MDC.)

Saturday 26th January: Taking today into account, our average attendance this month has been more than 250. This must reflect growing anxiety about the situation in Zimbabwe. Two-hundred-and-fifty people phoning home gives us a lot of information and we know conditions on the ground are not ready for free and fair elections. A group of 200 ROHR supporters demonstrated in Harare on Friday carrying banners demanding peace, justice and freedom. Riot police pounced and started beating people. Twenty-three were seriously injured including two women with broken arms.

Saturday 2nd February: A text message from ROHR in Zimbabwe read 'The whole country has no electricity. We are in total darkness. The government continues to lie to the people about the electricity situation. The truth is that failure to govern Zimbabwe is the sole cause. Police brutality is getting worse with each passing day. Zanu PF is once again using intimidatory tactics to rig the forthcoming imposed elections. If the MDC goes for the elections they are wasting people's time. We want real change not just change.'

Another message from Zimbabwe tells us: 'Hope you're fine. We're struggling. Now as you must have heard we're signing $10 billion cheques bro! Individuals and companies have had their cheque limits raised from $500 million to a whopping $10 billion. Not that it is really a lot of money. Looks bad, but its getting worse and we can't even imagine how deeper we have to sink before things start getting better. Prices of virtually everything have again gone up no less than two-fold since last week! We bought a quart of Castle lager for $3 million last week then $6 million on Tuesday and $7million yesterday! Civil servants who received even up to 6000% increments in some instances are galloping back to square one barely two months after the increments and who knows when the next pay rise is going to be! Basic commodities continue to be in short supply. In fact the economy is crumbling right in our eyes and we are helpless. Now we are headed for yet another disputed election which literally means a deeper catastrophe! And our rural folk are so scared of the ruling party the only political discussion you hear them partake in is about the Zanu PF primaries, as if that's the beginning and the end of the election. You ask them if they do not see how their lives have changed they collectively tell you not to put them in trouble by getting them to discuss anything to do with the MDC. But one by one they will tell you how much they have been threatened. The tragedy is that they are so convinced and they really believe it would be known and they would be in deep shit if they do anything outside Zanu PF, no matter how much they are also aware how that same Zanu PF has messed their lives and their children's. They have wounds and graves to show to justify their fear. They say its better to suffer alive than to see and endure what they have already seen and especially what they have been 'promised' this time round. What with chiefs driving brand new Mazdas filled with free fuel; new tractors which they fleece villagers with (they charge for tillage and pocket the money). And headmen have their new scotch-carts, ploughs, harrows, seed, fertilizer, etc. Agriculturally my brother, Zimbabwe is headed, not for a Mother of all Agricultural Seasons but the Grandmother of all Agricultural Disasters! Even the oldest granny in the rural areas tells you we are facing a dreadful drought. Crops are all waterlogged, most of them a complete right off! God help us. Sorry to take so much of your time updating you. But there is so much more happening everywhere you look. People no longer know how or where to adjust their lifestyles!'

Saturday 8th March: Singing and toyi-toying behind placards reading 'Dignity! Democracy Zimbabwe', a stream of people joined the Vigil after a rally in Trafalgar Square. The rally was organised by ACTSA (Action for Southern Africa) on International Women's Day in support of women in Zimbabwe and was addressed by Lucia Matibenga, Vice-President of the Zimbabwe Congress of Trade Unions who spoke to a specially-arranged meeting after the Vigil. She warned us that there was no way the elections could be free and fair. Everything had already been skewed in favour of Zanu PF. Ms Matibenga spoke of the importance of outside pressure and support and said when she got the newspaper, the

Zimbabwean, she turned first to the Vigil diary . . . and looked at the pictures.

Press release – Zimbabwe Elections – March: *'Zimbabwean exiles are to stage mock elections outside the Zimbabwe Embassy in London from 6am to 6pm on election day, Saturday 29th March. They say it is already clear that the results will be rigged. Members of the military have been filling in multiple postal votes and the voters' roll is in a shambles. The opposition has been denied access to the mass media and no election monitors are being admitted from the West, which has been feeding millions of people left starving by Mugabe's murderous rule. The mock elections are organised by the Zimbabwe Vigil, which has been demonstrating outside the Embassy in support of free and fair elections every Saturday since October 2002. They will be illustrating the methods used by Mugabe to steal the elections and will feature a giant transparent ballot box, people dressed in army and police uniforms and others acting as election observers. Counting of votes in the presidential election has been arbitrarily moved to a command centre manned by the army, despite protests from opposition candidates. They fear that, whatever the vote, it will be announced that Mugabe has won. He can expect the imprimatur of election observers from such bastions of democracy as Iran, China and Russia. As for African observers, election rigging is part of the continental norm. Although Mugabe is confident his armed forces can put down any protests, his remaining days in office are clearly numbered, however many votes he gives himself. The economy is in ruins and he can no longer offer pickings to the kleptocrats propping him up. Inflation, conservatively put at 100,000%, is probably now three times that and set to accelerate exponentially as a consequence of his election bribes. Businesses find that their foreign currency accounts have been 'borrowed' – the last twitch of the economic corpse.'*

Zimbabwe Mock Elections – Saturday 29th March: About 500 people came to the Vigil for our mock elections. We were outside the Embassy from 6 am to 6 pm, with some people joining us from a Prayer Vigil for Zimbabwe at Southwark Cathedral. There was a lot of press interest and while the Vigil was on we had telephone calls from people watching us on Sky and BBC television. The focus of attention was Fungayi Mabhunu wearing our Mugabe mask and accompanied by Grace.

Fungayi really got into the swing of things, mouthing Mugabe's vitriolic comments about puppet Tsvangirai, prostitute Makoni and the evil British while stuffing the giant ballot box with votes reading 'Mugabe for Murder', 'Mugabe for Torture', Mugabe for Starvation' etc. Also much photographed was a voter rising from a coffin to cast a vote for Mugabe, who was surrounded by people dressed as soldiers, policemen and green bombers as well as blinkered election observers from countries such as Sudan, Libya and Russia. After the long but exuberant Vigil we adjourned to the Vigil pub to count the votes. The results were:

- Presidential: Morgan Tsvangirai 273, Simba Makoni 31, Robert Mugabe 10, Langton Tounganga 5.
- Parliamentary / Senate: MDC (Tsvangirai) 252, MDC (Mutambara) 12, Zanu PF 8, Independent 12, Other Parties 5

The votes for Mugabe should be taken with a pinch of salt because they included the ones he stuffed in himself and others coerced by the police or deposited by dead voters. Not everyone voted because they couldn't get near the box because of the crush.

Wednesday 2nd April: Official results of the parliamentary elections showed Zanu PF had lost its overall majority in the House of Assembly but not in the Senate. The result of the presidential poll was delayed.

Saturday 5th April: Zimbabweans from all over the United Kingdom gathered outside the Embassy to express their anger at the manipulation of the voting in the elections. There has been massive publicity about the situation in Zimbabwe and everyone who passed by seemed to be very concerned. The Vigil's posters expressed our supporters' disgust: 'Mugabe Go Now', 'Mugabe Stop Rigging'. The Vigil's own President Mugabe – Fungayi Mabhunu in his mask – was on hand to warn people of the perils of voting for Mugabe, handing out ballot papers reading 'Mugabe for Starvation', 'Mugabe for Torture' etc. We have been overwhelmed with requests from the media for spokespeople over the past week. Dumi Tutani, Ephraim Tapa and Rose Benton were in constant demand and Dennis Benton has had daily calls from Vatican Radio and feels he is going straight to heaven. France 24 TV asked for speakers for debates in French and English. Bonny Adams bravely took on the French debate and found herself taking part in an hour long programme.

Saturday 12th April: A ROHR member from Zimbabwe came to the Vigil direct from the airport to give us a first hard account of what is happening at home. He said ROHR members were confronting the regime head on and Zimbabweans had responded by voting for the opposition without fear. But he warned that Zanu PF was now preparing to unleash terror, torture, violence and hunger. It would not be removed from power without a protest movement that would influence the international community to act.

Thursday – Saturday 17th – 19th April: Three days of demonstrations outside the Embassy culminated in the relaunch on Saturday of the Vigil's petition calling for action against the Southern African Development Community for their failure to hold Mugabe to agreed election protocols. Several well-known musicians joined the Vigil, among them Lucky Moyo, formerly of Black Unfolozi, and Willard Karanga, formerly with Thomas Mapfumo's band. Vigil supporters were also out in force on Friday for a demonstration organised by Action for Southern Africa to mark Zimbabwe's Independence Day. There were also representatives of Zimbabwean youth groups who earlier that day had invaded a meeting in London addressed by Vice President Ali Mohamed Shein of Tanzania, which is the current chair of the AU. They challenged him about the organisation's attitude to Zimbabwe. On Thursday, the MDC in the UK staged a protest outside the Embassy and South Africa House against the rigged elections. Earlier in the week, on Tuesday, the Zimbabwe Embassy itself had been invaded by a group of Zimbabweans.

Saturday 26th April: Supporters expressed growing anger at the reign of terror inflicted on opposition supporters. We had lots of new posters at the Vigil featuring victims of the violence and many people stopped to look at them. We learnt that ROHR activist Tichanzii Gandanga was abducted on Tuesday and found in the bush 80 miles East of Harare on Thursday very badly injured. Apparently he was forced to lie down on the road and then his abductors drove over his legs four times. The Vigil and ROHR resolved that next week's Vigil will be dedicated to our suffering, abused, starved and tortured brothers and sisters in Zimbabwe. We will be their voice and will run a petition calling on President Mbeki to intervene to stop the violence because we believe that only South Africa can bring it to an end. One of our supporters had a chilling experience at the Zimbabwe Embassy. She lost her Zimbabwean passport and had to visit the Embassy to get it replaced. She was thoroughly interrogated and shown a photograph of herself at the Vigil.

Friday 2nd May: Official results of the presidential poll showed Tsvangirai had gained 47.9% of the vote and Mugabe got 43.2%.

Saturday 3rd May: ROHR activists were at the Vigil in force to express their abhorrence of the violence being inflicted on opposition supporters. We were briefed on ROHR's plans for actions on the ground in Zimbabwe. Ephraim Tapa, a founding member of the Vigil and also the founder of ROHR, is currently in Johannesburg at the invitation of South African activists who want to join up with the ROHR project. To support our demonstration we displayed graphic images of the injuries inflicted by Mugabe's terrorists. They stopped passers-by in their tracks and people lingered to study cartoons about Mugabe's lunatic world.

Zimbabweans look to ROHR for freedom – Friday 16th May: Ephraim Tapa, just back from South Africa says that walking down the street in Johannesburg he came across a large gathering of Zimbabweans and found they were part of the Zimbabwean community supported by Bishop Paul Verryn of the Central Methodist Church. When he introduced himself he found that he was already well-known. He learnt that most Zimbabwean exiles in South Africa keep a close eye on the internet and the Vigil website among others. Ephraim had a number of meetings with sections of the Zimbabwean community and was welcomed as a guest of honour and invited to speak to a 1000-plus group. He received overwhelming support for what ROHR aims to achieve for Zimbabwe. While in SA he met many people with stories of the horrors of what was happening: an elderly man with his arm in plaster who had fled from the recent atrocities, a member of ROHR in Zimbabwe who had fled after sustaining broken ribs and being left for dead, 15-year-old girls turned prostitutes, victims in South Africa of xenophobic attacks, including women and children now encamped in the bush for fear of more violence, angry former soldiers of the Zimbabwe National Army and more. Ephraim also visited the Home Affairs Departments in both Pretoria and Johannesburg where thousands of Zimbabweans spend countless days and nights waiting in a futile attempt to get papers. Shortly after Ephraim left South Africa, he was pained to hear about further xenophobic attacks on Zimbabwean and other refugees in the Joburg townships, which resulted in several deaths.

Saturday 17th May: More bad news: Elliot Pfebve, who came with us to Lisbon, reports that his elderly parents were kidnapped and taken to a torture camp – he has no definite news about them but has been told to expect the worst. Other members of his family were attacked, their houses raised and property looted. Otherwise, on an unseasonably cold and wet Saturday, we had a remarkably good attendance. Some supporters came across two Zimbabweans down in London from Stoke-on-Trent who had apparently phoned the Zimbabwean Embassy to check if the Vigil was on! We didn't hear what their response was. So the Presidential run-off is to take place on 27th June. Of course we will be outside the Embassy on that day to run another mock election.

Two ROHR activists killed in cold blood – Sunday 18th May: A report received from ROHR in Zimbabwe: Godfrey Kauzani and Cain Nyeve, who were abducted by state security agents last week, have been found dead in Goromonzi. The two bodies were already rotting in the bush when they were found on Sunday. Both were ROHR activists who participated actively in demonstrations against Zanu PF rule. They were visiting Murehwa together with their colleagues Tedius Chimedza and Better Chokururama, their driver. The vehicle they were travelling in was intercepted by two Toyota Hilux cars that had no registration numbers. The cars blocked the road at the front and back and armed men in civilian clothes jumped out of their vehicles and kidnapped them in broad daylight. Tedius by some miracle managed to escape but Better was brutally murdered on the spot. He was stabbed several times until he passed out. Better was buried at Warren Hills in Harare, a funeral that was attended by ROHR members and other members of civil society. Godfrey Kauzani and Cain Nyeve went missing for some days until their bodies were found. Their eyes and tongues were missing, strong evidence they were tortured.

Monday 19th May: Another report received from ROHR in Zimbabwe: In a bizarre twist, a day after the recovery of Kauzani and Nyeve's bodies, the wives of both victims were abducted last night from their homes in Domboshava by suspected state security agents. Their whereabouts are unknown. The funerals of both Kauzani and Nyeve that were supposed to be held in Domboshava have been moved to Mabelreign because relatives in Domboshava have refused to gather there in fear for their lives. Tedius Chimedza, the only survivor, is in hiding and reports suggest he has sought asylum out of the country.

Zanu PF thugs stone mourners – Wednesday 21st May: More reports from ROHR In Zimbabwe: There was pandemonium at Warren Hills cemetery yesterday at the burial of Cain and Godfrey when a mob of more than 100 Zanu PF thugs, chanting war slogans, attacked mourners with stones and sticks. The burial was turned into a battlefield as the few MDC activists present tried to defend themselves with shovels and throwing stones back at the thugs. Most of the people present were elderly and ran for the thick bushes nearby, some tripping and falling on top of each other in the stampede. No one was left to cover the graves. This had to be left to city council workers.

ROHR Zimbabwe has learnt with shock of the murder of Tonderai Ndira (33) one of its members who was abducted from his Mabvuku home on 14th May 2008 by 9 heavily armed police. Tonderai was also the provincial secretary for security in MDC T. His decomposing body was found in Goromonzi where he is believed to have been brutally murdered at a Zanu PF base. The news of Ndira's death was received in Harare yesterday after failed attempts to establish his whereabouts. Family sources said they were not allowed to see the body at the Harare Parirenyatwa mortuary. So far more than 40 people from the opposition are known to have been killed in the post election political violence.

Saturday 24th May: People across the world are demonstrating their solidarity with victims of human rights abuses in Zimbabwe. The 'stand up for Zimbabwe' campaign organised by a coalition of African civil society organizations is calling on people to press the Southern African Development Community, African Union and the United Nations to act decisively to end systematic political violence in Zimbabwe and resolve the country's long-standing political crisis. The global day of action on 25th May, a day traditionally used to celebrate the establishment of the African Union, is the start of a series of campaign events planned to alert the world to Zimbabwe's crisis. The Zimbabwe Vigil embraces this campaign and held a 'Stand up for Zimbabwe' event at the Vigil. More than 200 people joined us. We held a mass 'lie down' as a way of graphically illustrating how many more people might die if the crisis isn't resolved. So many people wanted to take part that we had 3 waves of people lying down.

ROHR Statement on Africa Day: Zimbabwe Under Seige – Sunday 25th May: Africa day comes as a sad reminder of the deteriorating human rights situation in Zimbabwe, exacerbated by the political violence unleashed on the citizenry by Zanu PF after the March 29 election as a reprisal for voting for the opposition.

BACKGROUND: The ceaseless attacks on opposition members and human rights activists are consistent with the warnings Mugabe gave well before the elections that Zanu PF would never be removed through the ballot. The service chiefs also indicated that they will go back to the bush if any other political party won the elections. Many people dismissed these statements as mere threats. The sincerity of the threats is now surfacing. There are systematic arrests, detentions, heavy torture by police and daily kidnappings of opposition and human rights activists, and murders by well-funded Zanu PF operatives.

POST ELECTION VIOLENCE AND THE REALITY ON THE GROUND: Now the nation is bracing for a very painful presidential runoff, at a time when the nation is drowning in rivers of blood being shed by Zanu PF's network of war veterans, youth militia and state organs such as the army, CIO and police. In the Zanu PF campaign known as 'Operation Mavhotera papi?' (Who did you vote for?)', military bases have mushroomed from which where war veterans, youth militia and the army are terrorising people in the rural areas. To date more than 50 people from the MDC have been killed. Thousands have fled from their homes in the rural areas and reports of internally displaced people are still coming in. Hundreds have broken arms and legs, many rendered crippled for the rest of their lives. There are volumes of graphic pictures showing people who have been assaulted severely by Zanu PF supporters who are under specific instructions to intimidate people into voting for Robert Mugabe in the June 27 presidential runoff. Medical institutions are failing to cope.

THE HUMANITARIAN CRISIS – Effects of an Early Winter: Countrywide there are reports that people have fled their homes and are now living in the open. Many people interviewed in Masvingo have been sleeping in the mountains for more than a month now because their houses have either been burnt or they received credible threats to their lives from Zanu PF supporters. Winter has come at a time when thousands of people are not living at home. Most of the victims do not have blankets as they were burnt. Churches have been housing people since the beginning of the reprisal against opposition supporters and have been mobilising communities to assist the victims with food, clothes, blankets and other necessities, albeit not enough to deal with the humanitarian crisis. The government has not spared the churches either. Church pastors and ministers in Harare and Bulawayo are being victimised for keeping the victims in 'safe houses'. Although the MDC has had the primary responsibility of providing for the welfare of its people, it does not have enough resources. Some civic organisations are helping out but what can be done by organisations with limited funding in the face of a national onslaught by the State?

ABDUCTIONS AND KILLINGS IN ZANU PF BASES: Reports of abductions are coming in daily and the trend so far is proving that once a person is abducted, the chances of them coming back alive are very slim. The past few days speak volumes. On 21st May the nation buried Cain Nyeve and Godfrey Kauzani in Harare, who were abducted and killed in cold blood, their eyes gouged out and tongues cut out. On 17th May 2008, the MDC buried Better Chokururama, who was killed by the same people. On 22nd May 2008, Tonderai Ndira was confirmed dead after he was kidnapped in full view of his family in Mabvuku. He was found dumped in Goromonzi a week afterwards, his body already decomposed. His eyes and tongue were also removed. On 24th May the senatorial candidate for MDC in Murewa North, Shepherd Jani, who had been kidnapped from his office, was reported dead, killed by suspected state secret agents. Last Friday two men and one female were found dead in Uzumba, Mashonaland East, although their identity is not yet verified.

ZANU PF STRATEGY OF ELIMINATION AND INTIMIDATION AHEAD OF PRESIDENTIAL RUNOFF: The Zanu PF strategy to win elections is multi-layered. Firstly, it is apparent that displacing opposition supporters or anyone suspected to have voted for MDC from their home areas is aimed at disenfranchising the populace of their right to vote. The logic is simple. To date thousands and thousands of people have fled from their homes because they have either been beaten or had their houses burnt. The strategy is quite effective in the rural areas because, with the geographical arrangement of rural settlements, people know each other and in most cases their political orientation is known. Since the Zimbabwe Electoral Commission has announced that the Presidential runoff will be ward based, MDC will be robbed of hundreds of thousands of votes of people who fled from their constituencies who will constitutionally not be able to vote in their temporary residence where they are sheltered. Secondly, MDC might fail to launch an effective campaign in hot areas such as Mash East, Mash West and Central. In areas like Uzumba, Maramba and Pfungwe, Mt Darwin, Mutoko, Mudzi, Murewa etc, there is no illusion that MDC will succeed in sending people to campaign let alone send in polling agents on the day of elections. They have been informally declared MDC no-go-areas. The abductions and killings are not only aimed at intimidating people, but at paralysing the opposition, destabilising its structures and even weeding out its influential leadership. ROHR Zimbabwe national coordinator

Tichanzii Gandanga, who is also the provincial director of elections in MDC, is a case in point. He was abducted from his office in Harare and found three days later, having been stripped naked by more than 12 men in the middle of the night at some place in Mash East, beaten heavily by sticks and his legs run over by a 4x4 truck more than six times. Having been left for dead, Tichanzii Gandanga was lucky to be alive and is still struggling with his legs. He's in hiding and is no longer performing duties effectively. His wife is being tracked by unknown men and has gone into hiding.

SECURITY CONCERNS FOR OPPOSITION MEMBERS AND HUMAN RIGHTS ACTIVISTS: All the remaining human rights activists, journalists and politicians are on high alert because Zimbabwe is now dangerous terrain and that fact can never be over-emphasised. There comes a time when one has to think about one's own security. Once a member is taken, there is no more that organisations can do for them except to pray and hope that he or she will be found alive. The police are either apathetic or actively participating in the operation.

RECOMMENDATIONS: As Africa commemorates Africa day, serious thought should be given towards the plight of Zimbabweans who seem to have been left at the mercy of a marauding leader who is committing human rights crimes under the guise that it is a necessary measure to ensure that the gains of the revolution are protected. It is imperative, in the light of the current ongoing onslaught on the opposition and human rights groups, that there be a massive movement that calls for immediate International Intervention. The African Union and United Nations must step in decisively and deal with Zanu PF, which has lost all credibility and legitimacy so that life can be preserved. We categorically state that Zimbabwe can no longer afford to be held ransom by the illusion that Thabo Mbeki's purported SADC mandate to mediate will deliver anything meaningful for Zimbabwe. In the face of overwhelming evidence exposing the Zanu PF terror campaign, the victims languishing in hospitals and people being buried in shallow graves in the rural areas, Mr. Mbeki says 'there is no crisis in Zimbabwe' and that Zimbabwe can solve its own problems. The President of MDC, Morgan Tsvangirai was in exile, but SADC was comfortable with the notion. Thabo Mbeki recently admitted that he cannot solve the Zimbabwean problem. It is probably so because South Africa is even failing to get its own people to stop the xenophobic attacks on foreigners currently spreading around the country like a veld fire claiming more than 50 lives in the process.

CONCLUSION: Zimbabwe is probably at its darkest moment since the Gukurahundi massacre of Ndebele people in the mid 80s. The environment is not conducive to the holding of a free and fair runoff and we call for an end to the terrorism on the citizenry and the creation of a free environment where freedom of speech, expression and association are respected. We call for immediate international intervention to stop the killings and elimination of opposition members and human rights activists. The people of Zimbabwe can only hope that SADC, AU and UN will start acting and send observers to quickly deal with the crisis.

Hero's farewell for Tonderai Ndira – Wednesday 28th May: Report from ROHR in Zimbabwe: More than 1000 people from across Zimbabwe gathered at the Warren Hills cemetery to pay their last respects to Tonderai Ndira who was murdered on 14th May. Ndira will ever be remembered for his heroic activism in the struggle for the democratisation and restoration of people's freedoms in Zimbabwe. The funeral was attended by Morgan Tsvangirai and the MDC's top leadership, civil society members, MDC youths, friends and relatives. Tonderai's body showed signs of brutal torture. Morgan Tsvangirai urged youths not to be used by Zanu PF to engage in violence for money.

Saturday 7th June: The Mugabe regime's decision to stop aid organisations feeding the starving has led the news bulletins. Passers-by showed great sympathy, especially following Mugabe's cynical rhetoric at the world food conference in Rome. Many stopped to discuss the situation and also signed our special petition addressed to Mugabe's protector, President Mbeki: 'Following the recent attacks on Zimbabweans and other foreign nationals in South Africa we, the undersigned, call on President Mbeki to take action to ensure the safety of these endangered people and bring the perpetrators to justice. We urge President Mbeki to end his support of President Mugabe, allowing a resolution of the Zimbabwe crisis and the return home of exiled Zimbabweans. Zimbabwean blood is at your door.'

Zimbabwe a nightmare says Tutu – Monday 9th June: The former Archbishop of Cape Town and Nobel Laureate Desmond Tutu has asked for forgiveness on behalf of South Africa for the recent xenophobic violence against foreigners. He was speaking at St Martin in the Fields, Trafalgar Square. Turning to Zimbabwe, Archbishop Tutu said it used to be a showpiece in Africa: 'It has now turned into the most horrendous nightmare'. He accepted a copy of a petition from the Vigil calling on President Mbeki to stop supporting Mugabe and allow a change of government in Zimbabwe so Zimbabwean exiles can return home.

Thursday 12th June: The Vigil protested outside the South Africa High Commission on the day when the Zimbabwe situation was to be discussed by the UN Security Council. Unsurprisingly, South Africa insisted that only the humanitarian situation be discussed by the Council: the political situation was not important enough. The same attitude was reflected by the High Commission, which initially refused to accept our petition to President Mbeki. It was pointed out to them what bad public relations this was. Then they changed their mind and allowed one person to take the petition in to reception. Accompanying it was the following letter to President Mbeki: 'We have been horrified by the recent xenophobic attacks on Zimbabweans and other foreigners in South Africa and enclose a petition signed on Saturday 7th June by people passing by the Zimbabwe Vigil. The situation can only get worse if Zanu PF is allowed to cling to power. More and more Zimbabweans will have no choice but to flee.' The demonstration reached its height when, singing and dancing, all fingers were pointed accusingly at the South African High Commission.

(Russia and China vetoed a UN Security Council resolution to impose sanctions on Zimbabwe.)

Saturday 14th June: Everyone is worried about the atrocities in Zimbabwe. We fear for the safety those at the forefront of the struggle. We were joined by Lovemore Mukeyani who spoke about the violence his family had suffered both in Zimbabwe and South Africa. The family in Zimbabwe had been targeted because Lovemore has been involved in protests in the UK.

Saturday 21st June: The suffering in Zimbabwe as Friday's run-off election approaches has touched the whole world. Certainly, no one in the UK can miss the media coverage. There is a lot of anger too. One elderly gentleman signing our petitions said 'I would like to sign Mugabe's death certificate and I'm a doctor, you know'.

Sunday 22nd June: After a planned MDC rally in Harare was prevented by Zanu PF supporters, Tsvangirai announced at a news conference he was pulling out of the election because of the violence. He said that his supporters feared being killed if they voted for him. Wikipedia reports: *'According to Tsvangirai, a free and fair election was impossible for eight basic reasons: "state-sponsored violence" ("The police have been reduced to bystanders while Zanu PF militia commit crimes against humanity varying from rape, torture, murder, arson, abductions and other atrocities."); interference with the MDC's campaign, including its inability to hold rallies; the arrests of many members of the MDC, including important figures, thereby disrupting the party's organizational ability to campaign; Electoral Commission "partisanship" (although he said that the Electoral Commission was not really in control); media censorship, harassment of journalists, and the exclusion of foreign journalists; Mugabe's attitude and his suggestions that he would not accept defeat; and the existence of "an elaborate and decisive plan by Zanu PF to rig the elections", which included extensive intimidation, obstruction of MDC election agents, and ballot stuffing in the Mashonaland provinces. Tsvangirai said that the MDC would ultimately prevail and that its victory "can only be delayed". Despite Tsvangirai's withdrawal, Information Minister Sikhanyiso Ndlovu said that the second round would nevertheless be held.'*

Zimbabweans in London mourn the Death of Democracy – Press Release, Monday 23rd June: Zimbabwean exiles are to stage demonstrations in London on Friday 27th June outside the Zimbabwe Embassy, the South African High Commission and the Mandela concert in Hyde Park. The demonstrations follow the decision by the Zimbabwean opposition leader Morgan Tsvangirai to pull out of Friday's Presidential run-off because of the violence and vote rigging by the Mugabe regime.

Wednesday 25th June: Several Vigil supporters were among about a dozen demonstrators who gathered at Hyde Park as Nelson Mandela arrived for a dinner with leaders including Prime Minister Gordon Brown and former President Bill Clinton. They held up a banner saying

'Mandela ignores Mugabe's terror. Shame', 'Mandela speak out. Support a free Zimbabwe'. They were pleased when Mr Mandela waved at them.

Thursday 26th June: We had a wonderful encounter with Nelson Mandela today. Vigil management team member Fungayi Mabhunu joined human rights campaigner Peter Tatchell at Mr Mandela's hotel in London. They were there to alert people who might have pitched up for the planned picket cancelled because of Mr Mandela's welcome comments last night about a failure of leadership in Zimbabwe. Fungayi, speaking in hastily-learned Xhosa, said how pleased he was that Mr Mandela had spoken out about Zimbabwe and asked him to continue speaking out. The Vigil had planned to also picket the concert for Mr Mandela's 90th birthday in Hyde Park on Friday but in view of his support any message that we will give will be one of gratitude that he has spoken out.

Friday 27th June:
On election run-off day some 150 people gathered outside the Zimbabwe Embassy to protest against the death of democracy in Zimbabwe. The centre-piece of the demonstration was a black-draped coffin which was presented to the nearby South African High Commission, containing a second tranche of our petition calling on President Mbeki to stop supporting Mugabe. The South Africans would not allow our nominated person to present the petition because he was wearing our Mugabe mask so it was presented instead by his dear wife Grace dressed from top-to-toe in Harrods. The crowd outside the High Commission shouted "Mbeki must go, Mbeki out, out, out'. Vigil supporters had walked from the Zimbabwe Embassy to the South African High Commission behind the coffin. They carried placards reading 'Died for

Democracy in Zimbabwe.' (With Tsvangirai having pulled out of the runoff, Mugabe was declared the winner.)

Saturday 28th June: Vigil supporters are horrified at the type of violence emerging in Zimbabwe. They blame outside influences. Supporters say that cutting off lips, gouging out eyes, attacking genitals and cutting off arms have never been known in Zimbabwe. We had a Sky television crew with us all day, apparently waiting for the election result from Zimbabwe so they could interview us for reactions. We were ready to tell them 'How can anyone recognise Mugabe as President?' More and more people joined us as the day went on until there was a big crowd. The Independent newspaper ran a front page lead: 'Mugabe's secret war – in Britain. Tyrant uses threats, bribery and surveillance to silence his opponents in the UK.' We have had lots of experience of this at the Vigil. We are regularly filmed by the CIO who seem to be the main occupants of the Embassy.

Saturday 5th July: A big crowd attended the Vigil to launch our new petition calling on FIFA to move the World Cup from South Africa: "With the deteriorating situation in Zimbabwe and the likelihood of unrest spreading to South Africa we call upon FIFA to move the 2010 World Cup from South Africa to a safer venue. By the time the World Cup takes place South Africa's support of the Mugabe regime will have made the whole region unsafe because millions more refugees will flee Zimbabwe prompting further xenophobic violence in neighbouring countries."

Friday 11th July: Vigil members took a leading role today in a service at Parliament's own parish church, St Margaret's, next to Westminster Abbey, addressed by the Archbishop of York, Dr John Sentamu. The occasion was a service of prayer for the people of Zimbabwe called 'Restore Zimbabwe'. Chipo Chaya and Luka Phiri of the Vigil read lessons in Shona and Ndebele respectively. Chipo also conducted the Zimbabwean choir and Vigil Co-ordinator Dumi Tutani led dancing below the altar. Vigil members gave testimony as 'Voices of Zimbabwe'.

Friday 8th August: There was big media attendance at a demonstration outside the Chinese Embassy in London to coincide with the opening of the Olympic Games in Beijing. Television teams from British and foreign news organisations spent four hours with us. It was an uplifting experience working with other oppressed peoples in protest at China's support of dictators. It is difficult to say how many people attended because the Burmese and Tibetans mobilised at different times but the Zimbabweans and Darfurians were there from beginning to end. A highlight was a symbolic tableau depicting Mugabe, Bashir of Sudan and Than Shwe of Burma chained to a figure representing China against the backdrop of a black coffin representing the millions of victims of the three dictators.

August: Alarmed at the deteriorating situation in Zimbabwe, SADC sponsored talks on power sharing between Mugabe, Tsvangirai and the leader of the breakaway MDC faction Mutambara. The talks were led by President Mbeki and an agreement was signed on 15th September. But Mugabe and Tsvangirai could not agree on the control of key ministries and the agreement did not come into force until 11th February 2009 when Mugabe was recognised as President with Tsvangirai as Prime Minister and Mutambara a Deputy Prime Minister.

Saturday 20th September: Our doubts about the power-sharing agreement seem to have been borne out. The word we get from relatives and friends is that ZANU PF seem to have no understanding of what power-sharing means. Vigil representatives went to a meeting in London on 16th September organised by the Zimbabwe Human Rights NGO Forum. It was addressed by Jenni Williams of WOZA and Abel Chikomo, Executive Director of the Zimbabwe Human Rights NGO Forum. The meeting was attended by many people from Zimbabwean-interested organisations. A few people expressed misgivings about the power-sharing arrangement but Jenni and Abel and most of the audience were reasonably optimistic. Abel described it as a good first step and a starting point to rebuild. Jenni spoke of the need for national healing.

But Vigil members say they cannot be optimistic. People are suffering but Mugabe is going shopping at the UN, where he will probably be applauded by the General Assembly. As one passer-by said to us: "It's a farce". The Vigil ended with the good news of the resignation of Mbeki. There were cheers at the downfall of a man who has consistently supported the forces of darkness in Zimbabwe and coerced the MDC into an unfair agreement to preserve Mugabe and his evil regime. The management team had a meeting after the Vigil and agreed unanimously that we would continue campaigning for the ousting of Mugabe and for democracy and justice in line with our mission statement. Basically our message is that the MDC has done an unsatisfactory deal with Zanu PF. Why weren't the details sorted out before the so-called agreement was signed? The management meeting agreed to reinstate two petitions that we had put on hold in hope of real change in Zimbabwe. These are the petition to FIFA to move the 2010 World Cup from South Africa and the petition to EU governments to withhold government to government aid to SADC members until they uphold their human rights commitments to Zimbabwe. The meeting agreed that we should draw up another petition to SADC countries which would complement the petition we are submitting to the European Union. We cannot understand how our brothers and sisters in SADC can accept Mugabe as the legitimate president. The former Secretary-General of the UN, Koffi Annan, has now openly criticized the AU for accepting Mugabe's bogus credentials.

We publish here an email received by the Vigil on 8th September. We have made efforts to ascertain its authenticity and the general feeling is it smacks of the truth. 'I was in Zimbabwe recently and happened to be walking along Samora Machel just up from the Reserve Bank. It was about 1 pm when there was a Mercedes that sped out of the Reserve Bank gates. The car was stopped by police near the court buildings. We saw a crowd gathering and I went to see what the commotion was about. People were shouting and police with guns were on the scene to pacify the angry crowd. I noticed the boot open and someone said to me look at that. I could not believe my eyes .The whole boot was full of United States dollars. The young lady who was driving the car was shouting to all 'Do you know who I am'. I was very upset and shouted 'You are nothing more than a thief, shame on you'. The people became rightfully angry and threatened the young lady. The police then realized she was a top official's child and rallied to assist her. The police then drove off with her and that was that.'

Saturday 11th October: Friends from times past joined us in brilliant sunshine for the Vigil to launch our 7th year outside the Embassy. Unfortunately Glenys Kinnock MEP was unable to be with us to receive our petition to the EU so we are sending it to Brussels by post. Letter to the European Union: "The Zimbabwe Vigil wishes to submit a petition calling on European Union countries to suspend government-to-government aid to members of the Southern African Development Community (SADC) because of their failure to help the suffering people of Zimbabwe. As you will see, the petition has been signed by thousands of people from all over the world who have recently passed by our Vigil and share our anxiety about the crisis in our homeland. The Vigil condemns SADC for recognising Mugabe as President when SADC's own election observers criticised the polls this year as deeply flawed. Mugabe consequently feels free to disregard a power-sharing deal signed last month -- despite the deepening humanitarian crisis. The Vigil wants the money saved by our proposal – and it amounts to many hundreds of millions of pounds a year – to be used to finance refugee camps in South Africa, Botswana, Zambia and Mozambique to which Zimbabweans can flee for their lives without fear of prompting more xenophobic violence."

Saturday 1st November: Vigil supporters were shocked by the murder of Osborne Kachuru of ROHR. He was beaten to death at ZANU PF's offices in Fourth Street, Harare, after a peaceful demonstration during the SADC talks on Monday. We are told that the Zanu PF political commissar Eliot Manyika was responsible and the Vigil swears to leave no stone unturned to make sure he eventually faces justice. *(Press Report on 6th December: 'Elliot Manyika, the ZANU PF political commissar whose name is synonymous with violence, died on Saturday following a road accident along the Zvishavane-Mbalabala road.')*

Wednesday 26th November: Letter from the Zimbabwe Vigil to South Africa and the Elders: 'The dishonesty, hypocrisy and ignorance emerging from South Africa in the past week stabs at the heart of all those working for democracy in Zimbabwe. The group of three 'Elders' spent a couple of days in South Africa talking about Zimbabwe and say they have been shocked by what they have learnt. Where have they been for the past 10 years? Have they read nothing, heard nothing? Even though they were not allowed into Zimbabwe, they submitted a report to South Africa's President Motlanthe. He says he was shocked by the report and talks about 'quibbling over ministries'. Where has he been for the past 10 years? Has he read nothing, heard nothing? They say the situation is desperate – and so it is – but it is not helped by this dishonesty, hypocrisy and ignorance. They say the Zimbabwean party leaders must put aside their differences and join in a power-sharing government to resolve the crisis in Zimbabwe – as if another shortsighted and deceitful agreement like the one signed in September will do anything to improve the situation.

Contrary to the perception emerging from the talks in South Africa, the crisis in Zimbabwe is caused by Mugabe alone and is not the result of the failure to set up a power-sharing government and may well be worsened by it. If Zimbabweans see that their democratic will is again thwarted they may well be reduced to violence. There is no way through for Zimbabwe until there is real power-sharing and to treat Tsvangirai as a junior partner when he won the general election in March will do nothing to help Zimbabweans. If he joins the government as a puppet nothing will change. Is this what the Elders want? South Africa clearly does, as is evidenced by the insulting letter reportedly sent to Tsvangirai by the mediator Mbeki in which he apparently complained of his links with the West. Where does Mbeki think aid and investment will come from to revive Zimbabwe? China, North Korea, Burma, Iran, Libya, Venezuela, Cuba? The $30million offered by South Africa will not go far given the mendacity and greed of the Mugabe regime. If there is to be any real pressure for change in Zimbabwe it must be applied on the Mugabe regime. The Botswana government sees this clearly. The Southern African region must take its advice and isolate the regime. For our part the Vigil wants to see:
1. No recognition of Mugabe's illegitimate regime
2. Neighbouring countries to refuse visas to members of the regime
3. A freeze on the assets of members of the regime
4. Tighter UN sanctions on the regime
5. The establishment of refugee camps in countries bordering Zimbabwe where desperate Zimbabweans can seek food, medical attention, shelter and education no longer available at home.'

Saturday 6th December: The leader of the UK Liberal Democrat Party, Nick Clegg MP, visited the Vigil and called for international action to oust Mugabe. Addressing Vigil supporters, Mr Clegg condemned the brutality of the Mugabe regime. He said it was a stain on the conscience of the world. The UN, he said, must take any measures necessary to remove Mugabe. The Lib Dem leader paid tribute to the persistence of the Vigil and declared 'you will prevail in the end'.

Saturday 20th December: There was massive media presence because of the juxtaposition of cholera and Christmas. We were particularly pleased to have the SABC with us because our main message is addressed to South Africa. We are encouraged that the rest of the world seems to be coming around to our view – both our petitions are aimed at pressing South Africa to take action against Mugabe. Father Cholera, in the form of Vigil Co-ordinator Fungayi Mabhunu, had an exhausting time sweating behind his Mugabe mask. When he appeared in his Santa Claus outfit he was mobbed by television crews (Sky, CNN, Channel 4, Aljazeera and others). He cut down from the trees beautifully wrapped Christmas presents and handed them to Vigil supporters representing the people of Zimbabwe. They were labelled: cholera, anthrax, starvation, hunger, violence, murder, rape, torture, greed, injustice, destruction, death, corruption, lies, inflation, AIDS, malaria, devastation, kleptocracy, terror.

Father Cholera

2009

Highlights

January: Government allows use of foreign currencies to try to stop hyperinflation.
January: Roy Bennett returns to Zimbabwe after several years in exile
February: Tsvangirai sworn in as Prime Minister after protracted talks over formation of Government of National Unity.
13th February: Arrest of Bennett, designated by Tsvangirai as Deputy Minister of Agriculture.
March: Tsvangirai's wife killed in a suspicious car crash. He is injured.
March: Retail prices fall after years of hyperinflation.
18th April: Vigil protests at starvation in Zimbabwean prisons.
June: Constitutional review begins.
June: Tsvangirai tours Europe and US seeking donor support.
20th June: Tsvangirai booed by diaspora at meeting in London's Southwark Cathedral. Stomps out.
August: Police in Zimbabwe raid family home of Vigil supporter.
September: A year after power sharing deal, frustrated MDC complains of persecution and violence against its members.
September: Arrival of EU and US delegations. But both maintain targeted sanctions.
10th October: Vigil marks its seventh anniversary by sending a Mugabe impersonator shopping in Harrods.
November: MDC (UK and Ireland) suspended by Harare which speaks of 'financial irregularities'.

Vigil Diary Excerpts

Monday 12th January: From our Press Release: "A leading Zimbabwean political activist in the UK campaigning for human rights in Zimbabwe has been taken into detention and told he is to be deported. Luka Phiri was helping organise a demonstration in London for Tuesday 13th January calling for Zimbabwean failed asylum seekers to be allowed to work in the UK. Phiri is on the management team of the Zimbabwe Vigil. Phiri entered the UK in 2003 on a Malawian passport and it is apparently for this reason that the Home Office wishes to expel him. Vigil Co-ordinator Rose Benton said "There is no doubt that Luka is a Zimbabwean but the Home Office wants to send him back to Malawi, a firm supporter of Mugabe. Malawi will send him on to Harare where he will face retribution from the Mugabe regime."

Tuesday 13th January: Vigil supporters joined Citizens for Sanctuary in their demonstration for Zimbabwean failed asylum seekers to be allowed to work. A dossier of CVs collected from Zimbabweans in the UK who have skills that are going to waste was delivered to Downing Street.

Saturday 24th January: We phoned Luka in detention in Dover. The phone was passed around to many of his friends so he could talk to them all. Apparently the Archbishop of York's Office wrote to Phil Woolas MP, Minister of State at the Home Office, on behalf of Luka. Luka's bail hearing is on Wednesday and we hope he will be released then.

Saturday 31st January: The Vigil bought a cake to celebrate the return of Luka who was released this week. He joked that at least he was warmer in detention. Luka said he was deeply touched at the support he had received from the Zimbabwean community at large. Patson Muzuwa of the Vigil management team introduced the dance troupe 'Umbane' who, despite the icy weather, donned traditional tribal costumes and performed their close harmony Zimbabwean songs and athletic dances.

Saturday 14th February: 'Free Roy Bennett' (and other political prisoners) was the theme of the Vigil. Roy was one of the people who inspired the launch of the Vigil and visited us when he was released from prison in 2005, when we clothed him and wife Heather in our Vigil t-shirts. 'If they can arrest Bennett, they can arrest any of us if we return' said Patson.

Saturday 21st February: more than 360 people turned out for our mock 85th birthday celebrations for Mugabe. The Vigil worked on the basis of a report in the Times saying that Mugabe's party organisers had ordered 8,000 lobsters and 4,000 portions of caviar to be washed down by 2,000 bottles of champagne and 500 bottles of whisky. We had Vigil management team member Fungayi Mabhunu wearing our Mugabe mask and waving a Methuselah of champagne. He stood in the doorway of the

Embassy with his consort Grumpy Grace, dripping with diamonds and perched on designer shoes as she scowled at the TV cameramen covering the Vigil. Afterwards she headed off to Harrods to do some shopping armed with a fat cheque from the UN. Supporters held up posters saying 'Mugabe spends US$200,000 dollars while his people starve' and 'Zimbabwean life expectancy: men 37, women 34, Mugabe 85+'. A couple more points:

- A Vigil management member was asked about the way forward for Zimbabwe and suggested support for ROHR. The dumbfounded person had difficulty hearing in the midst of the exuberant gathering and said 'War? – not war!'
- Everyone who signed the register was angry that they have not been included in the bloated new unity government. 'This is discrimination. If they don't give us cars and allowances we will stop coming to the Vigil. Then where would they be?'

Saturday 7th March: Some wearing black bandanas or armbands, Vigil supporters mourned the death of Susan Tsvangirai in Friday's road crash, carrying placards saying 'The Vigil mourns with Tsvangirai' and 'More death in Zimbabwe'. We were at a loss to understand how this could be an accident. The feelings were summed up by two big banners brought to the Vigil: 'Sleeping with the enemy one was bound to be bludgeoned to death in one's sleep. Mugabe is a murderer' and 'The plot thickens in Zimbabwe. An attempt on Tsvangirai's life and he loses his wife in a highly suspicious road accident'.

Wednesday 11th March: Vigil supporters attended a meeting chaired by Kate Hoey MP, Chair of the All-Party Parliamentary Group on Zimbabwe, at Westminster. The speaker was Thabitha Khumalo, MDC-T MP for the Bulawayo constituency Mkokoba. She talked about how she and her constituents were trying to repair damage: filling in potholes, unblocking sewers. She had gone into a sewer, braving the unbelievable stench, to try and unblock it. She was more successful than she expected and was suddenly drenched by a fountain of sewage! She had to travel 5 kilometres to find water to bathe in.

Friday 20th March: Fungayi Mabhunu spoke about conditions in Zimbabwe during a visit to the Dolphin School in Battersea, south London, at the invitation of teacher Steve Garvey who had visited the

Vigil. The Year 4s have decided to take part in a sponsored event next month with all the proceeds going directly to one or two schools in Zimbabwe who desperately need it. The Year 4 teacher Mr Garvey has also decided to raise money by running the London Marathon next month on behalf of the Vigil.

Saturday 18th April: There was a lot of media interest in our Independence Day protest about the conditions in Zimbabwean prisons. Public attention was grabbed by graphic pictures of starving prisoners and bodies piled high in Mugabe's hell-holes. Many passers-by stopped to add their names to a special petition to SADC: "A petition to Zimbabwe's neighbours: We call upon the Southern African Development Community – as guarantors of the Zimbabwe power-sharing agreement – to put pressure on the new Zimbabwean government of national unity to stop the blatant abuse of human rights of prisoners in Zimbabwe who are dying of starvation, disease and torture."

Our protest was given added urgency by a report that cholera has begun to spread in prison. Patson Muzuwa explained the Vigil's demand that the prison population be reduced to a level where those incarcerated could be properly fed and housed. Otherwise we were looking at a genocide. Patson, who has been imprisoned several times for his activism, described the abuses of a gulag system in which innocent people could be completely lost to the outside world. (Some months later the Zimbabwe government agreed to our demand for an amnesty.) 362 people signed the register.

Saturday 6th June: The Vigil gave a great pom pom to a man who ran 26.2 miles for us. Steve Garvey did the London Marathon in 3 hours 26 minutes to raise funds for the Vigil. Steve came to the Vigil some months ago with some of his pupils (8 – 9 year olds) who have since raised more than £1,000 for school children in Zimbabwe.

Saturday 13th June: There was talk that Tsvangirai would be accompanied on a visit to the UK by two Zanu PF ministers, Foreign Minister Simbarashe Mumbengengwi and the Minister of Mines Obert Mpofu. Both of them are on the targeted sanctions list and the Vigil approached the Foreign Office to protest at granting visas to these two Mugabe cronies. The Vigil has been assured that Mr Mpofu will not be part of the delegation. Our assumption is that Mumbengengwi will be allowed in under a dispensation allowing for 'dialogue'. The Vigil does not accept the case for relaxing targeted sanctions against Mumbengengwi. But we think he makes a better companion for the Prime Minister than Tsvangirai's niece Dr Arikana Chihombori who accompanied him to the inauguration of President Zuma of South Africa. She is an American citizen and has a large medical practice in the US where she has lived for 30 years. Nevertheless, she has seen fit to try to dispossess a Zimbabwean farmer so she can have a holiday home.

Saturday 20th June: An extraordinary day which saw Morgan Tsvangirai stomping out of a diaspora assembly in Southwark Cathedral in south London when his speech was booed. The Vigil was there to greet his convoy when it arrived. Displaying our banners 'No to Mugabe, No to Starvation' and 'End Murder, Rape and Torture in Zimbabwe', we danced and drummed and chanted 'To save Zimbabwe, Mugabe must go'. The Prime Minister could not have failed to see our posters 'Protect Human Rights Activists', 'Restore the Rule of Law' and 'End Farm Invasions'. Our purpose was to welcome Tsvangirai but also to remind him of what people in the diaspora think needs to be done if Zimbabwe is to win the confidence of donors and investors and be a welcoming place for returning exiles.

Outside Southwark Cathedral

Tsvangirai was given a big ovation when he emerged in the cathedral after prayers and a reading from the Acts of the Apostles by Vigil management team member Gugu Tutani – 'I have surely seen the mistreatment of my people'. But he was jeered by the audience when he called on them to return home. As far as they were concerned he was telling them to go back to a place with no jobs or rule of law and continuing human rights abuses. There were chants of 'Mugabe must go'. The much-heralded meeting ended abruptly.

Despite this distraction, the Vigil outside the Embassy took place as normal. We were not surprised that Tsvangirai did not stop by on his way to a £75 a head dinner for exiled Zimbabweans. Some comments from the many disappointed and angry Zimbabweans who came on from the Cathedral to the Vigil, many of them first-timers:

- 'When Morgan said "the schools have re-opened" everybody cheered. When Morgan said "the hospitals have re-opened" everybody was silent. When he said "there is peace in Zimbabwe" everyone heckled and booed and you could taste the anger in the air. One lady asked the question "if there are goods in the shops and the schools have re-opened where will everyone get money to buy food and send their children to school" – this was not answered.'
- 'He was speaking like Mugabe. He is saying everything is now ok.'
- 'The MDC expects everyone to agree or they are treated as an enemy'.
- 'We have been betrayed by Tsvangirai'.
- 'Today Tsvangirai was shot down in flames by Zimbabweans in the UK diaspora.'
- 'How can Tsvangirai encourage people to go home when all his children are in the diaspora?'

Saturday 27th June: Vigil supporters were fired up about allegations on some loud-mouthed Zimbabwean exile websites that the Vigil and ROHR were behind the booing of Morgan Tsvangirai when he spoke to the UK diaspora in Southwark Cathedral. Anyone looking at videos of the occasion will see that the angry response was prompted by Mr Tsvangirai's remarks and was spontaneous and could not possibly have been planned. The meeting's organisers also sought to blame asylum seekers, accusing them of being selfish and not being up to date with the situation on the ground in Zimbabwe – the 'progress' that has been made. Well, frankly, with the abundant access to information that we have in the UK we sometimes feel that we have to tell people at home what is going on – that, for instance, the MDC Deputy Minister for Mines, Murisi Zwizwai, seems to have been co-opted by Zanu PF in claiming that there is no evidence of killings in the Marange diamond fields. What upset the Zimbabwean exiles at Southwark Cathedral was this type of half truth being peddled by the MDC leadership. We are not convinced that everything is ok, that Mugabe's grip on power is being loosened or that human rights violations and farm invasions are not happening.

The Vigil went ahead with our human rights demonstration outside the cathedral despite an extraordinary email to us from an MDC organiser talking about possible violence. What was this about? The Vigil has been staging demonstrations at least once a week for seven years without any trouble. Among the efforts to destabilise the Vigil are predictable allegations of the misuse of money, most recently accusations of 'selling' letters to support asylum claims. We have spelt out our policy before but here it is again: We do not have membership fees but we charge a small administration fee of £10 for letters that we feel able to write in support of asylum claims on the basis of attendance at the Vigil. Now what happens to this money? No one draws a salary. Some of the money goes on administration expenses, some of it goes on fares and welfare expenditure for our supporters. The bulk goes to help ROHR and other Zimbabwean human rights causes as agreed by the finance committee and Vigil management team. The role of the Vigil and ROHR was discussed extensively at our very well-attended monthly forum held after the Vigil. Ephraim Tapa, President of ROHR, said the organisation was non-party political and was working with many partners in Zimbabwe, South Africa and the UK.

Saturday 25th July: The Vigil gathered in the middle of three days of National Hypocrisy. The so-called 'healing' exercise announced by Mugabe failed to convince our supporters that he has any intention of reining in his thugs or allowing the rule of law. Our supporters wanted to know when there will be justice for the oppressed and an acknowledgement of the evil perpetrated by Zanu PF. As one supporter (Brian Sibanda) said 'what happens on day 4 . . . back to torture?' He was questioning Ephraim Tapa who told the Vigil that 15 ROHR members had been arrested in Harare today during a demonstration against Mugabe's hypocrisy.

Saturday 15th August: A spectacular performance by our friends the Afro Drum Generation was the highlight of the Vigil. Dressed in traditional animal skins, their high-stepping dancing, supported by marimba and drums, attracted many passers-by. The group hopes to take part in Zim Idol, a TV talent contest to discover Zimbabwe's music stars of tomorrow.

Saturday 22nd August: An alarming picture of life under the 'unity' government has emerged in the wake of a mention in the Vigil diary about 'people's poet' Brian Sibanda. We reported how he had brought along a banner expressing scepticism about the '3 days of national healing'. His take was '3 days peace. On day 4 bullet sent via post' – a reference to the bullet sent to MDC Finance Minister Tendai Biti. Brian says that within days of our report (accompanied by a picture of him) appearing in the Zimbabwean, his family home in Zimbabwe was raided by three policemen. They compared photographs of him there with his picture in the newspaper and spoke angrily about Zimbabweans in the UK. Today we launched a new petition aimed at the SADC meeting in Kinshasha next month which is due to review the Global Political Agreement: 'A petition to Zimbabwe's neighbours: We call upon the Southern African Development Community – as guarantors of the Zimbabwe power-sharing government – to put pressure on President Mugabe to honour the agreement. More than six months into the unity government, Mugabe is still resisting a return to the rule of law, deterring essential foreign development aid and investment.'

Saturday 26th September: Exuberant ululating greeted two members of the Vigil management team, Dumi Tutani and Luka Phiri, when they arrived at the Vigil after completing a 55-mile sponsored walk from Brighton on the south coast. Despite their exhaustion, they immediately joined in the celebratory dancing. The walk was to raise funds to help a Zimbabwean girl with a severe facial tumour who is coming to the UK for urgent medical treatment. The girl, Taremeredzwa Nomatter Mapungwana, is supported by the Zimbabwean charity Girl Child Network. Dumi and Luka were greeted at the Vigil by Betty Makoni, founder of Girl Child Network, who was warm in her praise. "Because of your walk people here have now heard of our work". Betty told the Vigil she had been forced to flee Zimbabwe because of her role in helping women victims of political violence. Rape had been used as a weapon of war since 2002 and women and their families were still being harassed and intimidated. Husbands would be taunted by the perpetrators, who believed they could act with impunity.

Saturday 10th October: President Mugabe and first lady 'Shopwell' Grace were not at all happy with their Harrods experience marking the Vigil's 7th anniversary. Two members of the Vigil impersonating the presidential couple went to this puffed-up shop to illustrate what will happen if the targeted sanctions against Mugabe and his cronies are lifted as demanded by Zimbabwe's neighbours. After learning about our proposed shopping spree, a pompous Harrods flunky phoned us and threatened to put Attorney-General Tomana on our case. 'You can't come in', she said. 'Can we take pictures outside?' we asked. 'No it's out of the question' Harrods replied, sensitive as always to the susceptibilities of their kleptocratic clients. Well, despite Harrods' hoity-toity response, Mugabe and Shopwell marched boldly into the bazaar. Among the media to capture the moment was an AFP photographer rewarded by us with a Zim$100 trillion note. Nevertheless President Mugabe (Fungayi Mabhunu) and his consort (Gugu Tutani) have decided in future to take their custom next door to Harvey Nichols. Another of Zimbabwe's celebrated 15-digit notes was given to Geoffrey Van Orden, Member of the European Parliament for Eastern England, who came to the Vigil to support us on our anniversary and accepted our petition to hand over to the European Union calling for punitive action against SADC because of its failure to honour its commitment to ensure that the global political agreement is implemented. The petition was given to him by President Mugabe himself who arrived with Shopwell by rickshaw after their Harrods expedition. Mr Van Orden called on President

Mugabe to stand aside and allow peace and prosperity in Zimbabwe through free and fair internationally-monitored elections. 268 attended the Vigil.

Saturday 14th November: The Vigil's petition to the EU calling for punitive action against SADC countries was presented in Brussels this week to the EU's Commissioner for Development and Humanitarian Aid, Karel De Gucht.

Wednesday 25th November: Vigil supporters attended a meeting in London attended by Jenni Williams and Magodonga Mahlungu of WOZA, fresh from their meeting with President Obama in Washington. Our supporters reported there was deep concern about the human rights situation in rural Zimbabwe. There was criticism that the MDC were not reaching these areas.

Saturday 28th November: The Vigil is not surprised that the MDC UK and Ireland Province has been suspended by the party's leadership in

Harare. A letter from MDC Secretary General Tendai Biti spoke of financial irregularities, poor performance and 'disfunctionality'. The Vigil could add many other reasons. Since former Assistant Police Commissioner Jonathan Chawora was foisted on the membership going on two years ago, the MDC in the UK has gone steadily downhill. All its efforts have gone into fundraising but it seems Harare has seen none of the funds. Where has the money gone? The Vigil has a good idea. Well, the party leaders in Harare are to send an investigating committee to find out. The Vigil can tell the committee that the disgraced UK executive has done nothing to publicise the plight of Zimbabwe or promote the party to the British public. Instead it has devoted its energy to trying to undermine the Vigil – sometimes with veiled threats of violence. Gertrude Hambara, General Secretary of the General Agricultural and Plant Workers Union of Zimbabwe, dropped in at the Vigil. Earlier in the week she had addressed the All-Party Parliamentary Committee on Zimbabwe and said the MDC needed to move into rural communities before they became 'no-go areas'.

Tuesday 15th December: Vigil supporters spoke to Ben Freeth at a private screening at the Foreign and Commonwealth Office of a documentary about his persecution 'Mugabe and the White African'. He also expressed thanks to the Vigil for our work in continuing to expose the absence of the rule of law in Zimbabwe. This award-winning film will be shown all over the world and will do much to puncture the propaganda by both Zanu PF and the MDC that things are returning to normal in Zimbabwe.

Friday 18th December: Vigil members attended a meeting addressed by the human rights activist Jestina Mukoko. She expressed gratitude to the Vigil for our support when she was in prison being tortured and spoke of 'unsung heroes'. Jestina warned that the Mugabe regime had learned nothing from her case and were continuing to perpetrate atrocities.

2010

Highlights

January: Prime Minister Tsvangirai calls for the easing of targeted sanctions, saying the Unity Government's progress should be rewarded.

January: Zimbabwe's High Court rejects a SADC Tribunal ruling against President Mugabe's farm seizures.

March: New 'indigenisation' law to force foreign-owned businesses to sell majority stake to locals.

12th June: Vigil walkout shows split with MDC over Government of National Unity.

14th June: New British Foreign Secretary William Hague assures Vigil no change of policy on Zimbabwe.

3rd July: MDC Deputy Prime Minister spurns Vigil.

10th July: Vigil diary expresses despair at British diplomacy.

24th July: MDC ministers 'descending like locusts' on London whitewashing the GNU.

29th July: Vigil attacked by MDC on front page of the Herald.

August: Zimbabwe resumes official diamond sales amid controversy over human rights abuses at the Marange diamond fields.

September: Prime Minister Tsvangirai says Zanu PF instigated violence at public consultations on new constitution.

October: UK ends moratorium on sending home failed Zimbabwean asylum seekers.

13th November: 'Chilling experience of back-slapping hypocrisy' – Vigil's description of UK's explanation of Zimbabwe policy.

December: Zanu PF nominates President Mugabe as presidential candidate in next elections.

Vigil Diary Excerpts

Saturday 9th January: Snow at the Vigil. It's our eighth winter protesting outside the Embassy but the first time it has snowed . . . To protect us from the elements we used two tarpaulins – one to catch the snow and the other as a windbreak. During the week the Vigil sent the following letter to the International Development Committee of the

British Parliament, which is to review the British government's aid to Zimbabwe. 'The Zimbabwe Vigil wishes to express its opposition to any dilution of the pressure on Mugabe and his cronies until they comply fully with the Global Political Agreement signed with the two MDC factions in September 2008. We believe, in particular, that to give development aid to the coalition government is premature and will send the wrong signals . . . '

Saturday 16th January: The Vigil has revived its petition to the international football federation to move the soccer World Cup from South Africa in response to President Zuma's cynical suggestion that the MDC should simply accept that Mugabe would not implement the agreement he signed 16 months ago. Zuma said the MDC should 'park' the issues in contention. The Vigil believes that, by not addressing the human rights issues in Zimbabwe, Zuma is putting the whole region in danger. He needs to take another shower (a reference to his defence against AIDS).

Saturday 30th January: With the failure of the SADC-mediated talks to resolve differences over the Global Political Agreement, the Vigil launched a new petition calling for elections as soon as possible. The petition to President Zuma read: 'After a year of the Zimbabwe interim government it is clear that it is going nowhere so we call on President Zuma as mediator for the Southern African Development Community to arrange free and fair elections as soon as possible.' We intend to submit the petition to the South African High Commission during President Zuma's state visit to Britain in March.

Saturday 6th February: This week we sent Morgan Tsvangirai a petition we have been running for several months urging the MDC to stop co-operating with Mugabe. The petition reads 'Petition to the Zimbabwean Prime Minister, Morgan Tsvangirai. We urge you to refuse to co-operate with President Mugabe until he respects the rule of law and complies fully with the agreement under which the Zimbabwean coalition government was formed last February.'

Mugabe Birthday Protest – Saturday 20th February: Swigging appropriately from a Methuselah of champagne, a swaggering (or was it swaying) Robert Mugabe, accompanied by Amazing Grace, celebrated his 86th birthday at the Zimbabwe Embassy. Mugabe (in the Vigil mask) visited the nearby South African High Commission to pay his disrespects ahead of President Zuma's visit to London displaying a sign reading 'No Zumabwe'. Presents for Mugabe were labelled Giles Mutsekwa (Co-Minister of Home Affairs), Elias Mudzuri (Minister of Energy and Power Development) and Murisi Zwizwai (Deputy Minister of Mines) – the MDC ministers being investigated by the party on allegations of joining the corrupt Zanu PF gravy train.

Saturday 27th February: The Vigil wrote to the South African High Commissioner in London requesting permission to present our petition to President Zuma when he calls at the High Commission during his State Visit in March. A copy of a Vigil letter to Zuma was included. "The Zimbabwe Vigil is pleased that you are supporting elections in Zimbabwe in 2011, as envisaged in the Global Political Agreement. We are aware that politicians in Zimbabwe don't want new elections until they have had their fill at the trough but we believe that the situation can only worsen until there is a democratically elected government in place. What Zimbabweans want to know from you is how SADC can ensure that the elections are free and fair, given that Zanu PF has already reactivated militia bases and refuses to implement the GPA."

Thursday 4th March: Vigil supporters attended a meeting at the Royal Commonwealth Society on 'The Role of the Media in Zimbabwe's Transition' at which the BBC journalist Sue Lloyd-Roberts spoke about her recent damning report 'The polarised lives of Zimbabwe's rich and poor'. The Vigil's Ephraim Tapa took part in a BBC radio debate. He wiped the floor with Blessing Miles-Tendi of Oxford University who had written a piece advocating the lifting of sanctions.

South Africa House protest to greet President Zuma – Friday 5th March: Our message was: elections cannot come soon enough provided that the international community can ensure that they are free and fair. Our petition outlining this was delivered to the High Comission. Mugabe (in the Vigil's mask) was present to greet his friend Zuma with the following placards: 'Thank you Zuma', 'Bring me my machine gun' and 'Have another wife on me'. Zuma's appeal for the lifting of targeted sanctions against Mugabe and his gang went down like a lead balloon. It made him seem out of touch with reality. Here's what the Times said in a leading article 'Jacob Zuma is hard to take seriously, but his support of Robert Mugabe is a disgrace'. The real message to Zuma was in the spontaneous booing from more than 100 Zimbabweans and the chant of 'Shame on you' when he arrived. We were joined by some South Africans who shouted something like 'Ag Ag Zuma is Kak', whatever that means.

Saturday 6th March: We were told that we were joined by actor Jeremy Irons during the singing of Ishe Komberera / Nkosi Sikeleli. Judge for yourself – picture 2128 in album Zimbabwe Vigil 06/03/2010 on our Flickr page which can be accessed from our website. Many famous actors have dropped by in the past including Tim Robbins, Emma Thompson and Simon Callow. We are grateful for their support.

Saturday 13th March: The Vigil launched a petition to the UN Security Council calling on it to ensure that the elections are not stolen again. The petition reads: 'We call on the Security Council to ensure that the next elections in Zimbabwe are free and fair. We look to the United Nations to supervise the electoral process and the handover of power to a new government and believe peace-keeping troops will need to be in place before, during and after the polling.' As we explained to President

Zuma, Vigil supporters believe that the situation in Zimbabwe can only worsen the longer elections are delayed. Our argument is that:

- After a year of the interim unitary government it is clear that it is making no progress. If anything it is going backwards. The Mugabe regime has shown that it is determined to cling to power and that it will block real change, such as a free media and independent judiciary, so new elections are the only way forward.
- The situation will steadily deteriorate as long as Mugabe and his gang remain in power. Finance Minister Tendai Biti has admitted his hoped-for foreign budgetary aid and external investment will not be realised and, on top of that, the national exchequer has seen zero benefit from the exploitation of the Chiadzwa diamond fields. The Vigil rejects the argument that lifting or suspending targeted sanctions will make the Mugabe regime more conciliatory. On the contrary, we are convinced that appeasing the regime will only encourage it in its intransigence. We believe that the Mugabe gang fears that any change will lead to their prosecution for human rights and other abuses and that it is up to South Africa – as their supporter over the years – to make arrangements for the future of these criminals.
- In particular, Vigil supporters reject the notion that sanctions should be lifted because they are misrepresented by the Mugabe regime as sanctions against Zimbabweans in general. We believe the proper answer to Mugabe's propaganda is to patiently convey the truth to Zimbabweans and deluded Mugabe sympathizers in Africa and elsewhere. The Allies in the Second World War did not defeat national socialism, Italian fascism and Japanese militarism by bowing to their odious propaganda.

Sunday 4th April: A special Prayer Vigil for Zimbabwe outside the Zimbabwe Embassy on Easter Day was attended by about 100 people. It took place after a procession from nearby St Martin-in-the-Fields Church where Vigil supporter Josephine Zhuga led the choir.

Independence Day Protest – Saturday 17th April: The Vigil marked Zimbabwe's 30th anniversary of Independence with a big attendance during which we left thirty candles at the South African High Commission to remind them of their obligation to help us achieve true independence. We were joined by Lovemore Matombo of the Zimbabwe

Congress of Trade Unions and Gabriel Shumba of the Zimbabwe Exiles Forum. Another visitor to the Vigil was Mr Mugabe (in our Mugabe mask). He joined us at the South African High Commission with a placard reading 'Thanks Comrade Malema'. He reappeared later outside the Zimbabwe Embassy with a bottle of wine and large glass and a placard reading 'Here's to another 30 years'.

Satuday 1st May: The Vigil marked May Day by supporting an appeal from Amnesty International for the Zimbabwean authorities to stop intimidating and harassing human rights activists. People at the Vigil carried placards reading: 'May Day Appeal - End Human Rights Abuses in Zimbabwe', 'May Day Appeal - Protect Human Rights Activists in Zimbabwe' and 'Vigil Supports Oppressed Trade Unionists in Zimbabwe'. Amnesty International official Shane Enright said: "It's so important that people around the world stand in solidarity with the brave human rights and trade union activists in Zimbabwe this May Day. Our message to the police and security services is that we are watching you and will call you to account, however long it takes."

Monday 3rd May: Many Vigil supporters attended the London Citizens and Citizens UK pre-election assembly with David Cameron, Nick Clegg and Gordon Brown at the Methodist Central Hall, Westminster. The immigration question was at the heart of the meeting. One of the questions raised was about the welfare of children detained with their parents in immigration centres and there were promises to look into this.

Saturday 8th May: The Vigil received an email from James Chidakwa about a commemoration for his friend and fellow activist Tonderai Ndira who was brutally murdered two years ago. Reports say that he had been shot in the heart, with multiple stab wounds, his eyes gouged, his tongue cut out, and his neck, skull, jaw and knuckles broken.

Tuesday 11th May: Vigil supporters attended a memorial for Tonderai Ndira. They reported that it was a moving occasion as they remembered the horrors meted out to Tonderai two years ago. Money was raised to support Tonderai's family.

Saturday 29th May: The Vigil sent letter to the Foreign Secretary William Hague calling on the new British government to support our demand for early elections in Zimbabwe and urging the British government to ensure peacekeeping troops are sent to Zimbabwe to prevent Mugabe from stealing the elections.

Saturday 12th June: Mugabe (in our mask) popped up at the Vigil to demand that the next World Cup should be held in Zimbabwe to celebrate his 90th birthday. The Vigil sported England flags and placards wishing the England football team good luck in the competition. We are also running a World Cup draw for Vigil supporters. Two prominent human rights activists from Zimbabwe visited the Vigil: Irene Petras of Zimbabwe Lawyers for Human Rights and Roselyn Hanzi, the Project Manager for both the Human Rights Defenders Unit and the Constitutional Reform and Policy Formulation Unit. Addressing the Vigil, Irene said Zimbabweans in the diaspora should hesitate to go home until the rule of law was restored and human rights were respected. During the week a number of Vigil supporters attended a House of Lords debate on Zimbabwe. Management team member Patson Muzuwa said that afterwards a number of peers who took part in the debate said they were very disappointed at the failure of South Africa to resolve the Zimbabwe crisis. Vigil supporters attended two events to launch 'Zimbabwe – Years of Hope and Despair' a book by Philip Barclay a diplomat who was based at the British Embassy in Harare from 2006 – 2009. Vigil people walked out of the first meeting, hosted by the MDC Central London Forum, when a Mugabe apologist was given a platform to spout Zanu PF propaganda at length. One Vigil supporter said she was not prepared to listen to someone who supported murderers, rapists and torturers. At the official book launch later in the week Mr Barclay said he had been interested to see this division in the Zimbabwean diaspora in London.

Media Release from the Zimbabwe Vigil – Monday 14th June:
Hague: New government to continue policy on Zimbabwe: Reply to Vigil letter from new British Foreign Secretary, William Hague. He made it clear there will no change of policy on Zimbabwe. 'I am aware of the good work the Zimbabwe Vigil does in keeping alive the pressure for reform in Zimbabwe. It is dispiriting to consider just how long the people of Zimbabwe have been waiting for the opportunity to express their views in free and fair elections and to be able to contribute to the revival of a prosperous and democratic country . . . I wish the Zimbabwe Vigil

every success in achieving their aim of a peaceful and democratic Zimbabwe.'

Saturday 26th June: The Vigil provided the choir and drummers for a church service in support of Zimbabwean victims of torture. Speakers at the service included the Rev Useni Sibanda (National Director of Zimbabwe Christian Alliance) who joined a procession to the Vigil where he paid tribute to the Vigil for carrying on the struggle for so long.

Saturday 3rd July: The Zimbabwean Deputy Prime Minister, Thokozani Khupe (MDC T), has spurned opportunities to meet the Vigil during her week long visit to London beginning on 4th July. This does not surprise us. We suspect we are seen as a noisy embarrassment by the MDC leadership as they burrow deeper into the fertile ground of Zimbabwean government corruption.

Thursday 8th July: The following piece appears in the Londoner's Diary of the London Evening Standard. *Zimbabwean deputy PM upsets exiles: 'What not to wear to the Commonwealth Society . . . Zimbabwe's Deputy Prime Minister Ms Thokozani Khupe, who was a popular anti-Robert Mugabe figure before she joined the government after the 2008 elections, is in London but has upset sometime supporters by demanding they put on their gladrags and pay up to get an audience with her. Ms Khupe spoke at the Royal Commonwealth Society in Northumberland Avenue last night. Members of the Zimbabwe Vigil, who demonstrate against human rights abuses outside the Zimbabwe Embassy in The Strand every Saturday, had been surprised to be invited to meet her face to face at a dinner after the event. The catch was the ticket price and the dress code. Leaders of the Vigil find it offensive that, with Zimbabwe producing more asylum seekers than any other country, diners were expected to pay £25 for the dinner and to wear lounge suits or cocktail dresses. "With 158,000 Zimbabweans seeking asylum from the coalition government in 2009, Khupe's dinner is just one more sign of how unreal the Movement for Democratic Change elite are becoming," writes Dennis Benton in the Zimbabwe Vigil Diary. "Not many of the Zimbabwean asylum seekers in the UK have a lounge suit or a cocktail dress. Those Zimbabweans likely to go to this event are well-connected Zanu PF people [Mugabe's party] of whom there all too many in the UK. Benton notes that, as a close MDC associate of former opposition leader and now Prime Minister Morgan Tsvangirai, Khupe was once a popular figure. "We repeat our* *invitation to Ms Khupe to come to the Vigil and talk to some of the ordinary Zimbabweans who can't afford £25," says Benton, a former BBC man.'* Unfortunately Ms Khupe did not attend the Vigil. Security issues were mentioned . . . As a representative of the Zimbabwe government she would have been perfectly safe outside her own Embassy and we are right next door to Charing Cross Police who would have policed the Vigil if we requested it.

Friday 9th July: Vigil supporters attended a meeting at Lancaster House at which Mark Canning, British Ambassador to Zimbabwe, spoke on "The politics and situation in Zimbabwe and the UK Government's response". (The meeting was held under Chatham House rules that there should be no direct attribution of any information and that it was for background use.)

Saturday 10th July: The immortal Dr Pangloss was a character in Voltaire's novel Candide – immortal not least because he is now working for the British Foreign Office. Pangloss was super-optimistic. Amid the chaos of the Lisbon earthquake 250 years ago he could still maintain 'All is for the best in the best of all possible worlds'. This appears to be the attitude of the Foreign Office towards the chaos in Zimbabwe. It sees steady progress (although at a 'glacial speed'). There are good things happening, we are told. In fact we should jolly well think of going back to enjoy them. A different picture emerges from a former British diplomat in Harare, Philip Barclay, in his book 'Years of Hope and Despair'. Barclay has been promoting his book in London and points to continuing disregard of the rule of law and the increasing acquiescence of the MDC within the unity government. Soundings at the Vigil suggest that Barclay's take is closer to reality than the line now being peddled by the Foreign Office. The diaspora cannot accept progress at a 'glacial' pace. We'll all be dead before we can go home. In that case why is the Home Office not told to let Zimbabwean failed asylum seekers work here? The Vigil does not believe that this is all that can be achieved. We think the British government should put renewed pressure on SADC countries to meet their obligations to Zimbabwe. In particular, we want to know what is being done to ensure free and fair elections. Britain should use its financial muscle. After all, it is British taxpayers' generosity that is helping to prop up these countries. The British government's softly softly approach is more surprising given a damning report by international legal bodies on the state of law in Zimbabwe which was launched recently at a meeting in parliament The report was compiled by a mission which included representatives of the Bar Council, the Commonwealth Lawyers' Association and Avocats Sans Frontieres among others. It says the power sharing deal has failed to stop extra-judicial killings, kidnappings and torture. The report adds that human rights abuses continue to occur and go uninvestigated by the authorities. 'Access to justice is virtually non-existent' it says.

Saturday 24th July: Senator David Coltart, the Zimbabwean Minister for Education, was given a friendly reception when he came to the Vigil at the end of his visit to London – a welcome that turned to cheers when he put on our bracelet 'Mugabe Must Go'. Surrounded by Vigil supporters, he said 'I know that many of you are very sceptical about this inclusive government. But I want to let you know that there is a group working very hard to make it work. Don't write it off. But you do need to continue the Vigil because things are by no means right yet. We are all looking for the same thing: a democratic Zimbabwe where everyone can hold their heads up high.' We were pleased that Senator Coltart took the trouble to join us – even though many of us don't share his optimism. Some Vigil supporters went to hear him during the week when he spoke at a meeting in Parliament about the dire situation in the Zimbabwean education system. Who could be against giving money towards education in Zimbabwe – even if Zanu PF gangsters are looting the country's own resources that should be paying for it? Senator Coltart was only one of a horde of MDC leaders descending like locusts on London with their begging bowls. It's all very well giving money to education but the two other MDC ministers and the Deputy Prime Minister Mutambara were shaking the can for investment. They seem to have difficulty grasping that people are reluctant to invest in a country with no rule of law. A large contingent of our supporters went to hear Mutambara speak at a London meeting after the Vigil. Apart from telling us about his massive intellect and brilliant education, he urged people with skills and capital to go home, brushing aside questions of violence and good governance, though he admitted a lot of work still had to be done. An unexpected addition to the ranks of the Pollyannas who see nothing wrong with Zimbabwe is the new Director of the British Council in Harare Jill Coates. She said "Zimbabwe is such a beautiful and peaceful country and not at all hostile like what is perceived in the UK media." The columnist

Muckraker in the Zimbabwean newspaper the Independent said 'What do we call these remarks? Naïve or downright stupid?' The British Council no doubt keeps the British Sunday Times in its library. She will see in its latest edition new revelations about the scandal of the Marange diamonds.

Thursday 29th July: The Vigil made the front page of the Zimbabwe Herald this week. We are mentioned in the Herald's interview with Hebson Makuvise, Zimbabwe's Ambassador to Germany. He reportedly says of activists in the UK "Every Saturday they gather at the Zimbabwean Embassy in the UK playing drums denouncing President Mugabe, Prime Minister Tsvangirai and the inclusive Government. They are then given some money by tourists who visit the embassy in the name of the suffering masses of Zimbabwe." He said he has tried without success to dissuade the activists from carrying out such activities . . . Makuvise, Tsvangirai's uncle and former representative in the UK, tried to control the Vigil as he did the MDC in the UK. We can't forget how he thundered down to the Vigil with his goons and, oblivious to the irony, waved his fist at the Vigil Co-ordinator saying 'How dare you accuse me of being a bully-boy!' The latest development is that Ambassador Makuvise says he is instituting legal proceedings against the Zimdiaspora website which has published a report said to have been leaked from Tsvangirai's office which detailed alleged financial irregularities in the MDC UK and strongly criticized Makuvise. (Nothing further has been heard of these legal proceedings . . .)

Saturday 31st July: While both Mugabe and Tsvangirai have been seeking support from apostolic Christians, the Vigil was surprised to be joined by a large group of Zimbabwean Christians. We were grateful for their prayers – and touched when they prayed for those on our register. Dressed in white robes, they said they had come to London to spread peace. They are members of Friday Apostles 'Johane Masowe We Chishanu' and have a base in Sheffield in the north of England. We were glad to be joined by a Vigil activist we helped to escape from Zimbabwe. He said he was picked up on a recent trip home and randomly beaten up on the way to the police station. He was held in cells for 2 days in indescribable conditions and would probably still be there if we hadn't got legal help to get him out. The experience left him 2 kgs lighter.

Saturday 7th August: 'Zuma Save Zimbabwe' was the theme of the Vigil as SADC prepares to hold a summit meeting in Namibia. Our banners urging South African intervention have so far failed to bear fruit but we were pleased that Mugabe's attempt to keep Zimbabwe off the agenda seems to have failed. As the recent AU Summit in Uganda showed, African leaders are all too willing to sweep Zimbabwe under the carpet on the basis that SADC has been handed the responsibility. Vigil supporters believe that, after eighteen months of Zanu PF arrogance in refusing to implement the GPA, South Africa and SADC must now force Mugabe's hand. The Vigil urges SADC to address the real issue: how to ensure that elections are free and fair.

Saturday 14th August: A strong supporter of the Zimbabwe Vigil has been a Swazi lady Thobile Gwebu, who in January started a Vigil outside the Swaziland High Commission in London in protest at human rights abuses in her homeland. We were shocked that the UK Home Office has seen fit to detain her for immediate deportation and people at the Vigil signed a petition to the Home Office on her behalf. *'The Zimbabwe Vigil is appalled that her asylum claim has been turned down and that she is to be handed over to this medieval despot, who would like to spend the country's meagre revenues on a Boeing to fly his 14 wives to the fleshpots of the world.'*

Saturday 21st August: We are glad to say that the deportation of our Swazi friend Thobile Gwebu has been halted although she is still in detention.

Thursday 26th August: Vigil Co-ordinator Dumi Tutani was on a panel at a screening of 'Mugabe and the White African' in London on Thursday. Director Lucy Bailey was very pleased to have a black Zimbabwean's views. Dumi stressed that the problems in Zimbabwe were not caused by the white farmers and the land issue but by a corrupt government determined to stay in power at all costs.

Saturday 18th September: *Protest to mark the second anniversary of the signing of the Zimbabwean Global Political Agreement.* Comrade Mugabe – despite reports of ill-health – was fit enough to join our demonstration outside the South African High Commission. But mentally he seems to have lost it, judging by the mis-spellings in the poster he was carrying: 'SADC Final: Mugabwe 10, Zumabwe 0'. But the scornful message was clear. The demonstration marked the expiry of the 30-day deadline given by SADC for the leaders of the unity government to settle the issues outstanding from the Global Political Agreement signed two years ago this month. We were happy to be joined by our Swazi friend and supporter Thobile Gwebu just released from detention.

Saturday 25th September: During the week the Vigil sent the following message to the South American so-called Anglican cleric who invited Mugabe to Ecuador to receive an honorary doctorate. 'Dear Revd Dr Walter Roberto Crespo: the Zimbabwe Vigil wishes to add our support to Genocide Watch in protest at your proposal to honour Robert Mugabe . . .'

Zimbabwe Vigil's 8th Anniversary – Saturday 9th October: Robert Mugabe drinking coffee out of an MDC mug and pouring in spoonfuls of salt was the centrepiece of our 8th anniversary Vigil – until he fell asleep. Featuring our well-used Mugabe mask, it was prompted by a report that Mugabe hadn't been able to taste the difference between sugar and salt at a recent reception for diplomats in Harare – and a picture of him fast asleep at the UN (along with some of his 79 companions!).

Saturday 16th October: The banners we have been displaying outside the London Embassy for eight years inspired posters we attached to luggage to represent the feared consequences of deportation hanging over failed Zimbabwean asylum seekers: 'Back to Murder, Rape and Torture in Zimbabwe' and 'Back to Mugabe and Starvation'. Given Morgan Tsvangirai's nauseating love-ins with Mugabe over the past 20 months, Vigil supporters were not surprised by the British government's decision to end the moratorium on returning failed asylum seekers to Zimbabwe. Whether Tsvangirai is currently flipping or flopping makes no difference now: he has been telling the world that the GNU is working and that Zimbabwe is a safe place so we could hardly expect any other decision by the British government.

Saturday 23rd October: Supporters signed the following petition to the Home Secretary, Theresa May: 'We the undersigned, members of the Zimbabwean Diaspora in the UK and sympathisers, express our grave disquiet at the UK government's announcement that failed Zimbabwean asylum seekers are to be deported – even before the hearing of a test (country guidance) case is concluded . . .'

Sunday 24th October: *MEDIA NOTICE – Zimbabweans in UK say 'Don't send us back to Mugabe'.* Zimbabwean exiles in the UK are to stage a demonstration against deportations at a meeting to be addressed by a senior Home Office official at Lancaster House in London on Wednesday, 27th October. Ephraim Tapa, a prominent Zimbabwean human rights activist in the UK, said 'It is deeply disturbing that the British government seems to have predetermined the outcome of the court case. We did not expect this in the UK.' Mr Tapa was sceptical about the findings of a British mission to Zimbabwe this year which found that 'Zimbabwe is for many people a safer and better place to live than it was in 2008'. Mr Tapa said 'the stolen elections of 2008 were drenched in blood. New elections are planned for next year and we expect similar bloodshed unless peacekeepers are sent to the country'.

No Returns before Elections! – Wednesday 27th October: About 300 Zimbabweans gathered at Lancaster House for a meeting to hear a senior Home Office official Phil Douglas answer questions on the sudden ending of the four year moratorium on sending home failed Zimbabwean asylum seekers. He dismissed fears that the move would influence the decision of a team of judges presently considering the Zimbabwe country guidance case. Few of his audience were satisfied by his explanations. There was laughter when Mr Douglas said that returned people could relocate to different areas. Many people expressed fears of renewed violence during next year's elections. There was a cry of 'blood on your hands'. The British government team suggested that Zimbabwean concerns about the policy should be channelled through an organisation of their creation, the Zimbabwe Diaspora Focus Group. The Zimbabwe Vigil / ROHR's views are that they do not want to be represented by any other group and this was reaffirmed at a briefing after the meeting to the large group of Zimbabweans who had waited patiently outside. Mr Douglas agreed to accept our petition and hand it on.

Saturday 13th November: If the British government has any strategy to ensure that the promised elections in Zimbabwe are free and fair it is not letting on. That's the conclusion reached by Vigil supporters who attended a meeting at the Chatham House think-tank in London addressed by the Minister for Africa, Henry Bellingham, and the British Ambassador to Zimbabwe, Mark Canning. The Chatham House rule, under which remarks are not attributed, was lifted for the occasion. There was no need: Chair Robin Niblett summed the speakers up as tiptoeing and cautious. There was nothing that wasn't diplomat-speak except, perhaps, the observation by the Ambassador that he had little doubt that most of the high grade diamonds from Marange were 'going out of the back door'. But that's pretty obvious. Apart from that, no one – including the third member of the panel Zimbabwean academic Knox Chitiyo – had anything to say except blithe platitudes: the unity government is making a difference, the economy is looking up, violence is down. In fact, there has been 'remarkable progress', according to Her Majesty's Ambassador – though he admitted that the 80 – 90% of people unemployed might not notice.

The panel was asked by Geoff Hill of the Washington Times whether there could be an election or hand-over of power given Zanu PF's control of the police, army, CIO and youth militia. The Ambassador dodged it by saying he didn't know when the election would take place . . . Gerry Jackson of SW Radio Africa stood up and asked, to applause, about the increasing violence in rural areas being reported to them by their contacts every day and the desperation of people to ensure that their vote was not a death sentence. Minister Bellingham, who had spoken of an improvement in the human rights situation, was stung to say that the UK wants a comprehensive election monitoring system – 'but it's not for us to say how it should be organised . . . ' His main interest, it appeared, was how Britain could boost trade. It was, all in all, a chilling experience of backslapping hypocrisy. Diplomacy used to be defined as being sent abroad to lie for your country. Now you only have to go to Chatham House in St James Square. Further light on the meeting was cast when we learnt that an honoured guest was Zanu PF's Tourism Minister Walter Mzembi, in London to launch an attempt to attract visits by rich, fat and stupid murungus. Mzembi, a firm supporter of the army's involvement in politics, was delighted by the supine gushing of Canning and Bellingham. He told NewZimbabwe the meeting was 'a sign that the British are now ready to engage constructively' and 'they want to be less critical of Zanu PF and President Mugabe'. A different view of the situation in Zimbabwe was given by the President of ROHR Ephraim Tapa when he spoke at the Vigil. He said Zimbabweans in the UK were being sold down the river by a British government more interested in trade than principle.

Saturday 4th December: It was good to be visited by Judith Todd, the Zimbabwean human rights champion, who was briefly in London. She said how encouraged she was that we were still going and how she looked forward to reading our diary every week.

Saturday 11th December: The day began well when we received a large box of money. Always welcome. The box came from an anonymous donor with the message: 'We heard your protest vigil needed some money – enjoy'. The message continued 'proudly printed in Zimbabwe and smuggled out to you by some brave friends'. It seems that Mugabe's personal bonker has started a new bank, the Reverse Bank. We now have a pile of new billion, trillion and zillion dollar notes all with pictures of Gono and Grace.

Saturday 18th December: Snow fell steadily in London during the morning and it was impossible to bring the Vigil paraphernalia by car. So for the first time ever we had to have a skeleton Vigil: no drums, tables etc – just the bare necessities, such as our banners reading: 'No to Mugabe, No to Starvation' and 'End Murder, Rape and Torture in Zimbabwe'.

2011

Highlights

February: EU eases sanctions by lifting the freeze of assets of 35 Mugabe people.

12th February: Vigil marks second anniversary of GNU: 'two years forward for GNU – 2 years backward for MDC'.

19th February: 'Mugabe' appears at Vigil to launch two-million person petition against sanctions.

26th February: 'Mugabe' reappears in Arab robes to show solidarity with Gaddafi.

1st March: mock execution of Mugabe at Vigil.

March: Prime Minister Tsvangirai says unity government rendered impotent by Zanu PF violence and disregard for power-sharing agreement.

21st March: demonstrations outside Embassy and SA High Commission over Zanu PF violence.

26th April: Vigil supporters help chase Swazi king from Mayfair hotel.

4th June: Vigil attended by one of UK's best-known poets Benjamin Zephaniah: He condemns Mugabe.

30th July: UK Border Agency apologises to Vigil.

August: one of Zanu PF's leaders, General Solomon Mujuru, dies in suspicious fire.

November: the Kimberley process, which regulates the global diamond industry, lifts ban on export of diamonds from two Marange fields.

December: Mugabe says he will run in the next elections and describes the power-sharing government as a monster.

Vigil Diary Excerpts

Saturday 15th January: We had to call for police help for only the second time in our eight years outside the Embassy. This time it was a demented pro-Mugabe Caribbean shouting abuse. The last time we had to call for police help was when Tsvangirai's uncle Hebson Makuvise, now Ambassador to Germany, tried to hijack the Vigil.

Saturday 12th February: As Egyptians celebrated the downfall of President Mubarak, the Vigil marked the second anniversary of Zimbabwe's Government of National Unity with posters expressing our disgust at how the agreement has rescued Zanu PF and emasculated the MDC. We are still bewildered why MDC leaders signed up to such a flawed document. 'Two years forward for GNU – two years backward for MDC' read one of our posters. We are angry that the agreement's SADC guarantors have allowed Mugabe to get away with murder. 'Two years of GNU – two years of violence and looting' read another poster. Vigil supporters are disgusted that the opposition is more occupied in fighting among themselves than against Zanu PF.

With the quasi-legitimacy conferred by the GNU, Zanu PF is making further inroads in the UK. We have always had the families of Zanu PF bigwigs here of course – for education, to look after investments etc. Then there are the dozens of CIO people working for the Embassy . . . The Guardian newspaper reported recently that 32 suspected Zanu PF war criminals are believed to be in the UK. Among the dubious Zimbabwean organizations springing up here is 'Zimbabwe Achievers UK' who have announced a 'short' list of about 160 nominees for awards in some 30 categories. Surprisingly there is not a specific category for 'Zimbabwe war criminal' or 'Zanu PF propagandist'. But Vigil supporters noticed the inclusion of long-standing Mugabe fan George Shire in the category 'Academic Award'. Diary readers may remember Shire from the Vigil's encounter with him in Lisbon in December 2007 when he mounted a rival demonstration in support of Mugabe who was attending an EU / AU summit meeting.

Saturday 19th February: The mystery of Mugabe's whereabouts as his 87th birthday approached was solved when he suddenly arrived at the Vigil to launch his planned two million person petition against the illegal sanctions which as you all know have done so much damage to our country by beating up innocent people, raping and starving them etc and generally sanctioning them with the aim of illegal regime change. The Commander-in-Chief and Head of Everything, Robert Mugabe (Dickson Munemo in our Mugabe mask) emerged tottering on walking sticks from Rymans Stationers next to the Vigil. He had apparently mistaken it for the optician's shop on the other side of the Embassy. Supported by First Lady Grace (played by Josephine Zhuga) he signed our petitions without looking at them saying 'Down with gay Bliar and all his friends' before falling asleep in our chair. The couple were greeted by Vigil supporters holding up placards saying: 'Mugabe's 87th Birthday – Time to Go', 'People Power in Tunisia, People Power in Egypt. Watch out Mugabe' and 'Ben Ali & the Forty thieves gone! Mubarak gone! Mugabe must go'. Asked how the President and Commander in Chef had evaded the illegal travel sanctions, Grace's personal helper, Reserve Bank Governor Gideon Gono, said the birthday boy had travelled very comfortably in Grace's fully-equipped shopping bag. Mr Gono, who is said to know something about these matters, seemed to think that all Zanu PF wives delisted from the illegal sanctions nightmare would soon be swooping on Harrods with the missing millions in diamond money.

We were pleased to be joined by two leaders of the Zimbabwe Human Rights Association (ZimRights): Kucaca Phulu (Chair) and Okay Machisa (Director). They are visiting London as part of a tour of six European countries to tell of what is going on in Zimbabwe. Mr Machisa launched into singing and dancing. He said every week he checked what was happening at the Vigil saying 'You at the Vigil are in our hearts'. For his part, Mr Phulu pointed to the Embassy and said 'One day freedom will walk out of that building and find you here.' He added he had been 'inspired and touched by the Vigil' and expressed his confidence that the wave of freedom would reach Zimbabwe.

'Mugdafi' at London Embassy – Saturday 26th February: The illustrious leader, icon, beacon, legend and philanthropist with telescopic foresight can't keep away from the Vigil. Tearing his illustrious self away from his adoring fans at his birthday celebrations, Mugabe suddenly materialized outside the Zimbabwe Embassy dressed in the robes of an Arab sheik to show his solidarity with his Libyan friend Gaddafi, who is apparently running short of power at the moment. Icon Mugdafi waved a pistol at our posters: 'Mugdafi = Mugabe + Gaddafi – Terrrible Twins' read one of them. Mugdafi said he was there to welcome the King of Kings of Africa who was expected to arrive in London at any moment to lead his promised revolution against Queen Elizabeth, who Gaddafi complained the other day had been in power even longer than himself but hadn't been subjected to the same illegal criticism. Mugdafi said he wanted to discuss with the King of Kings payment for the hundreds of Zimbabwean troops reported to have been sent to join the African mercenary force in Libya who have been shooting the 'drug-crazed' young people there. Of reports that a plane stuffed with gold was ready to take Gaddafi to Harare, the beacon and philanthropist said the great Libyan philosopher and prophet only wanted to visit his Ethiopian brother Mengistu Haile Mariam, who has been sheltering in Zimbabwe for many years, to discuss how ungrateful people are to their despots. The paranoia of the Mugabe regime has been illustrated by the arrest of more than 40 people for watching a video of the turmoil in the Middle East. This is apparently treason.

Mugabe 'executed' outside Embassy – Tuesday 1st March: President Mugabe was strung up from a tree outside the Zimbabwe Embassy in London today at a Vigil in support of an attempt to stage an anti-Mugabe demonstration in Harare. Security forces were beefed up to deter protesters from gathering at Harare gardens but in London some 50 people attended our mock execution of the aging tyrant. We were joined by a Reuters news team, apart from other journalists, and passers-by stopped to take photos with their mobile phones. Bus drivers hooted in solidarity as Terence Mafuva in our Mugabe mask and a white shroud dangled from the branch of a maple tree (discreetly supported by a small stool). The Vigil was pleased to get a message of encouragement from Passop, the Zimbabwe support group in South Africa, who were holding a solidarity demonstration outside Parliament in Cape Town.

Zimbabweans demonstrate in London against violence – Monday 21st March: Zimbabwean exiles in the UK and supporters demonstrated outside the Embassy and the South African High Commission in protest at the growing violence as Mugabe's Zanu PF prepares for new elections. Outside the Embassy prominent demonstrators included members of the Haldane Society of Socialist Lawyers who demanded the release of six Zimbabwean activists on trial for treason for watching a video about the uprising in Egypt. Amid drumming and singing, over a hundred demonstrators outside South Africa House carried banners reading 'Zuma where is our road map?', 'Blood on Zuma's hands', 'Zuma publish election dossier now', 'AU act now', 'Bloody SADC where are you? – wake up'. A deputation was sent to the Home Office to deliver a petition protesting at new moves to send home failed Zimbabwean asylum seekers.

Saturday 2nd April: The Vigil celebrated the imminent ousting of another illegal president – Laurent Gbagbo of Ivory Coast – whose clinging to power after losing the election last November has cost countless lives. Gbagbo's poisonous legacy – like Mugabe's – will blight his country for many years. But, mercifully, the victorious President Alassane Ouattara was not persuaded to accept the discredited Kenya / Zimbabwe model where the election winner is coerced into playing second fiddle to the incumbent loser – with the disastrous result we have seen in Zimbabwe. As Ouattara's forces closed in on Gbagbo in Abidjan, Vigil supporters played the West African drama out in front of the Zimbabwe Embassy in London. Fungayi Mabhunu, wearing our Mugabe mask, welcomed his Ivorian friend with the poster 'Zimbabwe – world of wonders: Mugabe, Mariam, Gbagbo? Gaddafi?' Gbagbo (played by Stanford Munetsi) bore on his back the poster 'G'bye G'bye G'bagbo'. Trailing behind the former Ivorian President was another Mugabe ally – Libya's Colonel Gaddafi – played by Paul Mathema in Arab robes.

Saturday 9th April: Vigil supporters were encouraged by indications of a change of attitude to Mugabe by SADC leaders meeting in Zambia. Have they been given the jitters by what is happening in North and West Africa? Mugabe's arrival by 'golf cart' at the Livingstone meeting with a huge entourage of 60 (including a large medical team) clearly exposed both his increasing frailty and the big-man arrogance of Zanu PF. (Zuma was accompanied by only 12 people.) Now that SADC leaders have been subjected to the vitriol spewing out of the Harare cesspit we hope they will be prepared for the next stage – how to confront Zanu PF's delaying tactics and arbitrary moves. As the Vigil has repeated warned, Zanu PF never changes: it always resorts to the same primitive but successful strategies of violence and vote rigging. Thanks to Fungayi Mabhunu for playing the role of Mugabe arriving at the Vigil on a municipal bicycle.

Saturday 16th April: Vigil supporters are disappointed that Mugabe's Ambassador to London has been invited to the Royal Wedding on 29th April. But the presence of Ambassador Machinga might be entertaining as he goes around Westminster Abbey soliciting signatures supporting the two million-person anti-sanctions petition. Zim Vigil regular, Swazi national Thobile Gwebu took a stronger line when she heard that King Mswati of Swaziland would be present at the wedding, travelling to London with an entourage of no less than fifty to stay at the super expensive Dorchester hotel. Thobile, who launched a Vigil outside the Swaziland High Commission in London modeled on our own protest, was able to reach a large audience by being interviewed on the BBC TV Newsnight programme which looked at the brutal repression of the recent unrest in Mbabane.

Monday 18th April: Some 150 people gathered outside the Zimbabwe Embassy to protest on Zimbabwe's Independence Day against increasing Mugabe violence. Ephraim Tapa summed up our mood on the 31st anniversary of independence: 'we have nothing to celebrate', he said. An anniversary card was delivered to the Zimbabwe Embassy calling for an immediate end to the violence, free and fair elections and justice for the people of Zimbabwe.

Wednesday 20th April: Following comments in the Vigil diary on 16th April, the London Evening Standard took up the matter of the invitation to the Zimbabwean Ambassador to attend the Royal Wedding of Prince William and Kate Middleton. After some research the newspaper concluded that the UK would be justified in withdrawing the invitation so the Vigil sent the following letter to British Foreign Secretary William Hague. *'Exiled Zimbabweans in the UK represented by the Zimbabwe Vigil wish to express their disappointment that the Zimbabwe*

Ambassador. Gabriel Machinga, has been invited to attend the Royal Wedding. President Mugabe and his corrupt coterie have rightly been placed under EU sanctions for their human rights abuses and Mr Machinga has always made it clear that he represents Mugabe and not the people of Zimbabwe or even their coalition government'.

Tuesday 26th April: ZimVigil supporters had to search Mayfair when Swazi despot Mswati and his entourage of 50 failed to turn up at London's deluxe Dorchester Hotel to stay for the Royal Wedding. About 80 demonstrators had gathered outside the hotel to support the Swaziland Vigil which had arranged a picket of protest against Mswati's oppressive rule – only to find that the Swazi freeloaders had gone to the nearby Four Seasons Hotel. Mswati had obviously got the message as members of his entourage at the Four Seasons were overheard talking about our demonstration, which had attracted much media attention with protesters carrying posters such as 'Swazi King parties while country starves' and 'Royal Wedding guests are human rights abusers'.

Saturday 30th April: Vigil supporters ended another busy week picketing the farewell reception given by Swazi King Mswati. No sooner had we ended our regular Saturday Vigil outside the Embassy than we were off to join our fellow human rights campaigners of the Swaziland Vigil outside the Four Seasons Hotel in Mayfair. Guests appeared uncomfortable when they saw the protest. The Swaziland High Commissioner Dumsile T Sukati jumped out of her car and hurried into the building. Despite the failure of our appeals to the British government to withdraw the invitations to the wedding extended to Mswati and the Zimbabwe Ambassador Gabriel Machinga, we were compensated by the widespread publicity for our joint human rights cause. The Foreign Office said in a letter to the Vigil 'Thank you for your letter of 20th April 2011 about the invite of the Zimbabwe Ambassador Gabriel Machinga to the Royal Wedding. Representatives from all countries that the UK has working relationships with have been invited to the Royal Wedding . . .'

Saturday 14th May: The demand for change is steadily moving down Africa judging from the reception given to Mugabe and other African leaders attending the installation for another term of Ugandan perpetual President Museveni. Their motorcade was assailed by stone-throwing protesters shouting 'Go to hell dictators' and 'You dictators: we are tired of you'. These messages were reflected in posters displayed by Vigil supporters. The traditional English dancers the Morris Men made their annual visit to us and gave us a good show. Vigil management team member Fungayi Mabhunu drew a laugh from them when he said 'it was good to see Englishmen dancing like Zimbabweans'.

Saturday 21st May: To help focus the minds of SADC leaders the Vigil has been pushing the British government to suspend aid to countries supporting Mugabe. This is a substantial amount. Britain is one of the very few countries – if not the only one – to honour the Gleneagles Agreement of 2005 under which the world's richest countries committed themselves to giving 0.7% of their national income in foreign aid. In Britain's case this will amount this year to £8.1 billion (rising to £11.5 billion in 2014 /15). All this is at a time of stringent budget cuts in the UK. Here is a letter the Vigil has sent to the Defence Secretary, Dr Fox, who wants a more nuanced approach to how British government aid is allocated. *'The Zimbabwe Vigil notes with interest your recent comments and fully supports demands for a more flexible approach to the UK's overseas aid . . . Of particular interest to us is budgetary aid given to member countries of the Southern African Development Community (SADC), amounting to many hundreds of millions of pounds a year. SADC has betrayed the people of Zimbabwe by pandering to the odious Mugabe regime for the past decade . . . Take, for instance, the notoriously corrupt regime in the Democratic Republic of Congo, which will feature among the top 10 recipients of UK spending in direct aid for 2012 / 2013 at £165 million. Or take Malawi, which this year is receiving £90 million of British budgetary aid, but has recently expelled the British High Commissioner for criticising President Mutharika for being intolerant of criticism. Mutharika has made no secret of his admiration for Mugabe, naming a new highway after his idol, who in turn has given the Malawian leader a stolen farm.'*

Saturday 4th June: One of Britain's best-known poets Benjamin Zephaniah joined us at the Vigil and condemned Mugabe and his betrayal of Africa. Zephaniah, born and brought up in the UK of West Indian parents, spoke to us of his disillusionment with Mugabe. He said 'I am friends with Mandela. I have only seen him angry once and that was about Mugabe when he spoke about failure of leadership in Africa.' (The Vigil remembers the occasion well because Mandela's comment followed a campaign by the Vigil and others to urge him to reject Mugabe when Mandela visited London to celebrate his 90th birthday.) The Vigil welcomes Zephaniah's support particularly highly because we have had such difficulty getting our message over to our Caribbean brothers. It has been difficult to disabuse them of the dream we all shared and convince them that Mugabe the liberator has turned into Mugabe the monster. It was great to have Vigil team member Patson Muzuwa with us again with a party from Leicester. He was most appreciative of the support Vigil members gave him on the recent death of his mother. But we were alarmed to hear that her funeral was invaded by two truckloads of Zanu PF who disrupted the proceedings. We understand this was a direct result of Patson's involvement with the Vigil.

Saturday 11th June: Vigil founder member Ephraim Tapa has been elected President of the recently-formed Zimbabwe 'Yes we Can' Movement. Ephraim is also President of our partner organisation Restoration of Human Rights in Zimbabwe. Yes We Can will be the political face of ROHR, Vigil and other organisations.

Saturday 25th June: Few Zimbabweans here have much respect for the

UK Home Office . . . What prompts this comment is a letter from a Home Office official to a lawyer acting for one of our supporters who is seeking political asylum. The official said this about a letter from the Vigil supporting the asylum claim: 'Objective evidence from www.nehandaradio.com raised public awareness that the Zimbabwe vigil was exploiting asylum seekers in the UK and would on the payment of a fee issue a letter to state attendance at the vigil. Therefore, no weight is attached to the production of this letter'. Our supporter's lawyer asked for our comment on this 'objective evidence'. Here is the response of one of our Vigil Co-ordinators. *'I attach a doc with the history of why Nehanda Radio wrote the article decampaigning the Vigil. As you will see on 20th June 2009 Morgan Tsvangirai addressed the Zimbabwean diaspora in the UK and was booed. The Vigil was accused of orchestrating this and we wrote this riposte in our diary of 27th June "But Vigil supporters were too fired up about another matter – the silly allegations on some loud-mouthed Zimbabwean exile websites that the Vigil and ROHR were behind the booing of Morgan Tsvangirai when he spoke to the UK diaspora in Southwark Cathedral last week. Anyone looking at videos of the occasion will see that the angry response was prompted by Mr Tsvangirai's remarks and was spontaneous and could not possibly have been planned." You will see that we also outline our policy on asylum letters in this particular diary - and our policy is still the same now. Nehanda Radio's article of 30th June 'ROHR & ZimVigil exploiting asylum seekers' is in retaliation for this. Even though we didn't mention them by name they recognised themselves. We are not an organisation set up to help asylum seekers: we campaign against human rights abuses in Zimbabwe and all we can write about asylum claims by our supporters is their visibility as activists because they attend our protests – the more they come the more visible they are. We are entirely self-funding: the charge of £10 for our letters is for admin costs to cover paper, envelopes, print cartridges, phone calls, postage etc. Anyone who works for the Vigil does so voluntarily - nobody is paid. For people who are good attenders the admin fee for letters is not charged.'*

Sunday 26th June: The London chapel of John Wesley – one of the founders of the Methodist Church – resounded to the sound of drums and African singing and dancing as exiled Zimbabweans and supporters gathered to mark the UN international day in support of victims of torture. The Vigil supplied the choir and drummers, who were energized by management team member, Patson Muzuwa, himself a survivor of torture. Our host at the Methodist world's 'cathedral' was the Reverend Jennifer Potter who has ministered in Botswana and Zambia and is Methodist 'companion' for Zimbabwe, visiting there every year. Jennifer prayed for a new dawn in Zimbabwe and reached out to Anglican friends in Zimbabwe who, she said, seemed to be particularly persecuted. The service was addressed by visitors from Zimbabwe including Irene Petras, Director of Zimbabwe Lawyers for Human Rights.

Monday 27th June: Vigil supporters provided the backbone for a protest by Action for Southern Africa (ACTSA) against violence in Zimbabwe. The Embassy refused to accept 1,300 cards ACTSA had collected calling for an end to the violence. The Embassy (as usual!) was closed so we stuck one of the cards under the door signed 'Zimbabwe Vigil' and listing our address as 'outside the Zimbabwe Embassy'.

Saturday 2nd July: We were visited by the Information Officer of the new Zimbabwe 'Yes We Can' movement, Arnold Magwanyata, who told Vigil supporters that the movement wanted to encourage Zimbabweans in the diaspora to join the struggle for change. Vigil co-ordinator Dumi Tutani, the Vigil's representative to the new movement, reported on a meeting it held in Manchester on 25th June. He said one strong message was a determination to empower women. Following on from our diary last week in which we wrote about criticism of the Vigil from the Home Office we have sent the following letter to Theresa May, the Home Secretary. *'A solicitor acting for one of our supporters asked for our comment on a letter from the Home Office which maligned the Zimbabwe Vigil. You will see further information in our diary of 25th June 2011 . . . We totally reject the implications and challenge the Home Office to substantiate this malicious slur.'*

Saturday 30th July: The Vigil has received an apology from the UK Border Agency for comments made when asylum was refused to a Zimbabwean refugee who offered a letter of support from the Vigil as evidence of activism. The comments suggested the letter was worthless because of allegations that the Vigil was a money-making organization ripping off asylum seekers. The Border Agency's Director of Appeals and Removals Phil Douglas replied to our complaint: 'I apologise at the outset for the offence this has understandably given.' Mr Douglas went on to say that the comments referred to were not based on information accepted by the Border Agency. The Vigil has also been assured by the British government that it is to try to overturn a legal decision to grant a CIO torturer permission to remain in the UK, which was given on the grounds he might be tortured if returned to Zimbabwe! Foreign Secretary William Hague said in a letter in response to our representations that the government's policy was that the UK should not be a refuge for war criminals.

Saturday 6th August: Details of how elements in Zimbabwe are trying to hi-jack our sister organisation ROHR were given at the Vigil by ROHR's President, Ephraim Tapa. He said ROHR was becoming increasingly prominent with its non-party political campaign for human rights but now that it was attracting the interest of potential donors a small group had unconstitutionally tried to take it over. Four people have consequently been expelled. One of our supporters Louisa Musaerenge said she had received the following threatening email apparently targeting Vigil supporters: 'Murikupedza nguva muchiimba ku London pasi peziso ra baba Mugabe kupusa chose ticha kubvumburisai one by one you want boiling oil over you heads your brain has bin frozen there come here we sort you out dogs of english man. They laugh you all the time this whities, you bin used to wipe ass come and agriculture here home is gud'.

Saturday 27th August: Africa's new King of Kings, President Mugabe, Defender of the Faith (except Anglican), emerged from the Zimbabwe Embassy in London on Saturday on his way to Tripoli in support of deposed King of Kings Muammar Gaddafi, who has fallen on hard times. Brandishing a rifle, Mugabe (played by Fungayi Mabhunu) was dressed in Arab attire so that he would not be mistaken for one of what Gaddafi describes as 'Libyan rats'. Before disappearing in his golf cart down one of the tunnels leading to Gaddafi's compound, Mugabe said everyone was happy in Libya until the Western gangsters started bombing the place to find more oil. 'Don't they know it doesn't spring from rocks?' Asked whether Gaddafi had been annoyed when Zimbabwe didn't pay its $360 million bill for oil, Mugabe said: 'That's all oil under the bridge now. I explained to him that Zimbabwe had no reason to pay as we had used up all the oil'.

Saturday 3rd September: The Vigil has been told by sources in the Swaziland High Commission how King Mswati was thrown into a panic by the April protests against him in London. Apparently, when the organiser of the Swazi vigil, Thobile Gwebu, was threatened with deportation from the UK, two senior Swazi police officers were sent over to London in the hope of taking custody of her. Fortunately she has been allowed to stay in the UK. We were also informed that the king's last minute change of hotels for the Royal Wedding in London was caused by the Dorchester asking him to go elsewhere because of the demonstrators.

Saturday 10th September: The Vigil was pleased to hear of plans for the Archbishop of Canterbury to visit Zimbabwe. Apparently he is seeking a meeting with Mugabe. This has been criticized in the British press, with some commentators saying it will provide a propaganda opportunity for Mugabe. We took a different view and sent the Archbishop the following letter: *'Dear Dr Williams: The Zimbabwe Vigil welcomes your planned visit to Zimbabwe next month in support of besieged Anglicans under the rod of the unelected president Mugabe . . . The persecution of Anglicans in Zimbabwe has continued too long with little condemnation from the Christian community at large. Even brother churches in Zimbabwe have scurried from the crucifixion . . . We disagree with those who question the wisdom of your visit. We are encouraged that you share our pain, though we have no doubt that Mugabe will seek to use your visit for propaganda purposes. We do not believe his regime – steeped in lawlessness, terror and greed – will make any meaningful concessions at your request. But we pray that your visit will highlight to the world the plight of our suffering brothers and sisters at home.'*

Saturday 1st October: The Zimbabwean diaspora in the UK is growing increasingly anxious at signs that the Home Office is stepping up efforts to deport Zimbabweans on the grounds that conditions at home have improved. One of the Vigil's regular supporters Shamiso Kofi has been detained and told a ticket to Nairobi has been booked for her on Kenyan Airways on 4th October. At the Vigil today, we ran the following petition to the UK Border Agency, part of the Home Office: "We, the undersigned, are worried about the proposed deportation of one of our regular supporters, Shamiso Kofi. She is one of our most passionate dancers and singers and . . . there are serious concerns about her safety . .

.' A harrowing picture of the Zanu PF mentality was given in a new play produced in London by Chickenshed Theatre and attended by a Vigil group. The play 'The Rain that Washes' was based on the experiences of Christopher Maphosa (who has attended the Vigil).

Saturday 8th October: Vigil supporter Shamiso Kofi was not deported to Zimbabwe as planned on Tuesday. After a harrowing experience, Shamiso was taken off the flight from Heathrow with her three escorts and returned to Yarl's Wood detention centre. We marked our 9th anniversary with Vigil management team member Fungayi Mabhunu, wearing our Mugabe mask, standing at the front desk with wife Grace (played by Josephine Zhuga). Mugabe was holding the following petition: 'Petition to the Unfair World: The oppressed people of Zimbabwe demand an end to the illegal and unfair sanctions against me and my Zanu PF cronies: We have redistributed farms to deserving nearest and dearest, we have transferred businesses to indigenous ministers, our security forces make sure there are no London-type riots (a reference to rioting which broke out after a London man was shot dead by police), we have cleared slums by pulling down houses, we have liberated our diamonds, we have nationalized the Anglican Church. NO TO ZIMVIGIL LIES – YES TO MUGABE'S REVOLUTIONARY TRUTH. Mugabe had managed to get signatures from Gaddafi (Libya), Gbagbo (Ivory Coast), Mubarak (Egypt), Ben Ali (Tunisia), Assad (Syria), Saleh (Yemen) and Mutharika (Malawi). Mugabe also promenaded around the Vigil with the following placards: 'Mugabe (estimated wealth $1 billion) supports the right of excommunicated Bishop Kunonga to seize Anglican churches', 'Mugabe says no to Western human rights: yes to murder, rape and torture', 'Mugabe scorns British aid: says starvation a product of neo-colonialism', 'Mugabe (16 farms) supports the right of West London nurse Irene Zhanda to seize a farm in Zimbabwe'.

Saturday 15th October: A new attempt is to be made on Thursday to deport Vigil supporter Shamiso Kofi despite the violent failure of the first attempt earlier this month. There is speculation that the UK and South Africa are making a concerted attempt to deport Zimbabweans to put pressure on the Mugabe regime. Shamiso is one of the first Zimbabweans to be targeted for forcible return since the UK ended its moratorium on sending back failed Zimbabwean asylum seekers. It comes amid reports from South Africa that hundreds of Zimbabweans are being sent back from there.

Saturday 5th November: The Vigil is appalled that the EU has cleared the way for Zanu PF to expand its diamond swindle. We believe the EU's craven capitulation to commercial interests will undermine any attempts to get Zanu PF to honour the GPA. With virtually unlimited funds at Zanu PF's disposal, Vigil supporters believe it is farewell to hopes of free and fair elections. The Vigil is happy to report that Shamiso Kofi has been released from detention after the government's failure to deport her. The Vigil has received a reply to our open letter to the Archbishop of Canterbury about his visit to Zimbabwe. The Archbishop expresses his 'deep and sincere gratitude' for our support. We were joined by about 100 uniformed members of the Chinese spiritual organisation the Falun Gong, whose demonstrations against communist oppression we have supported. We discussed with them our disquiet at Chinese involvement in the Marange diamond racket and other matters such as arms sales to Mugabe.

CIO at Vigil – Saturday 12th November: Three suspected CIO operatives were photographed at the Vigil. The three men were spotted emerging from the side door of the Embassy. They passed by the Vigil before coming back to the front table, where they asked questions and requested a flyer which explains what we are about. They read our petitions: one of them signed but the other two declined. They then crossed the road when they noticed we were taking pictures of them. Two of the men were later photographed entering the Embassy. Ironically, the photos were taken by Fungayi Mabhunu, who only this week received a chilling message from a contact in Harare, a musician who had gone to the police band at Morris Depot (next to State House) to get his alto sax tuned. He happened to ask them whether they knew Fungayi (a former member of the police band) and they said: 'Yes, he's the one who was on TV denouncing the head of state. We will get him.' Fungayi believes the reference was to his appearance on a BBC World television programme after the last elections. The message he got from our contact was 'don't come back'. Here is the Shona text of the email: *'Fungai haubatsire nekureba kwaNyazika nhunu vese vangaziva panaKenny here. At least daiwandiudza nechapapi coner nani, pakati here kana pamucheto. Iyo body yakauya here? Mafe akoeku polica band* *ndakatosvika pabasapavo ndichidaku chinusa Alto yangu, ndikanzi na Mudhara Knox Dhauya, Fungai ndomuziva mupfana wekumbare uyu akazenge obuda paTV achitaura zvisinabasa uyu. Akangouya kuno anomama tichadhila naye. Ndikati wakamakwa, ukadzoka kuno vanokusata. handinakuzombo taura kuti ndinokuzivirepi.'*

The incident comes amid widespread criticism of the Zimbabwe police. The Zimbabwe Lawyers for Human Rights condemned them this week for their arbitrary actions in harassing officials from the Oxfam humanitarian organisation: 'The contemptuous conduct of the police and the Department of Immigration officials portrays a government that is suffering from persecutory delusional disorder, which is typical of paranoid states,' ZLHR said in a statement. It goes on to say: 'ZLHR is extremely concerned at the unmistakable and extreme collusion between the police from the ZRP Law and Order Section and the Department of Immigration officials and their uncivilised conduct in harassing bona fide visitors, whose organisations' interventions have sustained livelihoods, health and the less privileged people of Zimbabwe, which shows an unacceptable disregard for the rule of law in our country.'

Saturday 26th November: To our disappointment there was no sign of the promised Zanu PF demonstrators when a Vigil supporter went to check outside the Prime Minister's residence, 10 Downing Street, just around the corner from the Zimbabwe Embassy. Mugabe fans in the UK, led by George Shire, Lloyd Msipa and Laurence C Mzembi (brother of Zanu PF Minister Walter), had said they were to present a petition today to Mr Cameron calling for an end to the vicious neo-colonialist, racist, destructive and ineffective illegal sanctions which have deprived Zimbabweans of electricity and water, destroyed agriculture, caused potholes, prevented drugs reaching the sick and the supply of spares for ambulances and caused the drought and floods. At the last count the petition had amassed 51 signatures so perhaps the weight of it delayed the planned march from Lancaster House.

Saturday 3rd December: With the sun setting as early as 4 pm, we at the Vigil need everything we can get to cheer us up as we stand out in the cold. One of the posters in the Embassy window did the trick. Part of the 'Wonders of Zimbabwe' tourist promotion campaign, it read 'Wonder what our cultural ceremonies are like?' We couldn't help but think of

Tsvangirai's on-off wedding. But a canvass of opinion among Vigil supporters showed that the affair was more than a laughing matter. People were alarmed that Tsvangirai appears to have walked blindly into a Zanu PF trap and has become a laughing stock. Although there is respect for the Prime Minister's heroic work leading the MDC for the past twelve years, it was felt that he should – as the saying goes – consider his position.

Friday 9th December: An article on 5th December on nehandaradio.com repeated several malicious accusations against the Zimbabwe Vigil and our sister organisation ROHR. The article is a cut and paste job from discredited Nehanda Radio articles, some dating back two and a half years, when the Vigil was blamed for Tsvangirai being booed at Southwark Cathedral in London. The latest attack is in response to our diary of 3rd December suggesting that Tsvangirai should consider his position as leader of the MDC, partly because of his lack of political acumen in having a relationship with a woman with known Zanu PF connections.

Saturday 10th December: Fresh from the Zanu PF conference in Bulawayo, Robert Mugabe materialized at the Vigil to demand immediate elections – preferably before his 88th birthday in two months' time. 'No time can be lost', he said. 'Zimbabwe is in moral danger. No woman is safe from Morgan Tsvangirai.' The aged leader, played by management team member Fungayi Mabhunu in our Mugabe mask, could still wield a nifty sjambok which he brandished at Fadzai Muparutsa of Gays and Lesbians of Zimbabwe. Fadzai was at the Vigil with Gideon Shoko, Deputy Secretary General, Zimbabwe Congress of Trade Unions. Gideon passed on to Vigil supporters greetings from the workers of Zimbabwe and said how encouraged he was that we were still 'pushing the struggle' after nine years outside the Embassy.

Saturday 17th December: The Vigil staged a demonstration outside the South African High Commission in London to urge President Zuma to force Mugabe to honour the Global Political Agreement. Vigil activists and MDC members stood in silence with banners reading: 'Zuma save Zimbabwe'. The demonstration reflected the Vigil's disgust at the ANC's offer to help Zanu PF in the next elections. Further evidence of the incompetence of the UK Border Agency came in a letter to a member of the Vigil Management Team who requested access to the file on her held by the UKBA. The letter said 'We have now completed the processing of that request, but, unfortunately, we have been unable to locate all of the UKBA records relating to yourself . . .'

Saturday 24th December: Inspired by videos on youtube showing North Koreans apparently weeping hysterically at the death of Kim Jong-il, the Vigil spent Christmas Eve outside the Zimbabwe Embassy practising public grieving for Mugabe. After all, we don't want to be found wanting when mourning comes. With notices explaining 'Zimbabweans practising weeping hysterically for the forthcoming death of Mugabe', Vigil supporters beat their breasts, pounded their heads against the nearest soft object (after all it was just a practice), wept controllably, heaved their shoulders and generally looked bereft at the sight of a prostate Mugabe (played by Fungayi Mabhunu in our Mugabe mask) lying wrapped in a shroud with a Father Christmas hat. We were further cheered by the vociferous support for us shown by Congolese demonstrators as they passed the Vigil on their way to Whitehall to express their outrage at the stolen presidential election in the DRC. One demonstrator broke away from the tightly-policed procession to hurl water in the face of Mugabe depicted on one of our banners 'Mugabe wanted for murder'.

Saturday 31st December: The end of the year is traditionally a time for reflection and at the last Vigil of 2011 we discussed likely developments at home in the next twelve months. Sadly they were rather pessimistic. Few people at the Vigil expect a happy outcome in Zimbabwe to 2012. There was agreement at the Vigil on the most likely options: (1) The situation could continue as it is for another year with halting progress on the constitution front, not helped by Mugabe spending most of his time flying to and from Singapore for medical treatment. (2) Zanu PF (and we include in this military leaders), desperate to see a dying Mugabe returned to office, could engineer elections by collapsing the government – for instance, arresting Tsvangirai.

2012

Highlights

February: EU lifts sanctions on some prominent Zimbabweans.
April: MDC complains of a rise in violence and says its rallies are being stopped.
21st April: Vigil hands petition to 10 Downing Street to be passed to UN calling on it to ensure free and fair elections in Zimbabwe.
16th May: Vigil demonstrates with Swazis outside London hotel of visiting King Mswati III.
6th June: Vigil demonstrates against London visit of President Sata of Zambia after his expression of support for Zanu PF.
21st July: Vigil demonstrates outside Russian Embassy over reported plans to sell Mugabe helicopter gunships.
4th August: 'Mugabe' appears at Vigil on Olympic super Saturday displaying gold medals for shooting, looting etc.
1st September: Vigil warns MDC it will lose next elections.
15th September: A dread-locked 'Mugabe' appears at Vigil to repeat his warning to Caribbeans to 'stop da ganja.'
October: Human rights activists say repressive structures instrumental in 2008 electoral violence are being reactivated. Tsvangirai threatens to pull out of unity government because of violence against MDC members.
6th November: MDC Treasurer Roy Bennett warns British government that Zimbabwe could become permanent basket case.

Vigil diary excerpts

UK Zimbabweans petition Zuma – Saturday 21st January: Zimbabweans from all over the UK gathered outside the South African High Commission calling on President Zuma to force Zanu PF to implement the Global Political Agreement. The demonstration marked the beginning of a campagn of monthly demonstrations by Zimbabweans in the diaspora, including those in South Africa and the United States. Over 300 people attended the Vigil at which a petition to President Zuma was launched.

Launch of Zimbabwe Action Forum – Saturday 4th February: As London was blanketed in the first snow of winter, Zimbabweans from several different groups met after the Vigil to launch the Zimbabwe Action Forum to discuss ways to help achieve democracy at home. Our sister organization ROHR earlier held a general meeting and expressed confidence in Ephraim Tapa as leader and elected a new UK Executive.

Mugabe's birthday gifts – Saturday 18th February: It was a special birthday party at the Vigil for Mugabe as he celebrated the easing of sanctions and news that Zanu PF is expected to sell India 11 million carats this year. That's a lot of diamonds. 'A big thank you to Baroness Ashton,' said Mugabe, referring to the EU's foreign affairs chief, who was at the centre of both developments, helping Zanu PF get Kimberley Process approval to unload its blood diamonds and getting sanctions removed on many of his cronies – despite Mugabe making it clear he has no intention of allowing free and fair elections. The birthday boy – 88 on Tuesday – was played by Vigil management team member Fungayi Mabhunu wearing our Mugabe mask and holding a candle in one hand and an empty water bottle in the other, representing Zimbabwe's liquidity problems: no water and no money . . . He was given gifts labeled looted diamonds, sanctions eased, illiquidity and typhoid. Posters proclaimed 'Mugabe's 88th Birthday – vote for me or DIE' and 'Vote MDC and die'. The Vigil was interested to see that Zimbabwe was the only African country to vote in favour of President Assad slaughtering his people.

EU 'economical with truth' – Saturday 25th February: The Vigil expressed to the European Parliament our puzzlement at remarks by the EU Foreign Affairs representative, Baroness Ashton, about the easing of sanctions on Mugabe's cronies. She said that the EU 'welcomes progress made towards the creation of a conducive environment for the holding of free, fair, peaceful and transparent elections' . . . she went on to speak of 'progress in the implementation of the GPA' and further commented 'the overall situation in Zimbabwe has improved'. The Vigil pointed out that it is now three years since the Government of National Unity was formed. As far as the Vigil can see there was some early progress – difficult and slow – but there has been none at all in the past year. In fact, there is strong evidence that the situation has deteriorated in the year that Baroness Ashton is speaking of. The Vigil believes that even the total lifting of the measures would not persuade Zanu PF to allow free and fair elections. They would simply invent some other excuse for clinging to power.

Saturday 31st March: The Vigil sent a letter to the British Prime Minister David Cameron thanking him for the commitment he gave during talks with Morgan Tsvagirai to help achieve free and fair elections in Zimbabwe. The Vigil asked for an opportunity to present Mr Cameron with the Vigil's petition to the UN for passing on to the Security Council. The petition, signed by more than 12,000 people who had stopped by the Vigil, called on the UN to ensure the next elections in Zimbabwe are free and fair.

Vigil presents petition – Saturday 21st April: The MDC in the UK joined the Vigil to mark Independence Day. After gathering at the Vigil, about 200 people walked to the South African High Commission to continue the Global Diaspora Campaign to get President Zuma to call Mugabe to account. People then moved on to Whitehall to present the Vigil's petition to the British Prime Minister to pass on to the UN calling on it to ensure free and fair elections in Zimbabwe. Five delegates from the Vigil were allowed into Downing Street to hand over the petition.

Saturday 28th April: We were glad to welcome Vincent Dlamini, National Organising Secretary of the Trade Union Congress of Swaziland and Secretary General of Swaziland's National Public Services Union. He expressed gratitude for our support for the Swazi Vigil which has been campaigning for democracy outside the Swazi High Commission in London.

What Vigil friends is this? – Wednesday 9th May: About a dozen people from the Vigil attended the Globe Theatre for a performance in Shona of Shakespeare's Two Gentlemen of Verona. It was part of a festival to mark the Queen's jubilee during which Shakespeare's thirty-seven plays were performed in thirty-seven languages. We were given free tickets for the play and were invited to join the two stars Denton Chikura and Tonderai Munyevu in the staff bar after the show. They had both been to the Vigil.

Saturday 12th May: The Vigil had its annual visit by the Westminster Morris Men, traditional English male dancers who perform around the Borough of Westminster every year on the second Saturday in May. They grabbed hold of Vigil supporter Francesca Toft, danced round her and at the end of their performance lifted her aloft and then announced that they had just performed a fertility dance . . . The predominantly elderly dancers kissed her on the cheek in turn at the end.

'Let them eat cow dung' – Wednesday 16th May: Vigil supporters joined the Swaziland Vigil in a demonstration outside a leading London hotel against the visit of King Mswati III of Swaziland – Africa's last absolute ruler – who was in the UK to attend a diamond jubilee banquet for the world's monarchs hosted by the Queen at Windsor Castle on Friday 18th May. Amid drumming, singing and chants of 'Mswati must go', the demonstrators carried banners reading: 'King Mswati buys £30m plane while his people eat cow dung', 'Mswati and his 30 strong entourage stay in £400 a night Savoy Hotel while his people starve', 'End human rights abuses in Swaziland', and 'Democracy now for Swaziland'.

'Shame on you' – Saturday 19th May: After the Vigil we processed from the Zimbabwe Embassy to the Savoy Hotel about 200 yards down the Strand to join the Swazi Vigil as guests arrived for a dinner hosted by King Mswati. We heckled them with cries of 'Shame on you, Shame on you'.

BBC Man arrested in Zimbabwe – Saturday 26th May: The Vigil broke the news to the world of the arrest in Zimbabwe of the BBC classical music presenter Petroc Trelawny. We were informed by relatives in Bulawayo that he had been taken into custody for taking part in the city's music festival without permission to work in Zimbabwe, even though he was not being paid.

Zimbabwe must speed up reforms – Saturday 2nd June: The British government has assured the Vigil that it is ready to help SADC in its efforts to ensure free and fair elections in Zimbabwe. The assurance came in a letter from the Foreign and Commonwealth Office in response to our petition submitted on 21st April calling for UN intervention in Zimbabwe. Here is part of their reply: 'We share your concerns over the potential for violence in the forthcoming elections in Zimbabwe and that the international community, particularly SADC, have a critical role to play in ensuring that this does not happen.'

Zimbabweans in UK protest at Zambian President's visit – Wednesday 6th June:

The Vigil staged two demonstrations against the visit to London of President Michael Sata of Zambia who was a guest at the Jubilee celebrations for the Queen. Vigil Co-ordinator Dumi Tutani said 'Sata is an unashamed supporter of Mugabe. His parroting "Pamberi ne Zanu PF (Forward with Zanu PF)" at last week's SADC meeting was disgraceful.' The first demonstration took place at Marlborough House where the Queen attended a lunch for Commonwealth leaders.

The demonstrators then went on the Zambian High Commission to deliver a letter deploring President Sata's interference in the internal affairs of Zimbabwe. President Sata, a former platform sweeper at London's Victoria station, was offered a new broom by the Vigil 'so that you can resume a profession for which you seem better equipped than your current one'. Zambian diplomats refused to accept the letter and broom so we posted the letter in a letterbox across the road.

Saturday 9th June: A Zambian website which carried a report about our demonstrations against President Sata soon had more than 80 comments – mainly supportive of our action. Someone even suggested regular Friday 'broom' days.

Zim fuss at Zambia House – Thursday 21st June: The Vigil's Mugabe mask made an appearance outside the Zambian High Commission for the sixth round of the monthly Free Zimbabwe Global Campaign aimed at pressuring SADC leaders into ensuring democratic reforms in Zimbabwe. Fungayi Mabhunu, wearing the mask, made another attempt to deliver a new broom for President Sata but once again Zambian diplomats spurned the gift. The Zambians seemed particularly unnerved by the Mugabe mask (not surprisingly!) and called the police for help. The police explained to them that we were acting within our rights.

Stop Mugabe's war plans – Saturday 21st July: Russian diplomats peeping out from behind the curtains of their London Embassy must have been surprised to see President Mugabe at a demonstration against Moscow's reported plans to supply helicopter gunships in return for Zimbabwean platinum deposits. Fungayi Mabhunu, wearing our Mugabe mask, carried a poster reading 'I want a Russian helicopter'. The demo caused quite a security stir as the embassy is in a sensitive location near Kensington Palace. There was a heavy police presence with appropriately enough a helicopter overhead. It is with great sadness that the Vigil reports the death of Bernard Hukwa, a faithful supporter who was also a member of our sister organization ROHR and the MDC. His body was found in the Thames. We know he was worried about being unable to support his family in Zimbabwe.

Mugabe wins again – Saturday 4th August: The European Union's new friend Robert Mugabe popped up at the Vigil on Olympic 'Super

Saturday' to display his array of gold medals. 'On to Rio 2016' he croaked, waving his COPAC medal for the prolonged and pointless constitutional outreach programme. Mugabe was given a wild card entry to the Games following the EU's announcement that sanctions were being eased. But he was still not satisfied with his haul: gold medals for Men's Skulls, Rowing (backwards), Shooting, Torture, Genocide and Looting – as well, of course, as the COPAC marathon, which involves 3.5 years going nowhere. 'The London Olympics are full of discrimination', he complained. 'I was not allowed to go for the women's skulls or white water rafting. They wanted me to do the hurdles or high jump – or even the dressage! They know I have been illegally sanctioned from Harrods and other dressage places.' Thanks to Fungayi Mabhunu for sporting our Mugabe mask and Vigil Co-ordinator Dumi Tutani who awarded the medals. During the week we received the following email from Harare: 'It is with great concern that we hear the self confessed CIO agent in London has been granted asylum by the British Government even after confessing to rape, torture, murder etc.

Is the Zimbabwe Vigil doing anything about getting this murderer sent back to Zimbabwe? Please let us know.' Our response was 'The Vigil is equally horrified but the courts here are subject to the European human rights laws and these often seem to produce ridiculous decisions. We haven't forgotten this rogue and if there is any opportunity to call him to book we will jump at it.'

Tuesday 21st August: Zimbabwean exiles demonstrated outside the Mozambique High Commission in London to urge the new SADC Chair, Mozambican President Guebuza, to keep up pressure to secure free and fair elections in Zimbabwe next year. The demonstration was part of the 21st Movement Free Zimbabwe Global Campaign which has seen protests around the 21st of each month since January. A letter was handed over to a Mozambican official by nine year old Leslie Nkanyezi representing the demonstrators from the MDC, the Vigil, ROHR and the Zimbabwe We Can (ZWC) movement. The letter noted: 'We are pleased to see that the summit in Maputo reaffirmed the decisions already taken on Zimbabwe but we see little evidence of urgency in the summit resolutions, particularly in preparing the ground so that the elections will be free and fair.'

Disappointment with MDC – Saturday 1st September: Vigil supporters gathered after our weekly protest outside the Embassy for a wide-ranging discussion of the threatening situation in Zimbabwe and the Vigil's role in the fight for freedom and democracy. Our monthly Action Forum thought almost unanimously that the MDC was unlikely to be in charge after the next election. Questions were asked why the MDC had allowed itself to be seduced by the ludicrous constitution-making process while nothing had been done to ensure free and fair elections. We have Tendai Biti touring the world expressing his admiration for Mugabe and saying how the economy is poised to power ahead. Yet now he tells a luxurious conference at the Victoria Falls that Zimbabwe has a per capita annual income of about $320. Our meeting noted that Professor David Hulme of Manchester University told the Victoria Falls conference that Zimbabwe had seen one of the biggest declines in human and economic development recorded among countries not in a war situation.

Marathon Mugabe – Saturday 8th September: On the second last day of the Paralympics, Vigil supporters saw off President Mugabe in the Marathon. He only agreed to take part if he was promised the gold medal and insisted that we give it to him before the race to make sure. He also demanded to start a day before the opposition, given that he is about the oldest contender in the dictator stakes. Furthermore, he insisted on starting at the Embassy which is only a short distance to the finishing line in the nearby Mall. Thanks to Fungayi Mabhunu for playing Marathon Mugabe wearing our all too frightening Mugabe mask. An earlier agreement on the constitution of the race drawn up after a vastly expensive international consultation exercise which has gone for years was rejected by Mugabe at the last minute because it did not reflect his wishes. On a happier note the Vigil was pleased to see that Tanzanian President Kikwete, the new Chair of the SADC Security Troika, has called a meeting for October 7 and 8 to deal with Zanu PF's refusal to accept the COPAC draft constitution they signed off on. The Vigil believes that the Troika has no alternative but to call Mugabe's bluff for disregarding the GPA. Vigil supporters are very appreciative of Botswana's generous loan of $70 million to Zimbabwe. But we would caution them that Zanu PF never pays its debts – from China to Iran, from Malawi to Zambia, Zimbabwe has yet to be recorded as paying up. The Vigil was interested to see that last week's diary featured in a Herald article: 'MDC-T to lose forthcoming election: Zim Vigil' We advise people to compare the Herald article with what we actually said. In particular, the Vigil is not anti-Tsvangirai as suggested. In fact we are taking up a collection to pay for expenses incurred if his former mistress Locadia succeeds in her claim for $15,000 a month maintenance 'because this is what she will need to maintain the standard of life she enjoyed with Mr Tsvangirai'. So far we have collected £0.07.

Stop da Circus – Saturday 15th September:
The Vigil didn't know whether Tsvangirai's latest wedding was on or off when we gathered outside the Embassy. We were confused by the court proceedings. But we were determined to celebrate either way – not because of the nuptials but because Mugabe has at last solved a perennial problem for us. Mugabe's intolerant comments about Jamaican Rastafarians (as our poster put it 'Mugabe's message to Jamaica: stop da ganja man and da strong drink and cut the hair') opened the eyes of Caribbeans to his true character. We have had endless discussions with our brothers in the British Caribbean community over the past 10 years but they have been firmly fixed on an unreal picture of Mugabe as a warrior for African liberation. Now they have been kicked in the groin by their hero's feet of clay. A dreadlocked Mugabe puffing a giant spliff featured prominently at the Vigil, where he welcomed the arrival of Tsvangirai's

rival brides by rickshaw. Mugabe then handed them to a kneeling Tsvangirai with a placard reading 'Morgan's Zanu PF brides'. Fortunately we had plenty of people to keep the two brides apart. They then tucked into the marriage feast including a cake emblazoned with 'Congratulations on your wedding MDC T & Zanu PF'. Thanks to Lindiwe Bare (bride Elizabeth), Philip Maponga (Morgan), Mary Ndoro (aspiring bride Locardia), Fungayi Mabhunu (Mugabe) and Georgina Makaza (bridesmaid).

For those who are thinking of going home on a visit, be warned. A Zimbabwean who has lived in London for a long time and wanted to go home on holiday had a salutary experience. After travelling around South Africa and Swaziland, he went to book his coach to Zimbabwe. He was strongly warned not to cross into Zimbabwe through a land border using a British passport because he would have to pay exorbitant bribes and if he could not afford these his passport might be cut up by the authorities. He decided not to go home. We noted with interest the economic philosophy of former Gutu South MP Shuvai Mahofa, one of the Zanu PF officials gifted with the Save Conservancy. She said 'In fact I am realising that farming is a waste of time, there is a lot of money to be made in hunting . . . You just sit and wait for whites to come and pay for hunting and make money.'

Saturday 22nd September: As the Vigil's contribution to the Zimbabwe Diaspora 21st Movement's Global Campaign, we took letters to the Tanzanian and Botswana High Commissions in London. Our letter to President Kikwete of Tanzania noted: *'On behalf of the millions of Zimbabweans driven into the diaspora by the collapse of our country's economy and the breakdown of the rule of law, we appeal to you as the new head of the SADC security troika to act speedily so that the ground can be prepared for free and fair elections. We recall that it was your predecessor, Julius Nyerere, who told Mugabe that he was inheriting the jewel of Africa. At that time Zimbabwe had the second most advanced economy in sub-Saharan Africa. Now after 32 years of Mugabe's misrule it is one of the poorest and most corrupt countries. Mugabe is seeking to delay progress to elections so that there are no essential reforms, such as a new voters' roll. It was confirmed this month that the current roll contains the names of 16,800 people born on 1st January 1901 – no doubt all Zanu PF members.'*

The letter to President Khama of Botswana said: '*Exiled Zimbabweans wish to express our gratitude for your support for the people of Zimbabwe. In particular, we applaud your comments at a recent banquet in Gaberone for President Zuma that "nothing less than free and fair elections in Zimbabwe should be acceptable to the international community. SADC, as the guarantor of the GPA, must ensure transparency not only of the elections but also of the process leading to the polls." We are particularly appreciative of your understanding of the need for international monitoring of the elections.*'

One of our members has contacted her relatives in Bulawayo to find out how they are getting on with synchronized toilet flushing (to prevent blockages during frequent periods of water rationing). We have asked them to let us know when it's happening so we can flush our toilets in sympathy.

Vigil reply to MDC – Saturday 29th September: A leading MDC figure in the UK, while thanking us for our help, complained that we were again criticizing the MDC. Here is our reply: 'We would like to assure you that we are not against the MDC. But we feel an obligation to be critical when the leadership is failing the party's members. To do otherwise would be following the example of Zanu PF . . . The Vigil applauds the many MDC members working bravely and unselfishly for change. Without the support of these members the party would not exist. They and you have every right, if not a duty, to criticize the leadership when it fails.'

Saturday 6th October: Thanks to the BBC and others picking up our Bulawayo lavatory 'scoop', we have helped launch the prospective Olympic sport of 'synchronised toilet flushing'.

Zimbabwe Vigil's 10th Anniversary – Saturday 13th October: Today marked the beginning of our 11th year outside the Embassy. It was certainly no celebration as our objectives are far from being achieved. Supporters went on after the Vigil down the road to the India Club in the Aldwych where Ephraim Tapa, one of the founder members of the Vigil, chaired a meeting to discuss the way forward. He mentioned the BBC interview this week given by the Zanu PF Justice Minister Chinamasa in which he made it clear that Zanu PF will never hand over power. Many people expressed despair at the situation at home.

Saturday 20th October: On the eve of the 2nd Stakeholders' Meeting on the new constitution, Zimbabweans exiled in the UK gathered outside the Zimbabwe Embassy to underline our fears that this ludicrous process would again be hijacked by Zanu PF. A petition was drawn up on the spot and signed by participants, including many MDC members as well as Vigil and ROHR supporters, and slipped under the Embassy's front door. It said: 'We deplore the upsurge in political violence and the arbitrary arrests of opposition members and warn you that we will continue our campaign until there are free and fair elections.'

Crumbling away: Saturday 3rd November: A UK daily newspaper The Independent has asked the Vigil to write a blog explaining what has kept us going for the past decade. Here is what we are sending them:

'The Zimbabwe Vigil recently marked – not celebrated – our tenth anniversary protesting outside the Zimbabwe Embassy in London against human rights abuses and in support of free and fair elections. Since 12th October 2002 Zimbabwean exiles and supporters have gathered every Saturday, come what may, overlooked by Jacob Epstein's sculptures slowly crumbling away on the Embassy's neo-classical façade.

When the Vigil started we were hopeful that the then newly-formed Movement for Democratic Change (MDC) would soon sweep away President Mugabe's sclerotic Zanu PF party which had ruled since independence in 1980. Robert Mugabe had taken over what had been described by President Nyerere of Tanzania as 'the jewel of Africa' but, despite achievements in expanding education, had steered the economy onto the rocks and increasingly resorted to violence to deal with opposition.

The invasion of white-owned farms, aimed at undermining support for the MDC, had destroyed commercial agriculture and prompted the exodus of millions of people. More and more Zimbabweans began turning up in the UK – not primarily the dispossessed white farmers, who could use their skills elsewhere, but impoverished black Zimbabweans, many of them professionals from towns which collapsed as large swathes of formerly productive land were looted.

As Mugabe increasingly subverted the judicial system and police force, the rule of law in Zimbabwe became the rule of force, backed by an increasingly politicized army and a subservient media parroting the Zanu PF mantra that the mounting economic woes were caused by 'illegal' Western sanctions imposed on a number of Mugabe's cronies. The fact that trade with the West continued to increase – along with Western aid – was conveniently ignored.

Developments at home were watched with growing dismay by Zimbabweans in London who formed a branch of the MDC. Encouraged by visiting speakers from Zimbabwe, including the MDC MP Roy Bennett, it was agreed to launch a regular Vigil outside Zimbabwe House, independent of the MDC, along the lines of the anti-apartheid protest which had been held outside the South African Embassy.

At our first Vigils we had a few posters and a petition to the UN Human Rights Commission and not much else. A report appeared in the UK newsletter of the MDC on 8th November 2002. The first two Vigils, it said, had been well-attended but on the third it rained steadily. 'But that Vigil was the best ever. If it rains, you have to sing and dance to keep your spirits up . . .' The report went on to say of the Vigil 'It's only going on for a limited period . . . all signs are that Mugabe is finished . . .' Such optimism! But we prepared for the future and bought a tarpaulin which we strung from the four maple trees outside Zimbabwe House and gradually became, in the words of the Observer newspaper, the largest regular demonstration in London.

In the early years a good proportion of Vigil supporters were white Zimbabweans – perhaps 40%. But, as hope died, this dwindled until the Vigil became a 90%+ black protest, now averaging about 60 people a week. In the intervening years we have carried out many demonstrations apart from the weekly Vigil. One of the first was to hire an open-top double decker bus, adorn it with our banners "No to Mugabe No to Starvation' and 'End murder, rape and torture in Zimbabwe', and tour London delivering petitions to Parliament, the Commonwealth and the UN. On another occasion, a group of about 25 went to Lisbon to protest at the presence of Mugabe at a meeting there.

As the Vigil enters its second decade, we remember friends who have supported us: Remus Makuwasa, the gaunt, dying MDC shadow minister who sat huddled silently in blankets for the whole of a bitterly cold Vigil, Archbishop Pius Ncube who came and comforted people at the Vigil kneeling at his feet, the silent benefactor who would from time to time stuff a wad of £20 notes into our startled hands, the Oxford music professor who joined us in a local pub to tutor us on singing, the film

stars such as Tim Robbins and Emma Thompson who signed our petitions, not to mention Simon Callow who stopped his taxi to get out and give us some money.
Zimbabwe is now a gangster state, its democracy a travesty, with impunity for the rich and powerful and poverty and disease for the majority. On one level there is a vibrant economy fed by money made serving Mugabe's corrupt mafia, on another there is mass unemployment, power cuts and water shortages. The Vigil has no doubt that there will be violence as Zanu PF seeks to steal the upcoming elections. We expect the same outcome as in 2008 with another 'government of national unity' denying true democracy.
But as Epstein's statues continue to crumble like Zimbabwe's towns, environment and wild life, we are determined to continue alerting the world to what is going on in the former jewel of Africa -- reduced to one of the poorest countries in the world. A recent South African report says that from being one of the most advanced economies in Africa, Zimbabwe's GDP per person is now the second lowest of 185 listed. (It is ironic that the country listed last, the DRC, is even richer in natural resources than Zimbabwe.)'

A clean break – Tuesday 6th November: Several Vigil supporters attended a meeting in Parliament addressed by Ben Freeth who, together with his father-in-law Mike Campbell, successfully took Mugabe to the SADC International Tribunal after they were evicted from their farm. The Tribunal was then suspended after pressure from Mugabe. The meeting was also addressed by the Archbishop of York, the Ugandan-born John Sentamu, and the exiled MDC T Treasurer Roy Bennett who said: 'There needs to be a clean break with the past in Zimbabwe – and very soon – or else the country will be a permanent basket case akin to the Democratic Republic of Congo or the Central African Republic, or any of the other forgotten and forsaken backwaters in Africa, distinguished only by occasional atrocities and marked by the utter, grinding poverty of their inhabitants.' Roy dismissed as a pipe dream the idea that Zimbabwe would gradually evolve towards democracy and prosperity by co-operating with a 'reformed' Zanu PF. He warned that if the MDC and civil society did not drive Zanu PF from office and 'complete the return to democratic normality' in the next three years or so it might be too late. 'Zimbabwe will degenerate into a Somalia. It will just be another perennial slum in Africa, a shantytown, a bantustan where the dream of the citizens extends no further than emigration. The privileged few will gorge themselves on the scraps.' For full text of Roy's speech, see: http://nehandaradio.com/2012/11/09/zimbabwe-could-degenerate-into-a-somalia-bennett/.

Saturday 10th November: Ben Freeth came to join us at the Vigil today and urged us to keep up the struggle. 'We are encouraged because every week we see you are still there.' After the Vigil he attended the monthly meeting of the Zimbabwe Action Forum. He recalled how his own house had been burnt down along with that of his father-in-law Mr Campbell. 'Zimbabwe continues to burn yet we are four years into the new government. The country has not really moved forward. Huge problems continue and no real reforms are taking place.' The Joint Operations Command was still in place, the election machinery was exactly the same as in the last elections with the same people in charge who had declared those elections free and fair despite the violence. The elections supremo Mudede claimed the voters' roll was perfect, although a third of those on it were dead or absent.

'We expect violence' Ben said, 'forced meetings, Zimbabweans leaving home, crimes against humanity and the plight of the Zimbabwean people being disregarded.' Ben said he looked to the Vigil for help in creating pressure and said our partner organization Restoration of Human Rights was part of the answer. One disturbing reminder of how difficult things were becoming in Zimbabwe was from a supporter at the forum who said her parents in Zimbabwe had appealed to her not to go to the Vigil because they had been threatened. People agreed that we must nevertheless focus on getting our message to relatives in Zimbabwe. They must realise how much the diaspora, with regular remittances, is helping to keep the country going.

Vigil co-ordinator Dumi Tutani expressed anger at reports that Morgan Tsvangirai was staying in a luxury hotel nearby, the Savoy, which charges a minimum of £400 a night. He asked why Mr Tsvangirai had not contacted the diaspora, who would have liked to have asked him why the MDC was denying them the vote. Dumi suggested that the Vigil should make the UK an uncomfortable place for anyone from the Government of National Unity. After the meeting he and several others headed off to protest at the Savoy.

Saturday 1ˢᵗ December: Vigil management team member Josephine Zhuga had happy news for us today. After a long battle – when she was told her papers had been lost – she has finally been granted indefinite leave to remain in the UK. Lindy Bare and Philip Maponga, who played the roles of Tsvangirai and his new wife Elizabeth in our mock wedding on 15ᵗʰ September, announced that they are to get married. They had never met before our event.

Saturday 8ᵗʰ December: Our sister organization the Restoration of Human Rights in Zimbabwe (ROHR) met in Birmingham to elect a new executive. Vigil founder member Ephraim Tapa, who set up ROHR in 2007, was confirmed as Chair. The conference resolved to relaunch programmes in Zimbabwe and start operations in South Africa. Signatures were collected for a petition to the UK Border Agency protesting at the treatment of Zimbabwean deportees.

Saturday 22ⁿᵈ December: On the shortest Saturday of the year, with darkness falling before 4 pm, and floods reported from many parts of the UK, we gathered in the rain to sing and dance outside the South African High Commission to petition President Zuma for tough action against Mugabe. The demonstration was part of the 21ˢᵗ Movement Global Protest launched in January which has seen monthly demonstrations by the diaspora under the banner 'Reclaim Zimbabwe'.

2013

Highlights

January: Mugabe and Tsvangirai reach deal over new constitution.
12th January: Finance Minister Tendai Biti (MDC T) tells London investors Zimbabwe 'safe and lucrative place to invest'.
February: Biti says upcoming elections will be free and fair.
23rd February: Vigil delivers letter to South Africa House warning President Zuma there's no hope of free and fair elections unless electoral reforms implemented.
2nd March: Vigil asks UN to demand UN monitors for elections.
16th March: Vigil marks constitution referendum day.
30th March: Justice Minister Chinamasa has to be restrained from attacking British MP Kate Hoey at London diplomatic reception.
4th May: MDC T says it expects landslide victory in elections.
June: Zimbabwe court orders elections by end of July.
15th June: SADC summit demands immediate electoral reforms.
22nd June: Vigil launches petition urging opposition to boycott elections if no reforms.
13th July: Vigil warns Zuma elections being systematically rigged.
20th July: 'Mugabe' demonstrates at Vigil how elections are rigged. AU says conditions are good for the elections.
27th July: Four days before the elections, the Vigil 'congratulates' Mugabe on his victory.
31st July: As Zimbabweans go to the polls Vigil calls for new elections.
August: US demands further political reforms before considering Southern African call for the West to lift Zimbabwe sanctions.
September: Opposition boycotts opening of parliament in protest at rigged elections.
24th October: Vigil's Restore Zimbabwe Conference in London.
8th November: Vigil demonstrates at London meeting addressed by Tourism Minister Mzembi.
9th November: Vigil writes to Israeli PM protesting at Israeli company's involvement in Zimbabwe election rigging.

Vigil diary excerpts

A bridge too far – Saturday 5th January: The first Vigil of the New Year was auspicious if only because it didn't rain! (2012 had been the wettest year since English records began.) The Vigil diary noted that the exiled Zimbabwean writer Chenjerai Hove reflected the Vigil's view that there had been no improvement on the election situation of 2008. 'Mugabe's party has not changed its approach one inch' he said. 'As the country faints under heavy economic and political burdens, the politicians would rather punch the air with empty slogans and worthless promises that are so unrealistic that even illiterate villagers wonder how a politician can be so dumb as to promise a bridge where there is not even a river'.

Boasting Biti – Saturday 12th January: On a bitterly cold day the Vigil kept warm by laughing at the reported remarks by Finance Minister Tendai Biti at a Zimbabwe investment conference here in London. 'Reported' remarks because we couldn't afford to go to the meeting to hear for ourselves at a cost of £90 for the cheapest ticket. Biti said that Zimbabwe had become 'a safe and lucrative place to come and invest in' and was 'pregnant with opportunities' . . .

The world must witness – Saturday 19th January: The Vigil delivered a petition to the South African High Commission appealing to President Zuma to ensure that international observers are sent to Zimbabwe for the upcoming elections and calling on him to get tough with Mugabe. Vigil founder member Ephraim Tapa said the diaspora were the victims of South Africa's failure to broker peace.

Open letter to Chatham House – Saturday 26th January: The Vigil sent an open letter to Chatham House, the influential London international affairs think tank, protesting at not being allowed to attend a meeting to discuss a contentious book defending Mugabe's land policy 'Zimbabwe takes back its land'.

Thursday 31st January: Vigil supporters demonstrated outside Chatham House. We had consulted leading economists in Zimbabwe for their opinions on the assertions made in the book so we were able to tell people going into the meeting the facts the authors had ignored. A friend who managed to get into the meeting noted in an email to us: 'Irony of whites on the platform largely justifying what happened after the land invasions and blacks outside protesting'.

'We are not white we're black' – Saturday 2nd February: One of the authors of the book, Dr Joseph Hanlon, came to a meeting of the Zimbabwe Action Forum after the Vigil to defend the book. He had a rough ride. Nobody accepted his arguments. Daizy Fabian said: 'My father was a farmer but we were taken over and lost everything and we're not white we're black!'

Hoping for a miracle – Saturday 9th February: Every week sees the 'credibility gap' between Harare and the outside world grow wider. Last week we were told that Zimbabwe's agriculture was powering ahead – despite another appeal for international food aid. This week we were told by Tendai Biti that the elections will be free and fair – despite the failure to implement any of the GPA reforms. We are accustomed to Biti's fantasies but were disappointed that President Zuma is apparently content to allow the elections to go ahead without the reforms 'provided there is commitment on both sides of the political divide that the polls would not be preceded by violence and anything that would produce a contested outcome'. So no plans to stop the security services interfering in the elections? No cleansing of the voters' roll? No purge of the partisan electoral commission? No opening up of the airwaves? In short, no guarantee of a level playing field? Under these conditions the Vigil believes the MDC leaders will need a miracle. One would think that all they want now is Government of National Unity Mark 2 and a luxury carriage on the gravy train.

Saturday 16th February: The Vigil met earlier than usual to support an Amnesty International protest on behalf of WOZA. The Vigil displayed a poster protesting at the brutal treatment of WOZA at their Valentine Day's demonstrations in Harare and Bulawayo. Roses were laid on the doorstep of the Embassy.

Bind Mugabe to GPA promises – Saturday 23rd February: On a bitterly cold day, we were joined outside the Embassy by President Mugabe, tearing himself away from his 89th birthday celebrations. Thanks to Fungayi Mabhunu who played the role of Mugabe in our mask, dozing off under the snowflakes. Vigil supporters tied him to his chair with the SADC bonds which we hope will produce free and fair elections: 'International Observers', 'Curbs on Partisan Security Forces', 'Impartial Electoral Commission', 'Reformed Voters' Roll', 'No Hate Speech' and 'Open Airways'. Vigil supporters then trooped off to the South African High Commission to deliver a letter for President Zuma warning him that unless the GPA reforms are implemented there is no hope that Mugabe will allow free and fair elections.

No observers, no elections – Saturday 2nd March: The Vigil urged the United Nations not to finance the Zimbabwean elections unless UN monitors are allowed to attend. We said in a letter to the UN Development Programme: *'The Zimbabwe Vigil understands that the Zimbabwe government has asked you to pay for the coming elections as it says it has no money. At the same time, Vice President Joice Mujuru has insisted that only observers from Southern Africa will be invited to monitor the elections. We believe that President Mugabe's Zanu PF cronies have syphoned off billions of dollars of diamond revenue and that the President could easily arrange to finance the elections. But if the UNDP is of a mind to squander donors' money on the Zimbabwean elections we believe it should be conditional on UN observers being allowed to monitor them. We suggest that the observers should be drawn from those countries such as the US and EU members which provide most of the funds.'*

Thursday 7th March: 19 Vigil supporters attended a Mike Campbell Foundation event 'Hope in a Desert' at the prestigious Royal Geographical Society. The meeting was chaired by Kate Hoey MP, Chair of the All-Party Parliamentary Group on Zimbabwe, who paid tribute to the work of the Vigil. One of the speakers at the meeting was Dr Craig Richardson, an American associate professor of economics, who spoke of the importance of property rights for the future of the Zimbabwean economy. The executive director of the Foundation, Ben Freeth, criticized two recent books by British academics which he said were white-washing the agricultural situation.

Saturday 9th March: The likelihood of election violence in Zimbabwe has prompted a petition to the British Government by Restoration of

Human Rights in Zimbabwe and the Vigil to protest at the deportation of Zimbabwean failed asylum seekers ahead of the elections.

Referendum no litmus test – Saturday 16th March: The main event of the day was the presentation of our petition to 10 Downing Street. Earlier, more than 100 Zimbabwean exiles gathered outside the Zimbabwe Embassy to mark Referendum Day. We were joined by Mark Beacon of ACTSA who said a peaceful referendum on the proposed new constitution was no guide to what would happen in the elections. He insisted that for the elections to be credible there would have to be an accurate voters' roll and international as well as regional observers. People were invited to write messages of hope for free and fair elections on red paper roses which were deposited in a voting box. The only sour note was cast by President Mugabe (played by Fungayi Mabhunu in our Mugabe mask) who – asked to vote for freedom – voted no. Fungayi later summed up the Vigil's view: 'The referendum is a charade. President Mugabe has once again outwitted the Movement for Democratic Change. Four years and more than $100 million have been wasted on this defective constitution when what is really needed is action to ensure free and fair elections'.

Police state – Saturday 23rd March: Spring snow didn't stop us as we trailed around central London visiting various embassies to protest against the harassment of those opposing Zimbabwe's police state. Displaying posters such as 'Free Beatrice Mtetwa' (a human rights lawyer), 'Stop harassment of Zimbabwean human rights groups', 'End police lawlessness' and 'Restore rule of law in Zimbabwe', we first delivered a letter to the High Commission of Tanzania (the Chair of the SADC Security Troika). Copies of the letter were also left at the High Commission of South Africa (the SADC facilitator on Zimbabwe) and at the Zimbabwe Embassy.

Slap in the face – Saturday 30th March: Britain's conciliatory approach to Zanu PF was rudely rejected by Justice Minister Chinamasa on his visit to London for talks with the international donor group known as the Friends of Zimbabwe. People were stunned when Chinamasa lunged at Kate Hoey, Chair of the All-Party Parliamentary Group on Zimbabwe, at a Foreign Office reception on Monday for the visiting ministerial delegation. The blustering bully had to be restrained by Zimbabwean

Ambassador Machinga, who apologised profusely to the British MP. 'Entirely in keeping with what I would expect from Zanu PF', said Hoey.

If donor countries thought that by lifting most sanctions (including the exclusion of Chinamasa) it would be reciprocated by Zanu PF concessions their illusions were dispelled by Chinamasa's intransigence. Despite the Friends of Zimbabwe donating $2.6 billion to Zimbabwe in the last four years they are still the enemy, as Chinamasa made clear in a communique after the talks on Tuesday. He said there was nothing to show for this aid 'in terms of development at grass roots level except high rise and expensive houses for staff of the NGOs' and insisted the aid should go direct to the government. He said the donors in any case would not be allowed to observe the elections as they were not 'objective' and that there would be no security sector reforms as this would just be a means of 'effecting regime change'. Chinamasa added that the international community must understand that SADC's role was just to facilitate and not supervise or impose a solution in Zimbabwe and that foreign radio broadcasts to Zimbabwe must be stopped.

Not many concessions there – not that the Vigil expected anything but North Korean-type paranoia. Our supporters, gathered outside the Tuesday meeting in the bitter cold, shouted 'thief' and 'murderer' when Chinamasa emerged from the talks. One of the Vigil founders, Patson Muzuwa, managed to smuggle himself into the Zimbabwe Embassy for a meeting on Friday attended by the three person Zimbabwe delegation representing the GNU partners. Patson said that by allowing Chinamasa into the country the UK had done us a favour: the whole world would now see at first-hand what a bigoted thug he is. Patson said it was clear that the delegation only wanted to meet selected members of the diaspora and people had tried to shut him up when he insisted on asking questions. When Chinamasa asked whether people had been ill-treated by Zanu PF, Patson dismayed everyone by standing up and saying 'Yes, I have been tortured'. Patson added that Chinamasa made racist remarks, saying Zimbabweans didn't want whites, and also made it clear that he didn't want Zimbabweans returning home.

Referendum rigged – Saturday 6th April: Vigil founder member Ephraim Tapa, who has just returned from an undercover visit to Zimbabwe, says he believes the result of the referendum on a new

2013

constitution was rigged. Ephraim, a former leader of the Civil Service Employees Union, has not been home since he was given political asylum in the UK after being tortured and fleeing Zimbabwe in 2002. Ephraim said the Zimbabwe Electoral Commission's report of an unprecedented high voter turnout was being disputed and its cooking of the figures was an indicator of things to come.

Wednesday 10th April: A Vigil delegation had a useful meeting with the Zimbabwe Desk at the UK Foreign Office. We told them that we expected rigged elections and Ephraim spoke of the tangible fear he detected in Zimbabwe. He predicted that disillusionment with the MDC would produce apathy during the elections. We were assured that the British government's only aim was to see free and fair elections resulting in a government of the people's choice. The Foreign Office expressed confidence in the facilitation of SADC.

Cockroach culture – Saturday 13th April: That prosecutors have now charged civil rights lawyer Beatrice Mtetwa with calling police 'cockroaches' shows an unexpected sensitivity. Mind you, the police do seem to be all over the place, scuttling away as soon as the light shines on them, only to re-gather in the dark. But their boss Patrick Chinamasa shows more than sensitivity. He says the UN cannot visit Zimbabwe to discuss funding the elections. To check if things are ok would, in his paranoid mind, be furthering the regime change agenda. The UN must instead just hand the money over.

33 years of oppression – Saturday 20th April: Waving a pistol at Vigil supporters, President Mugabe (played by Fungayi Mabhunu in our Mugabe mask) appeared outside the Zimbabwe Embassy to mark Independence Day. Carrying a poster reading '33 years in power', he was beset by Zimbabwean exiles with rival placards such as: 33 years of oppression, 33 years of looting, 33 years of lawlessness and 33 years of rigged elections. Vigil supporters signed a letter to President Zuma drawing his attention to moves underway for massive vote rigging. After the Vigil, Ephraim Tapa joined us at the bi-monthly Zimbabwe Action Forum to talk about his visit home. He spoke of the daily hardships of the people living the 'economy of the stomach' and how when he visited people's carefully kept homes in Harare their faces fell when he asked to use the toilet.

Saturday 27th April: We at the Vigil were glad to hear Morgan Tsvangirai insist that reforms laid out in the GPA must be implemented before the elections. But the Vigil wants him to go further and spell out that, if the reforms are not made, he will not take part.

Saturday 4th May: The scale of the challenge facing the opposition is becoming ever clearer as Zanu PF puts into action its well-practised plan to rig the vote. Eddie Cross, the MDC T MP, says he expects a landslide victory but the Vigil can't imagine an MDC victory with: a rigged voters' roll, obstacles to voter registration, intimidation of MDC voters, corrupt electoral commission, clampdown on civil society organisations, politicised security forces, biased judges, unreformed media, refusal to allow UN scrutiny, limits on election observers and total non-co-operation with SADC.

Saturday 11th May: The British newspaper the Guardian has run a full page on Zimbabwe by David Smith reporting from Harare. He predicts: 'The Zimbabwean president will retain power in this year's elections through fair means or foul; the poll will be relatively peaceful and deemed "credible" by the west; then sanctions will be lifted against Mugabe and his inner circle, ushering him back in from the cold.' The message from the Guardian is that the coming election must be accepted however flawed. The Vigil begs to disagree. We believe that SADC should stand by the Global Political Agreement it foisted on the MDC. And if it doesn't the MDC should refuse to take part in the charade.

Zanu PF Charm Offensive – Saturday 18th May: South Africa must 'go to hell with their treachery and leave us alone' fulminates Zanu PF politburo member Jonathan Moyo. His tirade follows the 'outrageous' remarks by South Africa's Deputy Foreign Minister Ebrahim Ebrahim who said that the MDC parties had 'a legitimate argument' in demanding further reforms before the elections. The Vigil sent the following letter to President Zuma: *'On behalf of oppressed Zimbabweans we apologise for the insolent remarks by Zanu PF functionaries about the comments by Deputy Foreign Minister Ebrahim Ebrahim suggesting that Zanu PF should implement the GPA. We trust that South Africa will spell out to Zanu PF the consequences of a rigged election . . .'*

Sanitising Zanu PF – Saturday 25th May: 'We are sorry and we pass our condolences to his family' said MDC T MP for Mazowe Central Shepherd Mushonga. Who was the noble soul he was lamenting? None other than Elias Kanengoni, the Deputy Director of the Central Intelligence Organisation, who was sentenced to seven years in prison for the shooting of former Gweru mayor Patrick Kombayi but was pardoned by Mugabe. The late lamented was also named by MDC T as one of the people responsible for the massacre of 14 party activists at Chaona village in Chiweshe in May 2008. The Vigil's exasperation with this hypocrisy was prompted by a sycophantic television documentary on the Mugabe family made for the SABC by Dali Tambo, son of South African liberation hero Oliver Tambo. 'Flowers, silver cutlery and a box of tissues adorn the spotless white tablecloth' reports the British Guardian newspaper, which was given a preview of the programme. 'Mum chortles' as the first family tucks in... 'You're very loving, you're kind, you're generous', she gushes to the President...'

Size 46B for Biti – Saturday 1st June: The Vigil applauds Tendai Biti's promise that an MDC government will firmly support action on corruption. All public officials will be required to declare their assets every year. 'Guys I have four underwear,' he told SW Radio Africa. 'Guys I've got four vests. Guys I've got four bras – size 46B.' We would like to check next year if Mr Biti is still size 46B but, sadly, the Vigil doesn't think it's likely that the MDC will form the next government, having allowed themselves to be out-manoeuvred by Zanu PF for four years to the extent that there is no time left to ensure a level playing field for the elections that Zanu PF's tame judges say must be held by the end of next month. The Zimbabwe Action Forum, at our fortnightly meeting after the Vigil, was told by Andy Moyse of the Zimbabwe Media Monitoring Project: 'Zanu PF will control the elections as they have always done'.

Time to be serious – Saturday 8th June: We disenfranchised Zimbabweans think that Zanu PF spokesman Gumbo can't be serious in describing President Zuma's advisor Lindiwe Zulu as 'a mad woman' for insisting on the promised reforms before elections. The Vigil hopes that Zuma will dismiss the decision of the aptly-named 'con'court (constitutional court) to order elections by the end of next month. No doubt the 'mad woman' will have informed him of the opinion of Deputy Chief Justice Luke Malaba that the ruling 'defied logic'.

The clouds part – Saturday 15th June: We arrived at the Vigil generally pessimistic about the SADC summit in Maputo but before the day was out our lives faced transformation. 'Good people, good, good people, it has been an incredible and unbelievable day' Tendai Biti said on his Facebook page. 'SADC rose to the occasion and scuttled the evil and Machiavellian machinations of the chaos faction of Zanu PF.' Mr Biti said all President Zuma's recommendations were adopted, including a demand that the Constitutional Court be requested to postpone elections for 14 days to enable reforms to be made. The security forces would be required to publicly affirm their commitment to the rule of law, SADC observers were to be deployed immediately and SADC representatives were to sit in JOMIC and not merely to receive reports as demanded by Zanu PF.

Tuesday 18th June: About 20 Vigil supporters attended a meeting in London at which a new film was shown 'Beatrice Mtetwa and the rule of law'. We were happy to be introduced to Beatrice, who said the new constitution would not of itself restore the rule of law. This would require full commitment by all parties. At present the voters' roll was in a shambles and perpetrators of political violence were still at large. Even if changes were made now there was not enough time left to affect people on the ground.

'No reforms, no elections' – Saturday 22nd June: After a brief ray of hope from the SADC Summit in Maputo, the week since then has seen prospects of free and fair elections again dimming as Zanu PF refuses to implement agreed reforms. The Vigil learns Morgan Tsvangirai and Welshman Ncube were left kicking their heels at State House for three hours on Friday, waiting vainly for Mugabe to pitch up for a crucial meeting. What the Vigil would have liked to see from Tsvangirai and Ncube is a decision to present an ultimatum to Zanu PF and SADC: no reforms, no elections. The Vigil was joined by MDC members. Their signatures quickly filled pages of our newly-launched petition: *'Zimbabweans in the diaspora and supporters call on political parties at home not to take part in the forthcoming elections unless Zanu PF implements the reforms demanded by SADC at its summit in Maputo on*

15th June 2013. We believe that, unless these reforms are made, the results of the elections will not be credible'.

Thursday 27th June: Vigil supporters took part in a demonstration outside the Embassy to mark the fifth anniversary of the abortive presidential run-off. Centrepiece of the demonstration was a stark 'tree of hope' on which were hung messages wishing for free and fair and non-violent elections written on red paper roses by people who had called at our regular Saturday Vigil. The tree was then taken to Southwark Cathedral and installed there by the Sub-Dean, Canon Bruce Saunders, who led us in prayers for peace and justice in Zimbabwe.

No good GNUs – Saturday 6th July: Someone defined stupidity as doing the same thing again and expecting a different result. The reverse could also be true: intelligence could be defined as doing the same thing and expecting the same result. On this basis the MDCs are stupid and Zanu PF intelligent. Since it's now obvious that the elections have already been thoroughly rigged and that none of the long-promised reforms will be implemented, the Vigil could challenge Tsvangirai and Ncube to honour their threats to boycott the elections. But it is clear to the Vigil that there is no chance they will do this. The Vigil has never been persuaded by the argument that the opposition had no alternative but to join the government of national unity after the last stolen elections. We believe it was a stupid thing to do and that it has prolonged the agony of Zimbabwe. The Vigil hopes the MDCs will show intelligence this time and work to restore their tattered reputation by forming a real opposition to the rotting carcass that is Zanu PF.

The publishers Chatto & Windus have given us several copies of the book 'We need new names' by NoViolet Bulawayo. We've asked supporters to review it and here is the first one by Vigil Co-ordinator Rose Benton: *'After 11 years of our fight against human rights abuse in Zimbabwe, I was often in tears reading this harrowing but compelling book: the devastation of Murambatsvina, father going to find work in South Africa and returning in the last throes of AIDS, political opposition brutally murdered, 11 year old girl raped and impregnated by her grandfather, hungry children raiding for guavas then stealing the shoes from a hanged woman to buy bread, the hope of the 2008 elections dashed, the insensitive and patronizing visit of an NGO lorry. Then escape to the dream country – the USA: the fight for papers, the demands for money from home, backbreaking hard work, years of living under the radar as an illegal, the sense of alienation, the loss of culture.'*

Friday 12th July: A large group of ROHR activists presented a petition calling for free and fair elections to the Zimbabwe Electoral Offices in Harare and the Home Affairs Ministry.

Stand up to Mugabe – Saturday 13th July: SADC: As we gathered for our weekly Vigil on the hottest day of the year so far (30 degrees) one of the management team was on the phone to his mother in Mbare who told us businesses were being closed and people forced by Chipangano thugs to attend a Zanu PF rally – 'or you know what will happen to you'. Other Vigil supporters also heard what was going on: such is the ease of communications today.

With only a couple of weeks before the elections, one would have hoped that SADC observers would be there on the ground to see this. But our hopes are not raised by a surreal Voice of America interview with SADC's Director of Politics, Defence and Security Co-operation, a former Lesotho military officer, the appropriately named Tanki Mothae, who we note gloomily was a SADC observer at the stolen 2008 elections. He said some SADC observers are in Zimbabwe but 'the bulk of other observers will be in Zimbabwe, as soon as member states are ready, which is what we are waiting on now. The SADC Secretariat is busy trying to put together a team that will go to Zimbabwe as the SADC poll observer mission.'

Let's hope they will make it on time! Mothae added 'We are convinced that the Zimbabwe Electoral Commission is ready. The referendum was a test case, which they managed very well, and I think everybody was happy to see that under these illegal sanctions that Zimbabwe has been put under, they managed to pull through and the referendum was a very well-managed process' So the problem for SADC is 'illegal' sanctions? Not the SADC election requirement that observers should be in place three months before the polls . . . ?

The Zimbabwe Human Rights NGO Forum accuses Mugabe of trying to intimidate SADC by threatening to withdraw from the organization.

Judging from Mothae's comments we don't believe intimidation is necessary . . . Either way, the Vigil believes the real problem is the stuffing of ballot boxes by Zanu PF and we were joined by Mugabe himself (in the form of Fungayi Mabhunu in our Mugabe mask) who showed us how to carry out this clever Israeli trick. Vigil supporters have written to President Zuma in the hope of putting some spine into SADC. Here's our letter: *'Dear President Zuma: On behalf of our fellow countrymen we apologise for the discourteous and ungrateful comments on South Africa's mediation efforts made recently by President Mugabe. We can assure you that his views do not represent those of the majority of Zimbabweans who, on the contrary, welcome particularly your concern for free and fair elections in Zimbabwe. President Mugabe has made it clear that he will not respect the requirements of the recent SADC meeting in Maputo and has continued to obstruct any attempt to implement the reforms he undertook to make under the Global Political Agreement. Furthermore, there is clear evidence that the elections on 31st July are already being systematically rigged. The Zimbabwe Vigil urges you not to recognise the results of disputed elections.'*

Thursday 18th July: The Vigil / ROHR had a meeting with the Zimbabwe desk of the British Foreign Office and we gave them our analysis of the situation at home. Ephraim Tapa said our delegation was dismayed that concern seems to have shifted from 'free and fair elections' to 'credible elections'.

Baba Jukwa unmasked – Saturday 20th July: A demanding Mugabe kept all of us at the Vigil hard at it stuffing ballot boxes for the elections set for 31st July. Unusually considerate, he saved us a bit of work by marking a cross against his name before handing out the ballot papers from a seemingly inexhaustible supply. 'Don't tell anyone, but I am Baba Jukwa' (an alleged Zanu PF informer), he confided. 'I popped over to show you how Zanu PF will win the elections. They're in the bag. In fact, lots of bags', he said, pointing at the sacks of rigged ballot papers that he brought. Baba Mugabe spent the whole afternoon with us and as time went on we could see how he bewitched Morgan Tsvangirai during their weekly 'china cup' tea parties and got Tendai Biti rhapsodising about his wisdom, Nelson Chamisa about his leadership abilities, Dave Coltart about his deep compassion and British Ambassador Deborah Bronnert about his charm. Ad nauseum. Baba Mugabe gave Vigil supporters an authentic taste of the Zimbabwean voting experience. Here are some of the comments while people queued to vote: 'The ballot box is getting full but the line is not moving', 'I slept here last night and can't get to the front of the queue but other people have voted twice or thrice', 'I will use my dead father's vote' and 'They say it's one man, one vote but why has it changed to one man, one million votes?'

The Vigil recalls how SADC approved the rigged elections in the DRC in December 2011. In the words of journalist Simon Allison: 'A range of international observers were watching, and uncovered a long list of offences: evidence of vote tampering; impossibly high rates of voter turnout in places known to be loyal to the president; strangely low turnouts in opposition areas; the mysterious disappearance of 2 000 polling station results in Kinshasa; and violence in the run-up to and during the campaign which killed 18 people, mostly committed by incumbent Joseph Kabila's presidential guard. 'And yet, SADC, along with the African Union and three other African observer missions, declared that the elections were "successful", duly confirming that the organisation's standards of fairness and transparency are very low indeed; and sending a message to other leaders, like Mugabe, that there is a fair amount of electoral mischief that they can get away with before the regional body will call them out on it. And if Mugabe is called out, he is well within his rights to point out SADC's hypocrisy — and ignore their verdict. Once again, somehow, Mugabe holds all the cards. There is a reason why he has lasted in power so long — and why he still got a little while to go' Our hopes were not raised by a statement from the African Union: 'The environment in Zimbabwe so far reassures us that that the conditions are good for the election to be held on July 31,' said Aisha Abdullahi, AU commissioner for political affairs.

'Credible' elections? – Saturday 27th July: With only four days to go before the elections, the Vigil 'commends' President Mugabe on his 'credible' re-election for another 5 year term as he approaches his 90th birthday. Despite overwhelming evidence that the elections on 31st July are being rigged, the SADC 'Summit' on 20th July had four 'commendations' and a 'credible' in its brief four-point communique released after meeting to consider complaints by the MDC about the election arrangements. For connoisseurs of bullshit, here is the communique in full:

'8. On the Republic of Zimbabwe
8.1 The Summit was pleased to note that all the political parties have committed themselves to ensuring that the forthcoming elections are held in a peaceful environment. Summit encouraged the Government, all political parties and leaders to continue with these commendable efforts which will help realize credible elections.
8.2 The Summit commended the Government of Zimbabwe for extending an invitation to SADC Member States to deploy election observers and the manner in which these (sic) Observer Mission has been received in Zimbabwe.
8.3 The Summit commended H.E. Jacob Zuma, President of the Republic of South Africa and SADC Facilitator, for his tireless efforts in ensuring that the Zimbabwe political stakeholders hold successful elections.
8.4 The Summit noted the problems that arose during the special vote on 14-15 July 2013 and would like to commend ZEC for taking these up as challenges to be overcome on the 31st of July, and called upon all political parties to cooperate as fully as possible with ZEC in order to ensure that it is able to meet these challenges.'

The Vigil 'commends' the observers who went to such pains to see that the elections were 'credible', including President Zuma's former wife, the AU Commission Chairperson, Nkosazana Dlamini-Zuma, who astonished Morgan Tsvangirai by saying he had told her he was 'happy' with the election environment. Tribute must also be paid to President Zuma himself and SADC's 'commendable' support for the elections without which the people of Zimbabwe would not be able to look forward to such a 'credible' disaster. The Vigil further 'commends' the security forces who ensured that President Mugabe was 'credibly' returned to power. Lastly, to the UK, the EU and the US: the Vigil was impressed by the weasel words by which they abandoned the standards of 'free and fair' for the slippery slopes of 'credible'. We look to them to support President Mugabe's 'credible' and 'commendable' nomination for the Nobel Economics, Peace and Literature Prizes.

Zimbabwean exiles call for new elections – Wednesday 31st July: As votes were cast in the Zimbabwe elections, Zimbabwean exiles and supporters in London called on South Africa to organize new elections in keeping with the agreed roadmap and election guidelines of SADC. The call came during a six hour demonstration by the Vigil outside the

Zimbabwe Embassy on election day, 31st July, in protest at the rigging of the vote by Mugabe's Zanu PF party. Vigil supporters were joined by members of ACTSA and representatives of the Trades Union Congress and the Labour Party. Also there was the human rights campaigner Peter Tatchell. The protest was covered by a variety of news organisations who showed particular interest in the Vigil's depiction of how Mugabe was stealing the elections.

A Vigil leader, Fungayi Mabhunu, wearing a Mugabe mask, was filmed stuffing ballot boxes with votes from large black bags labeled Nikuv – the Israeli company accused of helping Zanu PF rig the elections. As the demonstration got under way Fungayi received a text from Harare that an informant in the Zimbabwean Electoral Commission had disclosed that polling stations in MDC strongholds were being supplied with Nikuv pens with ink which disappeared after a few hours. During the afternoon Vigil supporters moved en masse around the corner for a boisterous demonstration outside the South African High Commission, where the following letter was delivered:

'Dear President Zuma
Zimbabwe elections not credible
Zimbabwean exiles and supporters deplore the refusal of President Mugabe to ensure the elections are free and fair. There is overwhelming evidence that the poll has been comprehensively rigged and we have no confidence that the results will reflect the will of the people. The Zimbabwe Vigil calls on the Southern African Development Community to organise new elections in keeping with the agreed roadmap and SADC election guidelines. We caution you that, as things stand, there will inevitably be a new mass exodus of desperate and impoverished people

fleeing Zimbabwe as the Mugabe mafia intensifies its looting, sending the country's economy into a cataclysmic decline'

'Incredible' elections – Saturday 3rd August: After the predictable failure of the MDC in the elections, Morgan Tsvangirai must consider his position. The custom in most countries is that a losing candidate stands aside – particularly if he has lost several elections. The Vigil believes that Tsvangirai must take responsibility for a succession of decisions which have been fatal to the opposition in Zimbabwe. We don't want to rub salt into wounds, but here are a few of the MDC decisions which have puzzled us, as we have clearly recorded in our diaries:
1. The mad split over the Senate.
2. Pulling out of the Presidential run-off in 2008.
3. Joining in the flawed GNU ('we demand an end to sanctions and foreign broadcasts') when there was an opportunity to form a government in exile in Botswana at a time when Mugabe was on his knees.
4. Failure to pull out of government when Mugabe immediately disregarded the GPA and showed that the MDC had no power whatsoever.
5. Being distracted by the ludicrous 4-year-long constitution-making exercise, which produced an abortion of a document that has proved completely useless, especially as a new constitution can be expected within a year. The MDC should have spent the time concentrating on getting a level playing field for elections.
6. Allowing vital roadmap issues to be delayed until they were impossible to implement.
7. Agreeing to take part in the latest elections when none of the MDC or SADC requirements had been met.

Tsvangirai has issued a statement after an MDC National Council meeting in Harare saying 'Given the illegality of this election, the MDC National Council resolved that it will not legitimize institutions created by an illegal election and therefore will not engage in institutions of government'. The Vigil applauds this decision and hopes that MDC MPs will refuse to take their seats in this rigged Parliament. We would hope that they would stand outside when parliament is convened with banners saying 'we object'. Sadly we do not believe that this will happen. We can't see them giving up perks for principles. It gives the Vigil no satisfaction that our prediction of a rigged election turned out to be true. We can't end the diary without lamenting the retirement of our tireless friend Barbara Goss who has for years produced the daily compendium of news, the Zimbabwe Situation. It has been an invaluable resource and we owe her deep gratitude for her hard work.

Call for diaspora unity – Saturday 10th August: There has been a call in London for a conference of the Zimbabwean diaspora to discuss the way forward following the rigged elections which have returned Mugabe to power for another term. The call came from Ephraim Tapa who said the MDC project had run its course and Zimbabweans were looking to the diaspora to come up with an alternative programme to save Zimbabwe. The Vigil was attended by 100 Zimbabweans from all parts of the UK.

Saturday 17th August: Supporters of the Vigil and associated groups have agreed to arrange an all-stakeholder meeting in London in October to give the diaspora an opportunity to discuss ways of working together to reclaim Zimbabwe. The decision was made at the Zimbabwe Action Forum held after the Vigil. The Forum was addressed by Dewa Mavhinga, Senior Researcher for Africa with Human Rights Watch and a former regional co-ordinator for Southern Africa of the Crisis in Zimbabwe Coalition. He was in Zimbabwe for the elections and gave us a firsthand account of how they were rigged. Mr Mavhinga, who has had meetings with the leadership of most SADC countries, said they had made it clear that, as long as the violence of 2008 was avoided, they would rubberstamp the election outcome.

Saturday 24th August: The Vigil launched a new petition calling on the UK and the European Union to follow the lead of the United States and continue sanctions. The petition, addressed to European Union governments, reads: *'Following the rigged elections in Zimbabwe, we urge the European Union to re-impose the targeted sanctions on Mugabe and his cronies. We further call on the EU to suspend government aid to all Southern African Development Community countries until they abide by their commitment to uphold human rights in Zimbabwe.'* Ephraim Tapa said: 'Altogether the EU gives billions of dollars each year to pay for the misgovernment and corruption of Southern Africa. Why?

Challenge Mugabe to deliver – Saturday 31st August: The Zimbabwean diaspora is puzzled that a month has passed since the stolen elections and a seemingly punch-drunk opposition has given no sign of a strategy to confront Mugabe, let alone stage demonstrations against Zanu PF's blatant chicanery. We at the Vigil are sorry that the MDC did not decide to boycott parliament to make a powerful statement to the world about the election rigging – especially necessary since the puzzling withdrawal of the MDC's legal challenge against the outcome. Mugabe had promised that civil servants and others would be given pay rises. We urge the MDC to support the legitimate demands of workers for this promise to be honoured.

Saturday 7th September: After the Vigil many supporters went on to our Zimbabwe Action Forum at which we discussed plans for an all-stakeholders' meeting of the diaspora to be held in London. It was proposed that the diaspora should be invited to coalesce around ideas such as: 1) Scrapping indigenisation and encouraging foreign direct investment, 2) Giving freehold title to farmers to enable them to get bank loans or sell their properties (economists say this would at a stroke stimulate agriculture), 3) Nationalising the diamond mines, 4) Privatising the parastatals, 5) Requiring senior elected and non-elected leaders to disclose their assets, 6) Replacing the judiciary and reforming the police and armed forces.

Saturday 14th September: A pom pom from the Vigil for NoViolet Bulawayo who has been chosen as one of the finalists for the prestigious Man Booker prize for best novel of the year written by someone from the Commonwealth (still including the Irish Republic and Zimbabwe!) NoViolet, whose book is titled 'We Need New Names', gave an interview to the UK's Guardian newspaper about a visit home in April – the first time she had been back for thirteen years. It is clear that she shares our fears as we face the consequences of another stolen election. 'It was a strange country,' Bulawayo told the Guardian. 'I went there in search of the Zimbabwe I knew and it was a shock: power cuts, water cuts, just driving down the streets the potholes were amazing, and 80% of the population not working. Just seeing the desperation; wherever you went people were struggling. That was a picture of the country that I never knew.'

Zanu-PF dapper in London – Saturday 21st September: While we sang 'Ishe Komberera Africa / Nkosi Sikelel' iAfrica' outside the Embassy at the end of the Vigil, Zanu PF supporters in the UK were attending 'official victory celebrations' elsewhere in London. Zanu PF supporters continue to claim asylum in the UK on the fraudulent basis of political persecution in Zimbabwe. The Vigil will continue to expose those who do this. We believe they should be sent home to pressure NoPresident Mugabe to clear up the mess there which has made it unpleasant for even Zanu PF people to live in. The bi-monthly Zimbabwe Action Forum agreed the planned All-Stakeholders' Conference for the Zimbabwe Diaspora would be held on Thursday 24th October.

Zimbabwe's 'quaternary' stage? – Saturday 5th October: At the Vigil we said a prayer for all those fleeing Africa. Our thoughts were of the hundreds of hopeful migrants who drowned when their vessel sank off the Italian island of Lampedusa, ending their dream of a better life in Europe. Italy declared a day of national mourning and there were widespread cries that 'something must be done' to end the carnage in the Mediterranean caused by people-smugglers cramming desperate migrants into unseaworthy boats. Short of Europe throwing open its borders (unlikely to say the least) the unpalatable truth is that sadly nothing will stop this trade until there is good governance in Africa, an end to institutional corruption there and an improvement in conditions for ordinary people. There is little prospect of this, despite economic growth in some African countries. These are the reasons why up to a quarter of Zimbabwe's people have fled the country – among them the best educated. Reading the Herald one can see the disastrous result of this exodus. 'Elementary studies of economics inform us that production occurs in three levels which are primary, secondary and tertiary and of the late, the fourth level which is quaternary', goes one article. The writer says a 'paradigm shift' in Zimbabwe is 'the panacea that will lift our nation from the doldrums of quagmire that the economic forces of this age have relegated us to'. The Vigil thinks that if the writer meant Zanu PF instead of 'economic forces' his ravings might make a glimmer of sense. But it's clear he doesn't. The reality is that the flight from Zimbabwe looks, if anything, like increasing as NoPresident Mugabe reneges on his election promises of pay rises, investment in industry etc and the economy moves from primary to secondary and tertiary then 'quaternary'. The Vigil was told by a Zimbabwean who teaches at a London college that he was shocked on a recent visit home to rural Matabeleland to see how thin, gaunt and small people are. Their physical condition was in sharp contrast to that of people just across the border in South Africa.

Disunited Nations – Saturday 12th October: With the UN Secretary-General Ban Ki-moon's congratulations on his election 'victory' ringing in his ears, NoPresident Mugabe ventured to join us at the Vigil as we marked our 11th anniversary. Played by Fungayi Mabhunu, wearing our Mugabe mask, he carried a poster reading 'Thanks UN'. Ki-moon's congratulations may just be a diplomatic courtesy but former UN Secretary-General Kofi Annan of Ghana twisted the dagger further in an interview with the British Guardian newspaper, saying that Mugabe probably could have won the elections even without rigging. The Ghanaian, notorious for sleeping on the job during the Rwandan genocide, said the world must work with Mugabe. 'Holding on to the past and who was right and who was wrong and all this doesn't help' he said. Annan would have made more sense if he'd argued for UN assistance to solve the 'technical' problem claimed to be responsible for the failure to publish the voters' roll even a month and a half after the elections. Betrayed by SADC, the AU, the EU and now the UN, Zimbabweans have been abandoned to our fate. How the diaspora can help the people at home was discussed at a meeting of the Zimbabwe Action Forum. The forum was addressed by Ephraim Tapa, who is to chair the 'Restore Zimbabwe' All-Stakeholders' Conference which is to be held in London on 24th October. The purpose of the meeting is to agree a common platform and strategy for diaspora action on the Zimbabwe crisis. Ephraim spoke of the Vigil's long struggle and promised it would continue until there were free and fair elections in Zimbabwe. He said that during his covert visit home before the elections he had been assured by the MDC that there was no possibility of rigging and asked what his plans were for returning home. All was going well he was told: there was a new constitution, a new Zimbabwe Electoral Commission, observers were in place. Celebrations were underway; why was he spoiling the party?

Saturday 19th October: The Vigil's initiative in arranging a diaspora conference in London has met with predictable abuse by Zanu PF trolls prowling the internet. We think every CIO agent – when they are not out beating people up – spends his office hours in cyber disinformation in the relentless war against truth. Zanu PF's latest flatulent blueprint: Zimbabwe Agenda for Sustainable Socio-Economic Transformation (Zim Asset) is no asset as far as we can see. It says: 'Government would among other things undertake a national blitz to rehabilitate water supplies, sewerage systems, roads, health facilities and schools in all urban centres, institute measures to improve processes at the Registrar General's Office by December 2013 . . .' Fat chance!

Restore Zimbabwe Conference – Thursday 24th October: Vigil founder member Ephraim Tapa opened the conference, saying that it was coming at a critical time. He had received a message from the US supporting the quest for a common platform for the diaspora. Ephraim said there was overwhelming evidence that the July elections were a sham. The opposition to Mugabe had been let down by a compromised and unstrategic leadership. He said there was every reason to be very depressed at the suffering in Zimbabwe: company closures, economy shrinking, hundreds leaving the country daily . . . A fully-fledged dictatorship was in prospect because Mugabe could ignore the opposition. Ephraim said that the diaspora must now assume greater responsibility for the democratic agenda. The 'pull him down' syndrome must end and the diaspora unite and agree on a common strategy to restore Zimbabwe. Ephraim said Zimbabweans were looking for leadership. They could not just wait for the death of Mugabe. 'The house is on fire', he said. 'We want our right to dream again'.

Ephraim introduced the speakers:
- Kate Hoey MP, Chair of the All-Party Parliamentary Group on Zimbabwe, with a message of support.
- Muzvare Betty Makoni, award-winning gender activist – exploring the role of women in the struggle for democracy in Zimbabwe.
- Wilbert Mukori, political analyst and contributor to SW Radio Africa – talking about how the diaspora can promote democracy in Zimbabwe.
- Jaison Matewu, unsuccessful candidate for MDC-T, and Bie Tapa, recently returned from six months in Zimbabwe – witness accounts of what happened in the elections.

Kate Hoey said the diaspora has an important role to play and must be united. It was sad that there had been international acceptance of the election results, knowing it was a sham. The opposition to Mugabe had been naïve in thinking that SADC would ride to the rescue. 'We will have to wait a long time for that.' Kate said the cleverness of Zanu PF had been underestimated: immediately after the GPA they had set out to win the 2013 elections – with the help of China and the Israeli company Nikuv. Some of the opposition leadership thought they were cleverer than they are. It was up to the diaspora to create a powerful voice to make the UK government listen – particularly about sanctions when they come up for debate in the EU in February. While they were in exile in the UK Zimbabweans must be enabled to acquire skills: 'We must find a legal way for you.' Kate said the diaspora had a responsibility to let the world know what was happening in Zimbabwe. She described the Vigil as 'a shining light these long years'. And added 'you have been right when politicians have been wrong'.

Betty Makoni said Zimbabwe will never be free until women are treated equally. It was not only the elections that had not been free and fair: the leadership in Zimbabwe had let women down. Women were the most vulnerable and were taking all the blows. She argued that women must share power if Zimbabwe was to be truly free. 'Men have not ruled the world, they have ruined the world'. To restore Zimbabwe it was necessary to restore women. Betty went on criticize churches in Zimbabwe for endorsing the patriarchal society and added 'Men can't rule alone. We must rule side by side'. In response to a participant who said we needed to be aware that the NGO community were talking more and more of the need for re- engagement with the ZANU PF regime, Betty replied that we needed to be aware that the NGO community were mainly concerned with protecting their own jobs. Those who were advocating re-engagement with the Zanu PF government had only recently said the elections were not free and fair and were starting from a premise of dishonesty and compromise. The NGOs were moving the goalposts to suit their own selfish ends. Betty added that she had worked in the NGO environment for 10 years.

Wilbert Mukori said the conference was a step forward for the Zimbabwean diaspora. A recent scene in the Zimbabwean parliament when Zanu PF blocked a debate on the elections showed that they knew that they had been rigged. The situation in Zimbabwe was desperate. Finance Minister Chinamasa had returned home from international financial institutions with nothing to show but his arrogance. Wilbert said the MDC had shot itself in the foot by withdrawing its court challenge to the election results. The diaspora should present evidence to the world so that it couldn't accept the election results.

There were eye witness accounts of the elections from Bie Tapa of the Vigil recently back from Zimbabwe, and Jaison Matewu who unsuccessfully stood for MDC T in Buhera West. Bie spoke of problems with voter registration and corruption. He said there was a widespread fear of the consequences if people did not vote for Zanu PF. Urban youths were prevented from voting. Jaison said that, on the face of it, going into the elections, things had looked ok, with an absence of violence. But he soon realised something was going on. Ballot papers were being doctored. There was multiple voting. If you dipped your finger in paraffin the ink would disappear. Three hundred blank ballot papers mysteriously ended up with a cross for Zanu PF. The MDC shouldn't go into new elections before reforms had been implemented.

We were grateful that Stanford Biti stepped forward to stand in for our scheduled speaker, Taurayi Chomboko, who was summoned at the last minute to a meeting of the MDC UK Executive with Tsvangirai who had suddenly popped up in Oxford, a move we took as a deliberate undermining of the Conference.

The day ended with a spokesman for the Vigil proposing the following resolutions: The conference:
1. Rejects the 31st July elections as rigged
2. Calls on the diaspora to unite in demanding new elections
3. Condemns SADC for not ensuring the GPA was implemented
4. Appeals to the AU to revisit its approach to the Zimbabwe crisis
5. Urges South Africa not to support the Mugabe regime
6. Advises the EU to continue the targeted sanctions against Mugabe and to expand them to include judges and officials of the Zimbabwe Electoral Commission who have demonstrated bias for Zanu PF
7. Demands the Zimbabwean opposition resist Mugabe at every step
8. Asks the UK government not to send home failed Zimbabwean asylum seekers

The Conference was attended by about 70 people and messages of support came from the US, South Africa, Australia and Zimbabwe. Among them were:
- Yours is a valiant effort to keep the struggle alive. We take comfort from Churchill's adage: "When you're going through hell . . . keep going!" Well done for taking the initiative and holding this Conference – Dale Dore, Zimbabwean economist.
- All the best. Please give me feedback – Vince Musewe, Zimbabwean economist.
- This is a really important initiative of yours – Ben Freeth, Mike Campbell Foundation. What you are doing is so important and we would like to support you – Claire Freeth, Mike Campbell Foundation.
- I would love to attend and I wish this meeting the very best of success – Christopher Maphosa, Chair of ZAPU Europe Province. His life story inspired the play 'The rain that washes'.
- Good Governance Africa (Joburg) is planning a conference on Zimbabwe: Where to from here? for early next year, to be held in Johannesburg and attended essentially by Zimbabwe civil society activists. We would be grateful to hear a report on your meeting – R W Johnson, journalist.

Saturday 2nd November: A meeting of the Zimbabwean Action Forum overwhelmingly endorsed the resolutions put forward by the Vigil at the Restore Zimbabwe conference.

Poisonous Mzembi – Friday 8th November: Police were called to the Royal Institute of International Affairs when Vigil supporters staged a demonstration protesting at the recognition given to Mugabe's visiting Tourism Minister (and farm looter) Walter Mzembi. Mzembi had been invited to speak during his visit to London for an international tourism conference. African diplomats in dapper black suits and shiny black shoes glared poison at the demonstrators outside as they went into the venue. Soon afterwards a police van arrived and a policeman went into Chatham House. He quickly re-emerged and gave us a friendly wave before driving off. (We had arranged police permission for the protest.) 1 – 0 to the Vigil.

Saturday 9th November: It is already clear that manipulation by the mercenary Israeli company Nikuv was a decisive factor in Mugabe's 'victory'. The Vigil is sending an open letter to the Israeli Prime Minister and the people of Israel: *For the last 33 years Zimbabweans have been fighting to end the Mugabe dictatorship so they too can enjoy the fruits of democracy and good governance. It is wholly unacceptable that their hopes for a better future were once again ruthlessly dashed because Mugabe had help from an Israeli company Nikuv. Nikuv corrupted the voters roll so that nearly one million voters were denied the right to vote on election day. It is no exaggeration to say it was Nikuv which delivered election victory to Mugabe considering the tyrant's winning margin was said to be one million.*

Saturday 16th November: At a meeting of the Zimbabwe Action Forum after the Vigil, it was agreed to approach Zimbabwe Lawyers for Human Rights for advice on legal options open to us to challenge the rigged elections. Also discussed were calls by some MDC leaders for the lifting of the targeted measures against Mugabe cronies on the grounds that these sanctions provided a fig-leaf for Mugabe's mis-governance. The Vigil's view is that sanctions should be continued and indeed extended to include those who rigged the elections.

Saturday 23rd November: As winter closes in on us at the Vigil, we are in despair at Zimbabwe's hopeless government. We read that MDC MP Eddie Cross says that nothing is being done to tackle corruption. He says: 'I cannot think of a single Minister (perhaps one and even he is questionable) that is not guilty of gross corruption.'

Friday 29th November: We are grateful to Wilbert Mukori for representing us at a conference in Holland organised by the Zimbabwe Europe Network. He said it was clear the EU wanted to lift sanctions and they were prepared to accept the elections even though they know they were rigged.

Saturday 30th November: The Vigil is launching a campaign to alert British MPs and other opinion formers to the deteriorating situation in Zimbabwe as the EU moves to lift the remaining targeted measures. Supporters are being asked to send the following letter to MPs etc: *Zimbabweans in the UK are grateful for the sanctuary we have been given here in these desperate days for our homeland . . . Our hopes of change were dashed in July when the elections were stolen with the help of the Chinese and the Israeli ballot-rigging company, Nikuv, ending the four year coalition with the Movement for Democratic Change . . . The end of the restraining MDC influence on the government and the exposure of the hollowness of Zanu PF election promises threaten to lead to a new lurch to a North Korean-type siege mentality.*

Mugabe grabs aid money – Saturday 7th December: As we mourned the death of Nelson Mandela, the Vigil was shocked to learn that the UN has apparently agreed to divert some of the aid going to help Zimbabwe's starving people to help pay for the illegal regime's pie-in-the-sky economic development plan. The Vigil is sending an open letter to the UK's International Development Secretary: *We appeal to the UK government not to allow any of its aid to be diverted to prop up the Mugabe regime and, in particular, we call on it to exercise vigilance to stop aid being denied to opponents of the Mugabe regime . . .* A large group of Vigil supporters joined mourners outside the nearby South African High Commission. We recall how when Mandela visited London in 2008 we confronted him with a banner saying: 'Mandela ignores Mugabe's terror. Shame / Mandela speak out. Support a free Zimbabwe'. That very evening he spoke of a failure of leadership in Zimbabwe.

A choice of frauds – Saturday 14th December: The man hired by South Africa to interpret the Mandela memorial proceedings to the deaf turns out to be a schizophrenic fraud. His gestures were apparently as meaningless as those of President Zuma, whom the Vigil remembers as a man who betrayed his promise to deliver free and fair elections to Zimbabweans.

MDC joins Vigil in demanding new elections – Saturday 21st December: The Vigil welcomes signs that the MDC is emerging from its catatonic state following the stolen elections. Five months after we at the Vigil demanded new elections the MDC has now come on board and demanded a rerun. In an end of year statement Tsvangirai said: 'The lesson from the July 31 poll is that all reforms, including security sector and media reforms, that were agreed to under the Global Political Agreement are mandatory'. Hallelujah!

Saturday 28th December: We appeal to western embassies in Harare to urgently investigate new reports that food aid is being refused to opposition supporters. This comes despite the announcement that the UK is pouring more money into feeding Zimbabwe.

2014

Highlights

28th January: Zimbabwean business delegation to London challenged by Vigil.
1st February: Vigil thanks Botswana for denouncing Zimbabwe's rigged elections.
15th February: Vigil calls on British Prime Minister to boycott EU / AU summit if Mugabe attends.
22nd February: EU climbdown over Zimbabwe sanctions.
1st March: UK gives extra $10 million for education in Zimbabwe while Mugabe holds $1 million birthday party.
2nd April: Vigil demonstrates against Mugabe at EU / AU Summit in Brussels.
26th April: Royal Institute of International Affairs say 'Mugabe is misunderstood'.
14th June: 'Life is getting better in Zimbabwe' says British theatrical giant.
21st June: EU Ambassador to Harare criticizes NGOs and says no leadership crisis in Zimbabwe.
19th July: Belgian Ambassador to Harare says 'Nothing amiss in Zimbabwe'.
August: Grace Mugabe nominated to lead Zanu PF's Women's League.
20th September: Vigil confronts Zanu PF Minister Christopher Mutsvangwa at Chatham House.
18th October: Columnist in UK Times says Zimbabwe safe and stable.
November: Court orders South African government to release suppressed report which concluded that Zimbabwe's 2002 elections were not free and fair.
29th November: Vice President Mujuru says exposure of corruption is aimed at destroying the government.
December: Mugabe sacks Vice President Mujuru and seven ministers after accusing them of being plotting to kill him.

Vigil Diary Excerpts

Another challenging year – Saturday 4th January: We at the first Vigil of 2014 were spared the worst of the storm which saw flooding in many parts of the UK. But it was still a bracing challenge spending four hours outside the Embassy protected only by a tarpaulin strung between four trees.

Saturday 11th January: With Mugabe's return from his latest Asian holiday he will be able to celebrate his 90th birthday in some style. His office has been allocated $206 million in Chinamasa's budget – nearly six times as much as he was given last year . . . $200 million or so should cover his travel costs this year – after all it is more than the combined allocations for: The Ministry of Industry and Commerce – $7.4 million, The Ministry of Energy and Power Development – £23.4 million, The Ministry of Mines and Mining Development – $8.6 million, The Ministry of Agriculture, Mechanisation and Irrigation Development – $155.2 million.

Saturday 18th January: A meeting of the bi-monthly Zimbabwe Action Forum held after the Vigil discussed plans to stage a demonstration in Brussels next month when the EU decides whether to renew the targeted sanctions. It was agreed to run a petition to the EU demanding that there should be no recognition of the illegitimate Mugabe regime.

Saturday 25th January: The Vigil is to protest at a Zanu PF-backed visit to London by a delegation of Zimbabwean business leaders. The demonstration will take place on Tuesday outside the Royal Institute of International Affairs at Chatham House where the delegation will be appealing for international investment and the removal of targeted sanctions.

Mugabe's delegation turns chicken – Tuesday 28th January: Mugabe's broiler chickens scampered off clucking in alarm as the Vigil pursued them into Chatham House. The Zimbabwe business delegation arrived in a people carrier but when they saw the Vigil protest outside they hastily made for a side entrance, losing a few feathers in the flurry. Why broiler chickens? The former Finance Minister Tendai Biti said last week: 'The biggest problem with Zanu PF is that they think that money grows on trees. People just believe in spending, spending, spending. It's like a broiler chicken. The broiler just eats itself to death'.

Mugabe's square egg – Saturday 1st February: A delegation took time out from the Vigil to go across London to the Botswana High Commission to deliver a letter of thanks to President Ian Khama for denouncing SADC's endorsement of Zimbabwe's rigged elections. The delegation carried posters reading: 'Zimbabwe Vigil salutes Botswana' and 'Thank You President Khama'. The letter read: *'Exiled Zimbabweans at the Zimbabwe Vigil in London were heartened to read that Botswana will refuse to participate in future SADC observer missions because of SADC's acceptance of vote rigging in Zimbabwe's elections last July. We agreed with your comment on Botswana national television that the elections were neither free nor fair and that SADC has breached its own election guidelines by letting Zimbabwe 'off the hook'. Like you, we fear that this makes it difficult to expect other SADC countries to abide by the election guidelines. We note that Botswana has called for an audit of the election results but we fear this is impossible as Zimbabwe's Supreme Court has just upheld a lower court ruling that there was no urgency in hearing the MDC appeal asking the Zimbabwe Electoral Commission to release the voters' roll. The voters' roll is the smoking gun to the election rigging by Mugabe. It was expected to be released at least one month before the elections but now, six months after the elections, its release is apparently not urgent! Mugabe has clearly decided to sit on it: he is a chicken who has laid a square egg.'* There was a lively meeting of the Zimbabwe Action Forum after the Vigil. Among the matters discussed was a campaign to secure the diaspora's vote in Zimbabwe's elections. It is reassuring that our meetings are considered of such interest that the CIO bothers to attend.

Financing Mugabe's looters – Saturday 8th February: The Vigil is advising the British government not to agree to Mugabe's request to pay for the education of 750,000 Zimbabwean primary school children. The Vigil's view is explained in a letter to Justine Greening, Secretary of State for the UK's Department for International Development (DFID). Our letter follows up DFID's response to concerns we expressed about development assistance to Zimbabwe falling into the hands of the rapacious Mugabe gang . . . DFID acknowledges that some British money had been routed through the regime in contravention of DFID's funding policy in Zimbabwe and said it was strengthening its controls 'to ensure that there can be no repeat of this kind of mistake in future'.

Boycott EU / AU meeting – Saturday 15th February: The Vigil is writing to Prime Minister David Cameron urging him to boycott the EU / AU Summit in Brussels on 2 / 3 April if Mugabe attends. We think he should follow the example of his predecessor Gordon Brown who refused to attend an EU / AU Summit in Lisbon in 2007. Our letter said: *We ask: what has changed since Mr Brown took his stand? We believe the situation has got even worse, with stolen elections in 2008 and stolen elections last year. Recent revelations in the official media in Zimbabwe confirm how totally corrupt the Mugabe regime is.*

Tell us the good news – Saturday 22nd February: The EU's fawning climbdown over sanctions has predictably been scorned by Zanu PF who will now harp on about the 'victimisation' of Mugabe and his wife. Baroness Ashton, the EU's foreign policy chief, says there has been progress in Zimbabwe. We have written to her asking: What is the good news from Zimbabwe that the EU uses to justify the suspension of targeted measures?

Vigil demonstration at Heathrow – Wednesday 26th February: A group from the Vigil went to Heathrow to demonstrate against the threatened deportation of our supporter Try Mahachi. We are relieved to say he wasn't put on the plane.

Vigil demonstration – Thursday 27th February: Vigil activists demonstrated at a London restaurant holding a Zimbabwean tourist promotion. The protestors carried our banner 'No to Mugabe, No to Starvation' and posters reading 'No Rule of Law in Zimbabwe' and 'Zimbabwe Tourism props up Mugabe'.

Aid for what? – Saturday 1st March: The British government's donation of an extra $10 million for basic education for poor children in Zimbabwe came as Mugabe was being feted at a $1 million 90th birthday bash and his daughter's wedding was being celebrated in equally lavish style. The Vigil suggests that our money would be better spent on funding change in Zimbabwe rather than propping up the regime. Our thanks to Fungayi Mabhunu for donning our Mugabe mask and playing the birthday boy in a tableau at the Vigil marking the wedding. Thanks also to Admire Mhindura for playing the role of a fawning Zuma who cancelled attendance at a Westminster Abbey memorial service for Nelson Mandela to go to the wedding.

Saturday 8th March: Prosecutor-General Tomana says that, despite Zimbabwe being bankrupt with only $0.5 million in the bank, it will continue to fund the legal action against the EU for imposing sanctions. We were delighted to be joined by our supporter Deborah Harry who has been released from detention. She was taken to the airport to be deported but at the last minute there was a reprieve.

Asset in Wonderland – Saturday 15th March: As Zimbabwe sinks back to the stone age those of us driven into exile can only shake our heads in resignation at the relentless idiocy of our rulers. One brief announcement summed it up: 'To make way for the Zim Asset Awareness Seminar, neither the National Assembly nor the Senate will meet on 12th and 13th March'. Zim Asset was cobbled up, we understand, by 'Professor' Jonathan Moyo to bamboozle voters in last year's elections. To pretend it is a viable plan offering a way out of our difficulties is, in the Vigil's view, to plunge down the rabbit hole into Wonderland. Zim Asset is merely a wish list, rather like the letters children write to Father Christmas. But perhaps Zanu PF believes in Father Christmas . . . Zanu PF's detachment from reality was shown in another announcement – that Zimbabwe is to review a tourism agreement with China signed in 2006. Despite the red carpet being laid out for them, only 5,000 Chinese visited Zimbabwe in 2012. And that is out of 83 million Chinese tourists who ventured abroad that year. Tourism Minister Mzembi says he is off to China next month to 'find a way of mainstreaming them to our destination' so that they can, no doubt, admire the old colonial infrastructure, the thriving farms and factories, the state of the art schools and hospitals, and perhaps pick up some ivory . . .

Vigil supports genuine asylum seekers – Saturday 22nd March: The Vigil has made a new approach to the Home Office over the sending back of asylum seekers to Zimbabwe. Our latest letter to Home Secretary Theresa May was delivered to the Home Office by Fungayi Mabhunu, enclosing a petition protesting at the proposed deportation of Trymore Mahachi.

EU finances Mugabe – Saturday 29th March: The Vigil will be protesting in Brussels against the invitation to Mugabe to attend the EU / Africa Summit on 2nd / 3rd April. The Vigil will be there to tell the world that things are not ok in Zimbabwe. Our message is that aid for Zimbabwe must not be aid for Mugabe and the military junta. We are very sad to report that, despite all our efforts, our supporter Try Mahachi was forcibly removed to Zimbabwe on Thursday. We are disturbed at reports of how he was treated when he was handcuffed and put on the plane.

Brussels demonstration – Wednesday 2nd April: Our Mugabe mask got another outing at an EU / Africa Summit when the Vigil demonstrated in Brussels against the EU's craven invitation to Mugabe to attend. The mask was first 'unmasked' in 2007 when Vigil supporters demonstrated in Lisbon against the EU's decision to allow Mugabe to attend the Summit there. The EU must have congratulated itself when Mugabe didn't pitch up for the Brussels meeting, complaining that the invitation did not extend to Grace. Our 'No to AU dictators' poster was particularly popular with the hundreds of Mauritanian protesters we were grouped with who showed great interest in our cause.

Saturday 5th April: We were glad that participants in the Brussels excursion were able to attend the Vigil today including Ruwimbo

Melody Tembo who left Stafford at 1.30 am for Brussels only getting back at 1.30 pm the next afternoon. More than 30 people attended our Zimbabwe Action Forum and heard Vigil founder member Ephraim Tapa report on a recent visit back home during which he had discussions with embassies in Harare. More importantly, he met prominent opposition leaders who suggested co-operation with the diaspora represented by the Vigil coalition.

Vigil welcomes new path – Saturday 12th April: The Zimbabwe Action Forum had a special meeting to discuss recent talks in Harare that Ephraim Tapa had with some leading politicians. The following resolution was passed: 'The Vigil notes with great interest the developments in MDC-T. The Vigil will work with any organisation whose aims are compatible with our mission statement to secure free and fair elections and end human rights abuses in Zimbabwe, while maintaining our own identity.' A second resolution was also approved complaining about the growing number of Zimbabwean failed asylum seekers being sent home at a time when the Zimbabwean economy is collapsing. The British government has expressed concern at the corruption in Zimbabwe. Their comment came in a letter to the Vigil in reply to one we had written to Prime Minister David Cameron urging him to boycott the EU / Africa Summit. The letter to the Vigil said the UK was supporting efforts to tackle corruption in Zimbabwe through a number of initiatives. It continued 'We believe that significant improvements in the electoral process are required along the lines proposed by international and domestic observers, if future elections are to be both credible and transparent'.

Craven Europe – Saturday 19th April: As Zimbabwe marked 34 years of independence amid deepening hopelessness, the Vigil received a letter from the European Union which confirmed our worst fears about their pusillanimous policy towards Mugabe. We had asked them what progress there had been in Zimbabwe that the EU used to justify the suspension of targeted measures? In their reply the EU cannot think of any progress beyond *'the generally peaceful manner in which the 2013 elections were conducted'* . . . It's rather like commending the generally peaceful manner in which the Nazis gassed millions of Jews. The EU letter says: *'Normalising the relationship with the government will enable the EU to play a stronger role in supporting the return to* *economic stability, improving the democratic environment, rule of law, respect for human rights, and the living conditions for ordinary Zimbabweans.*' The Vigil believes Europe's aid money would be better spent in promoting desperately needed change in Zimbabwe – not in propping up this geriatric mafia.

Zanu PF at Chatham House – Saturday 26th April: The Royal Institute of International Affairs in London at Chatham House claims to be an objective and independent-minded think tank. It is nothing of the sort, judging by the Vigil's experience of how it deals with Zimbabwe. Chatham House misses no opportunity to give a platform for Mugabe's propaganda. It has been happy to host, among others, the smarmy Zanu PF minister and part-time farm looter Walter Mzembi, who declared that Mugabe was misunderstood. Then there was the British academic Joseph Hanlon who said that land reform in Zimbabwe was a success (and that Mugabe was misunderstood). There followed a Zanu PF business delegation who said, guess what? Mugabe is misunderstood! Chatham House has just published a long report on Zimbabwe by Knox Chitiyo and Steve Kibble entitled 'Zimbabwe's International Re-engagement: The Long Haul to Recovery'. It comes as no surprise to the Vigil, given the involvement of Dr Chitiyo, that the report concludes that Mugabe is misunderstood. Dr Chitiyo is, after all, a former senior lecturer in History and War Studies at the University of Zimbabwe. So he should know.

The report betrays its bias from the outset: 'A landslide victory by the Zimbabwe African National Union–Patriotic Front in Zimbabwe's elections in 2013 resulted in its comprehensive recapture of the state. The endorsement of the results by the Southern African Development Community (SADC), the Common Market for Eastern and Southern Africa (COMESA), the African Union (AU) and the UN confirmed Zanu PF's grip on power. It also symbolized Zimbabwe's re-admittance into the international community . . .' The Vigil is not sure what the authors mean by 'confirmed Zanu PF's grip on power' – rubber-stamped would be at least more literate. As for the assertion that this so-called endorsement 'symbolized Zimbabwe's re-admittance into the international community' we at the Vigil scratched our heads over this. What on earth does it mean? Have they been welcomed back to the UN? We thought they had never been expelled. Have they been given money by the World Bank or the International Monetary Fund? No they still owe them billions. The short answer is, like so much else in the report, nothing but dubious assertions rather than facts.

Along with Botswana, the Vigil is convinced that the elections were comprehensively rigged and that Zanu PF has no mandate to govern Zimbabwe. Who is Chatham House trying to fool? We hope to have an opportunity to ask them. Chitiyo is to take part in a discussion on the report at Chatham House on 14th May. The Vigil was interested to note that he is to be joined by Dr Miles Tendai, lecturer in African History and Politics at Oxford – conveniently another Zanu PF supporter who also believes that Mr Mugabe is misunderstood. A Zimbabwean journalist based in the UK, Makusha Mugabe, notes the naïve tenor of the report. He says 'The recommended international engagement, including removal of remaining sanctions and targeted measures on President Mugabe and his wife and on defence equipment, cannot happen if it is contingent on improvement of the governance and human rights situation, because the violations are directly related to power retention. Without the ill-governance and the human rights violations Zanu PF would not retain power. . .'

Betraying the future – Saturday 10th May: Everyone who wishes Zimbabwe well must be worried at indications that Zanu PF, desperate for money to keep afloat, is preparing to mortgage the country's natural resources to secure a Chinese takeaway. We at the Vigil urge the many MDCs to at least unite on this one platform: warn China that when a democratic government comes to power any such deal will be repudiated.

Re-engagement with what? – Saturday 17th May: 'Re-engagement is the only game in town' was the message from the platform at a tightly-controlled meeting on Zimbabwe held at the Royal Institute of International Affairs in London. The meeting was to launch a report 'Zimbabwe's International Re-engagement: The Long Haul to Recovery' by Steve Kibble and Zanu PF apologist Knox Chitiyo. Another featured speaker was Zanu PF sympathiser Dr Miles Tendi, Lecturer in African History and Politics at Oxford University. A friend of the Vigil who managed to get in to the meeting said 'Various people in the audience brought up excellent reasons why the west's re-engagement is a bad idea but the bottom line was it doesn't matter about human rights abuses, it doesn't matter that there is no rule of law, it doesn't matter that Zanu PF is a criminal network (all points accepted by the panel) – their view was 're-engagement is the only game in town.' Our reporter says people were allowed only one question so it was impossible to get to the nitty-gritty of anything. Zimbabwe's Ambassador to London, on the other hand, was allowed the final word on everything. Our reporter added: 'I wanted to ask what message this sends out to other governments, and did they not think that re-engagement should be based on a moral imperative ie only when some reforms have been implemented. If you engage ahead of any reforms, the message appears to be that it doesn't matter what you do as a government, as long as you hold onto power long enough, through intimidation and rigged elections, eventually the west will come around and the west will still engage with you and throw money your way.' The Vigil is appalled by the tenor of the meeting. Re-engage Zimbabwe? Since when has the West stopped engaging Zimbabwe? There is a full pack of western ambassadors in Harare falling over themselves to feed the starving and support the hopeless. Only this week the French Ambassador, Laurent Delahousse, said Zimbabwe had imposed sanctions upon itself through corruption, violation of people's rights and other unacceptable behaviour and should stop blaming other countries. 'Zimbabwe should adopt a culture of accountability, deal with corruption, lack of transparency in diamond deals and an unclear indigenisation policy and avoid blaming the imagined Western sanctions,' he said.

A still birth – Saturday 24th May: The Vigil welcomes the belated court challenge to force the Zimbabwe Electoral Commission to release the voters' roll used in the last elections as required by the constitution. This week marked the anniversary of the signing into law of the new constitution providing for improved civil liberties. What a still birth! Zanu PF has simply refused to change the laws which allow it to deny people their – now constitutional – right to freedom of expression, association and peaceful assembly.

EU's policy stinks – Saturday 31st May: There was speculation at the Vigil that the eagerness of the EU to offer hundreds of millions of dollars to the Zanu PF regime may be linked to reports that Mugabe is to step down soon. Mugabe is said to have been told by the Joint Operations Command to leave it to the military to manage a takeover by Mujuru's rival, Justice Minister Mnangagwa. Vigil supporter Clifford Mashiri has appealed to the EU not to release the money to the Zanu PF regime until it allows the diaspora vote.

Saturday 7th June: As the EU embraces Zanu PF, the party's supporters in the UK are 'coming out' in force. Nehanda Radio displayed photos on its website taken at the launch of a new branch of Zanu PF in Bracknell, near London. The Vigil has put Nehanda Radio's photos on our flickr website and we ask people to let us know if they can identify anybody so that we can check on our database to see if any of them have come to the Vigil. If they have misrepresented themselves as human rights activists to get our support for permission to stay in the UK we would like to expose them to the Home Office and see these frauds sent back home to enjoy the paradise that Zanu PF has created.

Enter Fool Stage Left – Saturday 14th June: 'Life is getting better in Zimbabwe' reads the headline over a 'review' by a former director of Britain's National Theatre Richard Eyre. 'Many Zimbabweans are now prospering'. Mr Eyre says. Harare 'utterly failed to live down to my expectations. In spite of forceful government and forced land redistribution, if you walk around the centre and the suburbs of the city you will witness no violence and encounter universal courtesy.' Mr Eyre appears to be less than fully informed of the real situation he surveyed only from the verdant suburbs of Harare. We ask ourselves: did this theatrical giant bestride Chintingwiza? The Vigil today launched a new petition to the European Union calling for votes for the diaspora to be made a precondition for further re-engagement with Zanu PF.

Mugabe's EU cheerleader – Saturday 21st June: The Zimbabwe Action Forum, meeting after the Vigil, condemned pro-Mugabe comments by the EU's Ambassador to Harare Aldo Dell'Ariccia. 'Luckily we don't have a leadership crisis in this country', he said, sounding for all the world like Mugabe's spokesman. Dell'Ariccia went on to rebuke NGOs for being confrontational and unconstructive and added 'I have the impression that you are a little bit anchored in the past where instead of seeing NGOs one perceives AGOs – anti-government organisations'. The envoy went on to condemn civil society for being critical of Zanu PF's electioneering ZimAsset plan. The meeting voted to write to Dell'Ariccia's boss Catherine Ashton suggesting that she recall him 'for re-education in diplomacy'.

'Following the rot' – Saturday 28th June: Extroverts in tight dresses and bouffant wigs tottering along the Strand in high heels: it was Gay Pride Day in London. Mugabe would have loved it. He is so taken with gays that we could imagine him tottering along the Strand after them. A mad fancy? No madder than what is happening in Zimbabwe. Take the mad case of the 'Mujuru flies' (named after Vice President Mujuru). Secretary-General of the Progressive Teachers' Union Raymond Majongwe went to see for himself the plight of the 3,000 families displaced by the Tokwe-Mukosi floods five months ago. These desperate people have to share 36 latrines. Majongwe reports: 'There are large flies called Mai Mujuru flies which are ravaging the area'.

Home Office apologises to Vigil – Saturday 5th July: The Home Office has apologised to the Vigil for comments made by an official in a letter turning down an asylum request by a Vigil supporter. The official alleged that anyone could get a letter from the Vigil in support of their asylum claim on payment of a charge so the Vigil letter would be disregarded. We wrote to the Home Office complaining about this libellous accusation, which derived from a malicious web article, pointing out that the Home Office had admitted it was unfounded three years ago. Now, in an official letter, a Home Office manager says: 'We recognise the Zimbabwe Vigil as a UK-based pressure group representing the Zimbabwean diaspora.' It adds that officials have been reminded that they should disregard the article in assessing what weight to give to letters written by the Vigil. The Vigil was interested to see that the Zimbabwean all-white pro-Mugabe group has welcomed the EU's conciliatory policy to Zimbabwe. We wonder how they regard Mugabe's latest racist rant demanding that no white person should ever farm in Zimbabwe again, even working for a black boss.

Talks or chaos – Saturday 12th July: The Vigil is heartened by signs that people are beginning to accept that an all-embracing national dialogue is the only way forward to prevent chaos in Zimbabwe. Zanu PF spokesman Rugare Gumbo said: 'The economic transformation that we want to achieve requires the voice of everyone, including the opposition and civic society'. For our part, we want to reach out to everyone and were happy to be invited to take part in a demonstration in Birmingham organised by MDC T to draw attention to the Zimbabwe crisis. In our view the EU is not helping by dropping its objections to the lack of reforms and rushing to embrace Mugabe.

One hand clapping – Saturday 19th July: It came as no surprise to the Vigil that the Belgian Ambassador to Harare is quoted as saying 'there is nothing amiss in Zimbabwe'. He said Belgium is pushing for the removal in November of the remaining EU sanctions imposed on Zimbabwe because of human rights abuses. Mr Maricou Johan added that the President of the World Diamond Centre based in the Belgian city of Antwerp was soon to visit Zimbabwe – an indication of the reason for Belgium's hand of friendship to Mugabe. The Vigil observes that Belgium has not been noted for supporting human rights in Africa. Indeed it was famous for cutting off a hand of anyone in the Belgian Congo who objected to being owned by King Leopold.

Glasgow protest – Wednesday 23rd July: A Vigil leader Fungayi Mabhunu, who is married to a Swazi, helped organise a demonstration by our sister organisation the Swaziland Vigil at the opening of the Commonwealth Games in Glasgow. He hired a minibus and picked up exiled Swazis on the way to Scotland where they protested at the attendance of David Cruiser Ngcamphalala, Minister of Sport and a former head of the Riot Police, who is accused of torturing and killing pro-democracy activists.

EU position 'misunderstood' – Saturday 26th July: The European Union has distanced itself from reported remarks by its Ambassador to Zimbabwe, Aldo Dell'Ariccia. Addressing a meeting in Harare last month he was quoted as saying 'Luckily we don't have a leadership crisis in this country'. The Vigil complained to Mr Dell'Ariccia's boss, Catherine Ashton, and in a reply to the Vigil, the EU said: 'We have checked the circumstances, and came to the conclusion that the words of Ambassador Dell'Ariccia have been improperly quoted'. On another matter, the Vigil, acting at the request of Zimbabwean activists, approached the Foreign Office for further help in resourcing the means to convert a scanned copy of the 2013 voters' roll into an electronic text document. In reply to the Vigil the Foreign Office acknowledged the importance of the matter but said the budget for this has now run out.

Recall Ambassador –Saturday 2nd August: The Zimbabwean human rights activist Ben Freeth has written to the Vigil with information supporting our demand for the recall of EU Ambassador Aldo Dell'Ariccia because of his support for the Mugabe regime. Although the EU told us in a letter that Mr Dell'Ariccia had been misreported, Ben Freeth says he spoke to the Ambassador and he repeated that he did not believe that Zimbabwe had a leadership crisis (although he did distance himself from some of the comments he is reported to have made). Freeth said that Dell'Ariccia told him there would be 'blood on the streets' if there was a leadership crisis. In his letter to us, Freeth writes: *'When dictators lead their countries into evil nobody, in truth, can say that there is not a leadership crisis, however much they want to appease those dictators. We have seen genocide (Gukuruhundi) under our current leaders where 20,000 civilians, many of them women and children, were brutally murdered; we have seen Murambatsvina where 700,000 homes were callously destroyed by our current leaders; we have seen land invasions under our current leaders where over 300,000 people lost their livelihoods – and which brought about a situation where our current wheat crop in the ground is only 5% of what it was before the invasions; we have seen political violence under our current leaders where tens of thousands have been severely beaten and hundreds killed. We have seen per capita income fall from one of the highest in Africa to one of the lowest in the world. If all these crimes against humanity that have led to such poverty and suffering in Zimbabwe do not constitute a leadership crisis I have to wonder what a leadership crisis really is – by the definition of the European Union?'*

The Vigil marked the anniversary of the stolen 2013 elections by staging a tableau mocking the victory banquet in Harare this week held by Mugabe for his mafia henchmen. Fungayi Mabhunu, wearing our Mugabe mask, presided at a Vigil banquet flanked by supporters wearing red devils' masks amid posters reading: 'EU sups with devil Mugabe', 'Wake on anniversary of Zimbabwe's 2013 stolen elections', 'One year on, six years backwards', 'No rule of law, endemic corruption', 'Where are the two million jobs?' and 'What's happened to the new constitution?'

A voice silenced – Saturday 9th August: This weekend marks the end of SW Radio Africa which has been broadcasting high quality journalism to Zimbabwe for thirteen years. Coming at a time when the independent press at home is facing a growing financial squeeze, the Vigil believes the loss of this voice is a tragic blow to democracy. Supporting a peaceful democratic transition is proclaimed as one of the main objectives for Zimbabwe of the UK's Department for International Development, which must have given our country well over a billion dollars of aid during the lifetime of SW Radio Africa. It's a pity DFID didn't see fit to provide money to keep the radio station going as it filled the prescription for this. The Vigil is glad to hear that EU Ambassador to Harare Aldo Dell'Ariccia is returning home.

No joke – Saturday 16th August: Supporters at the Vigil beamed broadly in response to Mugabe's appeal to Zimbabweans to pretend that all is well to the SADC Summit at the Victoria Falls. Our smiles were so big we couldn't help laughing at Mugabe's request: 'We are asking you to smile and show the region that we are a hospitable people, that we can welcome visitors. Let us all smile and for just a moment forget our problems . . . albeit under the burden of sanctions.' To underline our joy at our desperate situation we held up smiley pictures with the posters: "Mugabe: 'Smile for the SADC Summit'" and "Mugabe: 'Smile, though your heart is breaking'". We are sure that our South African friends, in particular, will appreciate a smiley welcome at the Summit – after all they are connoisseurs in hypocrisy, as shown by their clutching at legal straws to continue preventing the publication of an explosive report said to expose the rigging of the 2002 Zimbabwe elections. 'We welcome Zimbabwe's return to a path of stability and prosperity and remain committed to cooperation and partnership with our valued neighbour', joked South Africa's Home Affairs Minister Malusi Gigaba, announcing a three-year extension of residents' permits for Zimbabwean refugees. His joke was spoiled by the Daily News on Sunday quoting a highly-placed source in Pretoria: 'It is not a secret that Zimbabwe is currently economically stressed and that things may get significantly worse soon. The growing fear is that this economic crisis will trigger ever larger volumes of economic refugees.' The joke was further exposed by ANC Secretary-General Gwede Mantashe. "Zimbabwe was a food basket of Africa but is a disaster today," he said as he reassured South African farmers that their land would not be seized forcibly and without compensation. The Daily News source will not be surprised by a report by Newsday that an undertaker has again been named as businessman of the year by one of Zimbabwe's leading business associations or that a leading Chinese insurance company is refusing to guarantee loans to Zimbabwean companies because of Mugabe's failure to meet repayments. For our part, the Vigil is not surprised that Zanu PF is now turning to the EU for investment. Newsday quotes a no-doubt smiling Foreign Affairs deputy minister Christopher Mutsvangwa as saying that Zanu PF is now prepared to generously allow the West to rescue the economy. 'They should not fear anything. Not at all. The Head of State is seized with the matter of revising laws which may be an impediment to foreign direct investment,' said Mutsvangwa. The Vigil has bad news for Mr Mutsvangwa: there is no real prospect of the EU seriously engaging in a country where Mugabe is seizing anything.

Zhing-zhong deal – Saturday 23rd August: As Mugabe and top ministers converged on Beijing in a desperate appeal for a financial bailout, the Vigil was alerted to indications that an illegal deal was being negotiated to rescue Zimbabwe from its economic torpor and pay the government's pressing running bills. Zanu PF's golden grail is $27 billion to fund the fatuous ZimAsset programme for economic development which formed the centrepiece of its 2013 election campaign but – a year on – has failed to get off the ground.

The empty vessel – Saturday 30th August: As Mugabe made his thirteenth visit to Beijing, his hosts must have found it Chinese torture to keep a straight face. A 21-gun salute for the empty vessel must have been the final straw, especially knowing they were expected to fill it with gold. The Chinese will remember that when Mugabe came to power in 1980 Zimbabwe's annual gross domestic product per head was rather more than theirs at US$1,295 compared to China's US$1,061. They will have observed in awe how he has managed to completely ruin the country so that in 2013 the GDP per capita figures were: Zimbabwe US$446 and China US$3,583. Like clockwork, Mugabe trotted out the tired cold war rhetoric: 'Down with colonialism, imperialism and capitalism' which must have seemed rather quaint to his welcoming group of Chinese capitalists, colonialists and imperialists. If Mugabe had expected them to join his chorus he must now realise that they no longer zhing from the same zhong sheet.

'Tax' the Mafia –Saturday 6th September: President Mugabe – having failed to sell Zimbabwe in Beijing – is now turning to street vendors in Chitungwiza to bail out his bankrupt regime: they are being told they must register to pay tax. The Vigil believes, however, that there is still an untapped source of funding available: how about cropping the Zanu PF bigwigs and their mysterious wealth? Vice-President Mujuru appears to be ready for plucking and if her rich supporter Didymus Mutasa and other cronies could also be 'persuaded' to cough up a billion dollars or so, Zanu PF could look forward to a well-fed congress. Thanks to Fungayi Mabhunu for donning our Mugabe mask for a tableau illustrating the financial desperation of the Zanu PF regime. He was shown with a bucket for donations from the passing public, flanked by posters such as: 'Bankruptcy sale' and 'Country clearance'.

A ZimAsset – Saturday 13th September: The Vigil is awed by the academic triumph of the First Lady – now to be known not just as Mother of the People but also as Doctor. And what could be more appropriate than the subject of her learned thesis: 'The changing social structure of the family: the case of children's homes in Zimbabwe'. Few could deny that Dr Grace is qualified on such a subject with her vast and ever-expanding 'orphanage' holdings in Mazowe. She may have been unsuccessful in her last academic venture – achieving 7% in her BA English course 'Approaches to Text' and 9% for 'Explorations in Literature' – but that was at a British university by correspondence. And, as the Vice-Chancellor of the University of Zimbabwe suggested at the graduation ceremony,' 'illegal sanctions have a lot to answer for'. What must be acknowledged is that Grace's mastery of orphanages is extraordinary and it is no surprise that she was able to complete her PhD dissertation in the two months since she registered for the degree. While the President slept, she would have burnt the midnight oil thinking philosophically after putting the orphans safely to bed. ROHR President Ephraim Tapa, just back from 12 days in Zimbabwe, told the Zimbabwe Action Forum after the Vigil that he had found a dispirited people who had lost faith in politics.

Tables turned – Saturday 20th September: People running away in fear: it must have seemed like old times for Zanu PF minister Christopher Mutsvangwa. Except this time it was the former CIO agent and director of the ZBC who was doing the running when he arrived with

Embassy flunkies to give a talk at the Royal Institute of International Affairs on Tuesday. A group from the Vigil was ready for Deputy Foreign Minister Mutsvangwa with our twelve foot banner 'No to Mugabe, No to Starvation' and posters such as: 'No to Mugabe Stooge Christopher Mutsvangwa'. 'No to Stolen Elections', 'No to Mugabe Mafia' and 'Free and Fair Elections in Zimbabwe'. Another poster recorded Mugabe's latest racist rant: 'Kick out remaining Whites'.

The Mutsvangwa group tried to avoid us by sneaking into Chatham House through a side door. But Vigil demonstrators got there first and blocked Mutsvangwa's entry, demanding to know what he was doing in London representing an illegal regime. By the time he got into the building he was visibly shaken. Chatham House, influenced by a ZANU PF sympathiser on their payroll who poses as an impartial academic, takes every opportunity to invite Mugabe representatives to tell the world how wonderful he is. They might like to know a bit more about Deputy Foreign Minister Mutsvangwa. He was, for instance, not at all diplomatic when he launched a reign of terror against opposition supporters after unsuccessfully standing for Zanu PF in Norton in the 2008 elections. Several people died at the hands of mobs he personally directed. In addition to setting up torture bases, he was also accused of involvement in illegal diamond deals. All in all, Mr Mutsvangwa is not an ideal candidate to put Chatham House straight about Zimbabwe. They might be interested to read the following:

- 'Mutsvangwa is reported to have ordered the CID to arrest (Costa) Mateta and his partners. The Homicide Squad detectives are said to have taken Mateta and two others to Granville Cemetery on the outskirts of Harare, where they brutally tortured them and shot them to death'.
- Gibson Nyandoro was summoned 'to a kangaroo court chaired by Mutsvangwa... His body was discovered floating in a local dam a few days later'.
- Moses Mutandwa . . . 'was heavily assaulted with sticks under the feet and all over the body'.
- Chris Kakanga . . . 'savagely assaulted with steel bars and logs until he sustained a fractured arm and leg'.
- John Kwangware . . . 'said his left eye is permanently damaged as they allegedly tried to remove it'.

- David Mupandasekwa . . . 'the mob hauled him blindfolded to a place where CIO agents heavily assaulted him and left him for dead'.
- Theresa Kamasula . . . 'was taken into the tent and subjected to terrible assault and torture. The youths threatened to kill her if they wanted. She was told they had orders from Mutsvangwa to 'kill' and it was up to them either to kill or spare her life'.
-

Zanu PF's forked tongue – Saturday 27th September: The Vigil notes Mugabe's restatement of his attitude towards the 'evil' donors who are trying to educate our children, maintain a health service and feed the starving. Mugabe told the UN General Assembly that, for daring to empower her people, Zimbabwe had become a victim of 'the evil machinations of Western countries'. Mugabe's rant exposed the hypocrisy of Deputy Foreign Minister Mutsvangwa who, according to the Herald, voiced a very different view of the West when he spoke at Chatham House. He was quoted as saying: 'why not do once again what Cecil Rhodes did in 1890 when he brought capital and business to Zimbabwe?'

Stop the tanks – Saturday 4th October: Anyone who has seen pictures of the teeming crowds of pro-democracy demonstrators in Hong Kong will be impressed by their courage. A photograph of an unarmed student standing defiantly in the path of a tank sent to put down a protest in Beijing 25 years ago has become an icon of courage. We at the Vigil welcome Tsvangirai's statement that he is to exercise his constitutional right and take to the streets to protest about the failure of the Zanu PF regime. Will he be the man to stop the tanks? The Vigil was graced by the presence of Dr Mugabe in her splendid new academic robes. She carried posters such as 'Let me lead you to the promised Guccis'.

Let them eat yoghurt – Saturday 11th October: On the Vigil's 12th anniversary we were blessed with a warm and sunny afternoon. We were not surprised by remarks by Dr Grace who told a rally in Gweru: 'Nobody will remove me from the farm which I took. Blood will be spilt if anyone attempts to remove me from that farm . . . Women, we need land, so let us take it. Even if we don't farm on the land, that is not a problem as long as you have it and it's yours.' At a rally in Harare she said: 'Nobody is buying my yoghurt. Business is very bad because of sanctions. You can't even find a person who can buy a packet of milk'.

Cognitive dissonance – Saturday 18th October: The British government has expressed concern at the lack of progress in reforming the electoral process in Zimbabwe. It says the newly passed Electoral Amendment Act still contradicts the new constitution, with no sign of further amendments being planned. The Foreign Office's comments come as the European Union is apparently preparing to make further concessions to Mugabe next month, despite Zanu PF's failure to allow free and fair elections and respect the rule of law. The Vigil's view of the situation in Zimbabwe is apparently far too negative according to a columnist of the London Times, Matthew Parris, who has had another happy holiday there and says 'Zimbabwe is a safe and ordered place with a stable economy: one of Africa's more advanced countries.'

Normalising the abnormal – Saturday 25th October: The Vigil seldom agrees with The Herald but we do have some sympathy with the paper's scepticism about the naïve remarks about Mugabe by Britain's new Ambassador to Zimbabwe, Catriona Laing. 'Obviously he's an iconic figure', she told The Herald. Commenting on the interview, the Herald argued that Britain and the West had to go down on their knees and show real repentance for the terrible things they had done to Zanu PF.

Leadership paralysis – Saturday 1st November: The Vigil can't get excited about the EU's decision to lift sanctions. We were told this was coming some time back. We simply point out that the sanctions were imposed because of Zimbabwe's rigged elections and lack of respect for the law. This has not changed and the EU knows it, though they talk blithely about 'progress' . . . Finance Minister Chinamasa says the indigenisation law is to be clarified to encourage foreign investment but everyone knows that no decisions are being taken while Zanu PF tears itself apart.

EU betrays Zimbabwe – Saturday 8th November: Zimbabweans exiled in the UK are to deliver a petition to the Prime Minister's official residence at 10 Downing Street on 15th November following the EU's lifting of sanctions. Fungayi Mabhunu, a spokesman for the Vigil, said: 'We are protesting at the EU's spineless capitulation to Mugabe even though he has made no reforms whatsoever . . . Now the new EU Ambassador says he 'had a lovely chat with Mugabe'. It is sickening.

Mugabe has turned the country into a death camp.' The Vigil notes that only this week a peaceful demonstrator Itai Dzamara was viciously attacked by police for exercising his constitutional right to protest in Harare's Unity Square. We have been contacted by supporters of Mr Dzamara in the UK who are planning to join us next week to protest at the assault.

Appeasing a dictator – Saturday 15th November: Vigil supporters toyi-toyied to Downing Street singing 'Vigil Yedu'. We displayed our banner: 'No to Mugabe, No to Starvation' while a delegation was admitted into the Prime Minister's residence to hand over a petition, protesting at the EU's decision to re-engage with the Mugabe regime. Here is the letter we delivered to accompany the petition: *'Dear Mr Cameron. Zimbabweans exiled in the United Kingdom are disappointed that the European Union is re-engaging with the illegitimate Mugabe regime although it has refused to make any reforms. The EU's sanctions were imposed twelve years ago because of the breakdown of the rule of law in Zimbabwe, human rights abuses and the rigging of elections. All the conditions which prompted the sanctions are still in place: there is no rule of law, human rights continue to be abused and all elections are rigged. In addition, no attempt is being made to implement the new constitution which was adopted after a lengthy and expensive process largely financed by the European Union. We would be grateful if you would facilitate the delivery of the enclosed petition to the European Union. It has been signed by some 12,000 people who have passed by the Vigil . . .*

The petition reads: Millions of Zimbabweans have been forced into exile by the brutality, incompetence and corruption of the Zanu PF regime of Robert Mugabe. Despite the absence of any reforms, including the holding of free and fair elections, the EU is moving to normalise relations with the illegitimate Zimbabwean regime, promising hundreds of millions of dollars in aid direct to Mugabe's party. We urge the EU to insist that the diaspora is guaranteed the vote in future elections, as ordered by the African Union, before re-engagement goes any further. *We understand that the only EU sanctions left now are entry restrictions on Mugabe and his wife and an arms embargo, which are to be reviewed next February. Vigil supporters urge you to keep these in force and ask: 'What does the EU hope to achieve by appeasing a dictator?'*

When the delegation returned to the Vigil we launched a new petition to the European Union: *'With Zimbabwe's new constitution being disregarded by Mugabe, we deplore the EU's scramble to re-engage with his illegitimate regime. We call on the EU, and the UK in particular, to insist that: the constitution is implemented, the rule of law is respected, the voters' roll is made available for public scrutiny as constitutionally required and the diaspora be allowed to vote.'*

The Vigil is seeking a meeting with the Foreign Office to explain to them why re-engagement with the Mugabe regime is futile if not counter-productive. We will point out that, for Zanu PF, investment is understood as meaning a gift of wealth to them personally. They have no concept of the public good. Similarly, any aid is seen as tribute to the rulers. The governor of the Zimbabwe Reserve Bank this week pointed to the growing culture of debt denial. It is becoming common, he complained, for no-one to pay their debts. The Vigil was reinforced in this view by the Harare economist Vince Musewe who, commenting on Zanu PF corruption, said: *'What makes this situation worse is that the West has decided to re-engage with them. I have desperately tried to understand their logic – but I am failing. Zanu PF has dithered in aligning the constitution with the laws and, if anything, that needs to be the ultimate measure of progress. The party, the army and all their cronies continue to entrench themselves in the economy whether through agriculture, mining or tourism – they remain the primary beneficiaries. I have not heard even one Western diplomat pushing for economic freedom and less state-sponsored predatory intervention in the critical resource sectors where the party is crowding out local people and creating market inefficiencies to fuel profiteering, corruption and economic inequality. Expect no fundamental change because it is business as usual for the corrupt, the greedy and the connected. They make more money when there is chaos. The system remains in place and is even getting stronger as the formal economy worsens.'*

The last Vigil diary reported the police attack on human rights activist Itai Dzamara for protesting in Africa Unity Square in Harare. We have been inspired by his courage and his confidence of change in Zimbabwe as expressed in his facebook page of Sunday 9th November: *'My time in hospital has afforded me huge spaces of quietness, reflection, introspection and meditation. I am left without any doubt about three things. First, a new Zimbabwe is very possible, out of civil, peaceful and resolute means. I have seen and experienced enough during the past three weeks, to know that, beyond any doubt. Secondly, l have come to understand and appreciate that really the majority of us Zimbabweans are convinced that this is not the Zimbabwe we want. Therefore, there is only one route to take – fighting for a better nation. We have to do it, if not for today or now, but certainly for our children and the future. The fight does not require bombs, knobkerries or machetes. It requires determination, peace and love. Lastly my presence in hospital bears testimony to the fact that there are elements and forces bent on resisting our struggle for a better Zimbabwe – including through murder. But I have just completed a set of gym exercises this morning, to the shock of everyone, bearing testimony to the power and grace that is beyond human instinct or murder plots – just three days ago I was left for dead. I am left without any doubt at all that a new Zimbabwe is possible through our genuine efforts and without shedding blood or breaking bones. I am ready to continue playing my part and hereby challenge you to step up and do your duty. Through civil, peaceful and resolute means, we can make it because: We are the people! We are the numbers! Let's go!'* (Itai Dzamara was abducted by intelligence agents on 9th March 2015 and has not been seen since.)

Lies and hypocrisy – Saturday 22nd November: Vigil founder member Ephraim Tapa, speaking outside the South African High Commission in London, appealed to South Africa to reverse its policy and stand with the people of Zimbabwe and support our demand for democracy and human rights. He was speaking as Vigil supporters delivered a letter to the High Commission about the findings of the South African Judicial Observer Mission sent to report on the 2002 Zimbabwe elections. This report has now been released on the instructions of the South African Constitutional Court after having being suppressed by the Pretoria government. As long suspected, the report concludes that the election could not be considered free and fair. Ephraim said: 'If the report had been published at the time perhaps we would have got rid of Mugabe a long time ago'.

Six impossible things before breakfast – Saturday 29th November: As Chinamasa delivered his fantasy budget, the Vigil turned to Alice in Wonderland for an insight into what is going on in Zimbabwe. After all,

like Alice in the book, we are in a world where we are required to believe six impossible things before breakfast. In our case:
1. 'We are not a basket case' (Chinamasa tells a Johannesburg business breakfast).
2. 'Zimbabwe's economic prospects are weighed down by sanctions' (Chinamasa's budget speech).
3. 'Corruption has been caused by sanctions' (Chinamasa tells Danish delegation).
4. 'The exposure of corruption in the media is the work of subversive elements trying to destroy the government from within' (Vice President Mujuru).
5. 'ZimAsset is the answer to our problems' (Zanu PF mantra).
6. 'The Khampepe (South African) Report (on the 2002 elections) is a mere private opinion' (official Zanu PF view).

As Zanu PF leaders run around in a circle like Alice in Wonderland's crazy caucus race, allegiances fade away like the Cheshire Cat, leaving only a grin floating in mid-air. In this topsy-turvy world it seems that Joice Mujuru is cast as Alice eating cake until she grows too big and Queen of Hearts Grace orders: 'Off with her head and the heads of all her supporters'. Mugabe himself is obviously the book's Dormouse, forever falling asleep at the Mad Hatter's eternal tea party as they try to stuff him into the teapot. Will they all wake up before it's too late? As Alice says, the Crocodile awaits (a reference to Mnangagwa):
'How cheerfully he seems to grin,
And neatly spreads his claws,
And welcomes little fishes in,
With gently smiling jaws!'

A Zimbabwean woman who dropped by the Vigil said she used to work for Air Zimbabwe and recalled that 15 years ago she witnessed a full plane preparing for take-off being unloaded so that Dr Grace could be flown on a shopping trip to Paris. They even reconfigured the passenger seats to put in a bed for her. We expect that when she is President she will need the whole fleet for her shopping expeditions.

Who cares about food? – Saturday 6th December: We are told that providing bread and circuses was the way Roman emperors kept the people satisfied. The Vigil thinks that Emperor Mugabe, despite his sweaty Oscar-worthy performance at the party congress, has fallen short in the bread department. Circus-wise he's done well. Now the congress is over Mugabe can take his usual well-deserved holiday until his birthday celebrations in February while the purged leadership gets on with the goal of the congress: 'Accelerated implementation of ZimAsset'. But since this programme is complete fantasy, all it requires is a letter to Father Christmas.

(**December:** Mugabe sacks Vice President Joice Mujuru and seven ministers accusing them of plotting to kill him. Mnangagwa named Vice-President.)

Senile Mugabe not voice of Zimbabwe – Saturday 13th December: The Vigil has delivered a letter to the Ghanaian High Commission in London apologising for the insulting remarks about Ghana made by Mugabe. We are particularly concerned because senile Mugabe is the President-elect of the African Union and is bringing the whole of Africa not just Zimbabwe into ridicule. Speaking at Zanu PF's Congress, Mugabe said: 'I have been to Ghana, 1958 – 1960, and when you look at them now and compare their present situation to that which existed in the 1960s, no change. There might be more people yes. There may be one road from the airport that has been well done. That's about all. No change.' Confirmation of Zanu PF's popularity in the UK came in a report in The Herald about corruption in the selling of Zanu PF membership cards. Zanu PF says about $400,000 can't be accounted for and cites, as an example, that South Africa received 3,000 cards but 2,881 of them had yet to be accounted for. In contrast, 'the United Kingdom received an equal number but sold all the 3,000 cards'.

Food for Embassy – Saturday 20th December: After learning that Zimbabwean diplomats were going without pay because of lack of funds at the Foreign Ministry the Vigil arranged an emergency Christmas food drop for Zimbabwe House in London. We left a pile of food and other supplies in the Embassy's doorway with the notice: **Christmas Appeal:** Zimbabwean diplomats starving. Leave food for them here. (Sorry – no GM foods). We also pushed under the door the following letter: *Dear brothers and sisters in the Zimbabwe Embassy. We Zimbabwean exiles in the UK who have gathered outside the Embassy every Saturday since 2002 are worried at hearing that Zimbabwean diplomats have* *apparently not been paid for the past 20 months It pains us to think of you going hungry at Christmas so we have brought some food and left it in your doorway as you have not answered your bell to us for twelve years. We trust that John the caretaker will give it to the Ambassador so that he can divide it fairly among you. We know it is not much but you will understand that many of us struggle financially as we are called on to send money home to our starving families from the little we earn as, in your words, 'bottom wipers' in the UK. We are comforted, however, that you at least have the Embassy to sleep in and do not have to make do with cardboard boxes to keep out the cold, which is the lot of some Zimbabweans here. Be assured that when Zimbabwe has received the $50 billion or so it has claimed for damages caused by illegal sanctions, the government of his Senile Excellency will once again be able to pay your salaries. Until then, we fear, there is scant hope so we suggest you apply for assistance from your nearest benefits office which we trust will smile at your request. The Vigil urges you not to pursue the way of the Gambian High Commission which has been turned into a tax-free tobacconist and has seen four of its diplomats jailed here. Best wishes for Christmas and may 2015 bring the 2.2 million jobs promised for last year.*

We had thought of the food drop as primarily a symbolic gesture to show up the failures of the Mugabe regime, with people supplying unwanted food from their own resources. But one supporter went to the supermarket to buy food specially and another brought sanitary towels and condoms. In addition, two passers-by went and bought extra food. This is our 13th Christmas in the cold outside the Embassy and, despite the Herald proclaiming 'there is hope the country will soon claim its rightful position as an economic giant in the region', all we see is massive delusion. Amid the charade of the Chinamasa budget and the Zanu PF Congress, we hear of hunger reaching further even in the towns. '"The current inability of the economy to address people's basic needs is leading to hunger in most urban households, with almost none of urban residents affording three meals a day nowadays," said Philip Bohwasi, chairperson of the Council of Social Workers.

2015

Highlights

17th January: Vigil demonstrates in support of Itai Dzamara's Occupy Africa Unity Square protest.
19th January: Call for UK Parliamentary debate on Zimbabwe.
January: Mugabe chosen to chair African Union.
4th February: Mugabe falls down carpeted stairs at Harare airport resulting in dozens of memes which went viral.
9th March: Itai Dzamara abducted by state security agents.
19th March: Embassy invaded by protesters demanding 'we want Itai'.
27th March: Another invasion of Embassy.
18th April: As 700 African migrants drown in Mediterranean, Vigil calls for UN protection zone in North Africa.
May: Expelled Zanu PF ministers disclose Zanu PF lawlessness.
May: Mugabe gives SADC 'poison for whites' speech.
13th June: AU summit in Johannesburg. South Africa allows Sudan's al-Bashir to evade extradition to face the International Criminal Court.
18th July: Vice-President Mnangagwa, visiting China, admits Zanu PF has screwed up.
15th August: 'Mugabe' visits British museum in search for skulls of Zimbabwean heroes.
September: ROHR demonstrates in Harare and Bulawayo.
15th September: Mugabe reads wrong speech at Opening of Parliament.
22nd / 23rd September: Vigil protests against Zimbabwean delegation trying to raise money in London.
27th October: Vigil demonstrates outside Nottingham NHS clinic of farm looter Dr Nyatsuro.
5th December: Grace Mugabe accuses NGOs of 'giving food to the hungry'.
26th December: UN compliments Zimbabwe on human rights.

Zimbabwe Vigil Excerpts

Dead hand at the tiller – Saturday 3rd January: On a cold and wet day we staged a little tableau inspired by pictures of Mugabe's holiday feast in Singapore, with Fungayi Mabhunu donning our Mugabe mask and tucking in to deep-fried Mujuru.

Rudderless regime – Saturday 10th January: It is becoming clear that there is no one in charge in Zimbabwe. No sooner does one minister make a policy statement than another contradicts it. After Finance Minister Chinamasa gave assurances that the indigenisation policy would be clarified to encourage foreign investment, the new Indigenisation Minister Christopher Mushowe said foreign investors would be lucky to get a 49% share in their business. It could be as little as 1%.

Being counted – Saturday 17th January: Zimbabweans came out in the cold in London in support of the protesters who have been campaigning in Africa Unity Square since last October. The Harare protesters, led by journalist Itai Dzamara, are demanding that Mugabe step down and allow an interim administration to prepare fresh elections to rescue the country. Vigil supporters were joined outside the Zimbabwe Embassy by UK members of the Occupy Africa Unity Square movement (OAUS). In a message to us, Itai Dzamara said that a new Zimbabwe was within reach. He told us: 'Your protest today is not in vain'. He added: 'Colleagues in other parts of the world are also seriously committed and more protests will follow your sterling effort today in other countries.' The message was read by Tendai Kwari, leader of OAUS-UK. He told Vigil supporters that he wanted to see more and more people joining the OAUS protests in Harare. 'The regime is collapsing', he said 'They cannot kill us all'. Mr Dzamara has been beaten up and arrested during his demonstrations but is not deterred. The Vigil applauds his example and we agree with the comment by the former student leader Freeman Chari that if the 100 or so NGO and human rights organisations in Harare were each to supply just one member to join Itai Dzamara at the OAUS demonstrations Zimbabwe would be free. Who knows, they might even get donor funding and then they might be joined by the MDC . . .

Following the emergence in public of a white group of Mugabe followers, we were interested to note the following in the January newsletter from Ben Freeth's organisation: 'On the Colletts' farm in West Nicholson invaders are trying to get them off their conservancy despite huge support from the local people, the chiefs and the war veterans in the area for them to stay . . . It appears that their neighbour Ken Drummond, a ZANU PF supporter, wants to extend his empire and is giving the invaders his vehicles etc. to cause mayhem.'

Call for UK parliamentary debate on Zimbabwe – Monday 19th January: The possibility of a parliamentary debate on Zimbabwe emerged at a meeting in a parliamentary committee room organised by the MP for Reading West, Alok Sharma, who was approached by Restoration of Human Rights in Zimbabwe Reading branch. The idea was supported by former Africa Minister Mark Simmonds, who spoke of 'small steps of progress' in Zimbabwe.

Progress? – Saturday 24th January: Ephraim Tapa, President of ROHR, disagreed with Mr Simmonds that there had been progress in Zimbabwe but welcomed the idea of a parliamentary debate. He told the Vigil: 'It is necessary to interrogate the British government's policy as it is not at all clear what it hopes to achieve'.

Forward to the Stone Age – Saturday 31st January: Mugabe is an appropriate choice as chairman of the African Union (AU). The South African head of the AU Commission set out the aims of the meeting at which Mugabe was chosen: 'Democracy, good governance and human rights'. Well they have found the man for the task. Prepare for a new African Renaissance: this one rebranded as the Stone Age. The AU is not the only useless international organisation. You could add the EU with its re-engagement with Mugabe policy. But first prize must go the United Nations. It says unemployment in Zimbabwe is 5.42%.

Campaign for parliamentary debate – Saturday 7th February: The Zimbabwe Action Forum, meeting after the Vigil, discussed a template letter people could send to their MPs calling for a debate on Zimbabwe. Part of the letter said: *In brief, all elections in Zimbabwe are rigged, there is no rule of law, corruption is rampant and the new constitution – largely paid for by the British taxpayer – is predictably ignored by the Mugabe Mafia. Yet Britain talks of 'progress' and is lifting sanctions! We want the debate to ask questions such as: What is the British Government's policy on Zimbabwe?*

Zanu PF arrogance – Saturday 14th February: Anyone really hoping for a turnaround in the Zimbabwean economy will be dismayed by the comment by Local Government Minister Ignatius Chombo. Speaking after a meeting with a 19-strong British investor delegation, he said there had been 'some little unpleasant disagreements'. Chombo was apparently outraged that the naïve investors wanted to know where Zimbabwe is going.

The carpet's to blame – Saturday 21st February:

Zimbabweans in the UK gathered in force outside the Embassy to mark Mugabe's 91st birthday. The increasingly confused tyrant was supposed to be in South Africa attending to his duties as supreme leader of SADC (and Africa in general) but seems to have caught the wrong plane and turned up outside the Embassy, where he demonstrated how Mai Mujuru hid under the carpet and almost caused him to fall. Thanks to Fungayi who donned our Mugabe mask and demonstrated Mugabe's fall to the assembled media. The demonstration brought together a wide range of diaspora groups. Apart from our sister organisations, they included MDC T, ZAPU, Occupy Africa Unity Square, Zimbabweans United for Democracy, Zimbabwe Social Democrats and the Swaziland Vigil.

A nauseating feast – Saturday 28th February: 'An event of truly spectacular moral ugliness' was how the Mayor of London Boris Johnson described Mugabe's 91st birthday party. Fungayi wore our Mugabe mask as we restaged the Victoria Falls feast.

No appeasement – Saturday 7th March: Strong support for the Vigil's criticism of the European Union's new policy of 're-engaging' with the Mugabe regime has come from American former Deputy Assistant Secretary of State for African Affairs Todd Moss. With President Obama renewing American sanctions for another year, Mr Moss says that it is perplexing that Europe is now choosing to break ranks and resuming aid, signalling a shift in approach from sticks to carrots. Europe, he says, is wilfully blind to what is happening and who is responsible for the worsening conditions in Zimbabwe. 'Any new support for the current government will likely only further entrench the current coterie around Mugabe.' On a lovely sunny day we marked International Women's Day in support of Women of Zimbabwe Arise who were beaten by police during a Valentine's Day protest in Bulawayo.

We are Itai Dzamara – Saturday 14th March: Exiled Zimbabweans demonstrated outside the Zimbabwe Embassy about the abduction of Itai Dzamara. There are mounting fears that Itai has been killed by state security agents because he was seen being bundled into an unmarked truck by 5 unidentified men – typical CIO behaviour. At the suggestion of the writer Vince Musewe, Vigil supporters carried posters 'I am Itai Dzamara' to show solidarity with a man Musewe said had 'a burning desire to do that which we must despite the personal cost'. Musewe asked: 'Where are our pastors and our bishops? Where are our churches, civic organisations, human rights activists and our NGOs, our prophets and prophetesses, our community leaders, our opposition political party leaders and all those amongst us and in the diaspora who claim that they stand for our freedom? Where are you all now because words alone will not do?'

Among those at the Vigil was Tendai Kwari, leader of OAUS-UK, who said he feared for Itai's life. He added that a citizen of Zimbabwe could not be allowed to just disappear. 'We are all now living in fear'. Ephraim Tapa said: 'Enough is enough. We must move the struggle to another level. The Zanu PF regime must be dismantled. People must demonstrate outside Zimbabwe's embassies abroad and use social media to encourage people at home to join the protest.'

Itai Dzamara has been arrested, assaulted and tortured several times during his protest which was launched last October when he called on

Mugabe to step down. A collection was taken at the Vigil for Itai Dzamara's wife Sheffa, who says her young children haven't stopped crying for their father to come home. Not troubled by Itai's fate, Mugabe set off with about 100 hangers-on for an obscure UN conference in Japan on 'Disaster Risk Reduction', riding roughshod over objections from the Japanese Embassy in Harare at the bloated delegation.

Embassy demonstration – Thursday 19th March: The Embassy went into meltdown when nine Zimbabwean expatriates charged in and demanded information about Itai Dzamara. With cries of 'We want Itai', 'Bring back Itai' and 'Zanu PF murderers', the group demanded to see the Ambassador. Frightened staff pointed to a door but a voice from inside that room shouted 'don't let them in'. In the meantime police – some of them armed – swarmed into the building summoned by a panic button. The protesters explained they were simply making a peaceful request for information from their Embassy. The police asked them to continue the protest outside. The Embassy then closed for the day.

Saturday 21st March: The protest against the feared murder of Dzamara continued at the Vigil with posters reading 'Where is Itai Dzamara?' and 'Release Itai Dzamara'. The Zimbabwe Action Forum agreed to send a letter to the Ambassador asking for a meeting to discuss the abduction and warned *'The Zimbabwe Vigil fears that the unbridled criminal behaviour by the Mugabe regime is stoking a fire which could consume our people. Because the Embassy has no letterbox we will deliver this letter in person.'*

Another Embassy protest – Friday 27th March: Ten people got into the Embassy and sang protest songs in the reception area, brandishing placards such as 'Bring back Itai Dzamara', 'Enough is enough' and 'Robert Mugabe and Zanu PF government must go'. Scared Embassy staff retreated and summoned the police who asked the demonstrators to continue their protest outside. The demonstrators went on to the nearby South African High Commission where they demanded that Mugabe should be replaced as chair of the AU and SADC.

Diaspora no to Mugabe – Saturday 4th April: If further evidence was needed that Mugabe is crazy it came with his appeal to the diaspora to give him more money – presumably for his non-stop travels in search of eternal life. Whatever Zanu PF in the UK says, no sane Zimbabwean here would dream of putting their money anywhere within Zanu PF's grasp, although the party's UK spokesman happily proclaims that 'the economic renaissance (is) already in motion'.

Deadly silence – Saturday 11th April: While Mugabe continues to flaunt himself abroad, there has been a deafening silence from the Zanu PF regime about the abduction of Dzamara despite a court order to search for him. Even ousted Vice-President Mujuru claimed to be outraged by Zanu PF's indifference to Dzamara's fate. Amnesty International says no credible investigation seems to be taking place.

Vigil protests – Friday 17th April: Exiled Zimbabweans demonstrated outside the Embassy and the South African High Commission in London in protest at the abduction of Dzamara and at the new upsurge of xenophobic violence in South Africa. The protests came as ambassadors of SADC countries were holding a meeting at Zimbabwe House. Barriers were placed outside the Embassy and police kept guard after several incidents in which demonstrators entered the building in attempts to deliver a letter. Once again the Embassy refused to accept the Vigil's letter asking to discuss the abduction of Dzamara and the demonstrators were told they could not even push it under the closed front door. So we posted it at the local post office.

Let them drown? – Saturday 18th April: News that some 700 migrants from Africa drowned when their rickety boat capsized in the Mediterranean off Libya came within hours of a meeting at which the Zimbabwe Action Forum discussed the failure of the European Union and the African Union to deal with the growing crisis posed by the headlong flight from Africa and the Middle East. Our day was spent outside the Embassy protesting at Mugabe's regime on the 35th anniversary of independence. But discussion at the Forum after the Vigil turned to wider issues of bad governance, prompted by our contempt of the African Union for electing genocidal Mugabe as their chairman. Anger was only marginally less against the European Union. The forum discussed the following ideas:
1. European countries will not agree to open their borders to all comers.
2. The lamentable state of African governments led by icons such as Mugabe will continue to drive a flood of refugees to Europe.

3. International aid to Africa is largely misspent.
4. Some of these billions of dollars could be directed at creating a UN protection zone, perhaps in north Africa, where rescued migrants could receive food and medical attention, and indeed schooling, while their asylum claims for Europe could be processed.

The Forum is to continue its discussion at its next meeting in two weeks' time but, in the meantime, as if to show how out of touch with reality Mugabe is, the Herald would have us believe that Zimbabwe is poised to become a land of milk and honey – or in the paper's topsy-turvy world honey and milk. It says: 'the Government, even in the face of harsh economic sanctions that have cost the country over $40 billion, has made significant and notable progress . . . Indeed through the leadership of President Mugabe, honey and milk will flow in all the corners of the country. ZimAsset is one policy which if embraced by all Zimbabweans will take this country to another level and position this country as one of the most performing economies in the world.'

For his part, Welshman Ncube says 'every true patriot must be hanging his or her head in collective shame at how we got ourselves to be the perfect caricature of a failed African state with its people beaten, defeated, and in grinding poverty, stoked daily by the spectre of hunger and in some cases starvation while scavenging for survival, pretty much like our ancestors would do before the dawn of organized state entities'. Like Professor Ncube, the Vigil does not share the Herald writer's sunny optimism. To us ZimAsset has from the beginning been pie in the sky. If it wasn't, Zanu PF would have eaten the pie anyway.

ROHR President Ephraim Tapa told the Vigil: 'On today's 35th anniversary of independence we salute those who sacrificed for our freedom. What we did not know was that the struggle was to be privatised. With this came the privatisation of Zimbabwe to the exclusion of all others. This explains why 3 million people have been driven into exile, the masses reduced to poverty and the health and education systems destroyed while Mugabe and his cronies continue to grow richer. It explains why Itai Dzamara has disappeared. On the anniversary of independence, the Vigil was joined by Mugabe himself (Fungayi in our Mugabe mask). He was surrounded by devils bearing the gifts he has given the Zimbabwean people in his long reign: unemployment, starvation and terror.

Mugabe's illegal sanctions – Saturday 25th April: The ignominious failure of the Mugabe regime's court challenge to the sanctions imposed by the European Union has escaped much attention. That the challenge was a ludicrous waste of public money was obvious to the Vigil from the start – thrown into comic relief anyway by the gradual removal of the targeted measures. Zimbabwe must now foot the entire bill for this legal circus. Before the Vigil there was another demonstration outside the South African High Commission against the latest xenophobic violence there.

A feast of hypocrisy – Saturday 2nd May: A massive power blackout ushered in SADC's summit in Harare at which fireworks over xenophobic attacks in South Africa burst the organisation's usual backslapping bubble of hypocrisy. President Khama left early to fly home to Botswana after joining President Zuma in asking the pointed question: 'Why are people fleeing their own countries?', lifting the lid on the forbidden topics of misgovernance and oppression. Zuma noted that he had been told by an immigrant: 'If you raise your voice (in my country) you disappear'. The hypocrisy of Mugabe and SADC is matched by the weasel words of the International Monetary Fund, which claims to have detected 'meaningful progress' in Zimbabwe.

Challenge Mugabe – Saturday 9th May: With senior US officials due to visit Zimbabwe for talks in the coming week, the Vigil calls on them to remain focused on human rights issues, in particular the abduction of Itai Dzamara. Despite a court order to investigate his disappearance, the police appear to have done nothing to look for him and it is feared that he has met the fate of so many awkward opponents of the regime: tortured and killed. The Zimbabwe Association's exhibition in London shows fascinating glimpses of the Vigil's 13-year history. The exhibition is to tour the country.

A ZimAsset – Saturday 16th May: Bananas are plentiful in KwaZulu Natal. So apparently are doctorates, judging by the PhD awarded to General Constantine Chiwenga by the university there. The armed forces commander has taken time out from his diamond looting, vote rigging, and widespread farming and business interests, apart from his day to day military chores, to gain a Doctor of Philosophy degree in – of all things – Ethics. He says he interviewed Mugabe for his research. The former

Zanu PF spokesman Rugare Gumbo, now ousted from the party, has suddenly seen the light and talks of 'illegal bugging, torture, intimidation and abductions'. Another of the walking dead, former presidential affairs minister Didymus Mutasa, speaks of 'complete lawlessness in Zimbabwe'

Mugabe's poison – Saturday 23rd May: President Mugabe has called on South Africans to direct their xenophobia at whites instead of blacks. 'I give poison not for you to swallow but to give to someone else' he told the applauding staff at SADC Headquarters in Botswana. Speaking as Chair of the African Union as well as of SADC, Mugabe said South Africa needed a second liberation which would transfer wealth to blacks. He also called on Africa to stop courting the West for financial support, arguing that even with the end of colonialism the oppressors were back in Africa in the form of NGOs.

Bullet brain – Saturday 30th May: After 35 years of Mugabe, Zimbabweans will not be surprised at Sepp Blatter still clinging on to office as president of FIFA. He is a soul mate of Mugabe's in corruption and manipulation. One of Mugabe's most devoted disciples is Transport and Infrastructural Development Minister Obert Mpofu. He has not had the opportunity to sell the World Cup to a desert country with little history of football. But his announcement that the government is planning to bring in bullet trains shows a similar level of delusion.

Sleeping on the job – Saturday 6th June: All Zimbabweans will be pleased that the veteran BBC foreign correspondent John Simpson thinks of Zimbabwe as 'intensely beautiful, calm and welcoming'. In an article in the British Daily Telegraph, Mr Simpson says Zimbabwe is going through 'a period of relative political stability'. The Vigil thinks Mr Simpson, instead of tossing off trite pieces for the travel pages, should do some research into what is happening in Zimbabwe before he next writes about it. He might even come across an article in the American 'Foreign Policy' magazine in which the authors say: *'Over the course of the past few months, we have witnessed an ominous series of warning signs: bitter political infighting within the country's ruling party, the worsening of already deplorable economic conditions, the abduction and disappearance of a prominent human rights activist, and a surge of inflammatory rhetoric and political violence.'* Perhaps Mr Simpleton is asleep like President Mugabe, wandering the world like the Flying Dutchman, treated in Nigeria a few days ago as a geriatric imbecile even before demonstrating the reality of this by snoring his way through President Buhari's inauguration.

Big issues – Saturday 13th June: There are big issues facing leaders at the African Union summit in Johannesburg. Women's empowerment is the public face of the summit. But behind closed doors more immediately troubling problems will be raised. The headline issue is the resurgence of xenophobia in South Africa but the Vigil hopes AU leaders will address the broader question of the global migration crisis. It should come up with ideas on how they can encourage people to stay at home and develop the continent rather than fleeing to the West. Today we launched a new petition: *'To the UK Prime Minister: Exiled Zimbabweans, supporters and friends, at the Vigil outside the Zimbabwe Embassy in London, record our disgust at the anti-white rants of Zimbabwe's illegitimate President Mugabe. We wish to affirm our unwavering support of Zimbabwe's constitutional requirement for non-racism.'*

Falling from the sky – Saturday 20th June: News that Mali is to donate $300 million to avert starvation in Zimbabwe would be warmly welcomed by the worried Zimbabwean diaspora, scrimping to send money home to help our families. But such manna from heaven is unlikely, to say the least. Mali's President Keita is all big talk. On a state visit to Zimbabwe, he was shown over one of Mugabe's collection of farms and said he was amazed by the 'success stories' of the land reform programme. As we gathered for our weekly Vigil we mourned the death of an African refugee who fell to earth from the undercarriage of a plane approaching London's Heathrow Airport.

No to Mugabe's poison – Saturday 27th June: The Zimbabwean diaspora turned out in force to present a petition to the Prime Minister's official residence protesting at racist comments by Robert Mugabe. In a letter accompanying the petition we assured Mr Cameron that Zimbabwean exiles in the UK wish to disown the comments.

Geriatric Genocidaire – Saturday 4th July: The Vigil has launched a new petition calling for the arraignment of Mugabe before the International Criminal Court. We know he will be protected by his

Security Council friends in Beijing and Moscow but we wish to focus attention on the evidence for the prosecution because Africa continues to honour this geriatric genocidaire. The Zimbabwean economist and opposition MP Eddie Cross recently looked at the population statistics and concluded that, even allowing for mass emigration, the population is some 10 million people short of what would have been expected by the historic growth trend – the result of misgovernance: starvation, disease and poverty.

Mugabe murdered Dzamara – Saturday 11th July: Exiled Zimbabweans and friends demonstrated outside the Zimbabwe Embassy to mark 4 months since the abduction of the civil rights activist Itai Dzamara. A letter accusing Mugabe of Itai's murder was pushed under the closed front door of the Embassy. Vigil founder member Ephraim Tapa announced that the Vigil would mark Itai's abduction every month on the nearest Saturday to the 9th of the month until his family's demands were satisfied.

Countdown to jubilation – Saturday 18th July: Suddenly Zimbabwe is back in the news. We thought the big news of the week was the remarkable volte-face by Vice-President Mnangagwa who, on a visit to China, admitted that Zanu PF had completely screwed up and would have to rethink everything. But what has propelled Zimbabwe up the news agenda is not the nitty-gritty of Zimbabwean politics but the human drama: who is going to take over from Mugabe. The question is discussed in an article in the UK Times today by the Zimbabwean journalist Jan Raath, who concludes: 'The day Mugabe dies, the entire nation may well be enveloped in an explosion of jubilation.'

Divine Grace – Saturday 25th July: With her magical spiritual powers Amai Grace Mugabe PhD miraculously manifested herself at the Vigil to mark her 50th birthday. Asked how she had transported herself here while simultaneously gracing a glittering dinner/dance at her Borrowdale Brook mansion, the First Lady simply pointed to the full-colour advertisement sponsored by Air Zimbabwe in a 14-page birthday supplement in the Herald. We understood immediately what she meant as we all know that the bankrupt airline is capable of miracles or it would have stopped flapping its wings a long time ago.

Where's the Pie? – Saturday 1st August: The second anniversary of the last stolen elections passed with little remark – though Zanu PF acknowledged for the first time the hollowness of its ZimAsset election manifesto. At the time it was unveiled the Vigil described the five-year economic programme as 'Pie in the Sky'. Now it's clear there is indeed no pie in prospect and Zanu PF doesn't even know the recipe to bake one. ROHR members organised a protest at the Vigil today in support of workers back home and the many job losses resulting from recent legislation on the termination of contracts.

Mugabe and Co – Saturday 8th August: One of the expelled Zanu PF leaders has complained that the party has been turned into Mugabe's private property and is inflicting 'untold misery' on Zimbabweans. Former Masvingo Minister of State Kudakwashe Bhasikiti was speaking in an interview with the Daily News. The Vigil welcomed unexpected visitors from Zimbabwe: Douglas Mwonzora, Secretary-General of MDC T, and Theresa Makone, the party's Treasurer. Mr Mwonzora spoke of reforms wanted by MDC T, including the diaspora vote.

Produce all skulls – Saturday 15th August: Sacked information minister Jonathan Moyo simply can't get out of propaganda mode. From his lowly perch as just one of the education ministers, Moyo is reduced to tweeting that the Zanu PF government can't concentrate on turning around the economy before the repatriation of the remains of First Chimurenga heroes from foreign museums. The Vigil managed to capture pictures of Mugabe visiting the British Museum in search of skulls. He was accompanied by his pet lion Cecil. The museum said it didn't have the skulls he was looking for but it would no doubt welcome his own as soon as possible for display in the dinosaur room. For our part, we urge Zanu PF to expand its search for skulls to include the 20,000 victims of Gukurahundi still haunting us today. And by the way where is Itai Dzamara?

Let them eat ice cream – Saturday 22nd August: All the reports we get at the Vigil suggest that the wheels are coming off Zimbabwe. This week we were sent several emails which in different ways graphically show how bad things are becoming. 'We live in a country with absolutely no rule of law', said one correspondent. 'There is no money and everyone, not only government, is desperate to find funds. Corruption and bribery are a way of life. They are ingrained and will be hard to get rid of.' Meanwhile Dr Grace has opened a new factory selling her dairy products, including ice cream. MDC spokesman Obert Gutu spoke of her extravagant display of wealth in a sea of poverty and said it was a clear sign that the Zanu PF regime was completely out of touch with the people.

The total liar – Saturday 29th August: 'There are lies, damned lies and statistics' goes the saying. Mugabe ticked all these boxes in his State of the Nation Address to Parliament. From his preliminary lie boasting of 'peace and stability', to his damned lie about tackling corruption to his ludicrous growth statistics, he was the total liar. Zimbabwean economist John Robertson said the State of the Nation Address was 'clueless'.

'What have we to lose?' – Saturday 5th September: This week the Vigil's sister organization Restoration of Human Rights in Zimbabwe took to the streets. They staged a demonstration in Harare against the Mugabe regime and joined in a protest march in Bulawayo against pre-paid water meters, which it is argued will worsen the situation of the poor. ROHR leader Ephraim Tapa said he had told members in Harare that it was their constitutional right to demonstrate regardless of what the police said. Ephraim, who was speaking at the Action Forum held after the Vigil, disclosed he had just made an undercover visit to Zimbabwe. He said plans were underway for demonstrations in other areas.

IMF says no money for Zimbabwe – Saturday 12th September: The International Monetary Fund says that even if the Zimbabwean government makes economic reforms it will take at least three years before it can expect loans from international lenders. For his part, the European Ambassador to Zimbabwe Philippe van Damme said Zimbabwe needed a return to the rule of law and respect for property rights if it is to attract foreign investment. These comments will be part of the message the Vigil will be presenting to any customers gullible enough to attend a Zanu PF fundraiser in London on 22nd September.

End of Mugabe era – Saturday 19th September: The fiasco of 91-year-old Mugabe reading the wrong speech at the opening of Parliament cannot be dismissed as 'a common era' as the Herald put it (before correcting its spelling error!). Zanu PF MPs clapped sagely, suggesting that anything Mugabe says is alright with them. The opposition, which had heckled the State of the Nation Address when it was first delivered, had received death warnings to behave so they tried to keep a straight face. Attempts to undermine the Vigil continue as the CIO reacts against the spreading wings of our sister organisation ROHR. After last week's demonstrations in Harare and Bulawayo, ROHR has reconstituted provincial structures in Manicaland, Mashonaland West, Harare, Masvingo and Midlands. It appears people are responding to the simple demand for respect for human rights as provided for in the unimplemented constitution.

London anti-Zanu PF demo – Tuesday 22nd September: A large group of exiled Zimbabweans protested in Central London outside a meeting at which a delegation representing the Mugabe regime tried to persuade people to invest in Zimbabwe. The delegation was led by Industry and Commerce Minister Mike Bimha and included leaders of some bankrupt parastatals. Displaying posters reading: 'Don't fund Mugabe', '51% tax on investment', 'Britain don't invest with Mugabe's govt of thieves' and 'Bring back Itai Dzamara', we handed out the following flyer as people went into the building:

*'**BEWARE:** A friendly warning to anyone thinking of investing in Zimbabwe. For every £100 invested you can immediately lose £51 because of Mugabe's indigenisation policy. Despite talk of relaxing the opaque indigenisation rules, Mugabe's nephew Patrick Zhuwao has just been appointed the new Indigenisation Minister and insists he will push ahead with the programme 'for black empowerment'. This requires white and foreign-owned businesses to cede a 51% stake to local black 'businessmen' ie Mugabe's Zanu PF cronies. For an overview of the financial situation in Zimbabwe see the article by Todd Moss and Jeffrey Smith published on the Center for Global Development website. Todd Moss is a former US deputy assistant secretary of state for Africa. Jeffrey Smith is an Africa specialist at the Robert F. Kennedy Center for Human Rights. They say 'Zimbabweans should not expect economic recovery while Mugabe's heartless and economically illiterate junta remains in charge'. So our message to you is: hold back on investment until there is a return to the rule of law in Zimbabwe.'*

Stony-faced Zimbabwean delegates and officials refused to take the flyer but others read it with interest. As the meeting got underway, they could not fail to hear us singing and dancing outside, punctuated with chants of 'Down with Mugabe'. Draped on the railings across the road they could see our banners: 'End murder, rape and torture in Zimbabwe' and 'No to Mugabe, no to starvation'.

Minister flees London demo – Wednesday 23rd September: Zimbabwean minister Mike Bimha and Zanu PF cronies had to change venues for a London conference because of our protest. The conference aimed at getting money from the diaspora was scheduled to be held at the Embassy. Vigil and ROHR demonstrators gathered ahead of the planned start and put up banners. But the Embassy remained quiet with the front door locked and no staff in sight. Later we were informed by a policeman that the conference had been moved to an hotel.

Mugabe's same old song – Saturday 26th September: For the second time in a few weeks Mugabe has delivered an old speech – this time recycling his clapped-out ideas at the United Nations, complaining that Zimbabwe lacks resources to implement the new UN development programme because of (the long-suspended) sanctions imposed by Western countries. After our weekday protests we had a lot of encouraging messages. One read: 'All the leaderless folks back home salute you for your courage and patriotism'.

Mugabe's prosperity gospel – Saturday 3rd October: A Zimbabwean website's story has been given splash treatment in the mass circulation Daily Mail here in the UK. The story taps into one of the few thriving industries in Zimbabwe – the prosperity prophet phenomenon. The prophet involved this time is Malawi-born Shepherd Bushiri who claims to have a private jet so private that nobody can see it and to be able to walk on air (presumably when he is not using his private jet). The website's video about the miraculous 'walking in the air' has gone viral after being uploaded to Youtube. But the Mail, along with others, points to the unexplained shadow of someone apparently helping to support the floating prophet. The hoax helps explain the superstitious support for false prophet Mugabe and his creed of 'believe in me: I can perform miracles'. A meeting of our Action Forum heard that ROHR has now, with the addition of Matabeleland South and Matabeleland North, set up new structures in all ten provinces.

Khama save Zimbabwe – Saturday 10th October: To mark the Vigil's 13th anniversary we launched a new petition warning that the situation in Zimbabwe is on a knife-edge because of threats by the army to wield 'the Zanu PF axe' against Mugabe's opponents. The petition is addressed to SADC Chair President Khama of Botswana and calls on SADC to intervene to stop a meltdown. We were sorry to see that about ten Zimbabweans saw fit to hold their own 'vigil' outside the Embassy at the same time as us – a sad example of how Zimbabweans can't seem to work together. Thanks to Fungayi Mabhunu for donning our Mugabe mask to be pictured standing in front of the 'anti-vigil' holding a poster 'thanks to Zanu PF vigil for your support'.

Expel British farm looter – Saturday 17th October: The Vigil has called on the British authorities to take action against a UK doctor who is attempting to seize a farm in Zimbabwe. It is the latest incident in which Zimbabwean exiles given refuge in the UK have revealed the hypocrisy evidenced in the growth of Zanu PF activities in Britain.

Confusion Award – Saturday 24th October: China's award of the Confucion Prize to Mugabe will be welcomed by all right-minded Zimbabweans. At last the confused leader is getting the recognition he deserves. The award comes at the right time for Mugabe. It brings in some money which will help the family's struggling milk business, which apparently has run into 'liquidity' problems. In short, some people have been milking him.

Nottingham demo against farm looter – Tuesday 27th October

About fifty people gathered outside a clinic in Nottingham run by Dr Sylvester Nyatsuro who is trying to seize a farm in Zimbabwe. Dr Nyatsuro, now a British citizen having lived here for more than 10 years, is trying to take over a farm from a white Zimbabwean Philip Rankin who bought theFarm afterIndependence with the approval of the Mugabe authorities. Vigil activists displayed posters reading: 'Down with farm looter Dr Nyatsuro', 'No to Mugabe supporters in UK'.

Zanu PF swaggers in UK – Saturday 7th November: Attempts to disruptthe Vigil as we embark on our 14th year are linked we believe to a growing Zanu PF mafia in the UK. It is clear that some Zimbabweans who have settled here are unrepentant Mugabe supporters. While the Vigil is busy challenging a British GP who is trying to take over a farm in Zimbabwe we ourselves are under siege from a determined group who are seeking to profit from the asylum industry. They are trying to hijack our brand for their own purposes. At the Vigil today we marked eight months since the abduction by state intelligence agents of human rights activist Itai Dzamara.

Zimbabweans protest again at looting British GP – Friday 13th November: Thirty people went to Nottingham to stage another demonstration outside the clinic run by Dr Sylvester Nyatsuro and his wife Veronica who are trying to seize a farm in Zimbabwe although they have lived in the UK for more than ten years.

Zanu PF's Fantasyland – Saturday 14th November: All Zimbabweans will have rejoiced that Zimbabwe is to produce its very own car and export it to the rest of Africa. The announcement in the Herald spoke of turning the country into 'a regional giant of exporting finished products'. A note of reality came in the American magazine 'Foreign Affairs', which questioned Zimbabwe's plan to borrow money from the international financial institutions so that it can begin to pay off the interest on its debts so that it can borrow more money which it will of course not repay. The Vigil expressed our solidarity with France after the terrorist attacks in Paris by wearing mourning bands.

Zimbabwe's 'perfect storm' – Saturday 21st November: With Christmas approaching, Zimbabwe seems to be facing all the gifts from hell: economic meltdown, simmering violence, a looming food crisis and a witch on the rampage. The South Africa-based think tank NKC African Economics says Zimbabwe is on the brink of total collapse and the infighting in Zanu PF could trigger unprecedented chaos. As Zanu PF gathers at Victoria Falls for its conference, Zimbabweans can only be grateful that mother of the nation Dr Grace will be there to hand out adult size 12 plastic shoes to the children.

Ugly budget – Saturday 28th November: The ugly situation in Zimbabwe was reflected in the pitiful budget of $4 billion announced by Finance Minister Chinamasa. To put it in perspective, the money involved is less than half the annual turnover of the South African food retailer Shoprite . . . The Vigil is sad that Zimbabwe is not under the leadership of someone with the vision of new Tanzanian President Magufuli whose first move was to cancel independence day celebrations to spend the money on a clean up campaign. This is not Mugabe's way. He went on from his Paris shopping trip to triumph at the Vigil's Mr Ugly competition, winning the Nikuv floating trophy.

Goblin economics – Saturday 5th December: Zanu PF says it has raised well over the $3 million it wanted for its conference at Victoria Falls. Most of this money will come, in reality, from state coffers. Our galaxy of parastatals – driven into bankruptcy by Zanu PF looting – paid up to $100,000 each for a boastful table at dinners in Harare and Bulawayo held to raise funds for the conference. First Lady Dr Goblin Mugabe accused non-governmental organisations of giving food handouts to hungry people 'year in and year out'. She continued 'this shows that they don't have the people at heart. They want us to be beggars for the rest of our lives.'

United for human rights – Saturday 12th December: Zimbabweans supported our friends of the Swaziland Vigil when they presented a petition to 10 Downing Street calling for the suspension of Swaziland from the Commonwealth until there is democracy and an end to human rights abuses. Nine months after Itai Dzamara was abducted, the Vigil held its monthly protest to ensure he is not forgotten.

Quoting Bible a crime – Saturday 19th December: The hypocrisy of the Zanu PF regime and the complicity of the outside world have been exposed by the solitary pilgrimage of Pastor Patrick Mugadza who took the road to Calvary from Kariba to protest against Mugabe at the Victoria Falls Zanu PF conference. Despite our lauded and expensive yet-to-be-implemented 2013 constitution which enshrined human rights, Pastor Patrick was thrown into prison for displaying a poster 'Mr President, the people are suffering. Proverbs 21, 13' ('Whoso stoppeth his ears at the cry of the poor, he also shall cry himself, but shall not be heard'.) The Vigil is particularly disappointed at the failure of the UK and the West to promote the new constitution for which they provided so much money in a time-consuming process which succeeded only in distracting attention from Zanu PF's stealing the last elections.

Mugabe's happy Christmas – Saturday 26th December: As we spent another Christmas in exile we were surprised to hear from the United Nations that 'Zimbabwe had done tremendously well' on the human rights front. We would never have known this if the Herald had not carried an article by the UN's acting resident co-ordinator Dr David Okello. The Herald quoted him as saying: 'Zimbabwe has made tremendous strides in living the spirit of the Universal Declaration of Human Rights'. The latest UN ravings must have cheered Mugabe as he set off for his annual holiday in the Far East after a celebratory banquet at State House for Zanu PF bigwigs. Zimbabwe now closes down for the next month or so until the geriatric reappears to replenish his funds for his 92nd birthday celebrations.

Glossary

ACTSA: Action for Southern Africa, the successor to the Anti-Apartheid Movement in the UK.
AU: African Union. Set up to replace the discredited Organisation of African Unity (OAU).
Baba Jukwa: Zimbabwean online blogger said to have disclosed inside information on Zanu PF.
Bennett, Roy: Former MDC parliamentarian, he was jailed for eight months after a fracas in Parliament with Zanu PF. He went into exile for several years before returning to take part in the Government of National Unity. Mugabe refused to swear him in as Deputy Mininster of Agriculture and he again had to flee the country.
Biti, Tendai: Finance Minister (MDC) in the GNU.
Chatham House: Headquarters of the Royal Institute of International Affairs think tank in London.
Chinamasa, Patrick: Zanu PF Finance Minister from 2013.
CIO: Central Intelligence Organisation.
COPAC: Constitutional Parliamentary Committee. Set up to drive the constitution-making process which led to the 2013 constitution.
Cross, Eddie: MDC T MP for Bulawayo South.
Freeth Ben: Zimbabwean farmer and human rights activist. Together with his father-in-law Mike Campbell, he was evicted during Mugabe's 'land reform' programme. They won a case at the Tribunal of the Southern African Development Community but the Tribunal's decision was ignored by Mugabe and Zimbabwe withdrew from the Tribunal.
G40: Generation 40. Group of younger Zanu PF politicians. Opposed to Mnangagwa's succession to the presidency. Believed to be led by Jonathan Moyo and the party's political commissar Saviour Kasukuwere and to support Grace Mugabe taking over from her husband.
GNU: Government of National Unity: a coalition between Zanu PF and the two MDC parties formed after the 2008 elections. Ended in 2013.
Gono, Gideon: Governor of the Reserve Bank of Zimbabwe during the time of hyper-inflation which ended with the adoption of the US dollar in 2009.
GPA: Global Political Agreement: the agreement brokered by South Africa which led to the GNU.
Gukurahundi: Shona for 'early rain that washes away the chaff'. Refers to an operation by the army's North Korean-trained Fifth Brigade

Glossary

between 1983 and 1987 during which Ndebele so-called dissidents were eliminated. An estimated 20,000 people died.

Hoey, Kate: British Labour Party politician and long-serving Chair of the All-Party Parliamentary Group on Zimbabwe.

JOC: Joint Operations Command. Shadowy group which co-ordinates state security. Said to be led by Vice-President Mnangagwa and includes commanders of the army, air force, police, prison service and CIO.

JOMIC: Joint Monitoring and Implementation Committee set up to oversee the GPA after the 2008 power-sharing agreement.

Lacoste Group: Supporters of Mnangagwa, who is known as 'the crocodile'. (Lacoste is a fashion brand which uses a crocodile logo.)

Mbeki, Thabo: Succeeded Mandela as South African President in 1999. Brokered the GNU after the rigged 2008 elections. Mugabe supporter. Replaced as president in 2008.

MDC: Movement for Democratic Change formed in 1999 from trade union roots.

Mnangagwa, Emmerson: Vice-President since 2014. Was Minister of State Security at time of Gukuruhundi.

Moyo, Jonathan: Minister of Higher and Tertiary Education. Formerly Minister of the Interior. Controversial politician with a murky background including various allegations of embezzling money.

Mugabe, Grace: Born in 1965, she married Mugabe in 1996 after being his secretary and divorcing her husband. Head of Zanu PF's Women's League since 2014.

Mugabe, Robert: Born in 1924. President of Zimbabwe since 1987, having previously governed as Prime Minister since Independence in 1980. Marxist and former teacher, he became leader of Zanu during the Independence War after spending 10 years in detention.

Mukuru, Joice: Former guerilla leader and wife of General Solomon Mujuru, she was appointed to the Cabinet at Independence and served as Vice-President from 2004 until she was dismissed in 2014 for allegedly plotting against Mugabe.

Murambatsvina: 'Drive out the trash'. Operation in which the homes and businesses of some 700,000 mostly poor opposition supporters were destroyed in an ostensible drive to clean up the cities.

Mutambara, Arthur: American-based academic who was chosen as the front man for the MDC by Welshman Ncube in 2006 and was Deputy Prime Minister during the GNU.

Glossary

Ncube, Pius: Roman Catholic Archbishop of Bulawayo, critic of Mugabe. Resigned his post after CIO agents revealed he was in a compromising relationship with a woman.

Ncube, Welshman: One of the founders of the MDC who split from Tsvangirai in 2005 over the creation of the Senate.

NEPAD: New Partnership for Africa's Development proposed by South Africa's President Mbeki in an attempt to allay Western complaints of African corruption and attract new investment and loans.

Nkomo, Joshua: An Ndebele and leader of Zimbabwe African People's Union (Zapu), a rival to Robert Mugabe's Zimbabwe African National Union (Zanu). They eventually merged to form Zanu PF (Patriotic Front), with Nkomo becoming Vice President of Zimbabwe. Died 1999.

ROHR: The Restoration of Human Rights in Zimbabwe. Human rights organization founded by Ephraim Tapa of the Vigil in 2007 to be the Vigil's face in Zimbabwe.

Royal Institute of International Affairs: See Chatham House.

SADC: Southern African Development Community consisting of 15 countries.

Tapa, Ephraim: Former leader of Civil Service Trade Union. Helped found the MDC. Tortured and driven into exile in 2002. Founder member of the Vigil and President of ROHR.

Tsvangirai, Morgan: Former leader of the Zimbabwe Congress of Trade Unions, he helped found the Movement for Democractic Change in 1999 and was chosen as its President. Served as Prime Minister during the Government of National Unity between 2009 and 2013.

WOZA: Women of Zimbabwe Arise: human rights group.

Zanu / Zapu / Zanu PF: See Nkomo, Joshua.

ZCTU: Zimbabwe Congress of Trade Unions

ZEC: Zimbabwe Electoral Commission: run by Zanu PF.

ZimAsset: Zimbabwe Agenda for Sustainable Socio-Economic Transformation. Unrealistic blueprint produced as Zanu PF's manifesto for the 2013 elections.

Zuma, Jacob: President of South Africa since 2009. Accused of corruption. Supporter of Mugabe.